THE
TWO-YEAR-OLD
GUIDE 2020

DAN BRIDEN
WITH MARTEN JULIAN

Marten Julian (Publisher) 2020 ©
69 Highgate, Kendal,
Cumbria, LA9 4ED

01539 741 007
rebecca@martenjulian.com
www.martenjulian.com

First published in Great Britain in 2020 by Marten Julian

A CIP catalogue record of this book is available from the British Library.

ISBN 978-1-9162387-9-4

Cover photography
Francesca Altoft Photography
www.francescaaltoft.co.uk

Internal photography
Francesca Altoft Photography
Photos: Bettys Hope, Dark Lady, Golden Horde, Oriental Mystique,
Pierre Lapin, Pinatubo, Positive, Quadrilateral, Raffle Prize, Satono Japan
& Under The Stars

Photo: Talent
Jodie Standing

Photo: Dubawi
Amy Lanigan

Layout:
Steve Dixon & Rebecca Julian-Dixon

Proof reading:
Ian Greensill & Richard Grummitt

Published by:
Marten Julian, 69 Highgate, Kendal, Cumbria LA9 4ED
Tel: 01539 741 007 www.martenjulian.com

CONTENTS

FOREWORD

It is a pleasure to be associated with this first edition of The Two-Year-Old Guide.

I know from my many years of writing Dark Horse Annuals how much time and effort goes into producing the final product, but Dan Briden has taken this a stage further in speaking to dozens of trainers about their two-year-olds and providing an in-depth analysis of their pedigrees.

I have had only a small part to play, providing a few insights about horses that for one reason or another catch my eye.

Thanks are very much in order to Dan for his painstaking devotion to every stage of this project and also to my daughter Rebecca, who has devoted hours in difficult circumstances to imposing the inevitable late amendments and the index.

Both Rebecca and Steve Dixon have done a great job with the design and layout while Richard Grummitt and Ian Greensill are thanked for editing the work.

I think you will agree that The Two-Year-Old Guide will prove a valuable source of reference through this season and beyond.

Bye for now

INTRODUCTION

I can hardly begin writing this without reference to the late Steve Taplin.

I sadly never had the pleasure of meeting Steve, but like many I enjoyed his Two-Year-Old publications which proved an invaluable guide through the season and beyond.

His untimely passing last September from prostate cancer meant that, purely from a literary point of view, there was a significant void left for a publication of this type. It certainly hasn't been the most ideal environment with the pandemic affecting our lives, including those within horse racing, and I am sincerely grateful to everyone that has contributed to this book for their valuable time. The patience shown and the help given is much appreciated.

It's not easy for a trainer, breeder or owner to give an accurate assessment in the spring but I attempted to include as many late-maturing/backend types as possible. On the whole I found people very receptive to the idea of a new book focusing on two-year-olds, while others felt unable to give an accurate guide on this year's crop but stated they would be more than happy to contribute to a 2021 edition.

Given the virus, all interviews were conducted via phone or email. I hope to visit a few stables next year, as some trainers have a significant number of juveniles and covering them in depth via electronic communication isn't viable in the long run for a number of reasons.

Regarding the contents of this book, I have attempted to filter each two-year-old's pedigree in a concise manner without sacrificing the most important elements of the page.

The horses included are a mixture of those I selected solely from pedigree and ones proffered by the people interviewed - a sort of process of elimination, which I felt was the best way to approach things given no-one really knew at the time of writing when racing would resume.

As you will see, my aim from each trainer is to get a feel of each two-year-old's physical development and their temperament/nature, along with where they stand in terms of homework.

The two-year-olds listed from stables that didn't participate were those I felt would be of most interest on pedigree, though again with the emphasis on later-maturing/three-year-old types.

I hope the book proves both an informative and enjoyable read and I thank everyone who helped along the way and made it all possible.

Dan Briden

HOW TO GUIDE

For each horse we have listed various items of information for your reference.

For example each horse appears in the following format:

BEYOND BOUNDARIES (IRE)
20/3 ch c Australia - What A Treasure (Cadeaux Genereux)
Owner: King Power Racing Co Ltd
Sales price: 280,000gns (SackvilleDonald)

This is what each part means:

Horse name - Beyond Boundaries
20/3 - Date of birth
Ch - Chestnut
C - Colt
Australia - Sire
What A Treasure - Dam
(Cadeaux Genereux) - Sire of Dam
After sales price in brackets is the name of the purchaser.

Please note that the information in the main body of the book, including names, was correct up to 7 May. After this point we continued checking for names to amend the index.

This means some horses appear as unnamed in the book yet in the index appear with their name. Consequently if you look up a horse in the index it may state a page number yet when you go to the page it will show as unnamed. This is because some horses were named after the layout was complete and because they are in alphabetical order we could not move them within the book.

Horses that this relates to have a (N) next to their name to help identify them and serve as a reminder.

Clients who buy the book direct from us, the publisher, will receive updates on horse names. If you have bought the book from a book shop please contact us for details on how to subscribe to our enhanced service. Proof of purchase will be required.

The book is split into three sections.

Section 1 covers trainers who spoke with Dan and shared their opinions and views on the two-year-olds they consider to be of particular interest. Marten adds his thoughts at the end of each trainer section.

Section 2 features a selection of owners, syndicate managers, breeders and bloodstock agents who spoke with Dan and shared their thoughts on the two-year-olds they consider to be of particular interest.

Section 3 relates to interesting two-year-olds that are with stables who were not able to speak with us.

There are four indexes; Horse, Sire, Dam and Trainer. Please note the index lists the main reference point, not every mention. For example if a sire is mentioned as being the sire of a horse it is listed in the sire index but if it is mentioned again within the write up this second reference will not appear. Please also note that if a page number has (2) after it this means the horse appears twice on that page as a main reference point.

ANDREW BALDING

BEYOND BOUNDARIES (IRE)
20/3 ch c Australia - What A Treasure (Cadeaux Genereux)
Owner: King Power Racing Co Ltd
Sales price: 280,000gns (SackvilleDonald)

Full brother to smart Irish 7-13f winner (including at Listed level)/Racing Post Trophy third Western Australia and half-brother to very useful 7-10f winner (including at Listed level) Hoarding. Dam a dual 7f 3yo winning sister to French 7f Group 1 winner Toylsome and a half-sister to 6f 2yo Group 3 winner Coral Mist; the family of 2013 St Leger winner Leading Light.

"A lovely, athletic individual, but very much one for the backend this season and middle distances next year."

DAISY WARWICK
26/3 b f Kingman - Our Poppet (Warning)
Owner: Hot To Trot Racing
Sales price: n/a

Half-sister to high-class sprinter Overdose, French 7.5f Listed winner Majestic Mount, Listed-placed French 6-6.5f winner Poppet's Treasure, useful triple 7f winner Poppet's Lovin and five other winners. Dam a once-raced maiden half-sister to 1m Listed winner Musicanna (later dam of UAE 1m Group 2 winner One Man Band), eight other winners including the great-grandam of 2019 Queen Mary Stakes winner/Cheveley Park Stakes runner-up Raffle Prize and the maiden dam of Group 3-placed 2019 dual 5f 2yo winner (including at Listed level) Alligator Alley (by Kingman).

"She is still with the pre-trainer but is a nice filly by all accounts."

DANCE AT NIGHT
13/3 b c Dark Angel - Strictly Dancing (Danehill Dancer)
Owner: Jeff Smith
Sales price: n/a

Half-brother to smart multiple 6-7f winner (including at Group 3 level) Dancing Star, Listed-placed multiple 6f winner Foxtrot Lady and useful 8-10f winner Dance Of Fire. Dam a useful 6f 3yo winner who was a half-sister to Listed-placed multiple 5f winner Verne's Castle, useful UK/US 7-10f winner Star Pupil and the unraced dam of Group 1-placed French 10-14f winner (including at Group 2/3 level) Norse King out of a Nunthorpe Stakes winner who was a half-sister to top-class sprinter Lochsong (later dam of Listed winners Loch Verdi (5f) and Lochridge (6f)).

"A family we obviously know very well going right back to Lochsong. For all he is only medium-sized, he's a nice-looking colt who possesses some scope and should make a two-year-old."

FIVETHOUSANDTOONE (IRE)
16/2 b c Frankel - Promised Money (Dark Angel)
Owner: King Power Racing Co Ltd
Sales price: 475,000gns (SackvilleDonald)

First foal of an Irish 5f 2yo Listed winner who was a sister to useful 2019 5-6f 2yo winner Praxeology and a half-sister to 5f 2yo Listed winner Beldale Memory and useful 7-8.5f winner Hacienda out of an Irish dual 5f 2yo winner who was a half-sister to 1m 3yo Listed winner/Irish 2000 Guineas runner-up Fa-Eq, 7.5f/1m Listed winner Corinium, very useful dual 5f winner Ellway Star and the dam of Group 2-placed multiple 6f-1m winner Birdman.

"A sharp colt who, though by Frankel, comes from quite a speedy family. He looks nice and should be running in six furlong races by the summer."

FLYIN' HIGH
20/3 b c Siyouni - Zee Zee Top (Zafonic)
Owner: Castle Down Racing
Sales price: 150,000gns (Vendor)

Three-parts brother to dual 10f Group 1 winner Izzi Top (by Pivotal) and a half-brother to Group 1-placed 8-10f winner (including at Group 2/Listed level) Jazzi Top, Grade 2-placed UK/US 7-8.5f winner Emaraaty and useful UK/UAE 8-11f winner Rock N Roll Ransom. Dam a French 10f Group 1 winning half-sister to top-class middle-distance performer Opera House, top-class stayer Kayf Tara and the dam of Irish 7f 2yo Group 1 winner Necklace.

"He obviously boasts an exceptional pedigree and though it is one that suggests he will do better with time and at three next year, I'm hopeful we will get to see him at some point later this year."

KING VEGA
9/2 ch c Lope De Vega - Moi Meme (Teofilo)
Owner: Apollo Racing & DTA Racing
Sales price: 350,000gns (Andrew Balding)

Second foal of a French 10.5f 3yo Listed winner who was a three-parts sister to Group 3-placed French 10-12f winner (including twice at Listed level) Toi Et Moi and a half-sister to Italian 10f 3yo winner/Italian Oaks runner-up Moi Non Plus and French 1m 2yo winner Parle Moi out of a French 9/10f 3yo Group 3 winner; good Italian family.

"This is a nice, rangy colt who has a bit more size about him than some by the sire tend to do. He also has a bit of quality about him and can hopefully do something before the end of the season."

MARINE (IRE)
27/2 b c Sea The Stars - Ignis Away (Gold Away)
Owner: Qatar Racing Limited
Sales price: €400,000 (David Redvers)

Half-brother to 2019 1m 2yo winner Heart Reef. Dam a maiden sister to Listed-placed French 12f winner Debutante and half-sister to King George/Arc winner Danedream, Chester Vase winner Venice Beach and Irish 9.5f 3yo Group 3 winner Broadway; the excellent family of Groom Dancer, Indian Rose, Left Hand, Plumania and Vert Amande.

"A nice colt who is one of the neater offspring from Sea The Stars, but he is looking the part and I would be pretty disappointed if he wasn't racing and indeed winning at two."

MELLOW MAGIC
15/4 b f Nathaniel - Lady Brora (Dashing Blade)
Owner: Kingsclere Racing Club
Sales price: n/a

Three-parts sister to fairly useful 2019 12f 3yo winner Inclyne (by Intello) and a half-sister to high-class 7f-1m winner (including at Group 1 level) Elm Park, Group 2/3-placed 9-10f winner Brorocco and fairly useful 7.5f-1m winner Highland Pass. Dam a 1m 3yo winner who was a half-sister to 11-12f Flat/very useful 2m 5f-3m 1f hurdle (including at Listed level) winner Tweedledrum; the family of dual 6f Listed winner Intransigent and 7f Listed winner Border Music.

"Another family we know all about. Although she's by Nathaniel and there's some stamina in the pedigree, her half-brother Elm Park was by a similarly stout influence in Phoenix Reach and enjoyed a very good two-year-old season, winning the Racing Post Trophy at the end of it. This is an athletic, scopey filly who isn't too dissimilar to him, and I hope she will be running by the latter part of the summer. She should have enough speed to start over seven furlongs."

MELODY OF LIFE (IRE)
1/3 b c Dark Angel - Tamarisk (Selkirk)
Owner: King Power Racing Co Ltd
Sales price: 425,000gns (SackvilleDonald)

Full brother to smart 6f-1m winner (including at Listed level) Happy Power. Dam an unraced half-sister to 7f 2yo Group 2 winner Cairns, Listed-placed German 11.5f 3yo winner Tanamia, useful UK/UAE 5-6f winner Machynleth and the once-raced maiden dam of high-class French 7.5f-1m winner (including at Group 2/3 level)/French 1000 Guineas and French Oaks runner-up Tamazirte out of a smart 5-6f 2yo winner/Cheveley Park Stakes runner-up.

"We have the brother who is very useful and debuted in May as a two-year-old, but he didn't really switch on until the autumn of his juvenile career and I can see this colt being quite similar in that regard. However, he is a bigger model than his brother and a better type overall, so we're quite hopeful about him."

NEENEE'S CHOICE
24/4 b c Paco Boy - Galaxy Highflyer (Galileo)
Owner: Mick & Janice Mariscotti
Sales price: 50,000gns (Andrew Balding)

Half-brother to Group 2/3-placed 6-7f 2yo winner Oklahoma City. Dam an unraced three-parts sister to dual Gold Cup/Irish St Leger winner Kayf Tara and

Eclipse Stakes/King George VI & Queen Elizabeth Stakes winner Opera House and half-sister to 10f Group 1 winner Zee Zee Top (later dam of dual 10f Group 1 winner Izzi Top and 10f 3yo Group 2 winner Jazzi Top) and the dam of Irish 7f 2yo Group 1 winner Necklace and grandam of 7f 2yo Group 2 winner Good Old Boy Lukey.

"Bred along the same lines as Flyin' High. We have had plenty of success with horses bought from Meon Valley Stud and it has usually been with purchases from the lower end of the market. Hopefully it can work again. This is a medium-sized, good-bodied colt who moves well. I suspect he will be one for midsummer over six and seven furlongs."

RIVAL
22/1 b c Iffraaj - Pamona (Duke Of Marmalade)
Owner: Highclere Thoroughbred Racing - Peter Curling
Sales price: 100,000gns (Jake & John Warren)

First foal of a Group 2-placed 7-14f winner (including at Listed level) who was a three-parts sister to Grade 3-placed Irish/US 6f-1m winner Kitty Hawk and a half-sister to Italian 1m 3yo Listed winner Prianca out of an Italian 6f 2yo Group 3 winning daughter of a 5f 3yo winner who was a half-sister to 1m 3yo Group 2 winner Danceabout and 6/6.5f Group 3 winner Pole Position; the family of smart juveniles Krayyan, Precocious and Pushy.

"The dam ended up staying middle distances for the owners, but this colt appears to have inherited his sire's speed as he is shaping up to be a reasonably early type. He goes nicely and should begin over six furlongs."

RUSHMORE
13/3 b c Lope De Vega - Qushchi (Encosta De Lago)
Owner: Qatar Racing Limited
Sales price: 500,000gns (David Redvers Bloodstock)

Half-brother to Grade 1-placed 8-12f winner (including at Grade 2/Listed level) Mrs Sippy. Dam a Grade 3-placed UK/US 7-12f winner (including at Listed level) who was a half-sister to five winners and out of a dual 10f Listed winner who was a half-sister to Dewhurst Stakes/St James's Palace Stakes winner Grand Lodge, dual 1m 3yo Listed winner Papabile (later dam of Listed-placed 5-6f winner Paco's Angel) and the dam of 6f 2yo Listed winner Dowager.

"This colt is rather typical of one by his sire in that he is medium-sized and quite forward. I could see him appearing in June or July over six or seven furlongs."

SKIBO CASTLE (FR)
16/5 b c Shalaa - Noelani (Indian Ridge)
Owner: Mrs Fitri Hay
Sales price: €130,000 (Alexander Cole)

Half-brother to Group 3-placed Italian 9-10f winner Sufranel and Irish dual 5f 2yo winner Natalisa. Dam a smart Irish 5-7.5f winner (including twice at Group 3 level) who was a full sister to very smart 5-6f winner (including at Group 1 level) Namid and a half-sister to Group 3-placed Irish 7f 2yo winner Natalis, Listed-placed Irish 7f 2yo winner Mandama and the dam of US 11f Listed winner Siberian Iris out of an Irish 5f 3yo Listed winner.

"He is the only Shalaa we have here, and is just going through a growing spell at the moment. He has done bits and pieces of work and has gone upsides. I would hope to see him in action by late June."

SPANISH COLT (IRE)
9/4 b c Kodiac - Fairywren (Approve)
Owner: Javier Maldonado
Sales price: n/a

Second foal of an unraced half-sister to Grade 2-placed UK/US 5-8.5f winner (including five times at Grade/Group 3 level) Sandiva, smart UK/Danish 7-9f winner (including at Listed level) Wentworth and Listed-placed Spanish/French 5f-1m winner Irish Cliff out of an Italian 7-11f winner; the family of Dewhurst Stakes/Derby winner Sir Percy.

"This colt is forward and looks like he will be a pretty early runner. He has only gone upsides so far, but looks to have ability and should be quick enough to start over five furlongs whenever we are back underway."

SPIRIT MIXER
21/2 ch c Frankel - Arabian Queen (Dubawi)
Owner: Jeff Smith
Sales price: n/a

First foal of a high-class 5-10.5f winner (including at Group 1 level) who was a sister to fairly useful dual 7f 3yo winner Cosmopolitan Queen and a half-sister to UK/French 8-14.5f winner Australian Queen and 2020 11-12f winner Arabian King out of a smart 8-12f winner (including at Group 2/Listed level) who was a half-sister to 1m 2yo Listed winner Doctor Dash, Listed-placed 8.5-12.5f winner Dashing Star and very useful 10-12f winner Dash Of Spice.

"Obviously he boasts an excellent pedigree and is the first foal of Arabian Queen. It is easy to forget that she was a sharp juvenile who won a Cherry

Hinton in July of her two-year-old career, and his sire was also obviously very smart at two. This is a strong colt with a lovely attitude. I have every hope we can achieve something at two, though we are certainly in no rush with him. I'd say he will be seen sometime in midsummer if he continues to go the right way. He could have enough speed to begin over six furlongs though will likely want seven furlongs before long."

SUNFLOWER SEED
25/3 ch f Showcasing - Sunflower (Dutch Art)
Owner: Nicholas Jones
Sales price: n/a

First foal of a 6f 2yo winner who was a half-sister to Group 3/Listed-placed 5f 2yo winner Life Of Riley (by Showcasing) and useful 6-7f winner Battered out of a 5f 2yo winning three-parts sister to Listed-placed prolific 5-6f winner Texas Gold out of a 6f 3yo Listed winning half-sister to the dam of 6/7f Group 3 winner Scarlet Runner.

"A strong, well-made filly who looks a real two-year-old type, just as her pedigree suggests. She shouldn't be long making an appearance once we are back racing."

TACTICAL
14/2 b c Toronado - Make Fast (Makfi)
Owner: The Queen
Sales price: n/a

First foal of a Listed-placed 6f 2yo winning half-sister to 2019 7f 2yo winner Cranberry (by Toronado) out of a smart 5-7f winner (including at Group 3/ Listed level) who was a half-sister to several winners including useful 8.5f 2yo winner Big Challenge and useful Irish 11.5f 3yo winner Hikari (later dam of 2019 10f 3yo Listed winner Raise You) out of an unraced half-sister to German 6f 2yo Group 2 winner Somethingdifferent out of a US 1m 1f Grade 1 winner.

"The dam was pretty useful for us, placing a couple of times at Listed level. This is a strong, precocious colt who will be out as soon as racing resumes and will have no problem with starting off over five furlongs."

UNNAMED (IRE)
27/3 ch c Lope De Vega - Queen Of Power (Medicean)
Owner: Apollo Racing & PDR Properties
Sales price: €56,000 (Fujimoto Racing)

Half-brother to Group 2/3-placed 5-6f winner (including at Listed level) Garrus. Dam a useful Irish 7f 3yo winner who was a half-sister to dual 5f winner

Richter Scale out of a maiden half-sister to Listed-placed 7-10f winner Hallhoo; the family of Irish 6/7f 2yo Group 1 winner Danehill Dancer and Coventry Stakes winner Buratino.

"A nice colt who is just cantering at present and showing up nicely enough. We don't want to rush him and will see where we are come June and July."

UNNAMED (IRE)
24/4 b c Lope De Vega - Rosie Cotton (King's Best)
Owner: Apollo Racing & PDR Properties
Sales price: €120,000 (Fujimoto Racing)

Half-brother to once-raced 2019 7f 2yo winner Seasony. Dam a Listed-placed French 1m 3yo winner who was a half-sister to smart French 12-14f winner (including at Listed level) King Of Arnor out of a thrice-raced maiden half-sister to very smart UK/US 7-9f winner (including twice at Grade 1 level) Aragorn and 6f 2yo winner Kaseema (later dam of Group 3/Listed-placed UK/UAE 7f-1m winner Zainhom); the family of Irish 6/7f 2yo Group 1 winner One Cool Cat.

"Another medium-sized Lope De Vega who isn't at all backward. He is nice and should be racing by midsummer."

UNNAMED (FR)   *King of the midlands*
1/2 b c Kingman - Spin (Galileo)
Owner: King Power Racing Co Ltd
Sales price: €600,000 (SackvilleDonald)

Full brother to 2019 French 8-8.5f 3yo winner Bowled Over. Dam a Group 3/Listed-placed 1m 2yo winner who was a sister to French 12.5f 3yo Listed winner Dirgam and Irish 7f 3yo winner/1000 Guineas third Moth, a three-parts sister to Group 1-placed 8-10f winner (including at Listed level) Rave Reviews, 12f 3yo Listed winner Fermion (later dam of 6f 2yo winner/Coventry Stakes runner-up Roman Soldier) and Cheshire Oaks winner Sail and a half-sister to smart 8-10f winner (including at Group 3/Listed level) Hearthstead Maison.

"A good-looking, quality individual who has plenty of depth to him. One to look forward to in the autumn."

Marten writes:

As a punter I think of Andrew Balding as a 'safe pair of hands'.

If he has a budding top-notcher he places it to achieve its optimum potential while, at the other end of the scale, if handicaps are the likeliest option for a horse to win then they will be brought along in an appropriate manner.

The trainer is not known for having precocious two-year-olds – his overall strike rate for juvenile winners to runners in the last five years is around 13 per cent – and the one that I like from those listed above is **Mellow Magic** even though the best may not be seen of her until next season.

Her half-brother Elm Park was a very tough two-year-old, suited to soft ground, who won four of his five starts culminating in the Racing Post Trophy. He raced a little keenly at three, thereby forfeiting his chance in the Derby, but he subsequently returned to winning ways in a 1m Listed race at Sandown.

This family is packed with winners including the gutsy long-distance hurdler Tweedledrum. Nathaniel is an influence for both speed and stamina and I expect this filly to show up nicely at the back-end before coming into her own over 10f or more at three.

RALPH BECKETT

CASUARINA
11/2 b f Sea The Moon - Caribana (Hernando)
Owner: Miss Kirsten Rausing
Sales price: n/a

Full sister to very useful 2019 12.5-14.5f 3yo winner Durston and a half-sister to Group 1-placed 8.5-12f winner (including at Group 3/Listed level) Cubanita, very useful 7-10.5f winner Aquarium and 1m 2yo winner Camagueyana. Dam a 9.5f 3yo winning granddaughter of a Yorkshire Oaks winner/Irish St Leger runner-up who was a half-sister to the dam of Park Hill Stakes winner Discreet Brief (herself later dam of Royal Lodge Stakes winner Steeler).

"A half-sister to a good filly we trained called Cubanita and though quite stoutly bred, she copes well with her work at the moment and is looking like she will come to hand a little earlier than her pedigree suggests."

CITY CODE
5/3 b c Kodiac - City Girl (Elusive City)
Owner: Jeff Smith
Sales price: n/a

Three-parts brother to UK/Spanish 6-7f winner City Gent (by Holy Roman Emperor). Dam a Listed-placed dual 6f winner/Lowther Stakes fourth who was a half-sister to dual 5f winner Olympic Runner and 6f 2yo winner Echo Ridge out of a Group 2/3-placed multiple 6-7f winner (including at Listed level) who was a half-sister to 5f Listed winner Loch Verdi (later grandam of Group 3-placed dual 6f winner No Nonsense) and out of top-class sprinter Lochsong.

"I trained the dam who placed at Listed level, but it's perhaps fair to say she has been a little quiet as a broodmare to this point. I would say this colt is her best chance of a decent one so far though, and he will more or less be ready for the second wave of two-year-old races when we're back underway as he is pretty forward."

FREE WILL
10/3 b f Lope De Vega - Free Rein (Danehill Dancer)
Owner: The Eclipse Partnership
Sales price: n/a

Sister to useful 7f-1m 2yo winner Fintas and half-sister to 2019 7f 2yo Group 3 winner West End Girl. Dam a 7f 3yo winner who was a half-sister to very smart 5-6f 2yo winner (including twice at Group 1 level) Reckless Abandon and Japanese 12f Listed winner Best Approach out of a Listed-placed UK/Canadian 6f-1m winning half-sister to US 9/10f Grade 1 winner Ticker Tape and 6.5f Group 1 winner Brando.

"A big, tall filly who has a good way of going. She is still immature and rather leggy but I hope she can do something over seven furlongs during the second half of the year."

ICONIC QUEEN
17/5 b f Invincible Spirit - Barshiba (Barathea)
Owner: Jeff Smith
Sales price: n/a

Half-sister to high-class 5-10.5f winner (including the Juddmonte International Stakes) Arabian Queen, fairly useful dual 7f 3yo winner Cosmopolitan Queen, UK/French 8-14.5f winner Australian Queen and 2020 11-12f winner Arabian King. Dam a smart 8-12f winner (including at Group 2/Listed level) who was a half-sister to 1m 2yo Listed winner Doctor Dash, Listed-placed 8.5-12.5f winner Dashing Star and very useful 10-12f winner Dash Of Spice.

"She was a little fiery to begin with but has now settled nicely into the rhythm of a training routine. Whilst not lacking for speed necessarily, it is a family that can often take a little time to come to hand. I like how this filly goes and would be surprised if she couldn't win a novice race at least during the second half of the season."

JUST TELLEM (IRE)
20/4 b c Bungle Inthejungle - Art Of Gold (Excellent Art)
Owner: Peter Mellett
Sales price: 80,000gns (A C Elliott, Agent)

Half-brother to very useful 7f-1m winner Kynren. Dam a maiden half-sister to a 6f 2yo winner out of a Listed-placed triple 5f 2yo winning half-sister to Group 1-placed Irish/UAE 5-6f winner (including twice at Listed level) Balmont Mast, Group 1-placed 6f 2yo winner Crazee Mental (later dam of multiple 7f/1m Group 2 winner Premio Loco) and the dam of high-class 7-8.5f winner (including at Group 2/3 level) Gregorian, Group 2-placed UK/Australian 7-12f winner (including at Listed level) Naval Warfare and Listed-placed 8.5f 2yo winner/1000 Guineas fourth Manderley.

"Quite a mature, forward colt who won't take long to make an appearance. He has just gone through a growing phase though, so we've eased off him a little at present."

STATE OCCASION
30/3 b f Iffraaj - Forest Crown (Royal Applause)
Owner: The Eclipse Partnership
Sales price: n/a

Sister to very useful 2019 multiple 10-10.5f 3yo winner Forest Of Dean and a half-sister to Listed-placed Irish 7.5f-1m 3yo winner Rionach, very useful multiple 8-8.5f winner Crowning Glory and 2019 French 7.5f 2yo winner Golden Crown. Dam a Listed-placed 6-8.5f winner who was a sister to Listed-placed dual 6f winner Riotous Applause (later dam of 6f 2yo Listed winner Invincible Warrior) and half-sister to Racing Post Trophy winner Crowded House, the dam of high-class pair Brando and Ticker Tape and the grandam of Middle Park Stakes winner Reckless Abandon.

"I have trained a few of this family including the dam, who didn't break her maiden until November of her two-year-old campaign. I suspect this filly won't be too dissimilar in that regard as she isn't overly forward, but she goes well at this stage and ought to be capable of making some sort of impact this year."

STORM DREAMER
10/4 b c Oasis Dream - Ombre (Galileo)
Owner: Khalid Abdullah
Sales price: n/a

Half-brother to Group 2/3-placed dual 6f 2yo winner Gavota. Dam an unraced half-sister to Listed-placed French 7f-1m winner World Ruler, Listed-placed French 5.5-6f 2yo winner Grand Vista and Listed-placed French 1m 2yo winner Disclose (later dam of 6f Listed winner Encrypted) out of a 1m 2yo winning half-sister to Group 3/Listed-placed 12f 3yo winner Singleton and very useful multiple 6-7f winner Brevity; the family of Irish 10f Group 1 winner Urban Fox.

"This colt has a good bit of size about him and is more of a three-year-old prospect. He has got a good way of going and is a horse I like, but we're certainly in no hurry with him. I imagine he'll want seven furlongs to begin with."

TIME SCALE

6/2 b f Charm Spirit - An Ghalanta (Holy Roman Emperor)
Owner: Qatar Racing Limited
Sales price: n/a

Half-sister to Grade 2/Group 3-placed UK/US 5-8.5f winner Bletchley. Dam an Irish 6f 2yo Listed winning close relation to Listed-placed Irish/UK 8-11f winner Bancnuanaheirann and a half-sister to Group 3/Listed-placed Irish 6f-1m winner Billyford and useful Irish 6f 2yo winner Move To Strike; the family of Dewhurst Stakes winner Parish Hall.

"We trained her half-sister Bletchley who finished second in the Albany Stakes at Royal Ascot as a two-year-old. This filly has come to hand similarly early and should be amongst our initial batch of two-year-old runners. She is incredibly strong - a real ball of muscle. I like her."

WILLIAM BLIGH

25/3 b c Territories - Arbella (Primo Dominie)
Owner: Chelsea Thoroughbreds Ltd
Sales price: 50,000gns (Ralph Beckett)

Three-parts brother to Listed-placed UK 7f 2yo/Irish 9.5f winner Lat Hawill (by Invincible Spirit) and a half-brother to Listed-placed 13.5-14f winner Bellajeu and useful 14f-2m winner Chocala. Dam a useful dual 12f winning half-sister to very useful 7f-2m 2f Flat/smart 2m-2m 3f hurdle (including at Grade 1 level)/2m-2m 3f chase winner Overturn; the family of Middle Park Stakes winner Primo Valentino, Cherry Hinton Stakes winner Dora Carrington and smart stayer Barolo.

"He is closely related to a horse called Lat Hawill who looked very good early on but never quite built on that initial promise. This colt was well bought at 50,000 guineas as he has size, scope and also goes well in his work. He should make a two-year-old and I can see him making an appearance around July or August time. Another that we like."

UNNAMED

23/4 b f Lope De Vega - Ennaya (Nayef)
Owner: Montcastle Racing
Sales price: n/a

Half-sister to Listed-placed French 9.5f 2yo winner Ebony and 2019 7f 2yo winner Encipher. Dam a French 1m 1f 3yo winner who was a half-sister to very smart 5.5f-1m winner (three times at Group 1 level, including the French 1000 Guineas) Ervedya and useful French dual 7f 2yo winner Eldena out of a Group 3-placed French 8-9.5f winner.

"A tall filly with a good pedigree who finds it all very easy at this stage. While she is coming to hand all the time, I suspect she will be one for the autumn like a few of the other Lope De Vega fillies we have trained in recent years."

Marten writes:

I have selected **Iconic Queen** here because this is a family that I have always liked.

Her dam Barshiba was a regular in Group races towards the end of her career, well handled by David Elsworth and winning seven of her 35 starts having raced for five seasons.

Blind in one eye, she tended to strike top form in midsummer. The best of her progeny to date has been Arabian Queen, who beat Golden Horn by a neck at 50/1 in the 2015 Juddmonte International, where there was an interesting aftermath when Elsworth refused to grant interviews having felt slighted by the lack of respect given by the racing press to the filly's chance beforehand.

Given the race's reputation over the years for producing shock results – famously back in 1972 when Brigadier Gerard met the only defeat of his career – I had a very modest interest on Arabian Queen, who had shown when third in the Group 1 Nassau Stakes on her previous start that she was entitled to be competitive in that grade.

Iconic Queen is bred along top-class lines, with Invincible Spirit likely to impose more pace into the family than was the case with the sires of her siblings.

MICHAEL BELL

AESTHETE
5/4 b c Muhaarar - Miss Brown To You (Fasliyev)
Owner: W J & T C O Gredley
Sales price: n/a

Half-brother to very smart 10f-2m 4f winner (including the Ascot Gold Cup) Big Orange and useful triple 12f 3yo winner India. Dam a 1m 3yo winner who was a half-sister to very smart 8-10f winner (including twice at Group 1 level) Military Attack, Group 2-placed multiple 5f winner (including at Group 3/Listed level) Almaty, very useful 7-10f winner Impeller and the maiden dam of Hong Kong Vase winner/Melbourne Cup runner-up Red Cadeaux.

"A completely different sort physically to his Gold Cup-winning half-brother, Big Orange. He is a good-moving, very well-balanced colt who shows speed and is quite forward. I should think he will begin over six furlongs at some point during the summer, and would be high on our list of two-year-olds at the moment."

ALEXI BOY
23/3 b c Kingman - Putyball (Silver Deputy)
Owner: Amo Racing Limited
Sales price: €220,000 (Elliott Bloodstock Services Limited)

Half-brother to French 9.5f 3yo winner Quantivator. Dam a French 1m 2yo Listed winner who was a half-sister to high-class French/US 8.5-11f winner (including at Grade 1 level) Ball Dancing, Listed-placed 9-12f winner Hayhaat, useful 10f-2m winner Gabrial The Hero and Listed-placed 12.5f-2m Flat winner/very useful 2m jumper Palomar; the family of Belmont Stakes winner Union Rags and Queen Anne Stakes winner Declaration Of War.

"A fine big colt who is very impressive to look at and boasts a smart pedigree. He is on hold at present given the current situation, but I would hope he could do something during the second half of the season over six or seven furlongs."

BIG KITTY
23/2 b f Bobby's Kitten - Bipartisan (Bahamian Bounty)
Owner: M E Pearlman
Sales price: 2,000gns (Richard Frisby Bloodstock)

Second foal of a dual 1m 3yo winning sister to 7f 3yo winner Binthere Dunthat and half-sister to 10f Group 3 winner Robin Hoods Bay out of an unraced half-sister to Listed-placed Irish 7f 2yo winner Pietra Dura (later dam of US 10f Grade 3 winner Turning Top), Listed-placed 2019 8-8.5f 3yo winner Bighearted, Listed-placed 13f 3yo winner Bite Of The Cherry and the dam of King George VI and Queen Elizabeth Stakes/Juddmonte International Stakes winner Postponed and Italian 10f Group 1 winner God Given out an Irish 7f 2yo Group 1 winning half-sister to the dam of dual 1m Group 1 winner Simply Perfect.

"She wasn't wanted at the sales but is actually a nice filly who will be one to aim at those novice auction contests - like the ones they stage at the Newmarket July course during the summer months. I imagine she'll start off over seven furlongs."

BOBBY ON THE BEAT (IRE)
7/2 b c Bobby's Kitten - Late Night Movie (Holy Roman Emperor)
Owner: The Fitzrovians 4
Sales price: 24,000gns (Richard Frisby Bloodstock)

Half-brother to 5f 2yo winner Jasi. Dam an unraced sister to French 8-10f winner Julius Quercus, close relation to Listed-placed Irish 11-12f Flat/2m hurdle winner Glitter Baby and half-sister to Group 2/Listed-placed Irish 7f 2yo winner Going Public, useful Irish multiple 7f winner Northern Rocked and French 7f 2yo winner Hiort out of a maiden sister to Group 3-placed Irish dual 1m 2yo winner Super Gift (dam of Irish 12f Group 3 winner Sense Of Purpose).

"Bobby's Kitten is a first-season sire I am very interested in, given the look of those we have here by him. This is a well-made colt who has created a favourable impression so far, and I'd be hopeful he can make up into a nice six and seven furlong horse this summer."

BOOKMARK
12/3 b f New Approach - Free Verse (Danehill Dancer)
Owner: The Queen
Sales price: n/a

Half-sister to useful 7-13.5f winner Frontispiece. Dam a very useful 6-7f winner who was a full sister to Listed-placed 6f-1m winner Quadrille out of a 10f 3yo Listed winning sister to smart 8-13.5f winner (including at Group 2/3 level) Phantom Gold (later dam of dual 7f Listed winner Golden Stream and Oaks runner-up Flight Of Fancy, herself the dam of dual 10f Group 3 winner

Fabricate) and half-sister to useful 1m 2yo winner Tempting Prospect (later dam of 14f Listed winner Tactician).

"This filly is one of the speedier New Approachs and would quite possibly have been my representative in the Chesham Stakes at Royal Ascot in a normal season. She skips along nicely and is an extremely good mover."

CLOSENESS
22/3 b f Iffraaj - Pack Together (Paco Boy)
Owner: The Queen
Sales price: n/a

Second foal of a Listed-placed 6f 2yo winner who was a half-sister to useful dual 6f winner Instalment and four other winners out of a useful 9-10f 3yo winner who was a full sister to high-class UK/UAE 7-9f winner (including at Group 1 level) Right Approach and a half-sister to useful triple 1m winner Benedict and useful 14f-2m winner Temple Way.

"This is a strong, well-made filly who is ready to do more work once we get a clearer idea about when we might get going again. She is very light on her feet and gets up Warren Hill with ease."

DUJAC
11/4 b f Muhaarar - All For Laura (Cadeaux Genereux)
Owner: Wood Hall Stud & Mrs I Corbani
Sales price: 42,000gns (Richard Frisby Bloodstock)

Three-parts sister to 6f 2yo Group 2 winner/Cheveley Park Stakes runner-up Misheer (later dam of 6f 3yo Listed winner Mistrusting) and 7f 2yo winner Night Song (both by Oasis Dream) and a half-sister to multiple 5-6f winner Storm Lightning and multiple 6f winner Hartwright. Dam a useful 5f 2yo winner who was a full sister to very useful 7f-1m winner Kehaar and out of a 1m 3yo winner who was a half-sister to Middle Park Stakes winner First Trump.

"She is closely related to a good two-year-old Clive Brittain trained called Misheer, while I had a half-brother who was only fair at best. This filly looks quite forward, although hasn't quite come in her coat yet. She should begin over six or seven furlongs."

HUMMING BEE
13/4 b c Oasis Dream - Humdrum (Dr Fong)
Owner: The Queen
Sales price: n/a

Half-brother to UK/Australian 8-12f winner Humbolt Current, 6f 2yo winner Husbandry, 2019 8.5f 2yo winner Cloud Drift and two other winners. Dam a very useful UK/French 7f-1m winner who was a half-sister to very useful multiple 6f winner (including at Listed level) Musical Comedy, useful 7-12.5f winner Full Toss and 6f 2yo winners Otago and Ring Of Truth out of a Listed-placed 10f 3yo winning half-sister to 2m 4f Grade 2 chase winner Locksmith.

"We have trained a few from this family including Otago who won at two last season. This colt looks quite forward and, like his siblings, is a fluent mover. I can see him making up into a summer two-year-old."

INVEIGLE
6/2 b c Dark Angel - Sand Vixen (Dubawi)
Owner: The Queen
Sales price: n/a

Half-brother to high-class UK/UAE 7-9f winner (including at Group 1 level) Dream Castle. Dam a smart 5-6f 2yo winner (including at Group 2/Listed level) who was a half-sister to Group 3-placed UK/UAE 6-6.5f winner (including at Listed level) So Will I and the maiden dam of Group 3-placed French multiple 5.5-8.5f winner King Of Spades.

"A big, strong, athletic colt who moves well and finds Warren Hill extremely easy to climb. He has a wonderful pedigree, and really fills the eye physically. He will make a two-year-old and I hope he could be quite good."

LADY SKYE
26/4 b f Acclamation - Chutney (Exceed And Excel)
Owner: Amo Racing Limited
Sales price: 95,000gns (Peter & Ross Doyle Bloodstock)

Third foal of a 5f 2yo winner who was a half-sister to US 8/8.5f Grade 3 winner Pickle (later dam of four-time 6/7f Listed winner Gusto and US 8.5f Listed winner Beauly), Group 3-placed 7-10f winner Auld Burns and useful French 6-7f winner Pivock out of a fairly useful 5.5-10f winner who was a half-sister to 11f Listed winner Ronaldsay (later dam of Group 1-placed 6-7f winner (including at Group 3 level)/Irish 2000 Guineas runner-up Gale Force Ten).

"A strong, well-made filly who shows speed, though we've not had a proper look at her just yet given all that's going on. She should make a summer two-year-old and will likely start off over six furlongs."

MASTERMAN (FR)
28/3 ch c Reliable Man - Quenching (Street Cry)
Owner: Amo Racing Limited & Mr S Hanson
Sales price: £50,000 (A C Elliott, Agent)

Full brother to 2020 French 6.5f 3yo Listed winner Quiet Times and very useful UK/Hong Kong 7-9f winner World Famous. Dam a French 1m 1f 3yo winner who was a half-sister to 2020 French 7.5f Listed winner Nature's Colors, very useful triple 6f winner (including at Listed level) Whitman and very useful French 8-9f winner Mount Pelion out of a Group 1-placed UK/US 7-10f winner (including at Group/Grade 3 level)/1000 Guineas runner-up.

"A strong, well put together colt who is a brother to a nice horse we used to train called Master Brewer over here (now named World Famous). He has been doing well in Hong Kong recently while his three-year-old sister Quiet Times won a Listed Race over in France earlier this year. This colt looks more forward and shows a bit more speed than his brother did at this stage."

MR RYDER
20/4 b c Pearl Secret - Jackline (Diktat)
Owner: Amo Racing Limited & A C Elliott
Sales price: 25,000gns (A C Elliott, Agent)

Half-brother to Italian multiple 5-7f winner Excellent Jack, 6f 2yo winner Epona and two other winners. Dam a maiden half-sister to smart 5-6f winner (including at Group 3/Listed level) Elnawin, useful multiple 5f winner Normal Equilibrium and useful multiple 5f-1m winner Elna Bright out of a useful 5-6f 2yo winner; the family of 2019 1m Group 2 winner Move Swiftly, 6f/1m Group 3 winner Satchem and 10.5f 3yo Group 3 winner Mulaqat.

"He is the one I am most frustrated about at the moment because he would have been running already in a normal season. He is the most forward of our two-year-olds, and though we haven't pushed any buttons given the present situation, I suspect the response once they are pressed will be pleasing."

STANLEY BALDWIN
7/3 br c Showcasing - Madame Defarge (Motivator)
Owner: W J & T C O Gredley
Sales price: n/a

Half-brother to useful 2019 14f-2m 2f winner Land Of Oz. Dam a Listed-placed 1m 2yo winner who was a three-parts sister to useful 7f-1m winner Foolin Myself and a half-sister to US 1m 1f Grade 3 winner Gender Agenda, Listed-placed 7-12f UK/Bahraini winner Unex El Greco and the dam of high-class triple 6f 2yo winner (including at Group 1 level)/Irish 1000 Guineas second Pretty Pollyanna out of a half-sister to Oaks/St Leger winner User Friendly.

"Another nice homebred of the Gredleys who is related to our star two-year-old of a couple of seasons ago, Pretty Pollyanna. This is a good-sized colt who has a nice temperament and pleases in all he does on the gallops so far."

SUN FESTIVAL
23/3 b c Toronado - Raymi Coya (Van Nistelrooy)
Owner: The Queen
Sales price: n/a

Full brother to 2019 7f 2yo winner Cranberry and a half-brother to Listed-placed 6f 2yo winner Make Fast. Dam a smart 5-7f winner (including at Group 3/Listed level) who was a half-sister to several winners including useful 8.5f 2yo winner Big Challenge and useful Irish 11.5f 3yo winner Hikari (dam of 2019 10f 3yo Listed winner Raise You) out of an unraced half-sister to German 6f 2yo Group 2 winner Somethingdifferent out of a US 1m 1f Grade 1 winner.

"A sizeable, lengthy colt who really covers the ground and moves easily. He has a lovely temperament and should make a nice summer two-year-old all being well."

TONY MONTANA
19/4 gr c Frankel - Tropical Paradise (Verglas)
Owner: Amo Racing Limited
Sales price: 500,000gns (A C Elliott, Agent)

Half-brother to fairly useful 6-7f winner Coral Sea and once-raced 2020 10f 3yo winner Fiji. Dam a smart multiple 6-7f winner (including twice at Group 3 level) who was a half-sister to smart Italian multiple 5-7f winner (including at Group 3/Listed level) Harlem Shake and Group 3-placed 7-10f winner (including at Listed level) Shenanigans; the family of Irish 12f 3yo Group 3 winner Dancing Sunset (later dam of Irish 6f 2yo Listed winner Lady Of Kildare) and French 12.5f 3yo Group 3 winner Don't Sulk.

"The concern with this page was the crossing of Frankel with a Verglas mare as it had the potential to produce a flighty one, but thankfully this colt seems to have a good mind on him. He has done well physically, but will obviously take a bit of time and is more one for the second half of the season."

VEDUTE

22/2 b g Holy Roman Emperor - Quads (Shamardal)
Owner: Richard Green
Sales price: £85,000 (Richard Frisby Bloodstock)

Second foal of an unraced half-sister to high-class 7f-1m winner (including at Group 1 level) Here Comes When, Group 2/Listed-placed 10-12f winner Melodic Notion and 10f 3yo winner Morant Bay out of a French dual 1m 2yo winner (including at Group 3 level) who was a half-sister to Grade 1-placed US 8-11f winner (including at Grade 2/Listed level) Bonapartiste, French triple 10-12f Listed winner Go Got and French 10f Listed winner Sablier Noir.

"He has already been gelded and is a precocious sort who would have run by now in a normal year. His skin looks great and hopefully he can have a good two-year-old campaign as he looks the type do well as a juvenile."

Marten writes:

The main reason that I have nominated **Stanley Baldwin** from Michael Bell's crop is because he is a half-brother to Land Of Oz, who won six races last season progressing from a rating of 58 to 93.

Placed with the finely honed skill we have come to expect from Sir Mark Prescott, Land Of Oz stays in training at four with the prospect of making further progress up the rankings.

Land Of Oz, the first foal of his dam, is by Australia and has won up to 2m 2f, but this younger half-brother is by Showcasing so should be sharper. The bottom line includes the dam of top-class two-year-old Pretty Pollyanna and Oaks and St Leger winner User Friendly, who I vividly recall catching my eye in the paddock as a big imposing filly before making a winning debut at Sandown way back in April 1992.

There are a lot of familiar names in this homebred colt's pedigree and I would expect him to show up well in a mid-season maiden.

GEORGE BOUGHEY

ASTIMEGOESBY
14/2 ch c Mehmas - Chantaleen (Falco)
Owner: Mrs Susan Roy
Sales price: £40,000 (A C Elliott, Agent)

Half-brother to once-raced 2019 5f 2yo winner Bomb Proof. Dam a French 10f 3yo winner who was a half-sister to Group 2-placed French/Italian 7.5-9f winner (including at Group 3/Listed level) Spoil The Fun out of a once-raced maiden three-parts sister to French 7f 2yo Group 2 winner Roi Gironde and half-sister to French 10.5f 3yo Group 3 winner Garendare, 10f 3yo Listed winner Port Vila and Listed-placed French 8-10f winner Glen Falls.

"His half-brother Bomb Proof won a good novice race at York last spring and was due to go to Royal Ascot before meeting with a setback. This is a nice colt who is also forward and would have been ready to roll during the early stages of the turf season."

SUSUCARU
11/4 b f Starspangledbanner - Sugar Hiccup (Refuse To Bend)
Owner: George Boughey
Sales Price: 14,000gns (Hurworth Bloodstock)

Third foal of a 12.5f Flat/2m-2m 4f hurdle winner who was a half-sister to Italian 14/15f Listed winner Ryan, Group 3/Listed-placed 6f 2yo winner Highland Daughter (later dam of Australian 6f Listed winner Highland Beat), useful 1m 3yo winner Rive Gauche (later dam of wide-margin 2019 6f 2yo debut winner Ultra Violet) and three other winners; the family of Group 1 winners Helene Mascot, Kinnaird and Laurens.

"A forward filly purchased fairly cheaply by Sam Haggas at Book 2 of the Tattersalls October Yearling Sale considering her extended family. She would have been ready to run during the first couple of the weeks of the intended season, but I imagine she will be seen to even better effect during the second half of the year in any case."

UNNAMED
15/4 ch c Toronado - Blossom Mills (Bahamian Bounty)
Owner: J R Boughey
Sales price: 36,000gns (Amanda Skiffington Bloodstock)

Second foal of a maiden half-sister to five winners including smart 10-12f winner (including at Group 2/3 level) Air Pilot out of an Irish 14f 3yo winning half-sister to French 10f Group 3 winner Mint Crisp; the family of 1m 1f Group 3 winner/Racing Post Trophy runner-up Charlie Farnsbarns and 6f 2yo Group 3 winner Angel's Hideaway.

"A really nice colt for the second half of the season. He's a gorgeous mover who has found it all very easy so far."

UNNAMED (IRE)
7/2 b c Ivawood - Lady Lizabeth (Lord Shanakill)
Owner: George Boughey
Sales price: €13,000 (Amanda Skiffington/George Boughey)

First foal of an unraced half-sister to useful UK/US 7-8.5f winner Mighty Empire, fairly useful 7-13f winner Freddy Q, Italian 7.5-9.5f winner Carimo and the unraced dam of smart Italian 5f-1m winner (including at Group 3/Listed level) Fontanelice out of an unraced half-sister to smart Japanese performers Manic Sunday and That's The Plenty.

"This is another lovely colt who I think was very well bought at €13,000 from Tattersalls Ireland. He is one for the summer onwards and has a bit of quality about him."

UNNAMED
19/4 ch f Australia - Queens Park (King's Best)
Owner: George Boughey
Sales price: 33,000gns (Avenue Bloodstock/George Boughey)

Half-sister to 2019 Irish 6f 2yo Listed winner Sir Boris. Dam an 8.5-9f 3yo winning half-sister to useful Irish 7f 2yo winner Singing Bird out of an unraced half-sister to French 10.5f 3yo Group 3 winner/French Oaks runner-up Abbatiale (later dam of four-time 6/7f Group 3 winner Bewitched), French 10.5f 3yo Listed winner Aubergade and the dam of high-class Irish/Australian 12-14f winner (including at Group 2/3 level)/St Leger third Southern France.

"She's a half-sister to a Listed winner and has a bit of class about her. Very much one for the backend and will make an even better three-year-old."

Marten writes:

George Boughey is one of the newest recruits to the training ranks, having been granted a licence last July following six years as assistant to Hugo Palmer, for whom he oversaw the trainer's 50-box satellite yard.

Before that he spent time with Gai Waterhouse and Lloyd Williams in Australia.

He has made a good start to his new career, with eight winners to date headed by four-times winner Three C's.

Astimegoesby is a half-brother to Jeremy Noseda's two-year-old winner Bomb Proof, who was going to head for Royal Ascot but didn't appear again. This son of first-season sire Mehmas comes from a strong French family packed full of winners.

I confidently expect this young trainer to build on his promising start.

KARL BURKE

BOOGIE TIME (IRE)
3/2 b c Kodiac - Get Up And Dance (Makfi)
Owner: Carl Waters & Mrs Elaine Burke
Sales price: £65,000 (Karl Burke/Carl Waters)

First foal of a 6f 3yo winning half-sister to Group 1-placed multiple 5f winner (including at Group 2/Listed level) Pearl Secret, useful 5-6f winner Batten The Hatches and 5f 2yo winner Secret Romance out of a 5f Listed winning daughter of a multiple 5f winner who was a half-sister to 5f Group 3 winner Palacegate Episode (later grandam of Middle Park Stakes winner Dutch Art and French 1000 Guineas second Up) and triple 5/6f Listed winner Palacegate Jack.

"A sizeable colt with a lot of scope. He won't be early but goes along nicely and will hopefully be running around June time. There is lots of speed in the pedigree and I imagine he will start off over six furlongs."

CELESTIAL QUEEN
30/1 b f Dark Angel - Agnes Stewart (Lawman)
Owner: Clipper Logistics
Sales price: 200,000gns (William Haggas)

First foal of a Group 1-placed 7f-1m 2yo winner (including at Group 2 level) who was the daughter of a useful 7-12f winner who was a half-sister to dual 6f 2yo winner Kuwait Station out of a 6f 2yo winner who was a half-sister to Irish 7f 2yo Group 1 winner/Irish Derby runner-up Definite Article, Dante Stakes winner Salford Express and Greenham Stakes winner Salford City.

"A beautiful, strong filly who has been cantering in the main, given she only arrived in March though has recently gone upsides. She is typical of her sire in that she'll likely want a bit of cut in the ground, so we will have to mind where we go with her. Hopefully she will be ready to start around the end of May or June if conditions are suitable."

H BOMB
26/3 ch c Pearl Secret - Mothers Finest (Tamayuz)
Owner: Titanium Racing Club
Sales price: £20,000 (Larry Stratton)

First foal of a useful dual 1m winner who was a half-sister to useful 10-12f winner Dame Lucy out of a maiden half-sister to US 1m 1f Grade 3/Irish 6f 2yo Listed winner Coney Kitty and four other winners including the dam of Dante Stakes winner/Derby second Libertarian, 10f Group 3 winner Prince Siegfried and French 12.5f Listed winner Bigzam.

"We trained the dam who was useful and probably black type standard though never quite achieved it. This is a smallish colt who goes nicely and is doing nothing wrong at present. I hope to have him out in late May or June."

HILARITY
28/4 b f Twilight Son - Light Hearted (Green Desert)
Owner: Cheveley Park Stud
Sales price: n/a

Three-parts sister to 5f 2yo winner Giddy (by Kyllachy) and a half-sister to 6f 2yo winner/Lowther Stakes fourth Merletta. Dam a 6f 3yo winner who was a full sister to smart 6-7f winner (including twice at Group 2 level) Byron and useful prolific 7-8.5f winner Gallantry, a three-parts sister to useful 7f-1m 3yo winner Resort (later dam of Listed-placed 5f 2yo winner Secret Venture) and a half-sister to the unraced dam of 6f 3yo Listed winner Mystic Dawn out of a Cheveley Park Stakes winning half-sister to the dam of Royal Lodge Stakes winner Al Jadeed.

"A good-sized, tallish filly who came in a bit later than some of our other two-year-olds. She is a lovely individual by Twilight Son, who is a first-season sire I am quite keen on. I would be disappointed if this filly couldn't win her maiden and/or a novice this year and she should be a sprinter looking at her pedigree."

INHALER
8/2 b c Elzaam - Desire (Kyllachy)
Owner: Abdulrazaq Mohamdi
Sales price: £32,000 (Federico Barberini)

First foal of a triple 7f winner who was a half-sister to Group 1-placed UK/ Hong Kong 5-6f winner (including at Group 2/Listed level) Frederick Engels, very useful multiple 6f winner Colonel Mak and fairly useful prolific 5-6f winner Piazon out of a maiden half-sister to useful 5f 2yo winners Montzando and Shuffling Kid.

"A nice colt who would likely have run by now under normal circumstances. He has some speedy relations and certainly looks like he will sprint himself. He goes well and I like him."

MISTER B
7/3 ch c Dandy Man - Days Of Summer (Bachelor Duke)
Owner: Ontoawinner 14 & Mrs Elaine Burke
Sales price: £48,000 (Karl Burke)

Half-brother to 6f 2yo winner Serradura. Dam a 6f 2yo winning half-sister to Irish 6f 2yo Listed winner Pharmacist (dam of US 11/12f Grade 1 winner Red Rocks and 10f 3yo Listed winners Galvaun and Medicinal), Listed-placed 7f 2yo winner Phariseek and the dam of 9/10.5f Group 3 winner Frankuus and French 1m 2yo Group 3 winner US Law.

"A lovely colt I bought from the Goffs UK Premier Yearling sale last summer. He is a big, strong colt with a fantastic mind on him. The slight negative would be Bachelor Duke as the damsire, but a lot of this family have won at two, and although he has the size and scope to train on next year, I'd be pretty disappointed if this colt couldn't follow suit."

NIGHT OF ROMANCE
14/2 ch f Night Of Thunder - Shohrah (Giant's Causeway)
Owner: Jeff Laughton & Elaine Burke
Sales price: 45,000gns (Karl Burke)

Three-parts sister to 8.5f 2yo winner Shaayeq (by Dubawi) and a half-sister to useful 6-7f winner Wahoo and 1m 2yo winner Bronte Flyer. Dam a useful 6f 2yo winner who was a half-sister to Listed-placed 7f 3yo winner Ma-Arif (later grandam of French 5f Group 2 winner Rangali) and five other winners including the dam of 7/13f Group 3 winner Wells Farhh Go out of a half-sister to Irish St Leger winner Ibn Bey and Yorkshire Oaks winner Roseate Tern.

"This filly perhaps hasn't grown as much as we'd have liked during the winter, but if she is good enough then she's big enough. We haven't pushed any buttons yet, but she is a lovely individual with a good temperament. She is related to a couple of two-year-old winners and the dam was also successful as a juvenile, so she really ought to be doing something this season."

NORTH OF AMAZING
20/4 b c Havana Gold - Princess Guest (Iffraaj)
Owner: Mrs Barbara Keller & Mrs Elaine Burke
Sales price: 125,000gns (Karl Burke)

Half-brother to 2019 5f 2yo winner/Norfolk Stakes third Dubai Station. Dam a maiden half-sister to very useful multiple 6-7f winner (including at Listed level) Imperial Guest, very useful multiple 6f-1m winner Excellent Guest and four other winners out of a 1m 3yo winner who was a half-sister to French 12f Listed winner Sibling Rival.

"He won't be quite as early as half-brother Dubai Station - who we obviously enjoyed a good two-year-old campaign with last year - but is a lovely individual who is coming to hand all the time and should be ready to run around July time. I like him."

RED FASCINATOR
16/2 b f Kodiac - Red Turban (Kyllachy)
Owner: Cheveley Park Stud
Sales price: n/a

Third foal of a 6f 2yo winner who was a full sister to 6f 2yo winner/Cheveley Park Stakes fourth Adorn (later dam of 6f 2yo Group 2 winner Saayerr and Group 2/3-placed multiple 5f winner Ornate) and 6f 2yo winner Furbelow (later dam of triple 6/6.5f Group 1 winner Advertise) and a three-parts sister to very useful US 5-8.5f winner (including at Listed level) Red Diadem out of a maiden daughter of a US 8.5f Grade 2 winner/1000 Guineas runner-up.

"She is a nice, refined filly who is already mature and looks like she should be a two-year-old. It is hard to know for sure at this stage as, like the other Cheveley Park filly, she only came in towards the end of January. We haven't got stuck into her yet but it's obviously a really nice pedigree and we certainly like what we see at this stage."

SHE'S SO NICE (IRE)
7/3 b f Mehmas - Elkmait (Trade Fair)
Owner: Carl Waters & Mrs Elaine Burke
Sales price: 110,000gns (Karl Burke/Carl Waters)

Half-sister to Group 1-placed UK/US 6f-1m winner (including at Grade 2 level) The Mackem Bullet and dual 6f 2yo winner Inuk. Dam a 6f 2yo winner who was a half-sister to Japanese 7f Group 2 winner Moonquake, Japanese triple 9/10f Group 3 winner Bounce Shasse, 2019 Japanese 8/9f Group 3 winner Contra Check and 2000 Guineas third Stubbs Art out of a maiden half-sister to smart 6f-1m winner (including at Group 2/3 level) Just James.

"A little on the small side but has grown a bit recently. She has just had a break and is now back in work. I think she has plenty of ability and will be very disappointed if she couldn't win a race or two this season."

SIMONS KING (IRE)
1/5 b c Kingman - Sanaya (Barathea)
Owner: Ecurie Normandie Pur Sang
Sales price: €140,000 (Ecurie Normandie Pur Sang)

Half-brother to French 9.5-11f 3yo winner Sanabad and French 1m 3yo winner Sannkala. Dam a Group 1-placed French/UAE 8-9f winner (including twice at Listed level) who was a three-parts sister to French Oaks winner/Arc third Sarafina (later dam of 2019 French 1m 2yo Group 3 winner Savarin) and a half-sister to smart French/UAE triple 1m winner (including at Group 3/Listed level) Sandagiyr and Listed-placed French 1m 2yo winner Sanjida.

"A lovely, scopey individual who we are very happy with so far. Given his size and pedigree, we are only just beginning to build him up in his work, so he's something of an unknown quantity at present. Having said that, I would be surprised if he wasn't capable of achieving something at two."

WIZARD D'AMOUR

21/5 gr c Dutch Art - Holistic (Pivotal)
Owner: Carl Waters & Mrs Elaine Burke
Sales price: 200,000gns (Karl Burke/Carl Waters)

Full brother to very useful 6-7f winner Diagnostic and a half-brother to useful dual 7f winner Homeopathic. Dam an unraced sister to 6f Listed winner Prescription and half-sister to 7f 2yo Group 3 winner Cupid's Glory, smart 7-8.5f winner (including at Group 3/Listed level) Clinical (later dam of 7f 2yo winner/Irish National Stakes third Lockheed) and 8/10f Listed winner Courting (later dam of 1m Listed winner Fury); the family of high-class sprinter Cassandra Go and Coventry Stakes winner/Irish 2000 Guineas second Verglas.

"A gorgeous colt who caught the eye of a few good judges at the sales, including Richard Fahey and Sir Mark Prescott. Sir Mark actually came up here recently and still really liked what he saw, so hopefully that bodes well. Being a May foal and coming from a fairly slow-maturing Cheveley Park family, we won't be in a rush with him. He is big and strong and we're just going through the motions at the moment. More of a three-year-old prospect."

UNNAMED

28/2 b c Showcasing - Blue Aegean (Invincible Spirit)
Owner: Clipper Logistics *Roadman*
Sales price: £150,000 (Joe Foley)

Second foal of a useful triple 5f winner who was a half-sister to 6f 2yo Group 3 winner who was the granddaughter of a Stakes-placed Canadian 6-8.5f winner who was a half-sister to US 5.5f 2yo winner Alba Daba Dou (later dam of US 1m 3yo Listed winner Alba Dabas Secret); the family of US triple 5.5-6.5f Listed winner Silver Expression.

"A good-sized colt who has a bit of a knee action on him so is another that will require some ease in the ground. Also like the other Clipper Logistics horse, he only came in fairly recently but I would hope to have him running by the end of May or June should ground conditions be suitable."

Marten writes:

I'm no lover of the name but I'm keen to nominate **H Bomb** as I know how highly the trainer rated his dam Mothers Finest, who I recollect being considered worthy of a high-class entry or two before she ran.

Connections persisted with her at a decent level, running her nine times from 13 starts in Listed contests, although the nearest she ever finished in that grade was fifth. She won her second race at two and her only other victory came in a 1m handicap from a mark of 92 as a three-year-old.

H Bomb comes from the first crop of the very useful Pearl Secret, whose yearlings caught the eye of some good judges in the autumn. I expect this colt would have fetched more money at the sales had he been a little bigger, but I still believe he will prove well bought at £20,000, leaving him with the option of running from a favourable weight in one of the sales races.

OWEN BURROWS

———— • ————

HOLWAH
5/4 b f Kingman - Shimah (Storm Cat)
Owner: Hamdan Al Maktoum
Sales price: n/a

Half-sister to very useful UK/UAE 5-7f winner (including at Listed level) Mushir, once-raced 2019 5.5f 2yo winner Raheeq and Irish 1m 2yo winner Moghamarah. Dam a Group 1-placed Irish dual 6f 2yo winner (including at Listed level) who was a half-sister to high-class 6-7f winners Haatef (including at Group 2/Listed level) and Walayef (including at Group 3/Listed level), Irish dual 6f 3yo Listed winner Ulfah and Irish 7f 2yo winner Mooqtar.

"A very forward individual who will be one of our first two-year-old runners. Her half-sister by Muhaarar won first time out for Roger Varian last spring and looks promising. This is a strong, compact filly who has thrived physically ever since she came to us and for all she can be a little bit hot, I am looking forward to seeing her in action."

KAWAALEES
12/3 gr c Havana Gold - Blanc de Chine (Dark Angel)
Owner: Hamdan Al Maktoum
Sales price: 115,000gns (Shadwell Estate Company)

Full brother to high-class multiple 5f winner (including at Group 1 level) Havana Grey. Dam a multiple 5f winner who was a half-sister to Group 3-placed triple 5f winner Fast Act, useful prolific 5f-1m winner Desert Opal and five other winners out of a French 5.5f 2yo winning sister to the dam of French 1m 1f 3yo winner Lateen Sails and grandam of 7f Group 2 winner Richard Pankhurst and 7f 2yo Group 3 winner Crazy Horse and half-sister to French 10f 3yo Group 2 winner Radevore.

"This colt has a bit of size but isn't too big and would be among our sharper two-year-olds. He has done a couple of good swinging canters and is forward mentally, which you would hope for given he is a brother to Havana Grey. I hope to have him running whenever we are given the go ahead to resume racing."

MAARAKAH (IRE)
4/5 gr c Markaz - Bunditten (Soviet Star)
Owner: Hamdan Al Maktoum
Sales price: 60,000gns (Shadwell Estate Company)

Three-parts brother to useful 5-6f winner Star Fire (by Dark Angel) and a half-brother to Coventry Stakes winner Rajasinghe, Listed-placed 5f 2yo winner Kurland, 5f 2yo winner Airborne Again, 6f 2yo winner Star Breaker and two other winners. Dam a Listed-placed 5f 2yo winner who was a half-sister to useful 5-6f winner Retainer.

"This colt has a precocious pedigree and is duly very forward both physically and mentally. He has done a couple of strong canters and moves nicely. He should be in action whenever we're allowed to start racing again."

MUBARMAJ (IRE)
13/2 b c Muhaarar - Kate The Great (Xaar)
Owner: Hamdan Al Maktoum
Sales price: €320,000 (Shadwell Estate Company)

Half-brother to Group 1-placed 5-6f winner (including at Group 3/Listed level) Eastern Impact, Group 3-placed Irish/Canadian 6-6.5f winner (including at Stakes level) Miss Katie Mae and very useful multiple 6f winner Summerghand. Dam a 5f 2yo winning close relation to Irish 5f 2yo winner Liberating and half-sister to Group 3/Listed-placed triple 6f winner/2000 Guineas fourth Bossy Guest and the dam of 1m Listed winner Another Touch.

"This is a quality colt but these Muhaarars caught everyone by surprise last year as they weren't as precocious as expected. He was always going to be a late summer sort of two-year-old, but suffered a minor setback which could see him appear even later in the season. He is bred to be a sprinter and should start off over six furlongs."

RASHEED (IRE)
20/2 b c Oasis Dream - Raaqy (Dubawi)
Owner: Hamdan Al Maktoum
Sales price: n/a

First foal of a useful 6.5f 2yo winner who was a half-sister to smart French/UK 7f-1m winner (including at Listed level) Mankib and 6f 2yo winner Rayaheen (later dam of smart 6-7f 2yo winner (including at Group 3/Listed level) Tajaanus and very useful 7-7.5f winner Motafaawit) out of a Cheveley Park Stakes and 1000 Guineas winner/French Derby third.

"A good-looking colt with a bit of quality. Barry Hills trained the dam to win first time out and she went on to finish third in a Listed Race, and it's obviously a good family that goes back to Natagora. He won't be overly early, but moves well and is one to look forward to in the second half of the season."

UNNAMED
29/1 b c Cable Bay - Conservatory (Observatory)
Owner: Hamdan Al Maktoum
Sales price: 140,000gns (Shadwell Estate Company)

First foal of an unraced sister to 6f Group 1 winner African Rose (later dam of 6f 2yo Group 3 winner Fair Eva) and Group 1-placed French 6f-1m 2yo winner (including at Group 3/Listed level) Helleborine (later dam of Coventry Stakes winner Calyx) out of a Group 3/Listed-placed 10f 3yo winner who was a half-sister to high-class 7-9f winner (including at Group 1 level) Distant Music and the unraced dam of French 15f 3yo Group 2 winner Canticum.

"A tall colt who is still a little immature and has some more growing to do - but we like what we see so far."

UNNAMED
11/3 ch c Lope De Vega - Dash To The Front (Diktat)   Moktasaab
Owner: Hamdan Al Maktoum
Sales price: 500,000gns (Shadwell Estate Company)

Three-parts brother to high-class 10-10.5f winner (including twice at Group 1 level) Speedy Boarding (by Shamardal) and a half-brother to very useful dual 10f 3yo winner Elwazir, useful dual 1m winner Next Stage and useful 8.5-12f winner Miss Dashwood (dam of 2019 Queen's Vase winner Dashing

Willoughby). Dam an 11f Listed winning half-sister to 10f 3yo Listed winner/ Yorkshire Oaks runner-up Dash To The Top (dam of 2019 Oaks winner Anapurna).

"This colt has more substance to him than his half-brother, Elwazir. It is obviously an excellent family but one that takes time. He is only cantering at present but moves well, and I'd hope to have him running by the autumn."

UNNAMED

23/3 b f Oasis Dream - Hedaaya (Indian Ridge)
Owner: Hamdan Al Maktoum *Hasanaat*
Sales price: n/a

Sister to 1m 3yo winner Bawaasil, three-parts sister to Listed-placed Irish dual 7f winner Tamadhor (by Arcano) and a half-sister to two winners. Dam an Irish 8.5f 3yo winner who was a half-sister to 6f 2yo Group 2/3 winner Memory (later dam of smart stayer Call To Mind and Acomb Stakes winner Recorder), Irish 7f 2yo Group 3 winner Remember Alexander and useful 6-7f winner Kafuu; the family of Group 3 winners Bin Rosie (7f) and Generous Rosi (10f).

"A filly with a lot of quality about her. She has a good mind and is very likeable. I would say she is more of a mid-season prospect as she hasn't done any fast work yet, but she is one we particularly like at the moment."

UNNAMED

12/4 b c Muhaarar - Path Of Peace (Rock Of Gibraltar) *Zaammit*
Owner: Sheikh Ahmed Al Maktoum
Sales price: 100,000gns (Shadwell Estate Company)

Half-brother to high-class UK/US 5f-1m winner (including the 2019 Breeders' Cup Turf Sprint) Belvoir Bay and 6-7f 2yo winner Peace Trail. Dam a 1m 3yo winning half-sister to 6f 2yo Group 2 winner Please Sing, Group 1-placed 7-10f winner Mountain Song and Group 3/Listed-placed 6f 2yo winner Raindancing (grandam of French 7f 2yo Group 3 winner Great Page) out of a sister to Solario Stakes winner/Kentucky Derby second Bold Arrangement.

"This is a very nice colt and would probably be the most forward Muhaarar I have dealt with so far. He has a willing attitude, and while he hasn't done anything too serious yet, he has handled everything we've asked of him very easily. His half-sister won the Breeders' Cup Turf Sprint last year so there is lots to like about him and I would be hopeful he'll be more or less ready to run once we're racing again. I imagine he will begin over six furlongs."

UNNAMED

30/4 b c Adaay - Place In My Heart (Compton Place)
Owner: Hamdan Al Maktoum
Sales price: £210,000 (Shadwell Estate Company)

Asad Jumeirah

Half-brother to Queen Mary Stakes/Flying Childers Stakes winner Heartache, Listed-placed 5f 2yo winner Heartwarming and useful 2019 5f 2yo winner Hand On My Heart. Dam a 5f Listed winner who was a half-sister to Irish 7f 3yo Group 3 winner/Irish 2000 Guineas fourth Leitrim House and very useful 7-9f winner Ace Of Hearts out of a useful dual 10f 3yo winner who was a half-sister to very useful multiple 5-7f winner Indian Trail and the dam of Group 1-placed multiple 5-5.5f winner (including at Group 2/3 level) Stepper Point and 2019 5.5f 3yo Listed winner Lady In France.

"It is a really good family that Clive Cox has done particularly well with in recent times. As the pedigree suggests he looks like he will be pretty forward, though is only cantering at the moment. Whilst we obviously await advice on when we will be racing again, I could see him making his debut at the end of May or in June."

Marten writes:

It's not easy trying to keep tabs on Hamdan Al Maktoum's horses over the years.

Occasionally I look up the derivation of the names he selects for his horses – I did so before buying one of his cast-offs at the sales for my racing club. His name was Nisaal, which in Arabic refers to a warrior, and the horse I have nominated from this yard is **Rasheed**, which in Arabic translates as 'wise' or 'prudent'.

Rasheed is the first foal of Raaqy, a daughter of Dubawi who made a winning debut as a two-year-old for Barry Hills. I recall there being quite high hopes for her at the time, but the nearest she got to winning again came when she ran second on her seasonal debut as a three-year-old in a Class 3 at Ascot.

This was disappointing, because Raaqy was a daughter of that admirably tough top-class performer Natagora, who won seven of her 15 starts and finished second and third in six of her other eight. Five of her victories came at two, culminating in a neck defeat of Fleeting Spirit in the Cheveley Park and then, at three, she won the 1000 Guineas and ran placed in four further Group 1 races.

I have hopes for Rasheed and am pleased to learn from the trainer that the colt moves well.

HENRY CANDY

COLOMBE (IRE)
21/3 b f Mehmas - Symbol Of Peace (Desert Sun)
Owner: Six Too Many
Sales price: £45,000 (Henry Candy)

Half-sister to 7f 2yo Group 3 winner Treaty Of Paris, useful 7-8.5f winner Mustarrid, useful 8.5-10f 3yo winner White Poppy and two other winners. Dam an 8-9.5f winner who was a half-sister to a handful of winners including useful 6-7f winner Loyal Tycoon out of a maiden half-sister to Grade 1-placed UK/US 9-10.5f winner (including at Grade 3/Listed level) Supreme Sound and the dams of 10f Group 3 winners Leporello (twice) and Stotsfold (four times).

"We were keen to secure her given she is a half-sister to our Acomb Stakes winner, Treaty Of Paris. She is an attractive filly with a good walk and finds it all very easy. She has gone back home for a brief holiday while all this is going on but will hopefully be a nice summer sprinter."

LUCKY BAY
15/1 b f Beat Hollow - Free Offer (Generous)
Owner: The Earl Cadogan
Sales price: n/a

Full sister to smart triple 1m 3yo winner (including at Listed level) Cape Peron and a half-sister to four winners. Dam a 7-10f winning daughter of a 1m 2yo winner who was a half-sister to US 11f Grade 2 winner Chelsea Barracks.

"Her brother, Cape Peron, won a Listed Race for us in France by a wide margin but was never sound thereafter. This filly finds it all very easy and is more precocious than her pedigree suggests. It was nice to see the mare return to Beat Hollow, and the initial signs point to it having worked again. One for the second half of the season."

POLLINATE
13/3 b f Oasis Dream - Spring Fling (Assertive)
Owner: Six Too Many
Sales price: n/a

First foal of a 5f Listed winner who was a half-sister to high-class multiple 6f winner (including twice at Group 1 level) Twilight Son, Group 1-placed 6-7f winner (including at Group 3 level) Music Master and useful 6-7f winner The Confessor, out of a 5-7f winner who was a half-sister to Listed-placed 6f 2yo winner Romantic Evening.

"This is the first foal of Spring Fling, who left it late to win a Listed Race. It's the Twilight Son family we know so well. This filly is improving quickly and has grown plenty, having been on the small side initially. She is another that has gone home for a break during this enforced absence, but should be racing by the summer all being well."

RUN TO FREEDOM
9/5 b c Muhaarar - Twilight Mistress (Bin Ajwaad)
Owner: Godfrey Wilson
Sales price: n/a

Half-brother to high-class multiple 6f winner (including twice at Group 1 level) Twilight Son, Group 1-placed 6-7f winner (including at Group 3 level) Music Master, very useful 5-6f winner (including at Listed level) Spring Fling and useful 6-7f winner The Confessor. Dam a 5-7f winner who was a half-sister to Listed-placed 6f 2yo winner Romantic Evening out of a 6f 3yo winning daughter of a useful half-sister to Queen Mary Stakes winner On Tiptoes.

"Like a lot of these Muhaarars he will need time. He is a big, scopey individual with a bit of class who finds it all remarkably easy at the moment considering his size, and the fact he's a May foal."

SONOROUS
27/2 ch f Pearl Secret - Speed Princess (Fast Company)
Owner: Andrew Davis
Sales price: £55,000 (Henry Candy)

First foal of an unraced sister to useful multiple 7f winner Fingal's Cave and half-sister to 1m Listed winner Audacia out of a maiden sister to Listed-placed dual 5f 2yo winner Indiannie Star and half-sister to very useful multiple 5-6f winner (including at Group 2 level) Ajigolo, Group 3/Listed-placed 5-6f winner Kickboxer and useful 6f-1m winner Silver Guest out of a 6-7f winner who was the daughter of an unraced sister to Irish 6f Group 3 winner Puissance.

"She is a ready-made two-year-old like the other Pearl Secret we have here. She goes nicely and has a willing attitude - she wants to do it. An out-and-out five furlong filly."

SOVEREIGN SLIPPER
6/5 b c Charm Spirit - Last Slipper (Tobougg)
Owner: D B Clark & Henry Candy
Sales price: 15,000gns (Vendor)

Half-brother to Listed-placed French 1m 3yo winner Slippers Best and useful triple 1m winner King's Slipper. Dam an unraced half-sister to Group 3-placed 8-12f winner (including at Listed level) Dansili Dancer, Listed-placed 6-7f winner Muhab, very useful 7-14f Flat/Grade 1-placed 2m-2m 4f hurdle (including at Grade 3 level)/2m 4f-2m 6f chase (including at Grade 1 level) winner Thari and the dam of triple 7f Listed winner New Seeker.

"He is a May foal who has grown a lot recently. He copes well with his work and is a good-looking individual, but it's a slow-maturing family and he will be one for the autumn."

TWILIGHT CALLS
30/1 b c Twilight Son - Zawiyah (Invincible Spirit)
Owner: Cheveley Park Stud
Sales price: £26,000 (Cheveley Park Stud Ltd)

Second foal of a close relation to smart 8-9f winner (including at Group 3/ Listed level) Kick On and Group 3-placed French 5.5-6f winner (including twice at Listed level) Sabratah and half-sister to smart UK/Australian 9-10f winner (including at Listed level) Raw Impulse and very useful UK/UAE 9-10f winner Nordic Lights out of a 6f Listed winner who was a half-sister to 7f 3yo Group 3 winner/Oaks fourth Sueboog (later dam of French 9.5f Group 1 winner Best Of The Bests and grandam of Melbourne Cup third Prince Of Arran).

"I liked him most out of all the Twilight Sons I saw at the sales last year and was delighted that Cheveley Park sent him this way. He can be a bit of a playboy but isn't at all unpleasant. He's a strong, attractive colt who finds it all very easy at the moment. He will be ready to roll as soon as we're back racing again."

Marten writes:

I am always encouraged at the sales when I find myself bidding against a sound judge, especially one that buys at my lower-end of the price bracket.

I gather that when Martin Pipe started to have some buying power he used to 'follow in' the proven judges, agents and trainers in the belief that they had done their research beforehand and so saved him the effort!

In a similar way I like to see whom I'm bidding against and if Henry Candy and his wife wander into the ring for a 'cheapie' then I know I'm bowling near the wicket.

Pollinate comes from a family the trainer knows well. She is the first foal of Spring Fling, who won three of her 19 starts competing at Listed and Group level as a six-year-old and winning a 5f Listed race at Ayr on her penultimate outing.

Spring Fling is related to a handful of winners, most notably Twilight Son, who won two Group 1 races for this trainer, six-race winner Shaded Edge and The Confessor, who won five.

Pollinate is bred to be useful and we can rest assured that she will be placed to optimum effect.

MICK CHANNON

AMY BEACH (IRE)
29/1 b f New Approach - Isabella Bird (Invincible Spirit)
Owner: Jon and Julia Aisbitt
Sales price: n/a

Second foal of a 1m 3yo winner who was a half-sister to German 2m Group 2 winner Raa Atoll and Group 3-placed 12f 3yo winner Moderah out of a French 11.5f 3yo winning sister to high-class French 10-12f 3yo winner (including at Group 2/Listed level) Moon Queen (later dam of US 12f Grade 3 winner Beauty Parlor and French 6f 3yo Listed winner The Brothers War) and Irish 14f Listed winner Rostropovich and half-sister to dual 12f Listed winner/Park Hill Stakes runner-up Innuendo (later dam of US 11/12f Grade 2 winner Criticism).

"A nice filly who moves well. She won't be early and will need seven furlongs or a mile."

AONACH MOR
6/4 b c Twilight Son - Royal Ffanci (Royal Applause)
Owner: Hunscote Stud Ltd
Sales price: £100,000 (Vendor)

Half-brother to smart 5.5-7f winner (including at Group 3 level) Dan's Dream. Dam an unraced half-sister to fairly useful 7f-1m winner Bountybeamadam and fairly useful multiple 8-8.5f winner Abidhabidubai out of a triple 1m winner who was a half-sister to Group 2-placed 6-7f winner (including at Group 3/Listed level) Penkenna Princess, Listed-placed 5f 2yo winner Mystery Ocean, useful 7f-1m 3yo winner Tirania and four other winners.

"A half-brother to our Fred Darling winner, Dan's Dream, but he is going to need plenty of time. I would be surprised if we saw much of him much before his three-year-old career, but he is a lovely horse and one that I hope will do very well in time."

ARCADIAN NIGHTS
10/3 b c Exceed And Excel - Lady Lahar (Fraam)
Owner: Jon & Zoe Webster & Partner
Sales price: 52,000gns (Gill Richardson Bloodstock)

Three-parts brother to Group 1-placed multiple 6-7f winner (including at Group 3/Listed level) Jallota (by Rock Of Gibraltar) and a half-brother to 1m 2yo Listed winner Classic Legend, Group 1-placed 8-10f 3yo winner Rawdaa, Listed-placed 10f 3yo winner Popmurphy and the maiden dam of French 1m 2yo/2020 UAE 10f Listed winner Certain Lad. Dam a Group 2-placed 6-8.5f winner (including at Group 3 level) who was a half-sister to Group 3-placed 5-6f winner (including at Listed level) Miss Lahar.

"Related to a smart horse we had here called Jallota. He is a quality individual who I'm hoping could be very good. I will look to start him over six furlongs around July or August time, perhaps somewhere like Glorious Goodwood."

ASTAPOR
24/5 b c Sixties Icon - Good Morning Lady (Compton Place)
Owner: M Channon
Sales price: n/a

Full brother to fairly useful 6f 2yo winner Azor Ahai. Dam a thrice-raced maiden half-sister to very useful UK/UAE multiple 7f winner Sirocco Breeze, useful prolific 5-6f winner Caustic Wit and useful multiple 5-6f winner Show Flower; excellent family of July Cup winner Anabaa, French 1000 Guineas winner Always Loyal, Gimcrack Stakes winner Country Reel, French 5f 2yo Group 3 winner Key Of Luck and French 1000 Guineas runner-up Baine.

"He will be one of our sharper two-year-olds. His brother was a winner for us at two."

CHATTRI
22/3 b c Sepoy - Sandreamer (Oasis Dream)
Owner: Jon and Julia Aisbitt
Sales price: n/a

Half-brother to useful 2019 7-7.5f 2yo winner Johan and useful 8-8.5f 3yo winner Why We Dream. Dam a Group 3-placed dual 6f 2yo winner (including at Listed level) who was a half-sister to Listed-placed Irish 8.5f 3yo winner Assume out of a 7f 3yo winner who was a half-sister to Rockfel Stakes winner Sayedah (later dam of very useful pair A Little Bit Me and Battle Of Marathon) and the 7f 3yo winning dam of Duke Of York Stakes winner Magical Memory.

"We trained the mare and she was a smart two-year-old. This colt is showing all the right signs and looks like he will be pretty speedy and precocious. He should get going at the end of May or the start of June."

DIAMONDS DANCING
29/4 b f Swiss Spirit - Crazee Diamond (Rock Of Gibraltar)
Owner: M Channon
Sales price: n/a

Half-sister to useful 5-6f winner Kinks. Dam a 6f 3yo winning close relation to Listed-placed 5-5.5f winner Thesme and a half-sister to useful multiple 5-6f winner Daffy Jane and useful 2019 triple 6f 3yo winner Last Empire out of a Listed-placed dual 5f winning sister to 5f 2yo Group 3 winner Castelletto, useful prolific 5-6f winner Hotham, useful triple 6f winner Lake Garda and dual 5f 2yo winner Princess Of Garda.

"Her half-brother, Kinks, won a nice handicap for us at Newmarket last summer, and this is a very nice filly who has a lot of quality. She works extremely well and will begin over six furlongs around June or July time."

JANIE JONES
13/4 ch f Le Havre - Coquet (Sir Percy)
Owner: The Megsons
Sales price: 120,000gns (Kilbride Equine/Paul Moroney Bloodstock)

Half-sister to useful 1m 2yo winner Glencadam Master. Dam a smart 8-10f winner (including twice at Listed level) who was a half-sister to multiple 10f-2m Flat/very useful dual 2m hurdle (including at Listed level) winner Cartwright, useful dual 12f 3yo Flat/useful dual 2m hurdle winner Midnight Oil and multiple 8-9.5f winner Genius Boy out of a 10f 3yo winning sister to Juddmonte International Stakes winner One So Wonderful and half-sister to Rockfel Stakes winner/Irish 1000 Guineas third Relatively Special and Craven Stakes/Dante Stakes winner Alnasr Alwasheek.

"A nice filly who is obviously bred to improve with time and a trip. I could see her beginning in that nice 7f fillies' maiden at Glorious Goodwood in August - if she has come to hand by then. In all likelihood, she is probably more one for the backend of the season."

MAHALE
19/2 b f Kodiac - Zarafa (Fraam)
Owner: Dave and Gill Headley
Sales price: 42,000gns (Vendor)

Half-sister to smart 5-9f winner (including at Group 2/3 level) Opal Tiara. Dam an unraced sister to fairly useful multiple 5-6f winner Bateleur and half-sister to fairly useful 12f-2m Flat/dual 2m hurdle winner Foster's Road.

"She is a half-sister to a lovely filly we trained called Opal Tiara. This filly wouldn't be the biggest, but that isn't untypical of the sire, and she shows all the right signs. I don't know at what level yet, but she'll win a race this year. I could see her beginning over six furlongs."

SAULIRE STAR (IRE)
26/2 b f Awtaad - Gallic Star (Galileo)
Owner: Jon and Julia Aisbitt
Sales price: n/a

Half-sister to useful 14f-2m winner Eden Rose and 1m 3yo winner Star Blaze. Dam a Group 2-placed 6f-1m winner (including at Listed level) who was the daughter of a 6f 2yo winning sister to smart 6-7f winner (including at Group

3/Listed level) Racer Forever and half-sister to useful 3yo winners Caribbean Pearl (10-12f) and Wrood (10f, twice).

"A big, tall filly whose half-sister needed time and a trip. I also trained the dam who was a bit sharper despite being a Galileo, but this filly looks like taking more after her half-sister. She will be nice one day I hope."

SOPHIGGLIA
29/4 gr f Sixties Icon - Myladyjane (Mastercraftsman)
Owner: Nick & Olga Dhandsa & John & Zoe Webster
Sales price: n/a

First foal of an unraced half-sister to useful 2019 6-6.5f 2yo winner Stone Circle out of a maiden half-sister to Listed-placed Irish 7-10f winner Valentina Guest and useful Irish 8-10f 3yo winner Bective Ranger out of a French 11f 3yo Listed winner who was a full sister to German 10f/French 10.5f Group 1 winner Kartajana.

"Quite a nice filly who is doing everything right. She will probably start over seven furlongs."

TEDDY B
27/3 ch c Sepoy - Effie B (Sixties Icon)
Owner: Bastian Family
Sales price: £600 (Vendor)

Half-brother to Listed-placed 5-6f 2yo winner Neola and 2019 5-7f 2yo winner Jeanie B. Dam a Listed-placed multiple 5-6f winner who was a half-sister to fairly useful 5.5-7f winner Willsy and dual 6f 2yo winner Miss Muga.

"He is a half-brother to a hardy sort we trained called Neola, whilst the year-older sibling won twice for us last season. This would be one of the sharper two-year-olds we have, and I'd be disappointed if he couldn't win a race this year."

UNNAMED (IRE) Smeatons Light
22/3 b c Dragon Pulse - Clenaghcastle Lady (Acclamation)
Owner: M Channon
Sales price: 28,000gns (Kilbride Equine)

Full brother to useful Irish/Hong Kong dual 7f winner Unicornbaby and a half-brother to useful multiple 7-8.5f winner Lord Clenaghcastle. Dam a maiden sister to 1m 3yo winner Brave Acclaim and half-sister to triple 7f winner Afkar out of a maiden sister to Irish 7f 2yo Group 2 winner St Clair Ridge (later dam of US 1m 1f Grade 2 winner Cat By The Tale); the family of 2019 7f Group 3/ Listed winner/Queen Elizabeth II Stakes third Safe Voyage.

"He will need a little bit of time but goes very well indeed. I think he could be smart."

UNNAMED (IRE) Knightoftentacles

27/1 b/gr c Sir Prancealot - Danamight (Danetime)
Owner: Six or Sticks 2020
Sales price: 40,000gns (Gill Richardson Bloodstock)

Half-brother to useful Irish 7f 3yo winner Queen Of Power (later dam of Group 2/3-placed 5-6f winner (including at Listed level) Garrus), dual 5f winner Richter Scale and Irish 1m 3yo winner Octavia. Dam a maiden half-sister to Listed-placed 7-10f winner Hallhoo and Irish 7f 3yo winner Secret Story; the family of Coventry Stakes winner Buratino.

"A strapping colt who will be one for the second half of the season."

UNNAMED Eerie Island

26/2 b f Sixties Icon - Ificaniwill (Mastercraftsman)
Owner: M Channon
Sales price: n/a

Second foal of an unraced daughter of an Irish 6.5f 2yo winner who was a half-sister to high-class 7f-2m 2f winner (including the Irish St Leger) Septimus, useful 10-12f winner Princess Caetani and 10f 3yo winner Channel Squadron.

"A very nice filly with lots of quality. She will start over seven furlongs and I'm looking forward to seeing her in action."

UNNAMED (IRE)

8/3 b c Kodi Bear - Subtle Affair (Barathea)
Owner: M Channon
Sales price: €29,000 (Kilbride Equine)

Half-brother to Listed-placed multiple 7-10f winner Imshivalla and seven other winners. Dam an 11-11.5f winner who was a sister to 1m 2yo Flat/2m Grade 3 hurdle winner Silk Affair and a half-sister to smart 12.5-14f winner (including at Group 2 level) Lochbuie; the family of Derby winner Slip Anchor and Hardwicke Stakes winner Sandmason.

"A really nice colt who has done everything we've asked of him so far."

Marten writes:

One of my happiest times in almost 50 years in racing came relatively recently, when I was asked to act as Mick Channon's private handicapper.

I'm not sure that I was much help, as Mick is a man of strong views and rarely swayed. No stranger to the liberal use of profanities, especially during first lot, the tirade would be followed by a turn of his head, as if to seek your approval, and a twinkle in the eye through a haze of blue bravado – because that was all it ever was.

Life was never dull and for all the fun and frivolity we have to respect that this is a man who has successfully scaled the heights in two highly competitive professions.

Samitar gave him his first Classic winner, taking the 2012 Irish 1000 Guineas, while Queen's Logic, unbeaten in five starts including the Cheveley Park, which she won by seven lengths, was the best filly he ever trained. She would have taken all the beating in the 1000 Guineas had injury not befallen her on the morning of the race.

It has not been easy selecting one from the bunch because he has close links to many of the families, especially the homebreds supplied by long-established owners such as Jon and Julia Aisbitt and the Websters.

Arcadian Nights has been chosen because when I was with Mick I held out high hopes for this colt's three-parts brother Jallota, who started his career in the yard. This son of Rock Of Gibraltar ran plenty of times, winning seven of his 52 starts, but despite landing a Group 3 in France for Charlie Hills I always thought he had the potential to do a little better.

The dam Lady Lahar won a Group 3 in Ireland for Channon while the related Certain Lad, a Listed winner in the UAE, is also trained at West Ilsley.

Arcadian Nights is bred to have plenty of pace and the early signs have been encouraging.

ROGER CHARLTON

BARN OWL
5/3 b c Frankel - Thistle Bird (Selkirk)
Owner: Nat Rothschild
Sales price: n/a

Half-brother to 7.5f 2yo winner Thorn and 2019 7f 2yo winner Bullfinch. Dam a high-class 8-10f winner (including at Group 1 level) who was a half-sister to Group 1-placed UK/Australian 7-10f winner (including twice at Group 3 level) McCreery and 10f 3yo Flat/smart 2m-2m 1f hurdle (including at Grade 2/3 level)/2m 1f chase winner Old Guard.

"The dam was a Group 1 winner for us, but this is a family that tend to be on the small side and that was certainly the case with her first foal, Thorn. We have her three-year-old, Bullfinch, here and he has more substance and looks a promising type. This colt would fall into the former category, but he is a good mover and has a sound mind. He should be ready to run come midsummer."

BEHELD
21/2 ch f Frankel - Tendu (Oasis Dream)
Owner: Khalid Abdullah
Sales price: n/a

First foal of a Group 3/Listed-placed 6f 2yo winner who was a sister to Gimcrack Stakes winner Showcasing and Listed-placed triple 6f winner Bouvardia and half-sister to Group 3-placed dual 6f winner (including at Listed level) Camacho and UK/US 6f-1m winner Westerland (by Frankel) out of a 6f 3yo Listed winning half-sister to Australian triple 8-10f Group 1 winner Foreteller, high-class French 7f-1m winner (including at Group 2/3 level) Modern Look and the dam of Musidora Stakes winner Shutter Speed.

"It is a family that extends right back to Andaleeb, who won a Lancashire Oaks for Jeremy Tree. This is a rangy, good-sized filly that shows promise."

BOLTAWAY
24/2 ch c Dubawi - Proviso (Dansili)
Owner: Khalid Abdullah
Sales price: n/a

Half-brother to US 8-9f winner Sailing Solo. Dam a high-class French/US 7-9.5f winner (including four times at Grade 1 level) who was a half-sister to very smart 8-10f winner (including at Group 1 level) Byword, smart French/ Australian 8-12.5f winner (including at Group 2/3 level) Finche and the dam of French 1m 3yo Group 3 winner Delaware out of a half-sister to smart UK/ Swedish 7-9f winner (including at Group 3/Listed level) Binary File.

"The dam has been rather unlucky so far - she lost a couple of foals early on and hasn't really had a chance to show what she can do as a broodmare as a consequence. Obviously Dubawi gives her every chance, and this is a good Juddmonte family that we know from the days of Jeremy Tree going back to Balabina, who was herself a daughter of one of Prince Khalid's foundation mares called Peace. This is an attractive, laid-back colt with a good temperament."

CREEDMOOR
27/3 b f Invincible Spirit - Vorda (Orpen)
Owner: H H Sheikh Mohammed Bin Khalifa Al Thani
Sales price: n/a

Half-sister to 2019 French 7.5f 2yo winner Saiga and French 7f 3yo winner Markhor. Dam a Cheveley Park Stakes winner who was a half-sister to French 7f 2yo winner Van Khan out of an Italian dual 5f 2yo winning granddaughter of an Italian 1000 Guineas/Italian Oaks winner who was herself a half-sister to Italian 10f Group 3 winner Verardi.

"The dam was a very smart filly and a top juvenile, who also did pretty well at three despite not winning. I would expect this mating to produce a sharper product than the dam's first two first foals. She is a good mover and has a good mind on her."

DESERT PIONEER
4/4 b c Dubawi - Lady Wingshot (Lawman)
Owner: Imad Al Sagar
Sales price: 100,000gns (Blue Diamond Stud)

Half-brother to French 6.5f-1m winner Expecting To Fly and 1m 3yo winner I Am Magical. Dam a smart Irish 7-7.5f winner (including at Group 3/Listed level) who was a three-parts sister to Group 2-placed UK/German 5f-1m winner (including at Group 3/Listed level) Bahama Mama and a half-sister to seven winners; the family of top-class stayer Yeats.

"He is a neat, good-natured colt with a typically solid outlook for one by his sire. The dam was stakes-placed at two, and he should make up into a mid-season two-year-old."

DOLPHIN
4/3 b f Sea The Stars - Dolma (Marchand de Sable)
Owner: Lady Bamford
Sales price: n/a

Half-sister to high-class 8-10f winner (including at Group 1 level) Thistle Bird, Group 1-placed UK/Australian 7-10f winner (including twice at Group 3 level) McCreery and 10f 3yo Flat/smart 2m-2m 1f hurdle (including at Grade 2/3 level)/2m 1f chase winner Old Guard. Dam a Group 1-placed French 6-7f winner (including three times at Listed level) who was a half-sister to the dam of 6f 2yo Listed winner/Cheveley Park Stakes third Madeline; the family of multiple 8/9f Group 1 winner Solow.

"She has recently come from pre-training with Malcolm Bastard. She is a well-grown, good-bodied, athletic filly. Her dam was speedy, but Sea The Stars has certainly given her some size and scope. It is a family that improves with age, and we hope to have her out around September time."

IN THE BREEZE
11/3 b c Harzand - Its In The Air (Whipper)
Owner: Inglett, de Zoete, Milln
Sales price: 35,000gns (Amanda Skiffington Bloodstock)

Half-brother to French 7f 2yo winner He's A Rock Star and US 1m 3yo winner Mutawasem. Dam an unraced half-sister to very smart UK/US 7-12f winner (including at Group/Grade 1 level) Storming Home, six other winners including useful 11-13f winner Desert Frolic (later dam of 7/9f Group 3 winner Dubai Prince), and the unraced dam of Australian 12f Group 1 winner Glencadam Gold; the excellent family of French 1000 Guineas winner Musical Chimes.

"An inexpensive purchase from Book 3, considering he is an attractive, athletic colt with a good temperament. He goes pretty nicely, though it's difficult to know quite what to expect yet. His pedigree leans towards stamina, but we'd hope to have him ready for when the seven-furlong races kick in."

JUMBY BREEZE
29/1 b f Dubawi - Annabelle's Charm (Indian Ridge)
Owner: Merry Fox Stud Limited
Sales price: n/a

Half-sister to smart triple 6f 2yo winner (including the Middle Park Stakes) Charming Thought and very useful 5-7f winner Spanish City. Dam a Group 3-placed 8-10f winner (including at Listed level) who was a half-sister to Listed-placed 7f 2yo winner Purple Sage out of a maiden sister to high-class 8-12f winner (including twice at Group 1 level) Ballingarry and Racing Post Trophy winner Aristotle and half-sister to St James's Palace Stakes winner Starborough and French 12.5f 3yo Group 3 winner Spanish Falls.

"This is a filly who has a good mind on her and is a nice model. The dam has been a little quiet since producing a Middle Park winner, but I am hopeful this promising filly can do well this season. I imagine she will be one for the middle of the summer onwards."

KEEPER
19/4 b c Frankel - Portodora (Kingmambo)
Owner: Khalid Abdullah
Sales price: n/a

Half-brother to Group 3-placed 2019 French 6-6.5f 2yo winner (including at Listed level) Alocasia, smart triple 1m winner (including at Listed level) Set Piece and useful multiple 7f winner Peril. Dam a dual 7f 3yo winning daughter of a Grade 2/Group 3-placed UK/US 8-9f winner (including at Listed level); the family of dual Group 1 winner Elmaamul and Oaks winner Reams Of Verse.

"A deep-bodied, strong colt who only arrived towards the end of February. He moves nicely and has a good pedigree behind him, but he's something of an unknown quantity as things stand."

LOVE IS YOU (IRE)
26/3 b f Kingman - Fallen For You (Dansili)
Owner: Normandie Stud Ltd
Sales price: n/a

Half-sister to high-class 6f-1m winner (including at Group 2/3 level) Glorious Journey. Dam a Coronation Stakes winner who was a half-sister to smart 7-10f winner (including at Listed level) Fallen Idol, Group 2/Listed-placed 1m 2yo winner Fallen In Love (later dam of French 10.5f Group 3 winner Loving Things) and the dam of smart pair Light Up My Life and Light Up Our World out of a 1m Listed-winning half-sister to Lockinge Stakes winner Fly To The Stars.

"This is a strong, attractive filly who only came in at the end of March. She obviously has a very nice pedigree as the daughter of a Group 1-winning half-sister to a good horse of Charlie Appleby's called Glorious Journey. I would hope she'll be ready to get started during the midsummer period."

LUCID DREAMER
24/2 gr f Dansili - Sleep Walk (Oasis Dream)
Owner: Khalid Abdullah
Sales price: n/a

Second foal of a 5.5-6f winner who was a half-sister to Group 1-placed 5-6f winner (including at Group 2/Listed level) Bated Breath (by Dansili), very smart 8-9f winner (including at Group 1 level) Cityscape, Listed-placed triple 1m 3yo winner Scuffle (later dam of 2019 St Leger winner Logician) and the unraced dam of smart sprinter Equilateral.

"Another family we know well. This is a very good-moving, active, athletic filly who should begin over seven furlongs."

LUDISIA
22/2 b f Frankel - African Rose (Observatory)
Owner: Khalid Abdullah
Sales price: n/a

Full sister to 6f 2yo Group 3 winner Fair Eva and useful 7-10f winner Herculean and a half-sister to useful 8-8.5f winner Hakka. Dam a very smart 6-7f winner (including at Group 1 level) who was a sister to Group 1-placed French 6f-1m 2yo winner (including at Group 3/Listed level) Helleborine (later dam of Coventry Stakes winner Calyx) out of a Group 3/Listed-placed 10f 3yo winning half-sister to high-class 7-9f winner (including at Group 1 level) Distant Music.

"She isn't here yet, but the reports from Juddmonte are positive."

PLEASANT MAN
21/3 b c Galileo - Melito (Redoute's Choice)
Owner: Brook Farm Bloodstock
Sales price: 140,000gns (Vendor)

Brother to Czech dual 1m 3yo winner Palazzo Corsini and a half-brother to Group 2/3-placed Japanese 8-10f winner Campbell Junior. Dam an Australian 6/7f Group 1 winner/Caulfield 1000 Guineas runner-up who was a half-sister to the dams of Australian dual 5.5f Group 3 winner Pariah and Australian 1m 3yo Group 3 winner You're So Good.

"He is a sizeable but sound individual with a good attitude. I hope he is as

*above-average as his pedigree suggests. The dam was sharp and won a
Group 2 in Australia fairly early on as a juvenile. I could see him making an
appearance once the seven-furlong races begin in earnest come June and July."*

QUILTED
19/4 b f Frankel - Nimble Thimble (Mizzen Mast)
Owner: Khalid Abdullah
Sales price: n/a

Full sister to 2019 Fillies' Mile winner Quadrilateral and a half-sister to
two winners. Dam a 9.5f 3yo winner who was a half-sister to Group/Grade
1-placed UK/US 6-8.5f winner (including at Grade 2/Group 3 level) Three
Valleys and six other winners; the exceptional family of Banks Hill, Cacique,
Intercontinental, Champs Elysees, Dansili etc.

*"She arrived towards the end of February. It is unfair to expect her to emulate
her sister, but if you were working from a blank sheet of paper and didn't know
who her sibling was, then you couldn't be happier with her. She is attractive
and has a charming nature, though I suspect she will need a bit more time
than Quadrilateral did."*

*Quadrilateral bursts onto the scene with this impressive success in a conditions event at
Newbury last September. She made it 3-3 when taking the step up to Group 1 level in her
stride in the Fillies' Mile at Newmarket the following month.*

TOURNESOL (FR)
9/4 b c Invincible Spirit - Fleur de Cactus (Montjeu)
Owner: H H Sheikh Mohammed Bin Khalifa Al Thani
Sales price: n/a

Half-brother to Group 3-placed 8-11f winner Pivoine. Dam a 13f 3yo winner who was a half-sister to Listed-placed 7f-1m winner Red Dune (later dam of Group 3/Listed-placed 7f-1m 2yo winner Feedyah and Listed-placed 7f-1m winner Red Mist) and the unraced dam of Melbourne Cup winner Fiorente out of a useful 7f-1m winner who was a half-sister to Group 1 scorers Islington (four times, 10/12f), Greek Dance (10f) and Mountain High (12f).

"He has an unraced half-brother in the yard who is showing good promise. This mating should work better as Invincible Spirit is more of a speed and precocity influence than what his mare has been paired with previously. He is well put together, has a good mind and is a laid-back individual."

Marten writes:

Roger Charlton belongs to a very select group. He is one of just three trainers who declined my support as an owner.

It would be indiscreet to name the other two, but I remember tentatively approaching him in the car park at Newbury as he was about to take over Beckhampton from Jeremy Tree to ask if he would be keen to accept me into the fold.

Graciously, as always, he explained that he would dearly love to train for friends but that at that time he was unable to accommodate me. Within a few months he won the Derby and Prix du Jockey Club with Quest For Fame and Sanglamore respectively and as a consequence was unlikely, I suspect, to have felt an opportunity had been missed in rejecting my advances the previous autumn.

There are certain trainers one tends to like, for whatever reason, and Charlton is one of them. He has since trained dozens of Group winners but has also shown with his deft handling of Withhold, to name but one, that he can 'do the business' when required.

I could have selected any of those listed above, but I've gone for **Tournesol** because he is a half-brother to Pivoine, a horse that I believe has never quite realised his full talent.

Pivoine began life with Sir Michael Stoute, winning his second start at two but then requiring a visor to help him home in a 1m 3f handicap the following season at Kempton. After winning next time at Doncaster he went to the sales as part of the Ballymacoll dispersal and fetched a staggering 340,000gns – a mighty sum for a 90-rated gelding.

Since then he has plied his trade at a reasonable level without, as I say, scaling the heights I had expected of him. He did, though, win £125,000 in prize money when landing the John Smith's Jubilee Cup at York last year and ran fourth in a Grade 1 at Woodbine.

Tournesol, by Invincible Spirit, is bred to have more pace than his sibling. From a family that traces back to the high-class Islington, Greek Dance and Mountain High, this is a horse I like on paper trained by a man who, all those years ago, showed he was as sound a judge of people as he is of horse flesh!

TOM CLOVER

APPRECIATE (IRE)
25/2 ch c Australia - Became (Giant's Causeway)
Owner: H Moorhead, C Fahy & J Collins
Sales price: €65,000 (Amanda Skiffington, Agent)

Half-brother to Italian multiple 7-9.5f winner Endlesscliffs. Dam an unraced half-sister to US 5.5-6f winner Uplifting and US 3yo winners Giocourgement (8.5f) and Mr Smee (5f) out of an unraced half-sister to US 7f Grade 1 winner Key Phrase (later grandam of US 7f Grade 2 winner Half Ours and US 1m 1f Grade 3 winner Khancord Kid and great-grandam of US 7f Grade 1 winner Bar Of Gold) and the dam of US five-time 7-10f Grade 1 winner Shared Belief.

"A strong, good-sized colt who has trained well. He is a typical Australia in that he won't be early and is a middle-distance three-year-old in the making, but we should see him in action towards the backend of the season with a clear run. He doesn't qualify for median auction races, so we'll have to be careful where to place him."

FAIRY DUST (IRE)
15/3 b f Gregorian - Dreaming Lady (Dream Ahead)
Owner: The Fairy Dust Partnership
Sales price: 12,000gns (JS Bloodstock/Tom Clover)

First foal of a maiden half-sister to Listed-placed 5-6f winner Ballymore Castle out of a US 8.5f Grade 3 winner who was a half-sister to US 6.5f 2yo Grade 3 winner Sunray Spirit and useful US 5.5-8.5f winner Dehere Of The Dog.

"We enjoyed great success with another daughter of Gregorian called Gypsy Spirit who was rated 97 at her peak. This filly is quite spirited and enthusiastic, but she covers the ground so easily and is very natural. I can see us having a lot of fun with her, and she'll also have a low weight in those valuable sales races. I like her a lot."

RAJMEISTER
5/2 b c Showcasing - Brilliant Sunshine (Pivotal)
Owner: R S Matharu
Sales price: 27,500gns (Tom Clover Racing)

Third foal of an unraced half-sister to smart 10-12f winner (including at Listed level) Ferdoos (later dam of Irish 10f Group 1 winner Nezwaah) and German 14.5f/Italian 15f Listed winner Brusco out of a useful dual 12f 3yo winning half-sister to Group 3/Listed-placed 8-9f winner Equity Princess and Listed-placed French 6f 3yo winner Blue Dream.

"It is a family my wife, Jackie, knows about as it produced a couple of smart fillies for Kremlin House in the days of her father, Michael Jarvis, and latterly Roger Varian, notably the Pretty Polly Stakes winner Nezwaah. We picked this colt up from Book 2, and he is a medium-sized individual who shows a fair amount of quirkiness but also good speed. If we can channel his energies in the right direction, he should be OK. I would say he'll begin over five furlongs."

ROGUE POWER
12/2 b c Pivotal - Strawberry Sorbet (Street Cry)
Owner: The Rogues Gallery Two
Sales price: 35,000gns (Jackson-Stops Bloodstock/Tom Clover)

First foal of a 1m 3yo winner who was a half-sister to Qatari 9.5f/French 10f winner Zamharer and French 10.5f 3yo winner Zalzalah out of a Group 1-placed multiple 8-9f winner (including at Group 2/3 level) who was a full sister to useful multiple 5-6f winner Wentworth Falls and a half-sister to four winners including 8.5-10f winner Strawberry Lolly (later dam of 1m 2yo Listed winner Tony Curtis and Italian 12f Listed winner Strawberry Martini).

"A strong colt who finds it all really easy at the moment. It is obviously a very good family and Pivotal can still produce a good one, even at his age. I would hope to see him in action by midsummer."

THE GUVNOR (IRE)
14/5 b c Frankel - Eva's Request (Soviet Star)
Owner: The Rogues Gallery Two
Sales price: 75,000gns (JS Bloodstock/Tom Clover)

Half-brother to 1m winner Heartstone and US 8.5f 3yo winner Sasini. Dam a smart 6-10f winner (including at Group 1 level) who was a half-sister to Irish 7f 2yo Group 1 winner Priory Belle (later grandam of Australian 12f Group 1 winner Opinion and Irish 7.5f 3yo Group 3 winner Anam Allta), Irish 7f 3yo Group 3 winner Wild Bluebell and the dam of 1m 2yo Group/Grade 1 winner Chriselliam and UAE triple 8/9f Group 2 winner Very Special.

"A good-sized colt who has a lovely long stride on him. He has done very well of late, but will need a bit of time as he is a late foal and it's a fairly slow-maturing family. More one for next year."

Marten writes:

The Guvnor looks well bought on paper.

The colt is by Frankel out of Eva's Request, a very tough mare who was kept busy by Mick Channon, running 27 times and winning seven.

As is often the case with Channon's horses she was quite ambitiously placed at two, winning a Kempton maiden on her second start before being beaten twice off 83 in two nurseries. That didn't discourage the trainer from stepping her up to a Group 3 at Goodwood, where she earned black type by finishing third, before ending her season with a Group 3 victory at the Curragh.

At three she ran with credit, winning a Listed handicap at Ascot in September, before running 11 times at four, winning a Listed race at Goodwood, a Group 3 at Epsom, a Group 2 in Turkey and a Group 1 in Italy – a long way off from being beaten off a mark in the low 80s at two and fully vindicating the trainer's decision to keep her in training for a third season.

At stud she has so far been disappointing, with Heartstone her only winner, which may be why this colt, by Frankel out of a Group 1 winner, did not fetch more at the sales. He is also a late foal, born in early May, so is likely to need time to come to hand.

Let's hope that he proves worth waiting for.

ROBERT COWELL

BUSINESS FLIGHT (USA)
7/2 b/br c Fed Biz - The Right Bird (Birdstone)
Owner: Tom Morley
Sales price: $27,000 (Robert Cowell)

Third foal of a maiden half-sister to US 8.5f 3yo Grade 1 winner Karlovy Vary, Grade 2-placed US 8.5-14f winner Rocket Legs, US 5.5-7f winner Mio D'Oro, US 1m 2yo winner Speedy Vanessa and four other winners out of a US 6f 3yo winning half-sister to US 6.5/7f Grade 2 winner Great Intentions and US dual 1m Stakes winner Sea Road.

"He is a strong-bodied colt with a good action. He works nicely and looks one for mid-season onwards."

DELIVER THE DREAM (USA)
18/2 b c Kantharos - Bellarada (Rockport Harbor)
Owner: Tom Morley
Sales price: $70,000 (Robert Cowell)

Half-brother to 2019 US 1m 2yo winner Savvy Gal. Dam a US 8-8.5f winner who was a full sister to very useful Canadian/US prolific 4.5-9f winner (including twice at Listed level) Banner Bill and a half-sister to Grade 2/3-placed US multiple 6-8.5f winner Zulu, Grade 3-placed US multiple 5-6.5f winner Third Chance, Stakes-placed US 5.5f 2yo winner Stormy Afternoon, US 5f 2yo winner Azevedo and six other winners out of a US 6.5f 2yo winner.

"Strongly-made, precocious colt. He isn't overly big, but knows his job and will be ready to run when racing returns."

RAZOR GLASS (USA)
31/1 b/br f Congrats - Lemon Splash (Lemon Drop Kid)
Owner: Tom Morley
Sales price: $35,000 (Robert Cowell)

Half-sister to US 7.5f-1m winner Lisa Limon. Dam a useful US dual 6f winner who was a half-sister to Grade 2-placed US 6-8.5f winner (including at Grade 3 level) Falling Sky, useful US 5-6f winner Last Dragoness, US 5-5.5f winner Hero Of The Sea and three other winners out of a Stakes-placed 4.5-5.5f 2yo winning half-sister to the smart All Giving.

"She needs to bulk out a little still, but I'd say she'll do so fairly quickly. She shows speed and is quite forward. A very likeable individual who won't be long in getting going when racing is back."

TAKE UP ARMS (USA)
11/2 b/br c Violence - Battle Axe (War Front)
Owner: Tom Morley
Sales price: $50,000 (Robert Cowell)

First foal of a US 8-9f winning half-sister to US 8.5f 2yo winner Bourbon Twist out of a US 8.5f 3yo winning half-sister to US 8-8.5f winner Soaringwitheagles and US 1m winner Happiest Memories out of a US 8.5f 3yo Grade 3 winner.

"Nice horse. He has a big frame, goes well and has a lovely stride on him. He should be an early enough two-year-old, though will be more of a six and seven-furlong type in time."

TRANQUIL BREEZE (USA)
3/3 b f Palace - Quiet Sunshine (Real Quiet)
Owner: Tom Morley
Sales price: $40,000 (Robert Cowell)

Second foal of a US 6-8.5f winning daughter of an unraced half-sister to Grade 3-placed US 7.5f-1m winner (including at Listed level) Dawn Before Dawn who was a half-sister to four winners including US dual 6f winner Imandra.

"She is yet another we bought at Keeneland last year. Unlike a few of those mentioned, she'll need a bit of time."

Marten writes:

I am not familiar with any sires of the five two-year-olds listed above.

Deliver The Dream is by Kantharos, who retired to stud at two after being unbeaten in three starts including a Grade 3 and Grade 2 success over six furlongs in the States. He has produced the useful World Of Trouble, winner of six races including Grade 1s at Belmont Park and Aqueduct.

This colt is a half-brother to a winner out of a full sister to Banner Bill from a family packed with useful performers.

On paper he looks to have the credentials to win races.

MICHAEL DODS

———— • ————

BLOWING WIND (IRE)
27/3 b c Markaz - Wojha (Pivotal)
Owner: Merchants & Missionaries
Sales price: 15,000gns (Michael Dods)

Half-brother to useful 2019 Irish 5f 2yo winner Punita Arora. Dam a 1m 3yo winner who was a half-sister to smart triple 7f winner (including at Group 3/ Listed level) Muthabara, Group 3/Listed-placed 7f 2yo winner Mustadeem and four other winners out of a 1m 3yo winning half-sister to 7f 3yo Group 3 winner Muqbil and Group 2-placed 6-7f 2yo winner Mostaqeleh (later dam of smart pair Matera Sky and Murillo); the family of St James's Palace Stakes winner Bahri and Champagne Stakes winner Bahhare.

"A nice, strong type who I think was well bought at the sales despite having the odd fault. He has the right sort of pedigree and I hope he can develop into a decent performer. I should think he will begin over six furlongs."

BOLD TERRITORIES (IRE)
27/3 ch c Territories - Amberley Heights (Elnadim)
Owner: TG Racing
Sales price: £20,000 (Barry Lynch/Michael Dods)

Third foal of a 6f 2yo winner who was a three-parts sister to Group 3-placed French 7f-1m winner (including at Listed level) Green Lady and French 6f 2yo winner Shamo and a half-sister to very useful 12f 3yo winner Entisar, useful UK/UAE 6f-1m winner Desert Realm and the maiden dam of high-class multiple 5-7f winner (including at Group 2/3 level) Balthazaar's Gift out of a smart Irish 7-10f 2yo winner (including twice at Listed level).

"He is a medium-sized colt who has just had a touch of sore shins. He will be one for the second half of the season, probably starting in August or September over six or seven furlongs."

HEAR ME ROAR (IRE)

2/3 b c The Last Lion - Dutch Heiress (Dutch Art)
Owner: P Appleton & Mrs Anne Elliott
Sales price: 26,000gns (Michael Dods)

Second foal of a useful dual 7f 2yo winning daughter of a maiden sister to useful 7f-1m winner Bobby Wheeler and half-sister to useful multiple 5-6f winner Regal Royale, Listed-placed UK/US 6f-1m winner Royal Banker and 7f 2yo winner Regal Riband (later dam of dual 7f Group 3 winner Regal Realm, herself the dam of 8/10f Group 3 winner/Eclipse Stakes runner-up Regal Reality) out of a twice-raced Cheveley Park Stakes winner.

"A good-looking colt who we are in no real rush with. He will make a lovely three-year-old, but equally I would hope he will be able to do something this season over six and seven furlongs."

MAGISTERIUM (IRE)

15/2 b f Elzaam - Dubaya (Dubawi)
Owner: Rjh Ltd And D Stone
Sales price: €35,000 (M Dods)

Half-sister to French 6f 2yo Group 3 winner Comedy. Dam an Irish 1m 2yo winner who was a three-parts sister to 10f 3yo winner Eolian and a half-sister to very useful 7.5f-2m 4f Flat/2m-2m 4f hurdle winner Ghimaar and useful UK/UAE multiple 7-10f winner King Charles; the excellent family of very smart milers Barathea and Gossamer.

"She is a half-sister to a three-year-old we train called El Naesri and, though he's a colt, this filly looks more masculine than him. She is quite sharp and should have enough toe to start out over five furlongs, though will stay six and seven furlongs."

SANDERLIN (IRE)

8/4 ch c Footstepsinthesand - Coppertop (Exceed And Excel)
Owner: David Richardson
Sales price: €42,000 (M Dods)

Half-brother to useful UK/Irish dual 7f winner Current Option. Dam a maiden three-parts sister to very useful Irish 5-8.5f winner (including at Listed level) Canary Row and half-sister to useful 8-12f winner Yabass out of an 11-12f winning daughter of a once-raced 10f 3yo winner who was a sister to Irish 7f 2yo Group 1 winner Preseli and a half-sister to Lingfield Derby Trial winner Kong, 14f Listed winner Mount Kilimanjaro and 7f 2yo winner/1000 Guineas runner-up Snowfire (later dam of US 8.5f Listed winner Model); the family of 7f 2yo Group 3 winner Dublin.

"A lovely colt we are bringing along steadily. He is by a good sire and the dam's related to plenty of good horses. I would be disappointed if he didn't improve into a decent three-year-old, but I can see him doing something this season from July onwards. He should have enough speed to begin over six furlongs."

TIGERALI (IRE)

15/3 b f Bungle Inthejungle - Dream Scenario (Araafa)
Owner: Mrs Theresa Burns & Michael Dods
Sales price: 7,000gns (Vendor)

First foal of a 5-7f winner who was a half-sister to Group 3-placed dual 5f winner (including at Listed level) Tropical Treat and 5f 3yo winner Place That Face out of a Listed-placed 5f 2yo winner; the family of Richmond Stakes/Champagne Stakes winner Sri Pekan and Railway Stakes winner/Coventry Stakes runner-up Daylight In Dubai.

"The fillies are sharper than the colts this year and this filly is the embodiment of that. She would almost certainly have run by now under normal circumstances. She will be ready to go over five furlongs whenever we resume."

UNNAMED (IRE) *Navajo Spring*
31/3 b f Charm Spirit - Clifton Dancer (Fraam)
Owner: Doug Graham
Sales price: £22,000 (Michael Dods)

Half-sister to fairly useful multiple 6f winner Avenue Of Stars and 6-7f winner Helen Sherbet. Dam a very useful triple 7f winner (including at Listed level) who was a half-sister to Group 3-placed 5f 2yo winner Bonnie Grey, very useful UK/Hong Kong 5-7f winner Cop Hill Lad and 2yo winners Bahamian Ceilidh (5f) and Okikoki (6f) out of a Listed-placed triple 5f winning half-sister to Group 2/3-placed multiple 5-6f winner (including at Listed level) Lord Kintyre.

"A sharp, strong filly who would have been racing by now. We like to run a filly at the first Beverley meeting in the middle of April, and I suspect this would have been our representative this season. She will be ready to go whenever we are able to race again and will start off over five furlongs."

Marten writes:

I am encouraged that the trainer says **Magisterium** is "quite sharp" given the stamina in her bottom line.

She is by Coventry Stakes runner-up Elzaam out of the Dubawi mare Dubaya, a winner on her debut from five starts and the dam of Comedy, winner of three of her six starts including a Group 3 at Deauville. Dubaya is a half-sister to Flat and staying hurdle winner Ghimaar and to a winner over 1m 6f, so there is abundant stamina in the pedigree.

Barathea and Gossamer, from one of the late Gerald Leigh's very successful bloodlines, also appear on the page.

There is a lot to like about this filly and I expect her to thrive when she is stepped up in trip.

ED DUNLOP

AJRAD
1/4 ch c New Approach - Princess Cammie (Camacho)
Owner: Hamdan Al Maktoum
Sales price: 160,000gns (Shadwell Estate Company)

Half-brother to 2019 Japanese 7f 2yo winner Prince Charm. Dam a 7f winning close relation to high-class 7f-1m winner (including at Group 2/3 level) Kodi Bear and half-sister to 6f 2yo winner Parsnip out of an unraced daughter of a 7f-1m winning half-sister to good broodmare Dievotchka (dam of triple 1m Group 1 winner Esoterique and French 10f Group 2 winners Archange D'Or and Russian Cross) and the dam of 6f 2yo Group 2 winner Cool Creek.

"A racy, good-moving colt with a bit of size. He is one that will require a bit of time, and is likely to remain cantering for a while in order to let him strengthen up and mature."

ALABLAQ (IRE)
8/4 ch c Lope De Vega - Tributary (New Approach)
Owner: Hamdan Al Maktoum
Sales price: 120,000gns (Shadwell Estate Company)

Second foal of an unraced half-sister to Grade 1-placed UK/US 7.5-12f winner (including at Grade 3 level) Strathnaver, UAE 1000 Guineas winner Siyaadah, useful 7-12f winner Bridle Belle, useful 8-10f winner Middle Kingdom and useful Japanese 7f-1m winner Fossamagna out of a smart UK/US 6f-8.5f winner (including at Grade 2/Group 3 level) who was a half-sister to Italian 7f 2yo Listed winner Kiralik and very useful 7.5f-1m winner Rio Riva.

"This colt isn't overly big and should be a relatively early two-year-old, though he is probably more a seven-furlong type. He moves well and is doing everything right so far."

DEW YOU BELIEVE (IRE)
18/4 b c Make Believe - Dew (Whipper)
Owner: Paul Turner
Sales price: 22,000gns (BBA Ireland)

Half-brother to useful 7f-1m 2yo winner Even Keel. Dam a maiden half-sister to Hong Kong 12f Group 2 winner Supreme Rabbit, Listed-placed Irish 7f 3yo winner Dangle, Listed-placed 6f 2yo winner Bahati (later dam of five-time 7f/1m Listed winner Tabarrak), useful 5-7f winner Zero Money and useful Irish 7f 2yo winner Devious Diva (later dam of triple 7/7.5f Group 3 winner Realtra); the family of Racing Post Trophy winner Seattle Rhyme.

"He is a neat, attractive colt whose pedigree suggests he will be relatively early. Obviously in light of the current situation we are only going gently with him at the moment. The sire has made a fantastic start to his career at stud."

JOHN LEEPER (IRE)
28/4 b c Frankel - Snow Fairy (Intikhab)
Owner: Anamoine Limited
Sales price: n/a

Third foal of a top-class 6-12f winner (including six times at Group/Grade 1 level) who was the daughter of a useful Irish 7f 3yo winning half-sister to smart 7-10.5f winner (including at Group 3/Listed level) Big Bad Bob and fairly useful 6-7f winner Bobbie Soxer (later dam of Grade 2/Listed-placed Irish 1m 3yo winner Mittersill); the family of 7f/1m Group 3 winner/Racing Post Trophy runner-up Elusive Pimpernel and 1m 1f 3yo Group 3 winner Palavicini.

"This is a beautiful colt who arrived from Ireland towards the end of March. He has size, scope and a good temperament. He is currently cantering gently, and is very likely to be a horse for the latter part of the year."

MAIDEN'S TOWER (IRE)
13/4 b/br f Golden Horn - Harlem Dancer (Dr Devious)
Owner: Jessica Ellen Ball
Sales price: 75,000gns (BBA Ireland)

Half-sister to Group 3-placed UK/UAE 5-6f winner (including at Listed level) Hototo and the maiden dam of smart Irish 7-12f winner (including at Group 3/Listed level) Who's Steph. Dam a useful French 10-10.5f 3yo winning daughter of a French 10f 3yo winner who was a half-sister to US 10f Grade 2 winner Globe, French 10f Group 3 winner Hoya, the dam of French 12f 3yo Group 2 winner Housamix and US/French 8/9f Listed winner Housa Dancer (herself

dam of 8.5f Group 3 winner Bushman) and the grandam of US 1m 1f 3yo Grade 1 winner Alexander Tango.

"A sizeable, good-looking filly who is very much a three-year-old prospect, but she moves well and has a good temperament."

SHAQEEQA
1/4 ch f Dawn Approach - Tabassum (Nayef)
Owner: Hamdan Al Maktoum
Sales price: n/a

Half-sister to Group 3/Listed-placed French/UAE 8-11f winner Jaaref, Listed-placed French/UAE 7f-1m winner Yaalail and 2019 French 7f 2yo winner Raamez. Dam a Group 2-placed dual 7f 2yo winner (including at Group 3 level) who was the daughter of a twice-raced 6f 2yo winning full sister to Canadian 1m 2yo Grade 3 winner Prussian.

"This is a neat, racy filly who moves well and has done all that has been asked of her so far, though has only been here since the end of March. She should make a two-year-old."

UNNAMED   Tashbeeh
28/3 b c Siyouni - Aristotelicienne (Acclamation)
Owner: Hamdan Al Maktoum
Sales price: £200,000 (Shadwell Stud)

Half-brother to 2019 6f 2yo winner Aussie Showstopper. Dam a useful French 6.5f-1m winning half-sister to smart 6-8.5f winner (including at Listed level) Ceremonial Jade and useful UK/UAE 6f-1m winner Innocuous out of a French 7.5f winning sister to French 1m 2yo Listed winner/French 1000 Guineas runner-up Firth Of Lorne (later dam of UAE 9.5f Group 3 winner Falls Of Lora and 7f Listed winner/St James's Palace Stakes second Latharnach) and half-sister to the dam of German 2000 Guineas winners Dupont and Pacino.

"A very racy, athletic colt who looks a pretty forward type. I think he will be one of our earlier two-year-olds."

UNNAMED (IRE)   Verraeux Eagle
10/2 gr f Free Eagle - Evening Frost (Invincible Spirit)
Owner: Mrs G A Rupert
Sales price: 62,000gns (BBA Ireland)

Half-sister to French 6f winners Primeravez and Top Chain. Dam a once-raced French 5.5f 2yo winner who was a half-sister to Irish 7f Group 3 winner Penny

Pepper, French 6.5f 3yo Listed winner Morning Frost, Stakes-placed UK/US 7-10f winner Shaan and 2019 5f 2yo winner Aim Power out of an Irish dual 6f Listed winner.

"A strong, powerful filly who I imagine will need a bit of time. She is currently cantering and causing no problems."

UNNAMED Uraib

19/3 b f Shalaa - Social Media (New Approach)
Owner: Hamdan Al Maktoum
Sales price: 110,000gns (Shadwell Estate Company)

First foal of a 2m winner who was a half-sister to smart 8.5-12f winner (including at Group 2/Listed level) Horseplay, 10f Listed winner More Mischief and useful 10-11f Flat/Grade 1-placed triple 2m hurdle winner Devilment out of a Group 3-placed 9.5-13f winner (including at Listed level) who was a half-sister to smart multiple 7f winner (including at Listed level) That Is The Spirit and Irish 6f 3yo Listed winner Khukri.

"A tall, leggy filly whose mother we trained. She ended up winning over 2m, but this filly in comparison is quite racy and is also by a speed influence, so she should prove a fair bit sharper."

Marten writes:

It is now accepted that owners like to reserve certain names for horses they think may be top class – we've seen that over the years with the Coolmore operation and more recently over jumps with Champ, named by JP McManus in honour of AP McCoy's great achievements.

I'm not sure if the name **John Leeper** was retained for something special because, as some of you will be aware, 'Leeper' was the middle name of Ed Dunlop's father, John.

It would be hard to imagine a more illustrious pedigree.

This colt is a son of Frankel and the third foal of the hugely gifted Snow Fairy, the winner of six Group or Grade 1 races including the English and Irish Oaks, the Queen Elizabeth II Cup in Kyoto, the Hong Kong Cup in Sha Tin and the Irish Champion Stakes, where she beat Nathaniel and St Nicholas Abbey.

Snow Fairy's first two foals, by Gleneagles and Elusive Pimpernel, proved disappointing but perhaps Frankel will bring a touch of magic into the job. He is a late foal so, as the trainer says, he may need time.

HARRY DUNLOP

DREAM CHASER (FR)
28/3 b c Dream Ahead - Avodale (Lawman)
Owner: Kirby, Gehring, Woodley
Sales price: €19,000 (Christina Dunlop)

Full brother to smart 5-7f winner (including at Listed level) Visionary, 7f-1m 3yo winner Forward Thinker and 2019 7f 3yo winner Attorney General. Dam a maiden daughter of a French 10f 3yo winning half-sister to Group 2/3-placed French/UAE 6.5f-1m winner (including at Listed level) Bashaayeash and the grandam of 7f 2yo Listed winner Boitron; the family of high-class juveniles Al Hareb, Baitha Alga and Myboycharlie.

"He is a racy type who should be ready when the 6f races begin. He qualifies for the French premiums so will run both at home and over in France."

FIRST PIROUETTE (IRE)
25/3 b f Acclamation - Ballerina Rose (Duke Of Marmalade)
Owner: Neil Jones
Sales price: n/a

Second foal of a maiden daughter of an Irish 13f Listed winner/Irish Oaks runner-up who was a sister to Irish 12f 3yo winner Dance The Classics (later dam of Irish 1m 1f 2yo Listed winner Call To Battle) out of a 12f 3yo Listed winning sister to St Leger winner Millenary and half-sister to Derby third Let The Lion Roar; the family of Spectrum.

"Another racy individual. I have her year-older half-brother, Lost Empire, who is quite a useful sort. We like this filly."

SEA OF CHARM (FR)
18/2 b f Charm Spirit - Sea Meets Sky (Dansili)
Owner: Elwes, Cooper & Deal
Sales price: 12,500gns (JD Moore)

Third foal of a 10f 3yo winner who was closely related to high-class 8-10.5f winner (including at Group 2/3 level) Multidimensional out of a Group 1-placed 6-12f winner (including twice at Group 3 level) who was a half-sister to Canadian 9-12f Grade 2 winner Strut The Stage and the dam of Canadian triple 12f Grade 3 winner Aldous Snow.

"Inexpensive purchase considering she comes from a good Niarchos family that Henry Cecil did well with. She will hopefully be a nice filly over 7f during the summer months and beyond."

TURACO
16/2 b c Kodi Bear - Hobby (Robellino)
Owner: Larksborough Stud
Sales price: 9,500gns (Not Sold)

Half-brother to 6f 2yo winner Cotinga and 12f 3yo winner Kasuku. Dam a Group 2/Listed-placed 7f 2yo winning daughter of an unraced half-sister to Irish 1m 3yo Listed winner Golden Temple; the family of high-class Irish sprinter Acushla and Oaks winner Intrepidity.

"He is a nice colt who will improve as the year goes on, but I'd be hopeful he could achieve something at two."

Marten writes:

Harry Dunlop displays a great deal of enterprise with the placing of his horses, often sending them overseas to plunder Group races which can be less competitive than in the UK.

There is no finer example than Robin Of Navan, all of whose six victories were achieved overseas – five of them at Pattern level.

Sea Of Charm looks very well bought on paper, given that she is out of a winning three-parts sister to Group 2 winner Multidimensional, herself out of a Group 3-winning half-sister to a useful Grade 2 winner in the States.

Henry Cecil thought highly enough of the dam Sea Meets Sky to give her a Ribblesdale entry, which suggests this filly offers a lot on the page for her 12,500gns purchase price.

We can safely rely on her underrated trainer to place her to good effect.

CHARLIE FELLOWES

ANGEL AMADEA
5/4 gr f Dark Angel - Keene Dancer (Danehill Dancer)
Owner: Graham Smith-Bernal
Sales price: £55,000 (Jill Lamb Bloodstock)

Third foal of a useful UK/French 8.5-9f winner who was closely related to high-class 7-11.5f winner (including at Group 2/3 level) Berkshire and Group 3-placed UK/Australian 7-10.5f winner (including at Listed level) Abdon and a half-sister to very useful 12f 3yo winner Ben Vrackie and 10-12f 3yo winner Keenes Royale (later dam of dual 6f 2yo Group 2 winner/Middle Park Stakes runner-up Ivawood) out of a French 10f Group 1 winner.

"She's quite narrow and weak right now, so is having a holiday. She had done everything easily and is an uncomplicated filly, but very much one for the second half of the season."

DEPUTY (IRE)
24/2 b c Lawman - Finagle (Azamour)
Owner: Highclere Thoroughbred Racing - Philip Blacker
Sales price: £33,000 (C Gordon Watson/Fellowes)

Half-brother to Listed-placed 2019 Irish 6f 2yo winner Nurse Barbara. Dam an unraced sister to Grade 1-placed 7f-1m winner (including at Listed level) Gifted Girl and half-sister to useful UK/UAE 8-10f winner Con Artist and Group 3/Listed-placed German 6f 2yo winner Muriel (later dam of German five-time 6-8.5f Group 3 winner Millowitsch) out of a unraced half-sister to Irish Oaks winner Margarula and Irish 1m 1f 2yo Listed winner Wild Heaven.

"Nice horse. I thought he was the standout lot of the sale he was in. He showed some temperament initially, but has got better and better as time has gone on. He looks an early sort and will be one of my first two-year-old runners when we're back underway. I should think he will start off over six furlongs and I really like him."

GEORGE SCOTT (IRE)
12/2 b g Zoffany - African Plains (Oasis Dream)
Owner: Offthebridle Podcast
Sales price: 20,000gns (C Gordon Watson Bloodstock)

Third foal of a maiden half-sister to 6f 2yo Group 3 winner Fair Eva, useful 8-8.5f winner Hakka and useful 7-10f winner Herculean out of a very smart 6-7f winner (including at Group 1 level) who was a full sister to Group 1-placed French 6f-1m 2yo winner (including at Group 3/Listed level) Helleborine (later dam of Coventry Stakes winner Calyx).

"His conformation isn't great, but he's very sound and has a cracking pedigree. We have recently gelded him as he was getting a bit boisterous, but he is a really good-looking horse who could prove to be very well bought if staying right. He should be out in June or July and will likely start over six or seven furlongs."

GOLDEN BEAR (IRE)
6/5 b c Kodiac - Golden Flower (Royal Applause)
Owner: Mrs Susan Roy
Sales price: 100,000gns (A C Elliott, Agent)

Full brother to useful 6f 2yo winner Mutawaffer and 2019 5f 2yo winner Harswell. Dam a dual 5f winner who was a full sister to 6f 2yo Group 3 winner Habaayib out of a US 6f-1m winning daughter of a US 6.5f 2yo Grade 2 winner.

"He's not going to be super early, but is a two-year-old through and through. He has a bit of physical development to do still and will be out in mid-season, probably June or July. He's a nice, straightforward sort of character."

WANNABE SAFE (IRE)
28/2 b f Oasis Dream - Wannabe Posh (Grand Lodge)
Owner: Normandie Stud Ltd
Sales price: n/a

Half-sister to smart 8-8.5f 3yo winner (including at Group 3 level) Wannabe Yours and useful 10-12f winner Wannabe Loved. Dam a Group 3-placed 11.5-12f winner (including at Listed level) who was a half-sister to Cheveley Park Stakes winner/1000 Guineas runner-up Wannabe Grand, smart Irish 7-8.5f winner (including at Group 3/Listed level) Wannabe Better, Irish 1m 3yo Listed winner Pirateer and Listed-placed dual 1m 2yo winner Assaaf.

"A lovely filly who has a lot of quality about her. I thought she would be precocious initially, but she went through a growing phase, so is having a little holiday at the moment. She has a smart pedigree, and could be quite nice if she's got the right attitude as the ability is most certainly there. I hope she will be ready around August or September time."

UNNAMED (IRE) *First Prophet*

5/5 b c New Bay - Lus Na Greine (Pour Moi)
Owner: Dexter Blackstock
Sales price: €50,000 (C Gordon Watson/Fellowes)

Second foal of an unraced half-sister to Irish 1m 3yo Group 3 winner/Irish 1000 Guineas third Rehn's Nest out of a very useful Irish 7f 2yo winner who was a half-sister to useful Irish 8-10.5f 3yo winner Coolcullen Times and Irish 1m 3yo winner Irish Question (later dam of French 1m 2yo Group 1 winner Loch Garman) out of an unraced half-sister to Irish 6f 2yo Group 1 winner Eva Luna and Irish 1m 2yo Group 3 winner Cois Na Tine.

"I liked this colt so much that I have kept a leg in him! Out of all the horses I bought last year he just has that bit of quality about him. I like the stallion and think he could be good in time. This colt finds everything easy at this stage, and should be in action by the middle of the season."

UNNAMED (IRE)

11/4 ch c Night Of Thunder - Mathanora (Anabaa)
Owner: Mohamed Obaida
Sales price: 85,000gns (C Gordon Watson Bloodstock)

Third foal of a French 11f winner who was a close relation to the dam of US 1m Grade 2 winner Rhythm Of Light and a half-sister to US 1m Grade 2 winner Little Treasure, US 8.5f 2yo Grade 3 winner Keep Quiet, Group 3-placed French 9-10.5f winner Harem Lady and Listed-placed French 1m 1f 2yo winner Annee Lumiere; the family of very smart miler Bigstone and French 7f 3yo Listed winner Blue Cloud (later grandam of Royal Lodge Stakes winner Mohawk).

"Big, scopey chestnut who does everything really easily despite his size. He has got a lovely attitude and is a really nice horse. I suspect we will see him from July onwards and I like him an awful lot."

Marten writes:

I was very taken by the physique of Lawman's stock when they first appeared on the market but it's probably fair to say that the Prix du Jockey Club winner's record, since retiring to the paddocks, has been disappointing.

He's had his moments, notably with St Leger winner Harbour Law and Irish 1000 Guineas winner Just The Judge, but generally speaking his progeny's racecourse achievements fail to match their good looks.

That may be the reason why **Deputy** did not fetch more money at the sales, because this colt has a very strong bottom line.

His dam is an unraced full sister to a Listed winner and a half-sister to four winners out of an unraced half-sister to Irish Oaks winner Margarula. Finagle was bred to stay beyond a mile and her first foal Nurse Barbara won on her debut for Ger Lyons last season and was then second in a 7f Listed race before running creditably in the Group 1 Cheveley Park.

I can quite appreciate why bloodstock agent Charlie Gordon Watson decided to take a chance with this colt and I hope to see his enterprise rewarded.

JAMES FERGUSON

LAZENBY (IRE)
6/4 b g Vadamos - Good For Her (Rock Of Gibraltar)
Owner: David Robert Seldon
Sales price: 45,000gns (Pamsel Investments/Clarke Bloodstock)

Half-brother to Listed-placed multiple 5-6f winner Sandra's Secret, multiple 6f winner Kyllach Me and 6-7f winner Pranceleya. Dam a maiden close relation to Irish 6f 2yo Group 1 winner Zoffany and Irish 6.5f 2yo Group 3 winner Wilshere Boulevard and half-sister to high-class Irish 7-12f winner (including at Group 2/3 level)/Irish Derby runner-up Rostropovich and useful UK/Irish 7-10.5f winner That's Plenty; the family of Broome, Claxon and Projection.

"A very backward gelding who is growing into a fine, big horse. He has a lovely pedigree with Zoffany and Rostropovich appearing in the second dam. Vadamos is an exciting first-season sire - they all looked fantastic at the sales and this horse was no exception. I am in no rush with him, and I would be looking towards the backend of the season before he starts to race. He will be a lovely staying type in time."

SMOOTH SPIRIT
24/2 b g Charm Spirit - Valonia (Three Valleys)
Owner: The Free Spirits
Sales price: £26,000 (James Ferguson)

Third foal of a Group 2-placed dual 6f winner (including at Listed level) who was a half-sister to useful multiple 6-7f winner Explain out of an Irish 6f 2yo winning half-sister to useful Irish 1m 3yo winner Ridiyara (later dam of French 11.5f 3yo Listed winner Ridaar) and the dam of Listed-placed multiple 7-9f winner Bronze Angel out of a Listed-placed Irish 8-9f winner; the family of French 10f Group 1 winner Ridasiyna.

"Despite already being gelded he has been straightforward from day one and moves nicely. He is a strong, fine-looking individual whose Listed-winning dam also placed in a Rockfel Stakes at two. All being well, I believe he will be ready to run around June time."

WHATITIZZ
22/2 br f Cable Bay - Wosaita (Generous)
Owner: Blackrock Racing UK And Mr G Bishop
Sales price: n/a

Half-sister to smart 7f-1m winner (including at Group 3/Listed level) Whazzis, 7f 2yo Listed winner Whazzat (later dam of Group 1-placed 6-7f winner (including at Group 2/3 level) James Garfield) and the dam of Group 2-placed 2019 7f 2yo winner Juan Elcano. Dam a maiden half-sister to French Oaks winner Rafha (later dam of 6f Group 1 winner Invincible Spirit and grandam of Italian 1m 2yo Group 1 winner Nayarra and 7f 2yo Group 2 winner Gustav Klimt) and the dam of Australian 6/7f 2yo Group 1 winner Pride Of Dubai.

"She comes with a very good pedigree from New England Stud. She looks strong but will need a bit of time to grow into herself. I am very interested in Cable Bay as a stallion and I think he gives her some class. I'm sure she can provide her owners with a lot of fun over the coming season."

ZOETIC
5/4 b f Kodiac - Zallerina (Zamindar)
Owner: Glentree Pastoral Pty Ltd
Sales price: £52,000 (Badgers Bloodstock)

Half-sister to dual 6f winner Zenovia. Dam an unraced half-sister to Group 3-placed 8-12f winner (including at Listed level) Surrey Thunder and Listed-placed Italian 5-6.5f winner Sgarzulina out of an unraced daughter of a French

1m 3yo Listed winning half-sister to the unraced dam of top-class 8-12f winner (including the French Oaks/Prix de l'Arc de Triomphe) Zarkava.

"A strong, typically sharp Kodiac with a nice pedigree who has impressed me. She was bought from the Goffs UK Premier Yearling sale by Badgers Bloodstock and was brilliantly broken in by George Peckham. This filly has good bone and is emerging as one who will be one of my earlier two-year-old runners. I will be looking to get her on a racetrack in late May if racing is on, and if not, she will be ready to rock whenever the season gets started."

UNNAMED (IRE) *Camelot Star*

3/4 b c Camelot - Sapphire Waters (Six Sense)
Owner: James Ferguson
Sales price: 62,000gns (Avenue Bloodstock/Clarke Bloodstock)

Half-brother to Italian 10f 3yo winner Bethany. Dam an unraced half-sister to smart Irish 12f-2m winner (including twice at Listed level) Rajik, Irish 1m 1f 3yo winner Rihla and French 12.5f 3yo winner Ridafa (later dam of French 10f 3yo Group 1 winner Ridasiyna) out of a Group 3/Listed-placed triple 12f 3yo winner who was a half-sister to Listed-placed Irish 8-9f winner Ridiya (later grandam of Listed winners Ridaar (11.5f) and Valonia (6f)).

"A Camelot colt who has really caught my eye. Physically he's the pick of my two-year-olds at the moment and moves incredibly well. Mentally he has come a long way since he was a baby, and has become more professional with each bit of work he has done. He would be my horse to watch for the future."

UNNAMED (USA) *Ridgeway Avenue*

16/5 ch c Kitten's Joy - Trensa (Giant's Causeway)
Owner: Lloyd J Williams
Sales price: $145,000 (Not Sold)

Full brother to very smart UK/UAE 7-12f winner (including twice at Group 1 level) Hawkbill and a half-brother to US 8.5f 2yo Grade 1 winner Free Drop Billy. Dam a Grade 3/Listed-placed US triple 8.5f winner who was a three-parts sister to US triple 8.5/9f Grade 3 winner Batique (later dam of Grade 3-placed US 8.5-9f winner Tejida) and the unraced dam of Group 2-placed 7f 2yo winner Alexander Castle out of a US 7f Grade 2 winner.

"He is a brother to Hawkbill who won the Eclipse for Charlie Appleby when I was assistant trainer there. This colt was purchased by my father at Keeneland and at first glance he looks very similar to Hawkbill, but being a May foal he needed to grow. He has certainly done that now, and has developed into a fine-looking individual who goes about his work in the right way. A really exciting horse to have in the yard."

UNNAMED (IRE) Francesco Guardi

19/3 b c Frankel - Trophee (Mr. Sidney)
Owner: James Ferguson
Sales price: 200,000gns (Amanda Skiffington)

First foal of a smart US 9-11f winner who was a half-sister to top-class French 8-12f winner (including the Prix de l'Arc de Triomphe twice) Treve and French 10f 3yo Listed winner Trois Rois out of a French 5.5f 2yo winning half-sister to Grade 1-placed French/US 6f-1m winner (including at Listed level) Tsigane out of a maiden sister to French 10f 3yo Group 1 winner Treble and half-sister to the dam of 6f Group 1 winner Tamarisk and grandam of 14.5f Group 2 winner Hi Calypso and smart middle distance/staying performer Warringah.

"Another very exciting horse to have in the yard being by Frankel and out of a half-sister to Treve. He has filled out physically and done very well since we've had him. I haven't pushed any buttons yet, but mentally he is showing all the right signs and I'm happy with the way he is progressing. I'd be looking to start him off mid to late season."

Marten writes:

How can anybody who follows pedigrees not be excited by a son of Frankel out of a winning half-sister to the dual Arc winner Treve?

This as yet unnamed colt is the first foal of Trophee, a winner in the States, tracing back to the family of top mare Trillion.

Treve was one of the great mares of recent years, winning nine of her 13 starts including the Prix de Diane, the Grand Prix de Saint-Cloud and those Arcs, finishing fourth to Golden Horn in her attempt to land the race for the third time.

I would not expect this colt to appear until the latter part of the season, with a pedigree that points to his suiting a mile or more.

WILLIAM HAGGAS

———— • • ————

AROUSING
29/4 b f Kodiac - Enticing (Pivotal)
Owner: Lael Stable
Sales price: n/a

Closely related to high-class 6-7.5f winner (including twice at Group 1 level) One Master (by Fastnet Rock) and useful multiple 6-7f winner Triple Chocolate (by Danehill Dancer). Dam a high-class multiple 5f winner (including at Group 3/Listed level) who was a half-sister to several winners, notably 1m 3yo Listed winner/Jersey Stakes second Sentaril.

"This filly isn't as strong as she perhaps looks. She has a big backside on her like her mother - a typical sprinting type. She is fairly sharp and will hopefully be in action by midsummer."

BACHAU
9/2 b c Kodiac - Margaret's Mission (Shamardal)
Owner: Julie And David R Martin And Dan Hall
Sales price: 120,000gns (Jill Lamb Bloodstock)

First foal of a fairly useful triple 1m winning sister to Group 3/Listed-placed UK/US 6f-1m winner Sharnberry and a half-sister to four winners including useful 5-6f winner Master Rooney out of a Listed-placed 5-6f 2yo winning daughter of a 5.5-8.5f US winner who was a half-sister to four-time US 8/8.5f Listed winner Baron De Vaux.

"He is a nice, strong colt who had a bit of shin earlier in the year but is over that now. He would have been a nice summer two-year-old in a normal year but should do well whenever we get back underway."

BEAUTIFUL NEWS
13/2 b f Shamardal - Besharah (Kodiac)
Owner: Sheikh Rashid Dalmook Al Maktoum
Sales price: n/a

First foal of a high-class 5-6f 2yo winner (including at Group 2/3 level)/ Cheveley Park Stakes third who was a half-sister to fairly useful 5-5.5f winner

Arzaak out of an unraced half-sister to smart US 6-8.5f winner (including at Grade 3 level) Kiss Moon and Grade 3-placed US multiple 8-8.5f winner (including four times at Listed level) Kiss Mine.

"Besharah was a filly we trained to win the Princess Margaret and Lowther Stakes and was a very good two-year-old. This is a small but well-made filly who will like fast ground and should give us some fun over the summer."

CANDLEFORD (IRE)
8/2 b c Kingman - Dorcas Lane (Norse Dancer)
Owner: Barnane Stud Ltd
Sales price: n/a

Half-brother to Listed-placed 8-12f winner Atty Persse. Dam a Group 2/3-placed 8-10f 3yo winner (including at Listed level) who was a half-sister to very useful 6f-1m winner Mutawaqed, prolific 6f-1m winner Mujood and 7-12f Flat/smart multiple 2m hurdle (including at Grade 1 level)/useful 2m 3f-3m chase winner Faasel out of a maiden sister to the dam of UAE 1m 1f Group 1 winner Tryster and half-sister to 1000 Guineas winner Harayir.

"A big, raw-boned horse, but he has got some speed and a bit of quality too. The dam stayed middle distances, but Kingman should add some pace, and he is one to the look forward to for the second half of the season."

CEDRIC MORRIS (IRE)
13/2 b c Fast Company - Big Boned (Street Sense)
Owner: Richard Green
Sales price: €90,000 (Richard Frisby Bloodstock)

Half-brother to Listed-placed UK/French 5-6f winner K Club and 2019 Irish 5f 2yo winner Back To Brussels. Dam a maiden half-sister to US 6f 3yo Listed winner Cool Bullet and US 7f-1m winner/Chesham Stakes third Casper's Touch out of a US 6f 3yo Listed winning half-sister to smart Irish 9-9.5f winner (including at Listed level) Sense Of Honour.

"We have never managed to have a runner in the Brocklesby, but if ever I was going to have one it would have been this horse, so it's unfortunate the current situation we're in meant there was no Lincoln meeting this year. He will be ready to go as soon as racing starts and should have a good two-year-old campaign if coping with faster ground conditions, having already shown he can handle a soft surface. He has been a natural from the moment he came in."

CHALK STREAM
8/2 b c Sea The Stars - Golden Stream (Sadler's Wells)
Owner: The Queen
Sales price: n/a

Half-brother to Group 1-placed 8.5-10f winner Invictus Prince. Dam a Group 3-placed triple 7f winner (including twice at Listed level) who was a sister to 7f 2yo winner/Oaks runner-up Flight Of Fancy (later dam of dual 10f Group 3 winner Fabricate and grandam of 10f 3yo Listed winner Momentary) and three other winners including the dams of 12.5f Listed winner Sextant (by Sea The Stars) and 13f Listed winner Daphne out of a 12/13.5f Group 2 winner.

"This is an extremely nice colt who is still rather unfurnished but has a lovely frame to fill. He is a good mover who I am very hopeful will be able to do something at two."

FIREWORKS (FR)
7/4 b c Kingman - Miss Plimsoll (Arch)
Owner: Ms Fiona Carmichael
Sales price: €850,000 (Amanda Skiffington)

Half-brother to Listed-placed French dual 1m winner Choice Of Raison and 6f 2yo winner The Paddocks. Dam a US 8.5f winner who was a sister to Group 1-placed 11-12.5f winner (including at Group 2/3 level) Pomology and a half-sister to very useful 6-7f winner (including at Listed level) Tommy Taylor, Grade 1-placed US 8.5-10f winner Sassy Little Lila and Listed-placed US 8-8.5f winner Sharbat; the family of very smart middle distance performer Apple Tree.

"A lovely horse who cost plenty, but he's still rather backward and is out for a break at the moment. He moves well and will hopefully have a run at the backend of the year. More of a three-year-old type."

GOOD AND PROPER
18/2 b f Dansili - Grace And Glory (Montjeu)
Owner: Nicholas Jones
Sales price: n/a

Half-sister to smart 7.5-10.5f winner (including at Group 3 level) Give And Take and useful UK/UAE 8-8.5f winner Alkaamel. Dam an unraced sister to very smart 1m-2m 4f winner (five times at Group 1 level, including the Irish Derby and Ascot Gold Cup)/Derby runner-up Fame And Glory and 10f 3yo winner Yummy Mummy (later dam of 1000 Guineas winner/Oaks runner-up Legatissimo); the family of Lockinge Stakes/Champion Stakes winner Farhh.

"A lovely filly with plenty of scope. She has a nice pedigree and is a half-sister to our Musidora winner Give And Take. She is with the pre-trainer at the moment, and under normal circumstances I would've hoped to have her out in July."

ILPHARE (IRE)
20/4 b f Fastnet Rock - Starship (Galileo)
Owner: Des Scott
Sales price: n/a

Full sister to high-class 7f-1m 2yo winner (including at Group 1 level) Rivet and Group 2-placed UK/Hong Kong 7-10f winner (including at Group 3 level) Booming Delight and a half-sister to Irish 10f 3yo Group 3 winner Alexander Pope. Dam a 7f-1m winning half-sister to Group 1-placed multiple 5f winner (including at Group 2/3 level) Superstar Leo (later dam of smart pair Enticing and Sentaril and grandam of French dual 7f Group 1 winner One Master (by Fastnet Rock)); the family of 2000 Guineas winner Footstepsinthesand.

"She isn't here yet. She is more backward than some of her siblings and likely won't run at two."

KADUPUL (FR)
5/5 b f Dark Angel - Cup Cake (Singspiel)
Owner: Al Wasmiyah Farm
Sales price: n/a

Half-sister to high-class 6f-1m winner (including at Grade 1 level) Suedois. Dam a Swedish 8-10f 3yo winner who was the daughter of a maiden half-sister to Group 1-placed Irish 6-7f 2yo winner (including at Group 3 level) Honours List, useful 6-8.5f winner Shahdaroba and useful Irish dual 6f winner Cnocan Gold.

"An attractive homebred filly who, although quite a late foal, is strong and well-made. She is out of a Singspiel mare and is the type to continue improving throughout her two-year-old season. One we rather like at the moment."

LIGHT REFRAIN
13/1 b f Frankel - Light Music (Elusive Quality)
Owner: The Queen
Sales price: n/a

First foal of Group 3-placed dual 7f 2yo winner (including at Listed level) who was a sister to very useful multiple 1m winner Sea Shanty out of a smart UK/

US 6f-1m winner (including at Listed level) who was a half-sister to useful 7f-1m winner Green Line and 6f 2yo winners Flower Market (dam of Australian 10f Group 1 winner Spillway) and Marching Song out of a 5f 2yo winning half-sister to 5f 2yo Listed winner/Queen Mary Stakes second Rowaasi.

"She is the first foal of a mare who won the Radley Stakes at Newbury for us as a two-year-old, and it has been a solid family overall. This is a strong, well-made daughter of Frankel who ought to be out in July or August."

LILAC ROAD (IRE)
14/2 ch f Mastercraftsman - Lavender Lane (Shamardal)
Owner: Jon & Julia Aisbitt
Sales price: n/a

First foal of a Listed-placed French 1m 3yo winning half-sister to smart French triple 10f 3yo winner (including at Group 2 level) Sumbal and French 10.5f 3yo Listed winner Lily Passion out of a Group 1-placed French 10-12f winning half-sister to French 10.5f 3yo Listed winner Fils De Viane and the dam of French 10f 3yo Listed winner Viane Rose.

"She is a homebred filly out of a Shamardal mare and is very straightforward and uncomplicated. She has got a bit of scope so will go on at three, and is an attractive, no-nonsense type of filly who should be running in July or August. I think she is one of the better two-year-olds we have."

MAIN EVENT
17/2 b c Frankel - Superstar Leo (College Chapel)
Owner: Lael Stable
Sales price: n/a

Full brother to 6f 3yo winner Yaraki, three-parts brother to 1m 3yo winner Curriculum (by New Approach) and a half-brother to eight winners, notably high-class multiple 5f winner (including at Group 3/Listed level) Enticing (later dam of dual Prix de la Foret winner One Master) and Group 3-placed 7f-1m winner (including at Listed level) Sentaril. Dam a Group 1-placed multiple 5f winner (including at Group 2/3 level) who was a half-sister to the dam of Racing Post Trophy winner Rivet; the family of 2000 Guineas winner Footstepsinthesand and Irish 2000 Guineas winner Power.

"This has been a phenomenal family for us, and this colt is the nicest foal that Superstar Leo has produced in a little while. It is quite remarkable that she was able to deliver a horse of this quality at the age of 20. She had a colt by Havana Gold last year and is now enjoying a well-earned retirement after

producing fifteen foals. This colt was a gorgeous yearling who has good bone and is very strong. I'd be looking to get him started around the end of July."

MARY CASSATT
15/2 b f Gutaifan - Quite A Thing (Dutch Art)
Owner: Richard Green
Sales price: 75,000gns (Richard Frisby Bloodstock)

Half-sister to smart Irish 7-7.5f winner (including at Group 3/Listed level) Yulong Gold Fairy. Dam a useful 5-6f 2yo winner who was a half-sister to very useful 5-6f winner (including twice at Listed level) Dazed And Amazed, useful UK/UAE 5-7f winner Stunned and the grandam of smart Irish triple 5f 2yo winner (including at Listed level) Sirici out of a maiden sister to dual 5f Group 3 winner Bishops Court and half-sister to four-time 5f Listed winner Astonished and the dam of Cornwallis Stakes winner Ponty Acclaim; the family of 6f 2yo Listed winners Saigon and Saxford.

"Not the biggest but, like Cedric Morris, she was bought to be a sharp two-year-old and should be exactly that."

MAWKEB
15/4 b/gr c Dark Angel - Best Terms (Exceed And Excel)
Owner: Hamdan Al Maktoum
Sales price: 425,000gns (Shadwell Estate Company)

Half-brother to Group 2/3-placed 7-12f winner (including at Listed level) Star Terms and French 10f 3yo Listed winner Fresh Terms. Dam a high-class 5-6f 2yo winner (including twice at Group 2 level) who was the daughter of an unraced half-sister to French 11f 3yo Group 2 winner Anton Chekhov, 2m Group 2 winner First Charter and 12f 3yo Listed winner/Italian Derby runner-up Private Charter; the family of Moyglare Stud Stakes winner Cursory Glance.

"This is a sharper horse than we would normally get from Shadwell, and it is such a shame that we've been held up as he would have been the type to start off at somewhere like the Guineas meeting. He is a good size and very strong."

MOHAAFETH (IRE)
26/3 ch c Frankel - French Dressing (Sea The Stars)
Owner: Hamdan Al Maktoum
Sales price: 350,000gns (Shadwell Estate Company)

Second foal of a 10.5f 3yo Listed winner who was a half-sister to US 12f Grade 3 winner Dalvina (later dam of 12/14f Listed winner Dal Harraild), 10f 3yo Listed winner Soft Centre (later dam of Nassau Stakes winner Sultanina) and useful 7f-1m winner Pretzel out of a Group 2-placed 6-10f winner (including twice at Listed level); the family of 5f 3yo Group 3 winner Extortionist, French 5f 2yo Listed winner Pursuing The Dream and 1m 3yo Listed winner Neebras.

"I really liked this colt as a yearling at auction and he cost plenty of money. He only came to us in March but is a nice mover and I'd be hopeful about him, for all he is very much the three-year-old prospect his pedigree suggests."

READY TO VENTURE
24/3 b f Kingman - Wonderstruck (Sea The Stars)
Owner: Lael Stable
Sales price: n/a

First foal of a Group 3-placed 12f 3yo winner who was a half-sister to very smart 6f-1m winner (four times at Group 1 level, including the 2000 Guineas) George Washington, very smart 7-11f winner (including three times at Group 1 level) Grandera, smart 10.5-14f winner (including twice at Listed level) Sun Central and five other winners.

"I suppose we're a bit biased given we trained the dam and want her to do well, but this filly is a nice model and isn't at all bad for the mare's first attempt. She is only medium-sized and not as scopey as her mother but should be OK."

SKYRUNNER (IRE)
26/3 b c Invincible Spirit - Maidservant (Seeking The Gold)
Owner: Graham Smith-Bernal
Sales price: 190,000gns (Jill Lamb Bloodstock)

Half-brother to Listed-placed Irish 5-7f winner Swish. Dam an unraced close relation to Listed-placed French 6.5-7f winner Waitress (later dam of Melbourne Cup winner Cross Counter) and half-sister to Group 3/Listed-placed French 1m 3yo winner Woven Lace (later dam of German 1m Listed winner Broderie) out of a French 6f Group 3 winning half-sister to Chesham Stakes winner Seba and the unraced dam of Irish 1m 3yo Group 3 winner Future Generation (later dam of French 12/15f 3yo Group 2 winner Brundtland).

"This is a racy individual who isn't quite as early as he looks, but he should make a two-year-old from midsummer onwards. He has got a good mind on him and whilst he was very cheeky when being broken, he has thrived on a bit of graft and should have a good year. Another with the scope to progress at three."

SKYTREE

4/2 b f Dark Angel - Tiptree (Duke Of Marmalade)
Owner: Michael & Mrs Michelle Morris
Sales price: n/a

First foal of a useful 7f 2yo winner who was closely related to Listed-placed 6f-1m winner Troubadour and Qatari 7f Listed winner Roman Legend and a half-sister to Listed-placed French 5f 2yo winner Agapimou out of a once-raced sister to Irish 1m 2yo Group 3 winner Equal Rights and half-sister to Australian 5.5f Group 3 winner Freedom Fields.

"A strong, well-made filly who showed promise before she went out for a break. She will be back here in May and should have a good season from August onwards. We particularly liked her when she was being broken."

SUBSTANTIAL

26/2 b/br c Siyouni - Sentaril (Danehill Dancer)
Owner: Lael Stable
Sales price: n/a

Half-brother to 2019 11.5f 3yo winner Magical Sight. Dam a Group 3-placed 7f-1m winner (including at Listed level) who was a sister to 7f 3yo winner Cloud Line, a close relation to fairly useful 8-10f winner Auspicion and a half-sister to high-class multiple 5f winner (including at Group 3/Listed level) Enticing (later dam of dual Prix de la Foret winner One Master) and six other winners out of a Group 1-placed multiple 5f winner (including at Group 2/3 level).

"A really gorgeous colt with a good temperament, and he would be the best that the mare has produced so far. Although still rather unfurnished at present, I'd be hopeful he can do something towards the backend of the season."

TARHIB (IRE)

14/3 b f Dark Angel - Allez Alaia (Pivotal)
Owner: Hamdan Al Maktoum
Sales price: 1,050,000gns (Shadwell Estate Company)

Half-sister to fairly useful 2019 5f 2yo winner Allez Sophia. Dam an unraced sister to high-class 7-10f winner (three times at Group 1 level, including the Irish 1000 Guineas) Halfway To Heaven (later dam of four-time 10-12f Group 1 winner Magical and 8/10f Group 1 winner/Oaks runner-up Rhododendron) and half-sister to 5/6f Group 3 winner Tickled Pink, 6f 3yo Group 3 winner Theann (later dam of US 8/10f Grade 1 winner Photo Call and 6f 2yo Group 2 winner Land Force) and Group 3/Listed-placed Irish 5f 2yo winner Fantasy.

"A very expensive purchase as a yearling. She hasn't been in all that long but is going the right way and has plenty of scope. One for the latter part of the season in all likelihood."

YAZAMAN (IRE)
17/2 b c Kodiac - Online Alexander (Acclamation)
Owner: Sheikh Ahmed Al Maktoum
Sales price: 185,000gns (Shadwell Estate Company)

Half-brother to useful 2019 6f 2yo winner Royal Commando. Dam a Listed-placed triple 5f winner who was a half-sister to three winners including fairly useful 8-10f winner Bnedel out of a 7f 3yo winner who was a half-sister to high-class 5-7f winner (including at Group 1 level) Red Clubs; the family of high-class sprinter Petong.

"A strong, good-bodied colt with a sound mind. Under normal circumstances, I would have been looking to get him out in May as he is bred to be pretty sharp."

UNNAMED   Alanmal
1/3 b c Siyouni - America Nova (Verglas)
Owner: Hamdan Al Maktoum
Sales price: 800,000gns (Shadwell Estate Company)

Half-brother to Group 1-placed UK/Australian 6-7.5f winner (including at Group 2/3 level) Weary, smart 6f-1m winner (including at Group 2/3 level) Nyaleti and smart French/US 7-8.5f winner (including at Grade/Group 3 level) Stellar Path. Dam a French 1m 2yo Listed winner who was a half-sister to French 12.5f 3yo Listed winner Cat Nova.

"This colt was very expensive as a yearling but is a gorgeous individual. He hasn't been in that long and I am slightly in the dark, but he is an extremely nice horse to look at."   Royal Address

UNNAMED (IRE)
17/2 br f Dandy Man - Barqeyya (Shamardal)
Owner: Sheikh Juma Dalmook Al Maktoum
Sales price: £45,000 (Blandford Bloodstock)

Second foal of a once-raced maiden half-sister to 1m 3yo winner Amaany out of an Irish 7/8.5f Listed winner who was a half-sister to Grade 1-placed French/US 6-10f winner (including at Grade 2/Listed level) Volochine, 12/15f Listed winner Kahtan, 5f 3yo Listed winner Sakha, 11f 3yo Listed winner

Ghataas and the grandam of Irish 1m Group 2 winner Red Tea out of a French 1m 2yo Group 3 winner; the family of Commonwealth Cup winner Eqtidaar.

"This filly was well bought at £45,000 as a yearling. She is strong, well-made and a real two-year-old type who would've been an early one for us under normal circumstances. We've had to take our time with her, but she has progressed nicely and should be running in auction events before going on to better things. I see her as an ideal candidate for the Weatherbys Super Sprint and the new EBF Ballyhane Stakes at Naas at the beginning of August."

UNNAMED

8/4 b c Muhaarar - If So (Iffraaj)
Owner: Sheikh Ahmed Al Maktoum
Sales price: 100,000gns (Shadwell Estate Company)

Half-brother to useful 2019 6f 2yo winner Final Option. Dam a useful multiple 6f winner who was a half-sister to very smart multiple 6f winner (including three times at Group 1 level) The Tin Man, very smart multiple 5-6f winner (including at Group 2/3 level) Deacon Blues, Listed-placed multiple 5f winner Holley Shiftwell and three other winners out of a useful 6-7f winner who was a half-sister to triple 7f Group 3 winner/Lockinge Stakes second Warningford.

"A lovely, scopey individual, who we have given a little break. The Muhaarars weren't as sharp as everyone was expecting last year, so I am keen to give this colt plenty of time as I don't want to get caught out again."

UNNAMED (IRE)

29/3 b f Sea The Stars - Kitcara (Shamardal)
Owner: Sunderland Holding Inc.
Sales price: 500,000gns (Mandore International Agency)

Second foal of a French 1m 3yo winner who was a half-sister to Group 2-placed French/Australian 9.5-12f winner (including twice at Listed level) Kapour out of a German 1m 3yo Listed winner who was a full sister to German 10f 3yo Group 3 winner/German Oaks runner-up Karavel and Group 2-placed French 10-12.5f 3yo winner (including at Group 3/Listed level) Kalla and a half-sister to high-class 7.5-12f winner (including at Group 1 level) Konigstiger out of a Listed-placed 10f 3yo winner who was a half-sister to King George VI and Queen Elizabeth Stakes/Irish Champion Stakes winner Pentire.

"Another homebred we have out of a Shamardal mare. She is a lovely filly who isn't in yet, but I saw her when she was being broken at Gilltown Stud in February. She will be one for later on, but is a sister to a three-year-old of ours we like called Al Aasy, and I hope she will develop into a similar kind of horse."

UNNAMED (IRE) *Titian*

15/2 b c Iffraaj - Lucelle (High Chaparral)
Owner: Michael Buckley
Sales price: €195,000 (Avenue Bloodstock)

First foal of a French 10-12f winning half-sister to high-class 8-12f winner (including at Group 2/3 level) The Black Princess (by Iffraaj) out of a once-raced maiden close relation to French Derby winner Lawman and half-sister to French Oaks winner Latice (later dam of 7f 2yo Listed winner/Racing Post Trophy third Fencing) and French 1m Group 3 winner Satri.

"I like him. He has just gone back home for a break, but is a really nice-looking colt who finds it all very easy."

UNNAMED

24/4 b c Iffraaj - Mamma Morton (Elnadim)
Owner: Sheikh Ahmed Al Maktoum
Sales price: 190,000gns (Shadwell Estate Company)

Half-brother to Group 2-placed UK/UAE 6f-1m winner (including at Listed level) Master Of War, useful dual 6f winner Muaamara, fairly useful 8-8.5f winner Rampant Lion, once-raced Irish 6f 2yo winner Aca Awesome and four other winners. Dam a maiden half-sister to eleven winners including Group 3/Listed-placed 10f 3yo winner Shaya and Listed-placed 7f 2yo winner Elshamms (later dam of Listed winners Flaming Spear (1m) and Taqseem (5f)).

"This colt was a beautiful yearling. He is a great mover with a solid outlook and should make a two-year-old."

UNNAMED (IRE) *Exchange*

21/4 ch c Night Of Thunder - Mon Bijou (Green Desert)
Owner: Sheikh Hamed Dalmook Al Maktoum
Sales price: 130,000gns (Stroud Coleman Bloodstock)

Half-brother to 7f 2yo winner Morlock. Dam an unraced close relation to useful UK/Australian 8-11f winner Yenhaab and half-sister to high-class 10-12f winner (including at Grade 1 level) Folk Opera out of a maiden half-sister to French/US 10/12f Listed winner Skipping, 7/10f Listed winner Innocent Air and Group 3-placed French 10.5f 3yo winner Minority (later dam of Prix Marcel Boussac winner Proportional and Irish 1m 3yo Group 3 winner/Irish 1000 Guineas third Vote Often).

"Another one that would have almost certainly been racing by May but for the current situation. He is a racy, forward type with a good mind and goes nicely."

UNNAMED (IRE)
21/3 b c Sea The Stars - Oojooba (Monsun)
Owner: Sheikh Ahmed Al Maktoum
Sales price: n/a

Half-brother to useful 8.5f 3yo winner Sharamm. Dam a Listed-placed 1m 2yo winner who was a sister to useful Australian 9.5-11f Flat/very useful multiple 2m hurdle (including at Listed level) winner High Bridge and a half-sister to four winners out of a 1000 Guineas winning half-sister to the unraced dam of dual 12f Listed winner Polly's Mark.

"He is a medium-sized, good-walking colt who is very uncomplicated. He is one of the best movers we have, and I hope he will be ready to go from September onwards. Whatever he does at two is a bit of a bonus because I can see him developing into a very nice horse next year."

Marten writes:

I love to see a horse with an old-fashioned staying pedigree.

I remember the late Major Dick Hern telling me how encouraged they were when the stoutly bred Sun Princess, who went on to win the Oaks and the St Leger, showed sufficient pace to run second in Ascot's Blue Seal Stakes as a two-year-old.

This is something that I have subsequently looked out for and it has served me well over the years. In the case of **Chalk Stream**, as a son of Sea The Stars out of a mare by Sadler's Wells, if he were to show up well in a maiden over six or seven furlongs one would have to be encouraged.

He is a half-brother to Invictus Prince, who won a maiden over an extended mile at two for the Queen with Sir Michael Stoute from a handicap mark of 81 on his three-year-old debut. He later went to race in Australia, once finishing second to the mighty Winx in a Grade 1 at odds of 150/1, but despite running well on occasions he failed to win again.

Chalk Stream comes from one of the Queen's most successful bloodlines, tracing back to Oaks runner-up Flight Of Fancy and the dam of the progressive Sextant, who is also by Sea The Stars.

The dam had the pace to win three times over seven furlongs and surprisingly appeared not to stay on her sole attempt at a mile and a quarter. She had the class to run second in a Group 3 at Goodwood.

I could have gone for half a dozen from the above list but I have a good feeling about this colt and look forward to seeing him run at the back-end of the season. He could be exciting over middle distances next year.

MICHAEL HALFORD

EBASARI (IRE)
3/2 b c Lope De Vega - Ebayya (Azamour)
Owner: H H Aga Khan
Sales price: n/a

First foal of a Listed-placed Irish 9.5f 3yo winner who was a half-sister to French 12.5f 3yo Group 3 winner Ebiyza (later dam of French 10.5f 3yo Listed winner Edisa) and Listed-placed Irish 10f 3yo winner Ebeyina out of an Irish 12f 3yo winning half-sister to Group 1-placed Irish/Hong Kong 8-9f winner (including at Group 3 level) Eyshal, Group 3/Listed-placed Irish/Hong Kong 6-7f winner Lotus Breeze and Group 3-placed Irish 12-12.5f winner Edelpour out of an Irish Oaks winning half-sister to very smart stayers Enzeli and Estimate and Irish 7f 2yo Group 1 winner Ebadiya.

"A big, backward colt but is well balanced and has a good attitude. He will be one for the second half of the season, but he is a grand sort who we like."

KALAROUN (IRE)
13/2 b c Starspangledbanner - Karalara (Shamardal)
Owner: H H Aga Khan
Sales price: n/a

First foal of a useful Irish 10f 3yo winning half-sister to French 1m 3yo winner Karishma out of a Group 3-placed Irish 7-12f winner (including at Listed level) who was a half-sister to Group 3/Listed-placed Irish 7f 2yo winner Kirinda and useful Irish 10-12f winner Kerisa out of a once-raced maiden half-sister to the dam of 6f Listed winner Rocky Ground.

"This would be the most forward of His Highness's two-year-olds at the moment. He is a strongly-built, powerful colt who shows speed in his work and also has a good attitude. I imagine he will begin over six furlongs."

RAYAGARA (IRE)
28/1 b f Dark Angel - Raydara (Rock Of Gibraltar)
Owner: H H Aga Khan
Sales price: n/a

Half-sister to once-raced 2019 Irish 7f 2yo winner Ridenza. Dam an Irish 7f 2yo Group 2 winner who was a half-sister to French 1m 3yo Listed winner Rondonia and useful Irish 11-12f 3yo winner Rayna out of an Irish 12f 3yo Listed winning half-sister to Group 1-placed 10-10.5f winner Roseburg; the family of Group 1 winners Kinnaird, Laurens and Helene Mascot.

"This is a nice filly, though a different type to her half-sister, Ridenza, which is only to be expected given their respective sires. She is a sweet, good-looking sort who has a nice action on her and has given the work riders a good feel. I'm hopeful she can do something in the second half of the season when there's some ease in the ground."

ROZIYNA (IRE)
11/2 b f Sea The Stars - Rayisa (Holy Roman Emperor)
Owner: H H Aga Khan
Sales price: n/a

First foal of a Listed-placed Irish 1m 2yo winner who was a half-sister to Group 2-placed Irish dual 7f winner (including at Group 3 level) Rehana out of a maiden half-sister to high-class Irish 6-7f winner (including at Group 3/Listed level)/Irish 2000 Guineas runner-up Rayeni out of an Irish 10f 3yo winning half-sister to Irish 7f 2yo Group 3 winner Rafayda, very useful Irish 9-11f 3yo winner/Irish Derby fourth Raypour and the dam of Irish 12f 3yo Listed winner Raydiya (herself later dam of Irish 7f 2yo Group 2 winner Raydara).

"This is a backward sort of filly, but she has a lovely attitude and is very straightforward. She is only cantering at this stage and still has a bit of developing to do, but His Highness's horses can blossom from the summer onwards."

TURBO SPIRIT

2/4 b c Charm Spirit - Bijou A Moi (Rainbow Quest)
Owner: Sammy Hon Kit Ma
Sales price: €72,000 (McKeever Bloodstock)

Half-brother to 10f Group 3 winner Robin Hoods Bay, dual 1m 3yo winner Bipartisan and three other winners. Dam an unraced half-sister to Listed-placed Irish 7f 2yo winner Pietra Dura (later dam of US 10f Grade 3 winner Turning Top), Listed-placed 13f 3yo winner Bite Of The Cherry and the dam of King George VI and Queen Elizabeth Stakes/Juddmonte International Stakes winner Postponed and Italian 10f Group 1 winner God Given out of an Irish 7f 2yo Group 1 winner who was a half-sister to Group 1-placed 7f 2yo winner Hotelgenie Dot Com (later dam of dual 1m Group 1 winner Simply Perfect).

"This is a nice, forward colt who should be ready to run once we are back racing. He was due to have an away day somewhere but that all went out of the window when the restrictions were put in place. He has a great mind on him, and is a good-looking type who has pleased in his work. I imagine he will want six furlongs to begin with."

Marten writes:

I have a soft spot for long-established homebred bloodlines and few can match the quality that the Aga Khan has consistently produced over the years.

In the case of **Ebasari** he is by Lope De Vega and the first foal of a winning daughter of Azamour, so I don't expect to see much of him this season.

Everything about his pedigree suggests he is one for middle distances next year, but it's encouraging that the trainer has already discerned that the colt has a "good attitude".

There are some well-known names on this colt's page, among them Ascot Gold Cup winner Estimate. All I want to see from him is a little bit of promise in a back-end maiden. That should set him up nicely for next season.

RICHARD HANNON

CLIFFCAKE (IRE)
1/4 b c Canford Cliffs - Cake (Acclamation)
Owner: Des Anderson
Sales price: n/a

Full brother to Listed-placed multiple 5-7f winner Tomily and fairly useful multiple 5f winner Drakefell and a half-brother to 6f 2yo Listed winner Fig Roll (later dam of 2019 French 5f 2yo Group 3 winner Al Raya) and useful 6-7f winner Typhoon Ten. Dam a Group 3-placed multiple 5f winner (including at Listed level) who was a full sister to very useful multiple 5-6f winner Embour and a half-sister to useful UK/UAE 7f-1m winner Suited And Booted.

"He is from a family we know loads about having trained the dam and most of her progeny to date. This colt is typical of the page - speedy and precocious. He goes well and will be out sooner rather than later."

COLLINSBAY
16/2 b c Cable Bay - Kinematic (Kyllachy)
Owner: The Queen
Sales price: n/a

Full brother to useful 2019 6.5f 2yo winner King's Lynn. Dam a 5.5f 2yo winner who was a half-sister to very useful multiple 6f winner (including at Listed level) Musical Comedy, useful 7-12.5f winner Full Toss, UK/French 7f-1m winner Humdrum and 6f 2yo winners Otago (by Cable Bay) and Ring Of Truth out of a Listed-placed 10f 3yo winner.

"A lovely, sizeable colt of Her Majesty's. He has done some nice work and I'd be hopeful about him."

COOPERATION (IRE)
30/3 b c Mehmas - Ripalong (Revoque)
Owner: Sheikh Abdullah Almalek Alsabah
Sales price: £82,000 (Peter & Ross Doyle Bloodstock)

Half-brother to smart 6f-1m winner (including at Group 3/Listed level) Shamwari Lodge (later dam of dual 7f Listed winner Oh This Is Us) and Irish

7f 3yo Listed winner Imperial Rome. Dam a maiden half-sister to 6f Group 1 winner Pipalong (later dam of Irish 6f 2yo Group 3 winner Walk On Bye), 6f 2yo Listed winner Out Of Africa, 5f 2yo winner/Flying Childers Stakes runner-up China Eyes and the dam of Irish 5/6f Listed winner Great Minds.

"We obviously know this family well having trained half-sister Shamwari Lodge, her son Oh This Is Us and of course the sire. He is a strong sort who looks to have taken after his father and should be racing over five and six furlongs pretty much once racing begins. He shows us plenty."

DILLYDINGDILLYDONG
22/2 b c Territories - Cephalonie (Kris S)
Owner: King Power Racing Co Ltd
Sales price: 110,000gns (SackvilleDonald)

Three-parts brother to French 1m 3yo Listed winner Arctic Gyr, Group 3-placed 6f-1m winner (including at Listed level) Festivale and useful 6f 2yo winner Simple Magic (all by Invincible Spirit) and a half-brother to Group 3/Listed-placed 6f-1m winner Tell. Dam a French 12f 3yo winner from the excellent family of Prix de l'Arc de Triomphe winner Bago, French Oaks winner Senga and very smart French two-year-old performers Denebola and Machiavellian.

"A big, strong colt who is plenty forward and done all that has been asked of him. He has a lovely temperament."

ENOUGHISGOODENOUGH (IRE)
19/4 b f Dark Angel - The Hermitage (Kheleyf)
Owner: King Power Racing Co Ltd
Sales price: €440,000 (SackvilleDonald)

Full sister to Group 2-placed dual 6f 2yo winner (including at Group 3 level)/1000 Guineas fourth Angel's Hideaway and Group 2/3-placed 6f 2yo winner Perfect Angel. Dam a Listed-placed 5f 2yo winner who was a half-sister to Group 1-placed 7-11.5f winner (including at Listed level)/Oaks third Crown Of Light (later dam of 14f/2m Listed winner Balkan Knight), 1m 2yo Listed winner Alboostan and the maiden dam of 1m 1f Group 3 winner/Racing Post Trophy runner-up Charlie Farnsbarns.

"She cost plenty of money, but is a nice filly with a smart pedigree. We haven't done much with her yet as she is one for the second half of the season."

FAST STEPS (IRE)
27/3 b c Footstepsinthesand - Inis Boffin (Danehill Dancer)
Owner: Saeed Suhail
Sales price: €280,000 (Blandford Bloodstock)

Full brother to very useful Irish 9.5-10f 3yo winner Qatari Hunter and a half-brother to French 1m 2yo Listed winner Paint Island. Dam an 8.5f 3yo winner who was a three-parts sister to useful 6f 2yo winner Winds Of Time (later dam of 6f 2yo winner/Richmond Stakes second The Paddyman) and a half-sister to useful 8-14f Flat/Listed-placed dual 2m hurdle/2m 4f-3m chase winner Debdebdeb and useful UK/Australian 8.5-13f winner The Baronet.

"A very nice colt with plenty of size, and will be one for the second half of the season. He'll likely want seven furlongs at least."

HAFEZ (IRE)
18/1 br c Dark Angel - Stellar Path (Astronomer Royal)
Owner: Amo Racing Limited
Sales price: 400,000gns (Peter & Ross Doyle Bloodstock)

Half-brother to French 6f 2yo winner Astral Path. Dam a high-class French/US 7-8.5f winner (including at Grade/Group 3 level) who was a full sister to Group 1-placed UK/Australian 6-7.5f winner (including at Group 2/3 level) Weary and a half-sister to smart 6f-1m winner (including at Group 2/3 level) Nyaleti.

"He cost plenty of money but rightly so as he is a smashing horse. He will start over six furlongs when those races are here and I am hoping he could be pretty smart."

HOST (IRE)
22/1 b c Mehmas - Mistress Makfi (Makfi)
Owner: Highclere Thoroughbred Racing - Katie O'Sullivan
Sales price: £52,000 (John & Jake Warren)

First foal of a twice-raced maiden half-sister to Group 2-placed Irish 7f-1m winner/Irish 1000 Guineas fourth Rare Ransom and Listed-placed Irish 10-10.5f 3yo winner Ransomed Bride out of a Group 3-placed Irish 10f 3yo winner who was a half-sister to Group 3-placed Irish dual 6f 2yo winner (including at Listed level) Warrior Queen (later dam of US dual 8.5f 3yo Grade 2 winner A. P. Warrior and grandam of US 8.5f 3yo Grade 2 winner Global View).

"A strong colt owned by Highclere Thoroughbred. He reminds me quite a bit of his sire as he is relaxed, uncomplicated and shows plenty of speed. Let's hope he can run like him too!"

LUXY LOU (IRE)

5/4 ch f The Last Lion - Dutch Courage (Dutch Art)
Owner: Merribelle Irish Farm/Sullivan Bloodstock
Sales price: €92,000 (Peter & Ross Doyle Bloodstock)

Third foal of a useful 6-7f 2yo winner who was a half-sister to Group 2-placed dual 7f winner (including at Group 3 level) Dandhu, Listed-placed 6-7f winner Maid A Million and useful Irish 10.5f 3yo winner Gustavus Vassa out of an unraced half-sister to 1m 3yo Group 1 winner Rajeem (later dam of Group 1-placed multiple 6f winner (including at Group 2/3 level) Invincible Army) and the unraced dam of Group 3-placed Irish 6f 2yo winner Jeanne Girl.

"A nice filly who has done really well of late. She won't be massively early but should be OK in time."

MEADOW SPRITE (IRE)

24/2 ch f Slade Power - Pivotique (Pivotal)
Owner: Sheikh Mohammed Obaid Al Maktoum
Sales price: n/a

Half-sister to Group 2-placed 2019 7f 2yo winner Cloak Of Spirits. Dam a maiden half-sister to once-raced 2019 1m 3yo winner Subaana out of an 8.5f 3yo winner who was a three-parts sister to Irish National Stakes/Irish 2000 Guineas winner Dubawi and a half-sister to several winners including Lancashire Oaks winner Emirates Queen.

"She is a half-sister to a very nice three-year-old we train called Cloak Of Spirits who we have really high hopes for this year, having looked smart at two. This is a nice type in her own right, but will need a bit of time."

MR TRICK (IRE)

17/2 b c Kodiac - Alkhawarah (Intidab)
Owner: Mr & Mrs R Kelvin-Hughes
Sales price: 82,000gns (Amanda Skiffington)

Half-brother to triple 7f winner Wilson and dual 10f Flat/2m hurdle winner Oceanus. Dam a maiden half-sister to Middle Park Stakes winner Hayil, Grade 2/3-placed 6-10f winner Tamhid, Grade 3-placed UK/US 6-8.5f winner Ghurra (later dam of Prix Morny and Middle Park Stakes winner Shalaa), Listed-placed 5-7f winner Ebraam, Listed-placed 7-7.5f 2yo winner Elnahaar, useful 6f 2yo winner Farqad and the grandam of Group 1-placed 6f-1m winner (including at Group 2/3 level) Dragon Pulse.

"A cracking colt who is from the family of Al Shaqab's good two-year-old, Shalaa. He is a typically forward and mature son of Kodiac who pleases in everything he does. We should have some fun with him this year."

MUMMY BEAR (IRE)
6/2 br f Kodi Bear - Shortmile Lady (Arcano)
Owner: Vincent Caldwell And Maneerat Caldwell
Sales price: £40,000 (Peter & Ross Doyle Bloodstock)

Half-sister to 2020 Irish 1m 3yo Group 3 winner Lemista. Dam a maiden half-sister to smart prolific 5-6f winner (including at Group 3/Listed level) Indian Maiden (later dam of 5f Group 3/Listed winner Maid In India and French 5.5/6f Listed winner Love Spirit); the family of 3yo Listed winners Free Roses (5f) and Lake Volta (7f).

"A lovely filly whose half-sister won a Group 3 over in Ireland at the only turf meeting staged so far this year. She is one I am looking forward to getting started."

RED DAWN (IRE)
11/5 b c Night Of Thunder - Dream Day (Oasis Dream)
Owner: Isa Salman
Sales price: 92,000gns (Warren/Doyle)

Half-brother to Listed-placed French 9.5f 2yo winner Delhi, fairly useful 5-7f winner Dark Side Dream and 6f 2yo winner Wedding Dress. Dam a Group 3-placed 6f 2yo winner who was a half-sister to Listed-placed 6f-1m winner Sabbeeh and Listed-placed Irish 10f 3yo winner Bongiorno out of a French 7f 3yo Listed winning full sister to Listed-placed UK/US 7-8.5f winner Leopard Hunt and half-sister to Listed-placed 6f 2yo winner Bring Plenty.

"A big, attractive colt who will definitely be more one for the backend, but he is a lovely type who moves well. Will want seven furlongs and a mile this year."

RIVER ALWEN (IRE)
2/4 gr c Dark Angel - Intense Pink (Pivotal)
Owner: Sun Bloodstock Racing Limited
Sales price: €145,000 (Sun Bloodstock)

Third foal of a Group 3-placed 6-7f winner (including at Listed level) who was a half-sister to 6f 2yo winner/Racing Post Trophy third Henrik, Group 2/Listed-placed 6-6.5f winner Sir Reginald, Listed-placed dual 6f 2yo winner Bishop's Lake (dam of Irish 10f Group 3 winner Euphrasia), very useful 10-12f winner Fractal and the dam of 1m 3yo Listed winner/2000 Guineas third Van Der Neer.

"A really nice colt who shows speed and has a lovely temperament. He is a typical Dark Angel and should be out by the summer."

SAUNTON (IRE)
14/4 b c Footstepsinthesand - Camellia Japonica (Zoffany)
Owner: Owners Group 061
Sales price: 58,000gns (Peter & Ross Doyle Bloodstock)

First foal of an Irish 6f 3yo winning sister to useful 5f 2yo winner Bahamian Flame and a half-sister to two winners out of an unraced half-sister to high-class 7-10f winner (including at Group 1 level)/1000 Guineas fourth Red Bloom (later dam of Hong Kong 1m 1f Group 3 winner Simply Brilliant), smart 10-13.5f winner (including at Listed level) Red Gala and the dam of 1m 2yo Listed winner Thanksfortellingme out of a 7f 2yo Group 3 winner/French 1000 Guineas third.

"This colt was going well and looked like being amongst our earlier runners until racing was stopped. He is on the back burner just now while we wait for it to all start up again, but I can see him giving his owners some fun this season. He is by our favourite stallion of recent times as he gave us Threat and Mums Tipple last year."

SIAM FOX (IRE)
19/2 b c Prince Of Lir - Folegandros Island (Red Rocks)
Owner: King Power Racing Co Ltd
Sales price: 260,000gns (SackvilleDonald)

Three-parts brother to Group 1-placed 6f-1m winner (including the 2019 German 2000 Guineas) Fox Champion (by Kodiac). Dam a maiden half-sister to Group 3-placed multiple 6-7f winner Dandy Boy and useful French 8-10f winner Complusory.

"This lad was a standout individual as a yearling and still is now. He is closely related to our German 2000 Guineas winner, Fox Champion, and I am extremely excited to see what this colt can do this season."

SIR RUMI (IRE)
9/3 ch c Gleneagles - Reine Des Plages (Danehill Dancer)
Owner: Amo Racing Limited
Sales price: €160,000 (Peter & Ross Doyle Bloodstock Ltd)

Half-brother to French 10.5f 3yo winner Cameo. Dam an unraced half-sister to Group 3-placed 7-10f winner (including at Listed level) Portage and Italian 10f 3yo Listed winner Cape Magic out of a maiden three-parts sister to French

1m 3yo Listed winner Mooring and half-sister to 6f 2yo Group 3 winner Wharf, French multiple 8-10f winner Docklands (later dam of Prix de l'Arc de Triomphe winner Rail Link) and the dam of French 10f 2yo Group 1 winner Linda's Lad.

"A smashing colt with plenty of scope who catches the eye in all that he does. He won't be overly early and will want seven furlongs, but we certainly like what we see so far."

SOUNDSLIKETHUNDER (IRE)
9/5 ch c Night Of Thunder - Dust Flicker (Suave Dancer)
Owner: Sheikh Juma Dalmook Al Maktoum
Sales price: €100,000 (Peter & Ross Doyle)

Half-brother to Group/Grade 3-placed UK/US 5-8.5f winner (including at Listed level) Sweepstake (later dam of 2019 Irish dual 10f 3yo Group 3 winner/ Derby fourth Broome) and three other winners. Dam a maiden sister to smart UK/French 7-12f winner (including at Group 3/Listed level) Dust Dancer (later dam of US 1m 1f Grade 2 winner Spotlight and grandam of Irish 6f 2yo Group 1 winner Zoffany and Irish 7f 2yo Group 2 winner/Irish Derby second Rostropovich) and half-sister to Fred Darling Stakes winner Bulaxie (later dam of smart pair Bulwark and Claxon).

"Dad trained the half-sister to win a National Stakes a few years ago now. This is a grand horse who has really grown into himself and put on plenty of bulk in the past few weeks. He is obviously by an excellent young sire and will be one for the six and seven furlong races."

VENTURA TORMENTA (IRE)
10/2 b c Acclamation - Midnight Oasis (Oasis Dream)
Owner: Middleham Park Racing IV
Sales price: £95,000 (Peter & Ross Doyle Bloodstock)

Three-parts brother to very useful multiple 6f winner George Bowen (by Dark Angel) and a half-brother to very useful 6-7f winner Mr Win, useful 6f-1m winner Mutahaady and two other winners. Dam a maiden three-parts sister to the dam of French 5f 2yo Group 3 winner Fly On The Night and a half-sister to smart 5-6f winner (including at Group 3/Listed level) Miss Anabaa (grandam of 6f 2yo Listed winner Enjazaat (by Acclamation)) and very useful 5-6f winners Move It and Out After Dark; the family of July Cup winner Owington and French 1000 Guineas second Nathra.

"A straightforward, uncomplicated colt who is very typical of his sire. You would hope he can do something at two."

UNNAMED (FR) *Longlai*

22/2 b c Shalaa - Mojo Risin (Lope De Vega)
Owner: King Power Racing Co Ltd
Sales price: €130,000 (SackvilleDonald)

First foal of a French 10.5f 3yo Listed winner who was the granddaughter of a Listed-placed French 1m 3yo winning half-sister to French 1m 1f 3yo Listed winner Palacoona (later dam of US 1m 1f Grade 3 winner Diamond Tycoon and 11f Listed winner Cassique Lady), French dual 1m 3yo Listed winner Palafairia and the dam of the smart Kendargent.

"Another very nice colt for King Power who has a bit of size, and while he won't be that early, the early signs look good. I would hope to see him racing by the summer."

Dark Lady makes her way to the start before her debut second at Newbury last July. The daughter of Dark Angel made rapid strides thereafter, going on to win the Group 3 Shadwell Dick Poole Fillies' Stakes at Salisbury in September.

Marten writes:

Richard Hannon has been lucky for me since taking over the licence to train from his father.

I was keen on the chances of his 2014 2000 Guineas winner Night Of Thunder and also 1000 Guineas winner Billesdon Brook. Both were long prices, but in both cases they had shown me enough to suggest they had the ability to win at the highest level.

In the case of Billesdon Brook the manner in which she won a nursery, albeit off 87, at Goodwood suggested to me that she was a filly with a special talent. It was one of the most remarkable victories I have ever seen and I took the view that although her subsequent form at two showed she was not an exceptional filly, what she did that day at Goodwood was indeed exceptional.

At 66/1 on Guineas day I argued that if she could replicate the ability she showed on that occasion at Goodwood then she would outrun those odds, which she duly did with something in hand.

It was good to see her return to top form last back-end when she won the Group 1 Sun Chariot Stakes at Newmarket.

The trainer is not afraid to aim high with his horses. His father did just that when Mon Fils won the 1973 2000 Guineas at 50/1, ridden by 46-year-old veteran Frankie Durr, and his son went close again when King Of Change was runner-up at 66/1 to Magna Grecia in last year's race.

Despite having over a hundred two-year-olds officially listed in training, there are few with middle-distance pedigrees from those nominated above. It's no surprise to see that he has a handful of youngsters by first-season sire Mehmas, having trained him to win four of his eight starts including two at Group 2 level and run placed in the Middle Park.

Mehmas was, unusually, retired to stud at the end of that season and his trainer will be keen to do well for him.

The one I've gone for is **Cooperation**, who is out of a maiden half-sister to the very useful Pipalong and other speedy types. Pipalong, who was trained by Tim Easterby, was kept busy winning 10 of her 37 starts including the Group 1 sprint at Haydock. She was particularly well suited to soft ground.

Hannon trained this colt's half-brother Shamwari Lodge and Oh This Is Us so the portents are favourably aligned.

JESSICA HARRINGTON

ANNA STRADA
3/4 ch f Havana Gold - Frequently (Dansili)
Owner: William Slattery
Sales price: 18,000gns (Vendor)

Fourth foal of an unraced three-parts sister to 2019 Prix Marcel Boussac winner Albigna and half-sister to Group 3-placed multiple 6f winner (including at Listed level) Polybius and useful triple 5f 2yo winner No Lippy out of a Grade 1-placed French 12-12.5f winner (including at Group 2 level); the family of Breeders' Cup Mile winner Domedriver.

"A fine big filly and not too dissimilar to Albigna, who is the dam's three-parts sister. She should be one for the six and seven furlong races and we quite like her."

BOHENIE (IRE)
15/3 b c Showcasing - Greenisland (Fasliyev)
Owner: Stonethorn Stud Farm Ltd
Sales price: n/a

Half-brother to very useful multiple 5-6f winner (including at Listed level) Shamshon, useful French 5.5-7.5f winner Shajjy and useful 7f 2yo winner Boerhan. Dam a Listed-placed 7f-1m winner who was a half-sister to 2019 Cheveley Park Stakes winner Millisle and very useful 11.5-12f winner (including at Listed level) Ithoughtitwasover.

"He has just come back in having had a breathing operation. He is related to our Cheveley Park winner, Millisle, and is a big, strong colt who should be ready to get started in June over six furlongs."

COOPER'S HAWK (IRE)
19/2 b c Awtaad - La Negra (Dark Angel)
Owner: Mill House LLC
Sales price: €64,000 (BBA Ireland)

First foal of an unraced sister to Group 1-placed 5-10f winner (including twice at Listed level) Gabrial and half-sister to useful 9-12f Flat/very useful multiple 2m hurdle winner Innocent Touch out of a French triple 10.5f 3yo winner who was a half-sister to US Grade 2 winners Iron Deputy (1m 1f) and Jaunatxo (9.5f) and the dam of Italian 1m Group 1 winner/French 2000 Guineas third Shamalgan and Italian 10f 3yo Listed winner Chardonney Tcheque.

"A nice, very strong colt who actually held an entry at the Curragh during the opening week of the season. He is ready to go and though he will want six and seven furlongs in time, he is likely to still start off over five furlongs."

DEPUTY SANDY (IRE)
8/3 b c Footstepsinthesand - Bayan Kasirga (Aussie Rules)
Owner: Zhang Yuesheng
Sales price: €60,000 (BBA Ireland/Yulong Investments)

First foal of a useful multiple 12-13.5f winner who was a half-sister to Group 2-placed UK/Hong Kong 7-9f winner Fortune Patrol out of a maiden half-sister to Group 1-placed 5-10.5f winner (including at Grade 2/Group 3 level) Barefoot Lady (by Footstepsinthesand) out of a 6f 2yo Listed winning half-sister to the dam of smart stayer Montaly.

"A fine big colt who does things easily so far. He should have no problem making an impact this year."

FLAUNTING (IRE)
25/3 b f Acclamation - Show Me Off (Showcasing)
Owner: Mrs P Myerscough & D Cox
Sales price: £38,000 (Vendor)

Half-sister to useful 2020 Irish 5f 3yo winner American Lady. Dam an unraced half-sister to smart multiple 5f-1m winner (including at Group 2/3 level) Loveleaves and 6-7f 2yo winner Tussie Mussie (later dam of useful Irish 5-7.5f 2yo winner Guessthebill) out of a 1m 3yo winning daughter of an unraced half-sister to 6f 2yo Listed winner Run For The Hills (grandam of Irish 6f Group 3 winner The Happy Prince) and the dams of US 1m 1f Grade 1 winner Stroll and

1m Group 2 winner Lady In Waiting, US dual 11f Grade 2 winner Grassy and high-class stayer Savannah Bay.

"A lovely filly who isn't quite long as some by the sire tend to be. She has a lovely way about her, and will be ready to go when the seven furlong races are here."

LAELAPS (IRE)
12/2 b c Exceed And Excel - Magen's Star (Galileo)
Owner: Newtown Anner Stud Farm Ltd
Sales price: n/a

Half-brother to smart Irish 7.5-12f winner (including twice at Listed level) Red Stars. Dam a useful Irish 11-14f Flat/very useful Irish dual 2m hurdle winner who was a half-sister to Listed-placed Irish 12f winner Really and the unraced dam of St Leger winner Simple Verse, Ribblesdale Stakes winner Even Song, and Group 3-placed 6-7f 2yo winner Maxentius.

"I think this is a smart colt. The dam's side has a good few middle-distance and staying types in it, but obviously his sire brings speed into play and he looks very much like he has inherited that. He is a tall, narrow colt with a long stride, and I hope to be able to start him off over six furlongs in the not too distant future."

LAY IT OUT (IRE)
11/3 b f Oasis Dream - Newsroom (Manduro)
Owner: The Long Wait Partnership
Sales price: €120,000 (Richard Ryan)

Second foal of a useful French 10f 3yo winner who was a half-sister to Group 1-placed multiple 5-5.5f 2yo winner (including at Group 2/Listed level) Signora Cabello, Listed-placed 6f 2yo winner La Presse, Listed-placed French 1m 3yo winner Emirates Girl (later dam of UAE 2000 Guineas winner Fly At Dawn) and very useful 7f-1m winner Paper Talk out of a Group 3-placed 6f 2yo winning half-sister to Flying Childers Stakes winner Sheer Viking.

"She is an early type who is pretty much ready to go now. She will enjoy top of the ground from what we've seen at home, and should have the speed to begin at five furlongs. A nice filly."

LOCH LEIN (IRE)
22/3 b f Invincible Spirit - Ashley Hall (Maria's Mon)
Owner: Epona Bloodstock
Sales price: 350,000gns (Vendor)

Full sister to Irish 5f 2yo winner Pedestal and a three-parts sister to 2019 5f 2yo winner Full Authority (by Kingman). Dam a US 5.5f 3yo winning half-sister to US 1m 1f 3yo Grade 1 winner Bandini, 7f 2yo Group 3 winner Discourse (later dam of 1m 2yo Listed winner Hadith, German 1m 3yo Listed winner Discursus and very useful 5-7f winner Blown By Wind (by Invincible Spirit)), useful 8.5-10.5f winner Serene Beauty, 7f-1m 2yo winner Najoum and 7f 2yo winner City Chic.

"A lovely filly who has a great long stride on her. She is fairly forward and should prove best at six and seven furlongs."

LOS ANDES (USA)
6/4 b c Karakontie - Candy Kitty (Lemon Drop Kid)
Owner: Flaxman Stables Ireland
Sales price: n/a

Third foal of a Grade 3-placed US 8-8.5f winner (including twice at Stakes level) who was a full sister to useful US 8-8.5f winner Brainwash and US 1m 3yo winner Worthy Turk out of a maiden close relation to US 1m/Canadian 8.5f Grade 2 winner Naissance Royale and half-sister to Group 3/Listed-placed 10f 3yo winner Spinnette (later dam of French 1m 3yo Listed winner Green Lyons and grandam of Irish 7f 3yo Listed winner Planchart).

"This is a tall, leggy colt who does it all very easily so far. I've only had one by the sire, but this looks like a very nice horse. He should be running by the summer over six furlongs to begin with."

MULAN VALOUR (IRE)
8/4 b f The Last Lion - Biaraafa (Araafa)
Owner: Zhang Yuesheng
Sales price: €50,000 (BBA Ireland/Yulong Investments)

Half-sister to dual 7f 2yo winner Doublet. Dam a 6-7f winner who was a half-sister to Listed-placed Irish 7f 2yo winner Pietra Dura (later dam of US 10f Grade 3 winner Turning Top), Listed-placed 8-8.5f 3yo winner Bighearted, Listed-placed 13f 3yo winner Bite Of The Cherry and the dam of King George VI & Queen Elizabeth Stakes/Juddmonte International Stakes winner

Postponed and Italian 10f Group 1 winner God Given out an Irish 7f 2yo Group 1 winner.

"A very good-looking filly who is sharp and was ready to run before the shutdown. One for the five and six furlong races."

NO SPEAK ALEXANDER (IRE)
14/4 b f Shalaa - Rapacity Alexander (Dandy Man)
Owner: Noel O'Callaghan
Sales price: €190,000 (Not Sold)

First foal of a French 5f 2yo Listed winner who was a full sister to high-class UK/Hong Kong 5-6f winner (including at Group 1 level) Peniaphobia and a half-sister to Group 3/Listed-placed 5f 2yo winner Safari Sunset out of an unraced half-sister to the grandam of Irish 1m Listed winner Lily's Rainbow; the family of 5f 2yo Group 3 winner Peace Offering.

"This filly is another who was more or less ready to go when we were forced to stop. She is a bit on the leg but looks precocious and has a good temperament. So far she does it all very easily and should make a nice sprinter."

OODNADATTA (IRE)
30/1 b f Australia - Bewitched (Dansili)
Owner: Robert Scarborough & Mrs John Magnier
Sales price: n/a

Three-parts sister to smart 10-12f winner (including at Listed level) Pablo Escobarr (by Galileo). Dam a smart multiple 5-7f winner (including four times at Group 3 level) who was a sister to useful Irish 5f-1m winner Peter Tchaikovsky and a half-sister to the dam of French 1m Listed winner Verglacial out of a French 10.5f 3yo Group 3 winner/French Oaks second who was a sister to French 10.5f 3yo Listed winner Aubergade and half-sister to the dam of Group 1-placed Irish/Australian 12-14f winner (including at Group 2/3 level)/St Leger third Southern France.

"She is compact and short-backed, so isn't your typical Australia. She is also very forward going, and has clearly taken after her mother. I think she is very nice and hope to have her running by mid-June over six or seven furlongs."

PROVOCATEUSE (IRE)
11/4 b f Pride Of Dubai - Malicieuse (Galileo)
Owner: Niarchos Family
Sales price: n/a

Second foal of a useful French 5.5f 2yo winning close relation to Group
3-placed Irish 7.5f 2yo winner Zabriskie and half-sister to top-class French
8-12f winner (five times at Group 1 level, including the Arc) Bago, very
smart French 8-10f winner (including at Group 1 level) Maxios and French
5f 2yo Listed winner Beta out of an unraced half-sister to French 1m 2yo
Group 1 winner Denebola (grandam of French Oaks winner Senga), French
6f 2yo Group 3 winner Loving Kindness and French 7f 3yo Listed winner Glia
(grandam of US four-time 8.5-10f Grade 1 winner Emollient).

*"I have three by the sire and this filly is big and strong like the other two. I like
what I have seen from her so far."*

VALLE DE LA LUNA
13/3 b f Galileo - Fiesolana (Aussie Rules)
Owner: Flaxman Stables Ireland Ltd
Sales price: n/a

Full sister to Group 3-placed 2019 Irish 8.5-9.5f 3yo winner (including at Listed
level) Up Helly Aa. Dam a high-class 6-10f winner (including at Group 1 level)
who was a three-parts sister to French 2m 3f Grade 1 hurdle winner Tidal
Reach and a half-sister to smart 5-10f winner (including at Grade 2/Group 3
level) Innit and French 2m 2f Grade 1 hurdle winner Tidal Fury out of a 1m 2yo
winner who was a half-sister to US multiple 1m Listed winner Davie's Lamb.

*"A beautiful, scopey filly, but she isn't bred to be a two-year-old, and is very
much one for the backend and next year."*

YULONG DE LEGEND (IRE)
26/3 b c Kodiac - Plum Sugar (Footstepsinthesand)
Owner: Zhang Yuesheng
Sales price: €62,000 (BBA Ireland)

Three-parts brother to Stakes-placed Irish/US dual 7f winner Ellery Lane
(by Holy Roman Emperor). Dam a useful Irish 1m 2yo winner who was the
daughter of a maiden half-sister to Ribblesdale Stakes winner Gull Nook
(later dam of King George VI & Queen Elizabeth Stakes/Irish Champion Stakes
winner Pentire), 12f Group 3 winner/Park Hill Stakes runner-up Banket, 13.5f
Listed winner/Irish St Leger runner-up Mr Pintips and the dam of Italian 1m
2yo Group 1 winner Konigstiger.

"A sharp colt who should be ready to run pretty much as soon as we're back racing. Six and seven furlongs will be his trip."

UNNAMED (FR) Taipan
22/2 b c Frankel - Kenzadargent (Kendargent)
Owner: Ms Fiona Carmichael
Sales price: €500,000 (Amanda Skiffington)

Half-brother to useful 2019 5-6f 2yo winner Brad The Brief. Dam a Grade 2-placed French/US 7-8.5f winner (including twice at Listed level) who was the daughter of a French 8-9f winning half-sister to French 1m Listed winner Bartex, very useful French multiple 6.5f-1m winner Plaisir Bere and the dam of US 8/9f Grade 2 winner Flamboyant.

"A gorgeous individual. He is big and strong and probably does it a little too easily at the moment because he will be one for mid-season onwards. I imagine he will start over seven furlongs but should stay a bit further in time."

Marten writes:

If, as the trainer suggests, the product of a Manduro mare may "have the speed to begin at five furlongs" then you have to sit up and take notice. This is what she says about **Lay It Out**, who probably gets the pace she apparently shows at home from her sire Oasis Dream.

Lay It Out is the second foal of a lightly raced half-sister to some very speedy types including Signora Cabello, who won four times at two including twice at Group 2 level before struggling at three. There are others in the family that shaped well at Pattern level.

Lay It Out has a blend of both speed and stamina in her pedigree, leaving me a little uncertain as to her optimum trip, but the early promise augurs well.

RICHARD HUGHES

AUSSIE STORMER (IRE)
22/2 b c Mehmas - Stormy Clouds (Sir Prancealot)
Owner: P Cook & K Lawrence
Sales price: £50,000 (Richard Hughes)

First foal of a Listed-placed 5-6f 2yo winner who was the daughter of a maiden half-sister to Group 2/3-placed 5-6f winner (including at Listed level) Danehill Destiny out of a 5.5f 3yo winning sister to useful triple 10f Flat/useful 2m-2m 4f hurdle/2m 1f-2m 4f chase winner Just In Time and half-sister to very smart 7f-1m winner (including at Group 1 level) Where Or When and smart 10-12f winner (including at Listed level)/St Leger fourth All The Way.

"He will be my first two-year-old runner when we're back racing. His mother won a valuable sales race at York for Richard Hannon. He shows plenty of speed."

BONNIE LAD
30/3 ch c Havana Gold - Bonnie Grey (Hellvelyn)
Owner: Bpc, Taylor & Young
Sales price: £11,000 (Richard Hughes)

Third foal of a Group 3-placed 5f 2yo winner who was a three-parts sister to 6f 2yo winner Okikoki and a half-sister to very useful triple 7f winner (including at Listed level) Clifton Dancer, very useful UK/Hong Kong 5-7f winner Cop Hill Lad and four other winners out of a Listed-placed triple 5f winner who was a half-sister to Group 2/3-placed multiple 5-6f winner (including at Listed level) Lord Kintyre and useful prolific 5-9f winner Highland Warrior.

"He is a grand little horse who didn't cost much, and would've been racing at the end of May under normal circumstances. I will be aiming him at those auction events."

DON'T LOOK BACK

15/4 gr c Oasis Dream - Ronaldsay (Kirkwall)
Owner: Clarke, Jeffries, Lawrence & Wakefield
Sales price: 38,000gns (Richard Hughes Racing)

Brother to Group 1-placed 6-7f winner (including at Group 3 level)/Irish 2000 Guineas runner-up Gale Force Ten and a half-brother to very useful UK/UAE 9-12f winner Eynhallow and useful UK/Swiss 9-12f winner Ulster. Dam an 11f Listed winner who was a half-sister to the dam of US 8/8.5f Grade 3 winner Pickle (herself dam of four-time 6/7f Listed winner Gusto (by Oasis Dream) and US 8.5f Listed winner Beauly); the family of top-class middle-distance performer Postponed and dual 1m Group 1 winner Simply Perfect.

"His sales price dropped dramatically from a foal to a yearling, but we haven't encountered any issues with him to this point. He has got a super pedigree as a brother to Jersey Stakes winner, Gale Force Ten, who also finished second in an Irish 2000 Guineas, and I rode a few of the family for Richard Hannon, including a nice horse called Gusto. This colt looks quite an early type and should be out during the first half of the season."

MISS DIAMOND (IRE)

12/3 ch f No Nay Never - Twinkling Ice (Elusive Quality)
Owner: Galloway, Lawrence, Merritt, Blake
Sales price: €72,000 (Richard Hughes)

Half-sister to 5f 2yo winner Pink Iceburg and 12f 3yo winner Kabrit. Dam a maiden half-sister to US 7f Grade 1 winner Forest Danger and Listed-placed US maiden Skipping Stars out of a US 6f 2yo Grade 2 winner.

"I trained the half-sister who was quite small and had a few quirks, such as box-walking and crib biting. Thankfully this filly has no such vices and is a good-moving sort who goes nicely so far."

SCHWARTZ (IRE)

7/3 b c Kodiac - Easy Times (Nayef)
Owner: Alex Smith
Sales price: 75,000gns (Richard Hughes Racing)

Full brother to Listed-placed 8-12f winner Al Hamdany. Dam an unraced half-sister to Listed-placed 7f-1m 2yo winner Easy Lover and 7f 2yo winner Pezula Bay out of an 11.5f winning sister to Oaks winner Love Divine (later dam of St Leger winner Sixties Icon) and half-sister to 1m Listed winner Dark Promise, 12f 3yo Listed winner Floreeda, Group 3-placed 12f 3yo winner Solar Sky and the once-raced maiden dam of triple 8/10f Group 1 winner Dan Excel.

"Bigger than your average Kodiac and I suppose that's why he went relatively cheaply at auction. I think he was well bought and although he's still got some growing to do, I really like him and hope he can do something this backend."

SHINE THAT LIGHT
21/3 b c Acclamation - Spotlight (Dr Fong)
Owner: Jaber Abdullah
Sales price: £20,000 (Richard Hughes)

Brother to 6f Group 3 winner Projection and a half-brother to useful 8-8.5f winner Up In Lights, dual 5f 2yo winner On The Stage and the dam of Group 2/3-placed Italian multiple 10f winner (including twice at Listed level) Elisa Again and Group 3-placed 2019 7f 2yo winner Berkshire Rocco. Dam a US 1m 1f Grade 2 winner who was a half-sister to the dam of Irish 6f 2yo Group 1 winner/St James's Palace Stakes runner-up Zoffany and Irish 7f 2yo Group 2 winner/Irish Derby runner-up Rostropovich.

"A nice colt and I'm really not sure why he didn't go for more at auction as it's a lovely pedigree. He hasn't put a foot wrong so far and is very easy to deal with, as are most Acclamations. I imagine he will be amongst our first two-year-old runners when we're back racing."

UNNAMED (IRE)
26/4 b c Showcasing - Canada Water (Dansili)
Owner: The High Flyers
Sales price: €70,000 (Richard Hughes)

Three-parts brother to useful multiple 5-6f winner Daschas (by Oasis Dream) and a half-brother to Group 3-placed French/UK 6f-1m winner Lawmaking. Dam a maiden sister to Prix de l'Arc de Triomphe winner Rail Link and half-sister to high-class French 10-12f winner (including at Group 2/3 level) Crossharbour, French 1m Group 3 winner Mainsail and French 10f Group 3 winner Chelsea Manor out of a French 8-10f winning half-sister to 6f 2yo Group 3 winner Wharf, French 1m 3yo Listed winner Mooring and the dam of French 10f 2yo Group 1 winner Linda's Lad.

"He isn't overly big and is still quite immature. His dam is a sister to an Arc winner and there are a few other middle-distance performers in the pedigree, so I'm certainly in no rush with him."

UNNAMED (IRE) *Crimson Sand*

8/4 b c Footstepsinthesand - Crimson Sunrise (Holy Roman Emperor)
Owner: Ms J A Wakefield
Sales price: 75,000gns (Richard Hughes)

Half-brother to 5.5-7f winner Chevalier Du Lac and dual 7f 2yo winner Kikini Bamalaam. Dam a useful Irish 6-8.5f winner who was a half-sister to very useful dual 6f 2yo winner You Never Can Tell out of a useful 5f 2yo winning half-sister to 5f 3yo Listed winner Double Quick and Group 3/Listed-placed dual 5f 2yo winner Speedy James.

"He doesn't have an overly-exciting pedigree I suppose, but he is a gorgeous individual who I hope to have running come the middle of the season. One for the six and seven-furlong races and should stay a mile in time."

UNNAMED (IRE) *Elektronic*

10/3 b c Kodiac - Elektra Marino (Mount Nelson)
Owner: Ms J A Wakefield
Sales price: £62,000 (Richard Hughes)

Half-brother to useful Irish/Hong Kong dual 6f winner Loving A Boom. Dam an unraced half-sister to two-time King's Stand Stakes winner Equiano, smart prolific 5-6f winner (including at Listed level) Encore D'Or, Group 3-placed 7f-1m winner (including twice at Listed level) Evita Peron and useful French multiple 6f-1m winner Orife.

"His half-brother is doing well in Hong Kong and it's obviously a strong pedigree in general. He is a tall, leggy colt who moves exceptionally well, and I hope to have him ready to run by the middle of the season."

UNNAMED *Lightening Shore*

23/1 br c Showcasing - Zora Seas (Marju)
Owner: The Heffer Syndicate & P Merritt
Sales price: 110,000gns (Richard Hughes Racing)

Second foal of a 1m 3yo winner who was a half-sister to Listed-placed dual 6f 2yo winner Al Aasifh, useful triple 5f winner Cowboy Soldier, useful 6-7f 2yo winners Chicago May and Invincible Gold and useful triple 1m winner Cordell out of a French 1m 3yo Listed winning daughter of a Listed-placed French 7f-1m winner who was a half-sister to French 10f Group 2 winner Gunboat Diplomacy and Listed-placed French dual 12f 3yo winner Honeytrap.

"A strong, gorgeous colt who is one my nicest two-year-olds at the moment. I will wait and see what some of our earlier juvenile runners do just to see where

we are with them, but I'd say he won't be long in making an appearance. He is high up the pecking order and I hope he's one to look forward to this season."

Marten writes:

I first met Richard Hughes in the paddocks at Mick Channon's yard a day or two after he arrived there from Ireland. I think it was the only time we've spoken but I have long admired him, both as a jockey and a communicator. He thinks before he talks and is a man of great insight, especially when discussing horses and their quirks.

As a trainer he needs a top-class horse to take the next step up – Derby entry Brentford Hope could fit the bill – and the one with the potential from those listed above may be **Schwartz**.

The son of Kodiac is a full brother to Al Hamdany, a winner three times for Marco Botti over 1m twice and 1m 4f. The family traces back to Oaks winner Love Divine so there is plenty of stamina in the bottom line to balance the sire's influence for speed.

I'm encouraged that the trainer says he is not going to rush him.

EVE JOHNSON HOUGHTON

BATINDI
23/4 b f Bated Breath - Rohlindi (Red Ransom)
Owner: Mrs C Vigors
Sales price: 18,000gns (Vendor)

Full sister to Listed-placed Irish 5f winner Mistress Of Venice and a half-sister to 8.5-10f winner War Of Succession and 2020 6f 3yo winner Tommy De Vito. Dam a maiden half-sister to 7f 3yo Listed winner Kalindi (later dam of high-class sprinter Medicean Man, Irish 6f 2yo Group 3 winner Abigail Pett and French 1m 3yo Listed winner Cerveza), Group 3/Listed-placed 5.5-6.5f winner Tayseer and the dam of Irish 7.5f Listed winner Fourpenny Lane.

"This is a nice filly who goes well and would've been an early runner under normal circumstances. She has gone home for the time being and is positively thriving there. I envisage her coming back here in June, and would hope to have her running by the end of the summer."

BHUBEZI
1/3 ch c Starspangledbanner - Lulani (Royal Applause)
Owner: Mr & Mrs James Blyth Currie
Sales price: £40,000 (Stroud Coleman Bloodstock)

First foal of an 8-9f winner who was a half-sister to fairly useful 7f-1m winner Caiya and French 6.5f 2yo winner Wedding Present out of an unraced half-sister to nine winners, notably 2000 Guineas winner Cockney Rebel.

"A lovely colt and a typically good-looking one by Starspangledbanner. He should be a sprinter initially and I had hoped to have him out around May or June time."

COCO BEAR (IRE)
22/4 br c Kodi Bear - House Of Roses (New Approach)
Owner: Trish & Colin Fletcher-Hall
Sales price: £15,000 (Highflyer/Eve Johnson Houghton)

Half-brother to 5-7f winner Primeiro Boy. Dam an unraced sister to Qatari triple 6f winner Court Life and half-sister to useful 5.5f 3yo winner Sunrise Star out of a Listed-placed French 6.5-7.5f winning half-sister to Lockinge Stakes winner Fly To The Stars and 1m Listed winner Fallen Star (later dam of Coronation Stakes winner Fallen For You).

"A very racy individual who should be amongst my earliest two-year-old runners when we're back underway."

DANVILLE
28/1 b c Muhaarar - Faustinatheyounger (Antonius Pius)
Owner: Viscount Astor
Sales price: 30,000gns (Highflyer Bloodstock/Eve Johnson Houghton)

Half-brother to 8.5f 3yo winner Mashaheer. Dam a maiden half-sister to US 8/9f Grade 2 winner Uncharted Haven (dam of 12f 3yo Group 3 winner/ Oaks third High Heeled and grandam of Irish 1000 Guineas winner Just The Judge), useful 7f 2yo winner Torinmoor and the maiden dam of US 1m Grade 2 winner Ferneley; the family of Irish 10f Group 2 winner Chancellor and 2019 Cornwallis Stakes winner Good Vibes.

"A lovely colt, but like most by his sire, he's a sizeable sort who'll do even better at three. One for the backend."

DARK ILLUSION
10/2 b c Equiano - Magic Escapade (Azamour)
Owner: The Kimber Family
Sales price: £20,000 (Vendor)

Half-brother to Group 3-placed 2019 5-6.5f 2yo winner Graceful Magic. Dam a once-raced maiden daughter of a maiden sister to French 10/10.5f Group 3 winner Trumbaka and half-sister to French 1m 1f 3yo Listed winner Arctic Hunt and 12f 3yo Listed winner Spirit Of Dubai (later dam of Gimcrack Stakes winner Emaraaty Ana).

"We obviously enjoyed a good season with his half-sister, Graceful Magic, last year. This colt shows us plenty in his work, and should make a decent enough juvenile himself. I hope to have him running in June or July."

DARK SHIFT
1/4 gr c Dark Angel - Mosuo (Oasis Dream)
Owner: H Frost
Sales price: 50,000gns (Highflyer Bloodstock/Eve Johnson Houghton)

First foal of an unraced half-sister to Juddmonte International Stakes/ Eclipse Stakes winner Ulysses and useful 11.5-12f 3yo winner Dr Yes out of an Oaks winning sister to the dam of French 10.5f Group 1 winner/French Derby/ Arc runner-up Cloth Of Stars and half-sister to 10.5f Group 1 winner Shiva and 1m 3yo Listed winner Burning Sunset (dam of Listed winners Smoking Sun (10f) and Zhiyi (1m) and grandam of 11/12f US Grade 1 winner/Derby second Main Sequence).

"This is a nice colt with a tremendous pedigree, albeit one that suggests he'll need plenty of time. He has really strengthened up and matured well, having been quite weak initially. I hope to get a run or two into him at the backend of the season."

ENDURING
5/2 b c Coulsty - Yearbook (Byron)
Owner: Marc Middleton-Heath
Sales price: £10,000 (Highflyer Bloodstock/Eve Johnson Houghton)

Half-brother to Group 3-placed 6f 2yo winner Mr Wizard and two other winners. Dam a maiden half-sister to Group 3-placed 7f-1m 2yo winner Day Of Conquest, Listed-placed 5-6f winner Day By Day, Listed runner-up Thought Is Free and the dam of Italian 1m 2yo Group 1 winner Hearts Of Fire; the family of Lord Shanakill, Forever Together, Haafhd etc.

"I like him. He is a strong, sharp individual who has grown a huge amount since we bought him and looks the part now. He does everything very easily."

JUMBY (IRE)
17/5 b c New Bay - Sound Of Guns (Acclamation)
Owner: Anthony Pye-Jeary And David Ian
Sales price: 45,000gns (Highflyer Bloodstock/Eve Johnson Houghton)

Half-brother to 2019 6f 2yo winner Jump The Gun and 2019 French 7.5f 3yo winner Ricochet. Dam a Group 2/Listed-placed 6f 2yo winning daughter of a Stakes-placed US triple 6f winner; the family of Cheveley Park Stakes winner Regal Rose.

"He takes the eye every time you see him canter. A lovely colt who I am looking forward to seeing run later in the year."

ROOFUL
26/3 b f Charming Thought - Roodle (Xaar)
Owner: Mrs R F Johnson Houghton
Sales price: 10,000gns (Vendor)

Half-sister to smart 6f-1m winner (including the Queen Anne Stakes) Accidental Agent and 2019 1m 3yo winner Madame Tantzy. Dam a useful 5-7f winner who was a half-sister to smart UK/US 6f-1m winner (including at Grade 2/3 level) Prize Exhibit and dual 7f Group 3 winner Mohaather out of a Listed-placed 5-7f winning half-sister to several winners, notably Group 1-placed 6-7f winner Gallagher and Listed-placed UK/UAE 7-10f winner Quick Wit.

"It is a family we obviously know extremely well, but this is a sizeable filly who isn't at all forward. I hope to have her out sometime in the autumn, but she's very much one for next year."

SCHILTHORN
10/3 b g Swiss Spirit - Wall Of Light (Zamindar)
Owner: The Mighty Mouse Partnership
Sales price: £9,000 (Eve Johnson Houghton)

First foal of a maiden half-sister to Group 1-placed 6-7f winner (including at Group 3/Listed level) The Cheka, Grade 2/Listed-placed 9-10.5f winner Wall Of Sound (later dam of 2019 7f 2yo Group 3 winner Boomer) and Irish dual 7f 2yo winner Leadership Race out of a maiden half-sister to French 1m 3yo Listed winner Arabride and five other winners including the dam of 6/6.5f Group 1 winner Regal Parade and 7f 2yo Group 3 winner Entifaadha.

"A rather plain sort who was getting very colty and a bit heavy topped, so we decided to geld him. His dam is a half-sister to a very good horse we had here called The Cheka and it's the primary reason I bought him. He shows speed and should do something this season, but looks sure to do even better as a three-year-old."

SOLDIER LIONS (IRE)
6/2 b c Equiano - Stylos Ecossais (Aqlaam)
Owner: H H Shaikh Nasser Al Khalifa & Partner
Sales price: £30,000 (Oliver St Lawrence Bloodstock)

Third foal of an unraced half-sister to smart 10-12f winner (including at Group 2/Listed level) Connecticut, German 11f Listed winner Fleurie Domaine and ten other winners out of a 7f 2yo winning half-sister to Cheshire Oaks winner Kyle Rhea, Park Hill Stakes winner Coigach and Group 2/3-placed 10-13.5f 3yo winner Applecross (later dam of Prix du Cadran winner/Ascot Gold Cup second Invermark and Princess of Wales's Stakes winner Craigsteel).

"For all there is plenty of stamina on the dam's side, this colt shows both speed and potential in his homework so far. I have high hopes for him and he should be one of our first two-year-old runners when we're allowed to race again."

STIGWOOD (IRE)
19/4 b c Kodiac - Time Honoured (Sadler's Wells)
Owner: Anthony Pye-Jeary And David Ian
Sales price: 42,000gns (Highflyer Bloodstock/Eve Johnson Houghton)

Half-brother to useful 10-11.5f winner Huge Future, useful UAE 7-9.5f winner Baroot, useful 7-10f winner Time Change and four other winners. Dam a 1m 2yo winner who was a half-sister to 12f Group 2 winners Time Allowed and Zinaad; the family of Queen Mary Stakes/Lowther Stakes winner Best Terms and Moyglare Stud Stakes winner Cursory Glance.

"This is a very nice horse. He could be the type to start off in one of those good maidens at Newbury, though they will obviously be ridiculously strong this season. He would've debuted over six furlongs had it been a 'normal' year, but that could change with the way things are at present. One to look forward to anyway."

TATTOO
16/3 b f Equiano - Belvoir Diva (Exceed And Excel)
Owner: Mrs J E O'Halloran
Sales price: £11,000 (Highflyer Bloodstock/E Johnson Houghton)

Half-sister to Listed-placed 2019 Italian 5f 2yo winner Penelope Queen. Dam a 6f 2yo winner who was a half-sister to useful multiple 5f winner Merry Banter out of a 6f 2yo winning sister to Group 3-placed multiple 5-6f winner (including twice at Listed level) Paradise Isle and half-sister to the dams of 1m 3yo Listed winner/Racing Post Trophy runner-up Van Der Neer and 7f 3yo Listed winner Intense Pink and grandam of Irish 10f Group 3 winner Euphrasia.

"As sharp and racy as her pedigree suggests. We had some success with a relation called Super Julius a couple of years back."

TIPSY LAIRD
2/4 b c Gleneagles - Lady Eclair (Danehill Dancer)
Owner: Mr & Mrs Nicholas Johnston
Sales price: 82,000gns (Highflyer Bloodstock/Eve Johnson Houghton)

Closely related to fairly useful 2019 12.5-14f 3yo Flat/Grade 2-placed 2m hurdle winner Lord Lamington (by Australia) and a half-brother to French 12f 3yo Listed winner Al Malhouf. Dam a very useful 12f-2m winner (including at Listed level) who was a sister to Irish 1m 2yo Listed winner Savethisdanceforme and a half-sister to French 12f 3yo Group 2 winner Crimson Quest, French 10f 3yo Listed winner Hijaz (later dam of UAE 8/9f Group 3 winner Deem), French 15f Listed winner Ballarat and useful 10.5f 3yo winner Bathilde (later dam of smart pair Al Shemali and Tungsten Strike).

"A big, backward colt who should make a lovely horse one day. He is currently with Hen Knight, who is doing a lot of basic groundwork with him and likes him a lot. He's essentially a middle-distance prospect for next year."

Marten writes:

There was a time, before the specialist racing channels and visual coverage in the betting shops, when the only way you could see a horse run was to go to the track.

The travelling got you down – I often drove from south-east Kent to Scotland, on more than one occasion there and back in a day – but it meant that you also got to see and meet the trainers, because they needed to be there as well.

These days the top trainers only turn up for the major meetings, or if special circumstances apply.

I get racing far less than I used to, but I do like to spend Wimbledon fortnight with a friend in Esher and that clashes with the Eclipse meeting at Sandown and a couple of Epsom meetings as well.

I like to attend if I can, and it was in July 2016 at a Sandown evening meeting that I first saw Accidental Agent. The colt stood out in the paddock, at least in the context of that race, not in terms of fitness but as a horse with the physical scope to progress and I earmarked him as a 'Sleeper' in my *Weekend Card*.

He put in an eye-catching run to finish sixth and went on to win a maiden next time at Chepstow before steadily progressing to scale the lofty heights of the 2018 Queen Anne Stakes at Royal Ascot.

I was tempted to feature his half-sister, Rooful, a daughter of Charming Thought, from the above list but instead I am nominating **Stigwood**, a son of Kodiac out of a Sadler's Wells mare that traces back to the family of Time Charter, a great favourite of mine.

Stigwood is a half-brother to a handful of winners including Huge Future, who cost €260,000 as a yearling and won three races for Godolphin. Others are 1m 4f winner Bona Fortuna, 1m 4f winner Infinitum and UAE winner Baroot.

The dam, Time Honoured, won the second of her only two lifetime starts and is a full sister to Jockey Club Stakes winner Time Allowed and a half-sister to Zinaad, out of the top-class mare Time Charter.

Given the quality of the page, and the number of winners in the family, I would suggest this colt looks well bought at 42,000gns. The fact his trainer considers he could have started over six furlongs in one of the better maidens is most encouraging because his pedigree points to his staying beyond a mile next season.

I have high hopes for this colt.

MARK JOHNSTON

CHICA BONITA
2/2 b f Lope De Vega - Hundi (Fastnet Rock)
Owner: Paul & Charles O'Callaghan
Sales price: 82,000gns (Johnston Racing)

First foal of a useful 6f 3yo winner who was a three-parts sister to Group 1-placed triple 7f winner (including at Group 3 level) Air Chief Marshal, smart 6-7f winner (including twice at Listed level) Misu Bond and very useful dual 6f winner/Irish 2000 Guineas runner-up Foxtrot Romeo and a half-sister to very smart 7-14f winner (including the Irish St Leger) Flag Of Honour and Group 3-placed 5-8.5f winner (including twice at Listed level) Slip Dance (grandam of Grade 1-placed dual 1m Listed winner Awesometank).

"She's not overly big but was in early and did plenty of work through January and February. We backed off her a bit during March, but she seems fairly precocious and that wouldn't always be the case for the sire. She is a nice enough filly who should prove best around six and seven furlongs."

HAPPY (IRE)
31/5 b c Galileo - Sent From Heaven (Footstepsinthesand)
Owner: Crone Stud Farms Ltd
Sales price: 80,000gns (Johnston Racing)

Three-parts brother to Listed-placed 7f 2yo winner Almania (by Australia). Dam a 7f 2yo Group 3 winner/1000 Guineas fourth who was a half-sister to 10f 3yo Group 3 winner Above Average, Group 3-placed Irish/Australian 10-12.5f winner Granddukeoftuscany, useful 2019 dual 7.5f 2yo winner Freyja, useful UK 6f 2yo/US 1m winner No Way Jose and five other winners; the family of Gimcrack Stakes winner Conquest and 7f 2yo Listed winner Victory Command.

"He was the standout horse at the December sales in terms of pedigree and physique and we certainly didn't expect to get a look in when it came down to buying him, so we were pleasantly surprised to pick him up for a relatively cheap amount. He is a lovely, strong horse but big and heavy with it, so will obviously need some time. However, I'd hope to see him in action at two, and he will likely prove best over seven furlongs and a mile."

HARLEM SOUL

23/2 ch c Frankel - Giants Play (Giant's Causeway)
Owner: Teme Valley 2
Sales price: 130,000gns (Johnston Racing)

Half-brother to Group 2-placed 10-14f winner (including twice at Group 3 level) Ispolini and Listed-placed winners Playful Sound (9-10.5f) and Vivionn (7-10f). Dam a US 10f Grade 2 winner who was a half-sister to US 12f Grade 3 winner Anjaz and 1m Listed winner Tearless out of a Fillies' Mile winner/Irish Oaks runner-up who was a full sister to Yorkshire Cup winner/Derby fourth Percussionist, a three-parts sister to Eclipse Stakes/King George VI and Queen Elizabeth Stakes winner Nathaniel and Irish Oaks winner Great Heavens and a half-sister to 8/14.5f Group 2 winner Echoes In Eternity.

"A lovely horse. I thought he should have made a lot more at the sales, but he does have quite bizarre markings - his body is covered in white and that might have put some people off. Almost everything in the family wants middle distances at least in time, but he has already done some bits of work and goes well for a backward two-year-old. He is a very big colt but flashy and nice with it."

JUMEIRAH BEACH (IRE)

4/4 b f Exceed And Excel - Dubai Sunrise (Seeking The Gold)
Owner: Sheikh Hamdan Bin Mohammed Al Maktoum
Sales price: n/a

Three-parts sister to 5-7.5f winner Chupalla (by Helmet) and a half-sister to Group 1-placed 7f-2m winner (including twice at Group 3 level)/Derby runner-up Dee Ex Bee and 2019 8.5f 2yo winner Gold Souk. Dam an unraced sister to top-class 8-10f winner (including three times at Group 1 level) Dubai Millennium and the unraced dam of 6f 2yo Group 2 winner Threading (by Exceed And Excel); the family of Timber County, Elnadim, Ribchester etc.

"This is the fourth foal in a row we've had from the mare. She is a little bit light and narrow at the moment, so we've given her some time to fill out. We haven't done anything serious with her so far."

MUTAZAWWED (IRE)
13/3 b c Muhaarar - Muteela (Dansili)
Owner: Hamdan Al Maktoum
Sales price: n/a

Second foal of a Group 3-placed 7f-1m winner (including twice at Listed level) who was a half-sister to high-class multiple 6f 2yo winner (including the Middle Park Stakes) Awzaan, Group 2-placed 6-7f 2yo winner (including at Group 3 level) Muraaqaba, Listed-placed 8-10f winner Hajras and very useful 6f-1m winner Khamaary out of a Group 3-placed 5-7f winner (including at Listed level); family of Listed winners Princess Loulou (10f) and Watching (5f).

"This colt is a nice size, and has been straightforward and easy to deal with since he came here. We haven't pushed any buttons yet, but he is about to move into fast work and looks like he could be fairly precocious."

POLAR FLEECE (IRE)
28/2 b c Frankel - Lacily (Elusive Quality)
Owner: Sheikh Hamdan Bin Mohammed Al Maktoum
Sales price: n/a

Half-brother to smart UK/UAE 5-6f winner (including at Group 3 level) Yalta. Dam a Listed-placed 1m 2yo winner who was a half-sister to Group 1-placed French 10.5-15.5f winner (including at Group 3/Listed level) Ley Hunter out of a very smart 8-12f winner (including the Irish Oaks) who was the daughter of a maiden sister to the dam of triple 7-10f Group 3 winner/Irish National Stakes runner-up Naheef and half-sister to Prince Of Wales's Stakes winner Faithful Son and Coventry Stakes winner Always Fair.

"A tall, lengthy, unfurnished horse with a considerable frame to fill. I doubt he will be particularly early as he still has quite a bit of developing to do, but he's a nice individual and there is certainly plenty to work with."

SHEM (IRE)
22/4 b c Kodiac - Noahs Ark (Charnwood Forest)
Owner: R Walker
Sales price: 52,000gns (Johnston Racing)

Three-parts brother to Group 3/Listed-placed Irish 6f 2yo winner After (later dam of 2019 Irish 7f 2yo Group 2/3 winner/Irish National Stakes runner-up Armory) and useful Irish dual 7f winner Gussy Goose (both by Danehill Dancer) and a half-brother to French 7f 2yo Listed winner/French 2000 Guineas fourth

Temps Au Temps. Dam a Grade 1-placed Irish 7f-1m winner who was a sister to Group 3/Listed-placed UK/German 7-9.5f winner Blueberry Forest; the family of Irish 7/9.5f Group 3 winner/Irish Oaks second Jack Naylor and 2019 7f 2yo Group 2 winner Daahyeh.

"We liked him at Book 2 and decided to give the mare another chance after his year-older brother The Weed Machine failed to live up to expectations. He is a fairly late foal but has shown plenty already, and would likely have run in the Brocklesby on the intended first weekend of the season. He goes nicely and will run as soon as possible."

SIR JOHN BOWDLER (IRE)
30/3 b c Exceed And Excel - Gotta Have Her (Royal Academy)
Owner: Paul Dean
Sales price: 50,000gns (Johnston Racing)

Half-brother to US 3yo winners Almithmaar (6-6.5f), Silver Beach (8-8.5f) and General Patton (8.5f). Dam a Grade 1-placed US 6.5-8.5f winner (including at Grade 2/3 level) who was a half-sister to US dual 1m winner Haka Girl (later dam of Listed-placed dual 6f 2yo winner Tutu Nguru) out of an unraced half-sister to smart trio Lady Blessington, Lowell and Red Cat and also the grandam of French 2000 Guineas/French Derby winner Lope De Vega.

"We would have expected him to be quite forward, but he looks as though he still needs a bit more time. He is a nice colt with plenty of scope who will hopefully prove worth the wait."

TRIBAL ART (IRE)
6/2 b c Farhh - Chaquiras (Seeking The Gold)
Owner: Sheikh Hamdan Bin Mohammed Al Maktoum
Sales price: n/a

Half-brother to Group 1-placed 6f-1m winner (including at Group 2/Listed level) Threading, useful UAE multiple 7f winner Beachy Head and 5f 2yo winner Camargue. Dam an unraced sister to top-class 8-10f winner (including three times at Group 1 level) Dubai Millennium and the unraced dam of Group 1-placed 7f-2m winner (including twice at Group 3 level)/Derby runner-up Dee Ex Bee (by Farhh); the family of Timber County, Elnadim, Ribchester etc.

"A very big horse - probably the biggest two-year-old we have here at the moment. He is lengthy, very tall and still unfurnished, so will need a bit of time to come together, but he's an interesting prospect and we like the stallion."

TWILIGHT LUCY
3/4 b f Twilight Son - Riva Royale (Royal Applause)
Owner: Nick Bradley Racing 17
Sales price: 52,000gns (Johnston Racing)

Half-sister to Listed-placed 6-7f winner Rivas Rhapsody, Listed-placed UK/ French 6-6.5f winner Stormbringer, Listed-placed UK/Hong Kong 6-7f winners Exciting Dream and Let Me Fight and useful 2019 5-6f 2yo winner Mrs Bouquet. Dam a 5-7f winner who was the daughter of an unraced half-sister to US 6f Grade 3 winner Prince Bobby B, smart 5-6f winner (including twice at Listed level) Notley and the dam of 6f Group 3 winner Knot In Wood.

"Her half-sister, Mrs Bouquet, had an excellent juvenile campaign for us last year, winning on four of her six outings. This filly didn't come in until quite late and in a normal year that would've been a disadvantage, but she hasn't missed out at all given the circumstances. She has been cantering away for a few weeks now and is around a month away from fast work. I liked her a lot at the sales - she's quite masculine and strong. One to look forward to."

VENTURA KINGDOM (FR)
16/3 bl c Dream Ahead - Fox Force Five (Araafa)
Owner: Middleham Park Racing XV
Sales price: €32,000 (F Barberini/Middleham Park Racing)

Half-brother to French 8-12.5f winner Tin Fox and once-raced 2020 1m 3yo winner Lexington Force. Dam a French 10f 3yo winner who was a half-sister to smart French 6-7f 2yo winner (including at Listed level) Ossun and Listed-placed French 5.5f 2yo winner Ladoga out of a French 8-10f winner who was the daughter of a 14f 3yo winning half-sister to Irish 7f 2yo Group 3 winner Isle Of Glass (later dam of French 10f 3yo Group 1 winner Limpid).

"He was bought by the Middleham Park team who own the year-older half-brother. This is a big, strong colt who is typical of the sire whose progeny we have done very well with. He came to us in February and is nearly ready to do his first bit of fast work. In his slower paces he looks a nice horse and has done everything asked of him so far."

UNNAMED (IRE) *King Frankel*
18/5 b c Frankel - You'll Be Mine (Kingmambo)
Owner: Mohamed Obaida
Sales price: 280,000gns (Johnston Racing)

Full brother to Group 1-placed 8-10f winner (including at Group 2/3 level)
Eminent. Dam a Group 1-placed Irish 7f 2yo winner who was a half-sister to
Irish 10f 3yo Group 1 winner/Oaks fourth Diamondsandrubies and Listed-
placed Irish 7f 2yo winner How High The Moon out of an Irish 7f 2yo Group 1
winner/Oaks runner-up who was a sister to Irish 1000 Guineas winner/Oaks
runner-up Yesterday and Irish 10f 3yo winner/Oaks third All My Loving (later
dam of 12f Group 2 winner Thomas Chippendale); the excellent family of
Group 1 winners Alborada, Aussie Rules and Coronet.

*"He is a late foal and was immature as a yearling. He is still quite weak and
unfurnished and is going to need some time to strengthen up and fill out. I
doubt we will see him until the second half of the season, but on paper he has
all the right attributes and it is an exciting pedigree to have in the yard."*

UNNAMED (IRE)
7/5 ch c Galileo - Zouzou (Redoute's Choice)
Owner: Matsumoto, Orpendale, Chelston & Wynatt
Sales price: €85,000 (Not Sold)

Full brother to 2019 Irish 8.5f 2yo winner Emperor Of The Sun and a half-
brother to Australian dual 6f Group 1 winner Zoustar. Dam an Australian 6f
winner who was a half-sister to Group 3/Listed-placed Australian 5f-1m winner
Crestfallen (later grandam of Australian 7.5f Group 3 winner Testashadow) and
the dam of Australian 7f Group 2 winner Dusty Star out an Australian multiple
6f-1m winner; the family of Australian 6f Group 3 winner Diamond Benny.

*"This is a nice colt who has done very well physically since arriving as he was
quite weak and immature to begin with. I wouldn't expect him to be early
because he doesn't show a lot of natural speed. He will want at least seven
furlongs, but is an exciting horse to look forward to in the second half of the
year."*

Raffle Prize narrowly edges out the Wesley Ward-trained Kimari to land the Group 2 Queen Mary Stakes at Royal Ascot last June. She followed up in the Duchess Of Cambridge Stakes under a penalty the following month, and signed off her 2019 campaign with a second place finish in the Group 1 Juddmonte Cheveley Park Stakes.

Marten writes:

Mark Johnston is listed as having 260 horses in training, almost half of them two-year-olds. Delegation skills must be a prime requirement working with such numbers, and having become the most successful British Flat trainer of all time when Poet's Society won at York in August 2018, his record when he does retire will be hard to match, let alone surpass.

With reference to my earlier point regarding the meaning of Arabic names I have no idea what **Mutazawwed** translates to. The reason I have selected him is that I like horses with bottom lines linked to the Dansili family. Furthermore he is out of a winning half-sister to the trainer's very useful Middle Park Stakes and Mill Reef Stakes winner Awzaan, from the family of Nufoos and Zafonic. The dam Muteela was useful, winning five of her nine starts including two Listed races and twice runner-up in Group 3 contests.

The sire Muhaarar was a top-class sprinter, winning seven of his 11 starts including four successive Group 1s in 2015 namely the Commonwealth Cup, July Cup, Prix Maurice de Gheest and British Champions Sprint Stakes at Ascot. Trainer Charlie Hills said of him, "He has the will to win, the most beautiful temperament and great looks. He has been a privilege to train."

Standing at £20,000, his yearlings have sold for up to 360,000gns, and last season's first crop included a Group-placed two-year-old. By Oasis Dream out of a Linamix mare, Muhaarar has a balanced pedigree and looks good value at his current stud fee.

Mutazawwed has the blend of speed and stamina that I like to see and I hope he does well.

PHILLIP MAKIN

CAPTAIN VALLO (IRE)
11/4 ch c Mehmas - Top Dollar (Elusive Quality)
Owner: Mrs Wendy Burdett
Sales price: €36,000 (Aidan O'Ryan/Phil Makin)

Second foal of a fairly useful 8-8.5f 2yo winner who was a half-sister to useful 7f-1m winner Tarteel out of a useful 7-12.5f winning half-sister to Grade 2-placed US 8-9f winner (including at Listed level) Dover Dere and useful 7f 2yo winner Wahsheeq; the family of six-time US 9-12f Grade 1 winner English Channel, US 1m 1f Grade 1 winner Pharma, four-time US 8-9f Grade 2 winner Hap and Rockfel Stakes winner/1000 Guineas runner-up Lucida.

"A sharp, likeable individual who is very straightforward. He has shown us plenty of speed, but possesses the scope to progress throughout the season."

MUKER (IRE)
22/3 ch c Mehmas - Naias (Namid)
Owner: Syps (UK) Ltd
Sales price: £27,000 (SYPS)

Half-brother to useful Irish multiple 5-6f winner Lady Mega. Dam a maiden half-sister to smart Irish multiple 5-6f winner (including at Group 3/Listed level) Snaefell, Group 2-placed Irish dual 6f winner (including at Listed level) Daganya (dam of 2019 Irish 1m 1f 2yo Group 3 winner Degraves) and Listed-placed prolific 5f winner Henry Hall.

"A strong, sharp colt who would almost certainly have been our first two-year-old runner had we been racing as usual. He is a straightforward character who shows plenty of speed."

PRINCE ALI

7/3 br c Twilight Son - Desert Liaison (Dansili)
Owner: Mrs Wendy Burdett
Sales price: £33,000 (Aidan O'Ryan/Phil Makin)

Three-parts brother to fairly useful 7-8.5f winner Gleaming Girl and 5-7f winner Little Miss Daisy (both by Arabian Gleam) and a half-brother to useful Irish 8-10f winner Wentwood. Dam the maiden daughter of a 7f 3yo Listed winner; the family of Irish 1m 3yo Group 3 winner Chanzi and 8.5f 3yo Listed winner Sharka.

"He is quite a tall colt who hasn't done much fast work yet, but he is a good mover. I see him as more of a seven-furlong, second half of the season type of two-year-old."

UNNAMED (IRE) *Cammy*

13/4 ch c Camacho - Swan Sea (Sea Hero)
Owner: Syps (UK) Ltd
Sales price: £31,000 (Aidan O'Ryan/Phil Makin)

Half-brother to triple 5f 2yo winner (including at Listed level) Titus Alone, fairly useful multiple 6-7f winner Ticks The Boxes and three other winners. Dam an unraced half-sister to Listed-placed Italian dual 1m winner Albinor.

"This is a good, athletic sort who moves well. He has needed a little time but is coming along nicely now. I would think he will want six furlongs."

Marten writes:

Prince Ali is bred to give his owner a bit of fun.

From the first crop of Haydock Sprint Cup and Diamond Jubilee Stakes winner Twilight Son, whose progeny fetched up to 135,000gns last autumn, he is closely related to four-race winners Gleaming Girl and Little Miss Daisy and a half-brother to dual winner Wentwood.

His dam Desert Liaison was disappointing in her four starts for Jeremy Noseda but she's done well at stud and wasn't cheap at the sales, having been acquired for €200,000, up from the 50,000gns she fetched as a foal.

The breeder sent his mare back to the sire – always a good sign – and the coupling produced a colt foal who fetched 17,000gns at the sales in November. If Prince Ali does well that could look a shrewd investment.

ROD MILLMAN

BONNY MISS MOLLY

21/3 b f Sayif - Glen Molly (Danetime)
Owner: Exors Late D Little The Links Partnership
Sales price: 8,000gns (Rod Millman Racing)

Sister to French 5.5-7f winner If I Say So and a half-sister to 5-6f winner Cuppacoco. Dam a 6-7f winner who was the daughter of a Listed-placed Irish 8-10f 3yo winning half-sister to UAE triple 7f/1m Listed winner Jaasoos out of an unraced sister to Group 3-placed 5f 2yo winner Glen Rosie (later dam of 7f 2yo Listed winner/smart hurdler Kings Quay) and half-sister to Irish 10f 3yo Group 3 winner Artema and the grandam of 12f 3yo Group 3 winner Hazel Lavery (herself dam of 2019 dual 1m Group 2 winner The Revenant).

"This filly is from the same stud as Bettys Hope, who was obviously a real star for us last season. She is a sharp, compact sort who would have been amongst our first runners as she had shown plenty of natural speed."

Bettys Hope wins the valuable Weatherbys Super Sprint at Newbury last July. The £3,000 daughter of Anjaal was very much the star performer for the Rod Millman stable in 2019.

FOUR ADAAY
29/1 b f Adaay - Sonko (Red Clubs)
Owner: The Four Adaay Syndicate
Sales price: £20,000 (Millman Racing)

Third foal of a fairly useful multiple 5f winner who was a half-sister to Group 3-placed dual 6f 2yo winner (including at Listed level) Terror out of a 7f-1m winning half-sister to prolific 5-6f winner Gone'N'Dunnett and 6f 2yo winner Deeday Bay out of a maiden half-sister to several winners, notably Group 1-placed multiple 6f winner (including at Group 2/Listed level) Indian Rocket and 6f 2yo Listed winner/Norfolk Stakes runner-up The Bonus King.

"She has a bit of size and scope about her, and while not as early as some of the sharper fillies, she is really beginning to come into her own now."

HURRICANE HELEN
17/2 br/gr f Gutaifan - Dame Helen (Royal Applause)
Owner: JPM Racing I
Sales price: 7,000gns (Rod Millman Racing)

Half-sister to 1m 2yo winner Voicemail. Dam a French 1m 2yo winner who was a half-sister to useful 9-12f winner Demolition, useful French/US 8.5-9.5f winner Golden Accolade and the dam of 6f 2yo Group 2 winner Blaine and 6f 2yo Listed winner Bogart; the family of Canadian 6f Grade 1 winner Lit De Justice, Racing Post Trophy winner Commander Collins, Royal Lodge Stakes winner City Leader and 2000 Guineas/Derby third Colonel Collins.

"Her sire made a solid start to his stallion career last year and this filly looks well bought at 7k. For all she shows speed, she has the scope to progress throughout the season and into her three-year-old campaign, which is obviously a big help given the current global situation."

ONARAGGATIP
11/5 b g Adaay - Onlyyouknowme (Martino Alonso)
Owner: Crown Connoisseurs
Sales price: £18,000 (Millman Racing)

Half-brother to useful 6f 2yo winner Ingenuity. Dam an Italian 6f Listed winner who was a half-sister to three winners in Italy including dual 10f 2yo winner Capitan Horlock; the family of smart juvenile performer News And Echo.

"Although he's a May foal, this son of Adaay is a strong sort who has been showing plenty of speed from an early stage on the gallops and was set to run around April time."

PRIDE OF HAWRIDGE (IRE)

12/1 b c Vadamos - Face The Storm (Barathea)
Owner: Eric Gadsden
Sales price: 105,000gns (Howson & Houldsworth Bloodstock/Rod Millman)

Half-brother to six winners, notably Group 2-placed 5-7f winner Roi De Vitesse and Listed-placed 6-7f winner Rebel Surge. Dam a 1m 2yo winning half-sister to 10f 3yo Listed winner Santa Isobel (later dam of smart stayer Whiplash Willie) out of an unraced daughter of a Fillies' Mile runner-up; the family of French 1m 2yo Group 1 winner Zafisio.

"He is an impressive-looking individual and our first six-figure purchase. We've enjoyed success with this family through half-brother Roi De Vitesse, who finished second in the Superlative Stakes back in 2009. The sire was a late-developing sort and with the shutdown he had a break to allow him to strengthen up and mature. He is back in now and cantering away."

Marten writes:

Pride Of Hawridge stands out here, if only because of the six-figure sum he cost as a yearling.

Rod Millman generally buys at the lower end of the market, doing very well with the stock that comes his way, so this 105,000gns purchase represents a significant step up for him, who will run in the colours of long-standing patron of the yard Eric Gadsden.

The sire Vadamos has that rock-solid middle-distance pedigree I like to see in a horse. Trained by Andre Fabre to win eight times, and although bred to stay well he ultimately proved most effective at a mile, winning the Group 1 Prix du Moulin as a five-year-old where he apparently recorded a sensational final furlong time of 10.47 seconds.

As a son of Monsun, out of a middle-distance-winning daughter of Peintre Celebre, Vadamos has a pedigree packed with stamina so I would not be expecting him to produce precocious stock.

Pride Of Hawridge comes from a very successful bottom line. The dam Face The Storm, herself stoutly bred, only raced at two, winning once from four starts for John Gosden. She has since done much better at stud, producing five winners including Roi De Vitesse, the winner of six races including two for this trainer, Rebel Surge, winner of three, and dual winners Rise Up Lotus and Cavort.

Everything about this colt screams out middle distances, so if he can show anything in a back-end maiden, connections are entitled to hold out high hopes.

HUGHIE MORRISON

BEARAWAY (IRE)
14/4 b c Kodiac - Fair Sailing (Docksider)
Owner: Michael Kerr-Dineen & Martin Hughes
Sales price: 115,000gns (H Morrison)

Closely related to smart 6-7f winner (including at Listed level) Windfast (by Exceed And Excel) and a half-brother to Group 3/Listed-placed 1m 2yo winner Montalcino and 2019 Irish 7f 2yo winner Windracer. Dam a maiden half-sister to Italian Derby winner White Muzzle, German St Leger winner Fair Question and Irish 10f 3yo Listed winner Elfaslah (later dam of Dubai World Cup winner Almutawakel and 1000 Guineas runner-up Muawakleh).

"He is a nice, racy sort, though perhaps not your typical Kodiac whose progeny can be very sharp and precocious. He has a good temperament and I'd like to think he will be out around June or July time."

CIDER APPLE
21/2 b f Charm Spirit - Golden Delicious (Cadeaux Genereux)
Owner: Nicholas Jones
Sales price: n/a

Half-sister to useful UK/Australian 7.5-12f winner Sir Pippin. Dam a useful 6.5-7f winner who was a half-sister to Japanese 7f 3yo Group 2 winner No One and 6-7f winner Imperial Delight out of a maiden sister to useful 10f 3yo winner Drama Class (later dam of Irish 10f 3yo Group 2 winner Eleanora Duse and 10f 3yo Listed winner/Irish Oaks runner-up Scottish Stage) and half-sister to high-class 9-10.5f winner (including at Group 2/3 level) Stage Gift.

"As to be expected given her sire, she is much more forward and mature than her siblings. We'll find out more in the next six weeks but hopefully she will be ready to start come June upon the recommencement of racing."

EQUISENTIAL
30/3 b f Equiano - Broadlands (Kheleyf)
Owner: Pickford, Collett, Morrison & de Zoete
Sales price: 55,000gns (H Morrison)

Half-sister to Group 2-placed 2019 7-7.5f 2yo winner (including at Listed level)

Romsey and useful triple 7f winner Indian Viceroy. Dam an unraced half-sister to 14f Listed winner Twitch, useful 1m 2yo winner Kaloor and 10f 3yo winners Maracuja and Myopic out of an unraced sister to very smart 6-12f winner (including eight times at Group 1 level) Viva Pataca and half-sister to high-class Irish/US 8-11f winner (including twice at Grade 1 level) Laughing.

"Her half-sister, Romsey, did really well for us last season and we also trained another sibling called Indian Viceroy to win a couple of times at two. She isn't quite as 'together' as them, but has a good temperament and will hopefully be ready to run in late summer or early autumn."

KING OF CLUBS
19/4 b c Intello - Queen Arabella (Medicean)
Owner: Castle Down Racing
Sales price: 19,000gns (Not Sold)

Half-brother to 10f 3yo winner Garden Oasis. Dam an unraced half-sister to smart 8-10.5f Flat (including at Group 3/Listed level)/2m hurdle winner Poet, Group 3-placed French dual 6f 2yo winner Hothaifah and five other winners including the dam of Irish 7f 3yo Group 3 winner/Irish 2000 Guineas runner-up France and 10.5f Listed winner Hippy Hippy Shake (herself later dam of 2019 French 1m 3yo Listed winner Twist 'N' Shake) and grandam of Oaks second Shirocco Star (later dam of 2019 Dante Stakes winner Telecaster and Group 3-placed 2019 7f 2yo winner Al Suhail).

"We have enjoyed success with this family through Shirocco Star and more recently her son, Telecaster. This colt is obviously bred to stay pretty well but is an attractive, easy-moving sort. One for later on but we like him."

LEGENDARY DAY
9/4 b c Adaay - Dubai Legend (Cadeaux Genereux)
Owner: A N Solomons
Sales price: 32,000gns (H Morrison)

Half-brother to 7f 2yo winner Show Legend. Dam a 6f 3yo winning daughter of an unraced half-sister to very smart 7f-1m winner (including at Group 1 level) Where Or When, smart 10-12f winner (including at Listed level)/St Leger fourth All The Way and the dam of Group 2/3-placed 5-6f winner (including at Listed level) Danehill Destiny.

"He isn't as forward as his page indicates. He has had immature knees but moves well and is straightforward. We won't push him too hard and I hope to have him out around July and August time."

MARSABIT (IRE)
19/3 ch c Mehmas - Masela (Medicean)
Owner: P C J Dalby & R D Schuster
Sales price: 42,000gns (James Toller)

Half-brother to Listed-placed multiple 6f winner Smokey Lane and triple 5f winner Loumarin. Dam a maiden daughter of an Irish 7f 3yo winner who was a half-sister to Listed-placed Irish 8-9.5f winner Masani and the dam of 10f Listed winner Elbereth; the family of Breeders' Cup Filly And Mare winner Dank, 10f Group 1 winner/Derby second Eagle Mountain, Prix Marcel Boussac winner Sulk and Irish 10f 3yo Group 2 winner Massyar.

"He was bought to be an early two-year-old and would've been but for this enforced break. We have backed off him for the time being, but I should think he'll be ready to get going when racing resumes."

ROOSTER
17/4 ch c Showcasing - Slatey Hen (Acclamation)
Owner: Michael Kerr-Dineen & Martin Hughes
Sales price: 78,000gns (H Morrison)

Half-brother to dual 5f winner Gold Stone and 2019 6f 2yo winner Foad. Dam a 5-6f winner who was a half-sister to smart multiple 5-5.5f winner (including at Group 3/Listed level) Masta Plasta and 5f 2yo winner Kheleyf's Silver (dam of Cheveley Park winner/1000 Guineas third Tiggy Wiggy) out of a maiden half-sister to Listed-placed 6f 2yo winner Ras Shaikh (dam of 7f Group 3 winner Racer Forever and grandam of 1m 2yo Listed winner Gallic Star).

"Smallish colt who we've had to take a pull with given the current situation. I suspect he will be out in midsummer."

ROSEMARY AND THYME
9/3 b f Camelot - Scarborough Fair (Pivotal)
Owner: Paul Brocklehurst
Sales price: 30,000gns (H Morrison)

Half-sister to 6f 2yo winner Barend Boy. Dam an unraced half-sister to high-class 7-11.5f winner (including at Group 2/3 level) Berkshire, Group 3-placed UK/Australian 7-10.5f winner (including at Listed level) Abdon, very useful 12f 3yo winner Ben Vrackie and 10-12f 3yo winner Keenes Royale (later dam of dual 6f 2yo Group 2 winner/2000 Guineas third Ivawood) out of a French 10f Group 1 winner; the family of six-time 8/10.5f Group 1 winner Laurens.

"A nice filly who is sharper than her pedigree might suggest. She was quite cheap at auction because she wasn't the biggest, but she has developed nicely since we got her, and I rather suspect she has even more growing to do".

SPANGLER (IRE)
19/4 gr c Starspangledbanner - Sixpenny Sweets (Dalakhani)
Owner: Michael Kerr-Dineen & Martin Hughes
Sales price: €55,000 (Hugh Morrison)

Half-brother to useful 8-8.5f winner Contrive and 2019 10f 2yo winner Kipps. Dam an unraced half-sister to smart 8-11.5f winner (including at Group 2/Listed level) Knight To Behold and Irish 10f 3yo Group 3 winner Beauty O'Gwaun out of an unraced sister to smart 8-10f winner/Derby third Let The Lion Roar and half-sister to very smart 11f-2m 2f winner (including the St Leger) Millenary and Group 2-placed dual 12f 3yo winner (including at Group 3 level) Head In The Clouds (later dam of Irish 13f Listed winner/Irish Oaks runner-up Roses For The Lady).

"He's a half-brother to Kipps, who is a very nice three-year-old we have here for these owners. This colt is a nice prospect in his own right, but I'd be surprised if we see him before the autumn."

SWEEP THE STARS
1/2 b c Iffraaj - Sweeping Up (Sea The Stars)
Owner: Ben & Sir Martyn Arbib
Sales price: n/a

First foal of a Group 3/Listed-placed 12-14f winner who was a half-sister to smart 8-10f winner (including at Listed level) Under The Rainbow, useful dual 12f 3yo winner/Park Hill Stakes runner-up Starfala (dam of Group 2-placed 10-12f winner (including at Listed level) Star Rock) and 1m 2yo winner Swingland out of a French 12f 3yo Listed winner who was a half-sister to smart performers Alpine Rose, Fragrant Mix, Fracassant and Fraloga.

"We know the family well and this is the dam's first foal. It is a stamina-based page but Iffraaj should inject some speed and precocity into the equation. He still needs to grow up a bit, but is a lovely-looking individual who should be racing in the autumn."

THUNDERCLAP (IRE)
13/5 b c Night Of Thunder - Former Drama (Dynaformer)
Owner: Sir Thomas Pilkington & Mr R A Pilkington
Sales price: 70,000gns (Stroud Coleman Bloodstock/H Morrison)

Half-brother to five winners including Irish 1m 1f Listed winner Champagne Or Water. Dam a maiden half-sister to Group 1-placed 6f-1m winner (including twice at Group 2 level) Endless Drama and useful multiple 6f winners Always A Drama and Histoire out of a 5f 3yo Listed winner; the family of smart performers Ghaiyyath, King's Drama and Rosinka.

"A big, strong colt who we like. One for the backend and next year, who will probably require a bit of dig in the ground."

Marten writes:

I've always liked the way Hughie Morrison trains.

The days of the great dual-purpose trainers have sadly passed – Peter Easterby and Reg Akehurst were two of my favourites – but from the current crop the only one from those days to have trained top-class horses both on the Flat and over jumps is David Elsworth.

There are others around, but Hughie Morrison must rank high having had Cheltenham Festival winners. I'll never forget the sublime ride that Paul Carberry gave Frenchman's Creek to win the William Hill Chase in 2002 while Marble Arch went close in that season's Champion Hurdle.

His Flat successes include two July Cups, with Pastoral Pursuits and Sakhee's Secret, and a handful of handicap winners at Royal Ascot, notably on three occasions in the Duke Of Edinburgh Stakes with Waverley, Cill Rialaig and Arab Dawn.

The trainer has some promising three-year-olds for the current season, among them Kipps, and that is why I am keen to nominate his half-brother **Spangler** from this section.

Kipps is by War Command, so more stoutly bred than this colt, as he showed when winning over 1m 2f last December. He carries a Derby entry and will prove useful at least.

Spangler is by top-class sprinter Starspangledbanner, a winner over 6f to a mile in Australia before winning the July Cup and Golden Jubilee here as a three-year-old.

The dam Sixpennny Sweets is an unraced half-sister to Harry Dunlop's Knight To Behold from the family of Let The Lion Roar and St Leger winner Millenary, a family handled over the years by John Dunlop. Another half-sister won a Group 3 over 2m 1f in Japan.

Given the quality of performers on this page I expect Spangler to prove well bought at €55,000. Whether he takes after his sire or dam remains to be seen, but he is very likeable on paper and I have high hopes for him.

WILLIAM MUIR

REINFORCER
28/4 ch c Lethal Force - Heavenly Dawn (Pivotal)
Owner: Foursome Thoroughbreds
Sales price: 35,000gns (William R Muir)

Half-brother to 2020 7f 3yo winner Lottie Marie and 12f 3yo winner Dawn Choir. Dam a Listed-placed dual 1m winning sister to US dual 10f Grade 1 winner Megahertz, Group 1-placed 7-9f winner (including at Group 3/Listed level) Heaven Sent (dam of very useful pair Firmament and Seven Heavens) and useful multiple 5-7f winner Orion's Bow and a half-sister to the unraced dam of Grade 3-placed UK/Canadian dual 7f winner (including at Stakes level) Endless Light and very useful Irish 6f/UAE 7f 2yo winner Van Der Decken.

"A lovely, big colt who I liked at the sales, and was the most expensive of the yearlings we purchased last year. He reminds me a lot of Clive Cox's Golden Horde, who is obviously by the same sire and was a top juvenile last year. He had a minor setback, but is over that now and I am looking forward to running him sometime in the autumn."

SHUV H'PENNY KING
16/1 b c Twilight Son - Cardrona (Selkirk)
Owner: Martin P Graham
Sales price: 32,000gns (McKeever Bloodstock)

Half-brother to Irish 1m winner Treble Cone. Dam a maiden full sister to smart 6f-1m winner (including twice at Listed level) Selinka (later dam of Irish dual 5f

Group 3 winner Hit The Bid) and half-sister to 7f 2yo winners Swanky Lady and Tidal Wave out of a dual 6f Listed winning half-sister to Group 3-placed 6f 2yo winner Umniya and the dam of 6f 2yo Listed winner/Norfolk Stakes runner-up Log Out Island and 2019 6f 3yo Listed winner Khaadem.

"A big, strapping colt who looks the part and moves very well. We are excited about what he's showing at the moment - there is plenty of natural ability there. As with all our two-year-olds, we won't rush him, but I hope he can do something of note this season."

UNNAMED *Mitrosonfire*
24/3 gr c Lethal Force - Blaugrana (Exceed And Excel)
Owner: John O'Mulloy
Sales price: 10,000gns (William R Muir)

Half-brother to 6f 3yo winner Ashwaaq and 9.5f 3yo winner Mojika. Dam a 6f 3yo winning half-sister to useful 10f 3yo winner Contradict (later dam of French 1m 3yo Listed winner Orbaan and Group 3/Listed-placed 7f 2yo winner Momkin) and 1m 1f 3yo winner Damascene out of a 12f 3yo Group 3 winning half-sister to several winners, notably 6f Group 1 winner Invincible Spirit, Italian 1m 2yo Group 1 winner Massarra and 12/13.5f Group 3 winner Sadian.

"I thought he was really well bought at 10,000 guineas from Stowell Hill Stud. Lethal Force is a stallion I particularly like, but they aren't quite as sharp as some people believe them to be, and this colt will certainly take a bit of time. However, he is a lovely, strong, robust individual, who moves nicely and could be anything."

UNNAMED *Country Pyle*
27/3 b f New Approach - La Pyle (Le Havre)
Owner: Knox & Wells Limited & R W Devlin
Sales price: n/a

Half-sister to 2019 1m 2yo Listed winner Pyledriver. Dam a French 10.5-11.5f 3yo winner who was a full sister to smart French/Irish 7-10f winner (including at Group 3/Listed level) Normandel and a half-sister to French 12f 3yo Group 1 winner Mont Ormel out of an Irish 7f 2yo winning half-sister to 8/10f Group 1 winner Linngari.

"This is a beautiful filly who is big and tall, and not unlike her half-brother, Pyledriver, who was a good two-year-old for us last year. We will be looking to give her a similar sort of campaign, and start her off in the second half of the season. She moves beautifully and is good limbed. The mare has an Oasis Dream yearling colt and is due to foal to Frankel before visiting Kingman, so hopefully this filly can help out the page some more in the meantime."

UNNAMED   *Anjella*

18/4 b f Anjaal - Lookslikeanangel (Holy Roman Emperor)
Owner: Frank Hope & Gary Hope
Sales price: n/a

Second foal of an unraced half-sister to useful 7f-1m winner Brownsea Brink, fairly useful dual 6f 2yo winner So Brave and two other winners out of a Listed-placed French 6f 3yo winner who was the daughter of a twice-raced maiden sister to French 1m 3yo Listed winner Cheyenne Dream (later dam of French 10f Listed winner Indian Choice) and half-sister to French 12f Group 3 winner Short Pause and the dams of French 12f 3yo Group 1 winner Zambezi Sun and July Cup/Prix de l'Abbaye winner Continent.

"She was bought privately, and didn't come in until a bit later than one or two of the others. Even so, I would hope she'll be our first two-year-old winner, as she is a strong, good-moving filly that shows up well."

UNNAMED   *Inter*

26/2 b g Oasis Dream - Savvy (Verglas)
Owner: Mrs Yvonne Jacques
Sales price: 28,000gns (Not Sold)

Second foal of a 12f 3yo winner who was a full sister to useful Irish 7f-1m 2yo winner Cest Notre Gris and a half-sister to 5/5.5f 2yo Group 2 winner/Prix Morny runner-up Gutaifan, useful triple 7f winner Silk Fan (later dam of Group 3/Listed-placed 5-6f 2yo winner Haikbidiac and promising 2019 6-7f 2yo winner Dance Fever) and four other winners; the family of 2019 Lockinge Stakes winner Mustashry and two-time Hardwicke Stakes winner Maraahel.

"I was really pleased to be sent this two-year-old by Mrs Jacques. He wasn't overly big as a yearling but has grown and developed really well of late. I had the year-older half-sister and she was absolutely tiny, but this is a strong, butty individual who could be nice if continuing to go the right way."

Marten writes:

As you will by now be aware, I like speed on top of stamina in a pedigree, and the one that fits the bill here is the unnamed gelded son of Oasis Dream out of the Verglas mare Savvy.

Savvy, who was trained by Jeremy Noseda, was unraced at two and took seven outings to win, her victory coming from a mark of 59 in a 1m 4f Class 6 contest at Wolverhampton.

Savvy is a full sister to the useful Cest Notre Gris and a half-sister to five winners from the family of Mustashry and Maraahel, who both won Group races for Sir Michael Stoute and Hamdan Al Maktoum.

Given time this gelding could be useful.

JEDD O'KEEFFE

ABUNDANT MOON (IRE)
7/2 b f Galileo - Replete (Makfi)
Owner: John Dance
Sales price: €250,000 (Vendor)

First foal of an unraced half-sister to French 10f Group 1 winner Romantica (by Galileo), Group 2-placed French 10-12.5f winner (including twice at Listed level) Ideal World and the dam of 2019 10f 3yo Group 3 winner Sangarius out of a Breeders' Cup Filly & Mare Turf winner who was a full sister to Group 1/ Grade 1 winners Cacique, Champs Elysees and Intercontinental and very smart miler Dansili and a half-sister to US 8/9.5f Grade 1 winner Heat Haze.

"A medium-sized filly with a sweet nature. She won't be early, but is a nice mover who is coping well with her work. One for the second half of the season."

CLANSMAN
15/3 b c Nathaniel - Pearl Dance (Nureyev)
Owner: John Dance
Sales price: 80,000gns (Jedd O'Keeffe)

Half-brother to smart French 8-9f winner (including at Group 3 level) Sparkling Beam, very useful UK/Hong Kong 6f-1m winner Born In China, Group 1-placed 1m 1f 3yo winner Rainbow Springs, useful 2019 7.5f-1m 3yo winner Be More, UK/US 6f-1m winner Ridge Dance and the dam of 10f Listed winner Snoano.

Dam a Group 1-placed 6f 2yo winning half-sister to German 10.5f Listed winner Ocean Sea and the dam of Melbourne Cup winner Delta Blues.

"He hasn't been in all that long, but we like him. He is a tall, lengthy sort who will need time, but he has a nice page and I'm sure he will be capable of doing something this year."

COLTON
8/3 gr c Lethal Force - Lady Poppy (Kyllachy)
Owner: T S Ingham & Mrs Liz Ingham
Sales price: n/a

First foal of a multiple 5f winner who was a half-sister to Grade 2-placed UK/US 7-9f winner Patentar, useful dual 7f winner Khamry and three other winners out of a 7f-1m winning half-sister to high-class sprinter Overdose, French 7.5f Listed winner Majestic Mount and Listed-placed French 6-6.5f winner Poppet's Treasure out of a once-raced maiden half-sister to 1m Listed winner Musicanna (later dam of UAE 1m Group 2 winner One Man Band).

"George Moore trained the dam initially - she was very quick and won a decent nursery at York, though she wasn't quite at her best when we got her towards the end of her racing days. This colt is her first foal and was shaping up to be one of our earlier runners until racing was suspended, so we've had to take a pull for the time being. He is a strong sort and, like his dam, an out-and-out sprinter. We hope he'll be ready to roll upon the resumption of racing."

SANDHOE (IRE)
27/1 b f Gutaifan - Odyssee (Teofilo)
Owner: H Alexander, D Powell
Sales price: €18,000 (Vendor)

Third foal of a French 1m 1f 3yo winner who was a half-sister to Grade 2/3-placed French/US 7-9f winner Urban King, Listed-placed French 7.5f 3yo winner Victoria College (dam of smart performers Lucky Look and Millfield) and French 12f 3yo winner Uruguay (dam of French 7f 2yo Group 3 winner Dame Du Roi) out of an Italian 6f 3yo Group 3 winning half-sister to 12f Listed winner All The Aces; the family of 6f 2yo Group 2 winner Anjaal.

"She has taken everything in her stride so far, and will be ready to go when racing resumes. She has plenty of speed."

UNNAMED
16/3 ch c Bated Breath - Novellara (Sadler's Wells)
Owner: Highbeck Racing 2
Sales price: 20,000gns (Arthur Walker)

Three-parts brother to smart UK/Australian 9-11.5f winner (including at Group 3/Listed level) Disclaimer (by Dansili). Dam a 14f 3yo Listed winner who was a half-sister to Fillies' Mile/Oaks winner Reams Of Verse, Eclipse Stakes winner Elmaamul, Yorkshire Cup winner Manifest and several other winners including the dams of very smart middle distance performer Midday and Nell Gwyn Stakes winner Hot Snap and 1m 1f Group 3 winner Confront.

"This is a well put together individual who comes from a very good family. He had a period out of training, but has come back in and found everything coming easily to him. For all he will undoubtedly progress with age, he should win a race this year."

UNNAMED
11/4 b c Nathaniel - Riot Of Colour (Excellent Art)
Owner: Highbeck Racing 1
Sales price: 11,000gns (Arthur Walker)

Third foal of a useful 7f 3yo winner who was a half-sister to 6f 2yo Listed winner Invincible Warrior and useful 7-8.5f winner Crowdmania out of a Listed-placed dual 6f winner who was a half-sister to Racing Post Trophy winner Crowded House and the dam of high-class sprinter Brando and grandam of Middle Park Stakes winner Reckless Abandon.

"I think he was very well bought at 11,000 guineas as we liked him a lot at the sales. He is a good size and a nice-looking type. He had coped easily with his initial work, but we've backed off with him presently given the hiatus. He is one for the second half of the season anyway, so it shouldn't inconvenience him too much."

UNNAMED (IRE) Jian 21
16/2 b f Acclamation - Shuttlecock (Dubawi)
Owner: Geoff & Sandra Turnbull
Sales price: n/a

Second foal of an unraced half-sister to useful multiple 6f winner Huntsmans Close out of a smart 6-7f winner (including at Listed level)/Cheveley Park Stakes third who was a half-sister to Group 2-placed 7f 2yo winner Fox, Group 3-placed 6-7f winner Cala, useful 7f-1m winner Rafferty, useful 1m 3yo winner

Badagara, useful dual 7f 2yo winner Ballantrae, 1m 2yo winner Badalona and the grandam of 2019 Irish 6f 3yo Group 3 winner Gustavus Weston.

"Not overly big but was doing everything right until racing was suspended. Geoff Turnbull has taken his two-year-olds back home during this period of inactivity, but we look forward to having this filly back here."

UNNAMED (IRE)
16/2 b f Flintshire - Spinamiss (Lilbourne Lad)
Owner: The City & Provincial Partnership
Sales price: £60,000 (Jedd O'Keeffe)

First foal of a Grade 3-placed Irish/US 7f-1m winning half-sister to Group 2-placed UK/UAE 5-6f winner (including twice at Listed level) Spin Cycle, 7f Group 3 winner San Sicharia, smart French/Hong Kong 7-10f winner (including twice at Listed level) Same World and Irish 1m 2yo Listed winner Spinacre; the family of French 2000 Guineas winner Vahorimix, French Oaks winner Valyra, Breeders' Cup Mile winner Val Royal and Queen Anne Stakes winner Valixir.

"A medium-sized, good-topped filly with a tremendous outlook. She won't be early but should be OK in time."

Marten writes:

Clansman is the one I like from the four named horses.

He is a son of Nathaniel, who had the misfortune to bump into Frankel on his racecourse debut in a 1m maiden at Newmarket in July 2010. I remember thinking at the time that I had witnessed a decent maiden – indeed, the third Genius Beast was rated on 110 the following June – but I never expected the first two to scale such lofty heights.

Nathaniel has since evolved into a very successful sire, with Enable and top French performer Channel currently leading the way.

Clansman is a son useful Pearl Dance, who won on her debut at 33/1 before finishing in the frame in the Group 2 Cherry Hinton Stakes and the Group 1 Moyglare Stud Stakes. She ran her best race when fourth to Six Perfections in the Prix Marcel Boussac but then ran just twice down the field at three. At stud she has done very well, producing six winners including the high-earning Hong Kong winner Born In China and seven-race French winner Sparkling Beam.

Clansman has a strong pedigree but it may not be until he tackles a mile or more that we see the best of him.

HUGO PALMER

BRUNNERA
15/2 b f Dubawi - Romantica (Galileo)
Owner: Khalid Abdullah
Sales price: n/a

Second foal of a French 10f Group 1 winner who was a half-sister to Group 2-placed French 10-12.5f winner (including twice at Listed level) Ideal World and the dam of 2019 10f 3yo Group 3 winner Sangarius out of a Breeders' Cup Filly & Mare Turf winner who was a full sister to Group 1/Grade 1 winners Cacique, Champs Elysees and Intercontinental and very smart miler Dansili and a half-sister to US 8/9.5f Grade 1 winner Heat Haze.

"This is a typically nice Dubawi who moves well. Like all of the Juddmonte horses she has only been here since the end of February, but is finding things quite easy at this stage and could be anything. One for later on and next year."

CHOCOYA
9/3 ch f Sepoy - Silver Games (Verglas)
Owner: Christopher Wright
Sales price: n/a

Half-sister to Listed-placed UK/US 6-7.5f winner Chiringuita. Dam a useful 7f-1m winning half-sister to 1m 3yo Group 1 winner Nahoodh (later dam of 1m Listed winner Hawkesbury), useful 2019 5.5-6f 2yo winner Makyon and UK/Qatari multiple 6f winner Thahab out of an unraced half-sister to French 12f Group 3 winner Not Just Swing.

"A sharp, strong, muscular filly who goes nicely and will be amongst our earliest two-year-old runners. We have enjoyed past success with this sire, with our German 1000 Guineas winner Unforgettable Filly one of his best performers to date. She has a bit of character like most Sepoys, but thankfully handles the stalls well so far."

DANTORA
10/2 b c Dansili - Rostova (Arch)
Owner: Khalid Abdullah
Sales price: n/a

First foal of a French 1m 3yo Listed winner who was a sister to 1m 3yo Listed winner Pavlosk (later dam of useful 2019 10-12.5f 3yo winner Derevo (by Dansili)) and half-sister to Italian 10/12f Group 3 winner Exhibit One out of a Listed-placed French 12f 3yo winning half-sister to very useful multiple 6f-1m winner Bravo Echo and the unraced dam of 1m 2yo Listed winner/French 1000 Guineas runner-up Irish Rookie; the family of 2000 Guineas winner Zafonic.

"This is a lovely, good-moving colt. They don't make them by the sire anymore and we obviously had a really nice one by him for Juddmonte called Set Piece. He is a Derby entry who is very much one for next year - the kind of horse that could have you dreaming in twelve months. Again, he has only been here since the end of February, so I anticipate he will begin to find life easier the more work he does. I would hope he can make an appearance at two."

ECHO BEACH
11/3 b c Adaay - Last Echo (Whipper)
Owner: Kremlin Cottage Ix
Sales price: 18,000gns (Philippa Mains)

First foal of a dual 12f 3yo winner who was a half-sister to useful 8-12f winner Manjaam out of an Irish 13f 3yo winning half-sister to French 12f 3yo Listed winner Kiltubber (later dam of Australian 12f Group 1 winner Opinion and Group 3 winners Anam Allta (7.5f) and Fox Hunt (14f, twice)) out of an Irish 7f 2yo Group 1 winner who was a half-sister to Italian 10f Group 1 winner Eva's Request and the dam of 1m 2yo Group/Grade 1 winner Chriselliam.

"He is the only Adaay we have here, and I like him quite a bit. He looks just like his grandfather Kodiac and I suspect had he been by him, he'd have fetched more than he sold for last autumn. We've done well for this syndicate, and I hope this will be another sharp, fun two-year-old for them as he finds it all very easy at this stage."

ECOSSE
18/3 b f Acclamation - Dumfriesshire (Oasis Dream)
Owner: Khalid Abdullah
Sales price: n/a

Fourth foal of an unraced half-sister to French 10f Group 1 winner Romantica, Group 2-placed French 10-12.5f winner (including twice at Listed level)

Ideal World and the dam of 2019 10f 3yo Group 3 winner Sangarius out of a Breeders' Cup Filly & Mare Turf winner who was a full sister to Group 1/Grade 1 winners Cacique, Champs Elysees and Intercontinental and very smart miler Dansili and a half-sister to US 8/9.5f Grade 1 winner Heat Haze.

"Another Juddmonte homebred with a typically spectacular pedigree. She is muscular and strong but attractive with it, and looks very much like a six and seven furlong two-year-old performer in the making. Her work has pleased me so far."

GLESGA GAL (IRE)
14/3 ch f Lope De Vega - Crystany (Green Desert)
Owner: New Wave Racing & Partners
Sales price: €120,000 (Avenue Bloodstock/Hugo Palmer)

Three-parts sister to French 1m winner Sapphirine (by Shamardal) and a half-sister to useful Irish 1m 3yo winner Vivianite and multiple 7f winner Smugglers Creek. Dam a Listed-placed 6f 2yo winning half-sister to very useful 8-10f 3yo winner High End, useful UK/US 7-11f winner Treasury Devil and the unraced dams of French 10f 3yo Group 2 winner Ocovango and Group 3/Listed-placed 6.5-7f 2yo winner Glitter Girl out of a Fillies' Mile winner/Irish 1000 Guineas runner-up who was a half-sister to 12f Group 3 winner Dubai Success.

"I adore this filly. She is beautiful to look at and very light on her feet. She isn't overly big but is still growing, and should be a nice size once she has finished developing. Whilst she hasn't done anything serious yet, she moves well and will hopefully make up into a lovely filly during the second half of the season."

KIZOMBA
13/3 b f Kodiac - Zulema (Shamardal)
Owner: Khalid Abdullah
Sales price: n/a

Fourth foal of an unraced half-sister to Racing Post Trophy/St Leger winner Brian Boru, French 12.5f Group 2 winner Moon Search, UK/Australian triple 12f Group 3 winner/St Leger third Sea Moon, Irish 1m 3yo Listed winner Kitty O'Shea (later dam of US 12f Listed winner/Moyglare Stud Stakes third Kissable), the unraced dam of Derby/Arc winner Workforce and the grandam of German/Australian triple 12f Group 1 winner Best Solution (by Kodiac).

"A typically strong, forward Kodiac filly who finds it all rather easy at present. She is very much a two-year-old in the making and certainly looks the part. She is bred on the same cross as our smart sprinter, Gifted Master, and the Danehill sireline has had a very positive influence on this family, so there's plenty going for her."

LOCKDOWN
19/3 b c Charm Spirit - Bounty Box (Bahamian Bounty)
Owner: Qatar Racing Limited
Sales price: 45,000gns (David Redvers Bloodstock)

Half-brother to useful dual 6f winner Fuente, 2019 Irish 5f 2yo winner Corrienthes and two other winners. Dam a smart multiple 6f winner (including twice at Listed level) who was a full sister to useful French dual 1m 1f 2yo winner Bahamian Box and a half-sister to Listed-placed 6f 2yo winner Vive Les Rouges (later dam of very useful 5.5-7f winner Dougan and 6f 3yo winner/ Middle Park Stakes fourth Speedfiend) and three other winners.

"I am very keen on him as he is a lovely mover and a strong, mature individual who likes to get on with it. He finds it all extremely easy at the moment and will be one of our first two-year-old runners."

LOVELY BREEZE (IRE)
20/3 b f Sepoy - Power Of Light (Echo Of Light)
Owner: Dr Ali Ridha
Sales price: n/a

Half-sister to 2019 May Hill Stakes winner/Fillies' Mile runner-up Powerful Breeze. Dam a Listed-placed 1m 2yo winner who was a half-sister to 5-6f winner Escrick and 7f 3yo winner Power And Peace out of a 6f-1m winner who was a half-sister to useful 7f-1m 2yo winner Vanguard Dream out of a Listed-placed 7-10f winner.

"She is the third one we've trained from the mare. I thought the first foal would be really good in her younger days, but I think we went too soon with her and she suffered a knee injury and never quite achieved what she should've done. The opposite can be said of Powerful Breeze. Had you told me 12 months ago she was going to be as good as she turned out to be, I would've been very surprised. This filly is a different type to her but no less attractive. I like the way she goes but will be bringing her along steadily with the second half of the year firmly in mind."

MUSED
13/2 b f Charm Spirit - Stroll Patrol (Mount Nelson)
Owner: Qatar Racing Limited
Sales price: n/a

Half-sister to 2019 6f 2yo winner Hot Touch. Dam a Group 3-placed 6-6.5f winner who was a full sister to Group 3/Listed-placed UK/UAE 7f-1m winner Hors De Combat and a half-sister to four winners including 6f 2yo Group 3 winner Yourtimeisnow (by Charm Spirit) out of a thrice-raced maiden half-sister to US 1m 1f Grade 1 winner Stroll.

"This filly is a fair size so we will bring her along gradually. She is an attractive sort who could make up into a useful performer during the second half of the season at around six furlongs if progressing as expected."

NOMAN (IRE)
28/2 b c Shalaa - Mathool (Alhaarth)
Owner: Al Shaqab Racing
Sales price: 70,000gns (Avenue Bloodstock/Hugo Palmer)

Half-brother to Irish 8.5f 3yo Listed winner Erysimum, very useful 10f-2m winner Rhombus and two other winners. Dam a maiden three-parts sister to Group 2-placed 8-12f winner (including at Listed level) Sahool (later dam of 12f Group 3 winner Laraaib) and half-sister to the dams of Italian 12f 3yo Group 1 winner/St Leger runner-up Ventura Storm, two-time Hardwicke Stakes winner Maraahel, 5/5.5f 2yo Group 2 winner Gutaifan and 2019 French 5f 3yo Listed winner/Queen Mary Stakes third Shades Of Blue and the grandam of 2019 Lockinge Stakes winner Mustashry.

"This is a gorgeous colt who moves exceptionally well in his work. He is essentially a bigger version of his sire and I am delighted Al Shaqab decided to acquire him, as I loved him at the sales and still do now. He would be high on my list at the moment and should make a two-year-old as he is very mature. For all he ought to stay further in time, I suspect he will begin over six furlongs if he continues to show up well."

NORTHBOUND (IRE)
17/1 b c Fast Company - Natalisa (Green Desert)
Owner: Kremlin Cottage Ix
Sales price: n/a

Fourth foal of an Irish dual 5f 2yo winner who was a half-sister to Group 3-placed Italian 9-10f winner Sufranel out of a smart Irish 5-7.5f winner (including twice at Group 3 level) who was a full sister to very smart 5-6f winner (including at Group 1 level) Namid and a half-sister to Group 3-placed Irish 7f 2yo winner Natalis, Listed-placed Irish 7f 2yo winner Mandama and the dam of US 11f Listed winner Siberian Iris out of an Irish 5f 3yo Listed winner.

"He is one of the sharpest two-year-olds we have and is working away now. I joked to the owners that he was well named, given he will be spending a lot of his time venturing up north in search of easier ground as he moves like he will want it. He'll require six and seven furlongs in time, but will probably begin over five furlongs. He ticks all the boxes."

SET POINT (IRE)

4/2 b c Sea The Stars - Hot Sauce (Peintre Celebre)
Owner: John Livock
Sales price: 220,000gns (Vendor)

First foal of a Listed-placed Irish 9.5f 3yo winning half-sister useful Irish 10.5-12f Flat/Grade 2-placed 2m 1f hurdle winner Cardinal Palace out of an unraced half-sister to high-class multiple 5-6f winner (including at Group 1 level) Prohibit, French 6/6.5f 3yo Listed winner Prior Warning and Group 3-placed French dual 7f 3yo winner (including at Listed level) Emergency out of a Group 2/3-placed 6f 2yo winning sister to 1m 3yo Listed winner Out Of Reach.

"He is only the second Sea The Stars we've had here and is a lovely individual. He is all about the backend and next year but has found it all incredibly easy to date and works with the sprinters without any issue whatsoever. Hopefully that is a positive and he should make it out for the seven furlongs and mile races sometime in the autumn. I like him."

UNNAMED (IRE)

17/4 gr c Mastercraftsman - Atlantic Isle (Tamayuz)
Owner: Military Syndicate & Clodagh McStay
Sales price: €45,000 (Not Sold)

Second foal of a German 7f-1m winner who was a half-sister to Group 3-placed French 7f 2yo winner Atlantic High and the unraced dam of Listed-placed maiden Teofilo's Princess out of a useful 6f 2yo winning close relation to Craven Stakes/Dante Stakes winner Alnasr Alwasheek and half-sister to 10.5f Group 1 winner One So Wonderful (later dam of US 8.5f Grade 2 winner Sun Boat) and Rockfel Stakes winner/Irish 1000 Guineas third Relatively Special (later dam of Listed winners Blue Gold (10f) and Just Special (7f)).

"A straightforward, good-moving colt who I would be aiming to start in June or July over six or seven furlongs under normal circumstances. He has got a tremendous attitude, and I am pleased with how he goes."

UNNAMED (IRE)

24/2 gr/ro f Mehmas - Crystal Snowflake (Danehill Dancer)
Owner: For Sale
Sales price: €22,000 (Amanda Skiffington/Hugo Palmer)

Third foal of an unraced sister to 5f 2yo winner Snow Angel and three-parts sister to Listed-placed Irish 5f 2yo winner Snowflake Dancer out of a maiden sister to very useful French 1m 2yo winner Welimina and half-sister to high-class French 5-6f winner (including at Group 1 level) Kistena; the family of Dewhurst Stakes/Lockinge Stakes winner Belardo.

"A very forward filly who would have been our first two-year-old runner during the first couple of weeks of the intended season. She is a nice size but sharp and fast, and I like what she's doing at the moment. I keep hearing good things about the sire, so hopefully this filly can be one of those to help him along early on."

UNNAMED

17/2 b c Showcasing - Dam Beautiful (Sleeping Indian)
Owner: For Sale
Sales price: €65,000 (Avenue Bloodstock/Hugo Palmer)

Half-brother to 2m winner Looking For Carl. Dam a useful dual 5f winner who was a half-sister to very useful 7f-1m winner (including at Listed level) Peach Melba, Listed-placed multiple 6-7.5f winner Major Crispies and useful multiple 5-6f winner Bosun Breeze out of a 7f-1m winning half-sister useful multiple 10-13f winner Art Man.

"He is a strong colt with a good attitude and is hard to fault. Another who is pretty much ready to run."

UNNAMED   *Lockdown over*

31/3 ch c Shamardal - Lovely Pass (Raven's Pass)
Owner: Dr Ali Ridha
Sales price: n/a

Half-brother to 2019 11f 3yo winner Lovely Approach. Dam a Group 3-placed UK/UAE 6f-1m winner (including at Listed level) who was a sister to useful 7f-1m winner Almoreb and half-sister to smart 8-8.5f winner (including at Listed level) Spirit Raiser out of a smart 8-10f winner (including at Group 2/Listed level) who was a half-sister to 6f Group 3 winner Pistachio, 1m Listed winner Captivator and Group 2/3-placed UK/UAE 6f-1m winner Azarole.

"We don't get many Shamardals as they aren't readily available outside the Godolphin operation. This a strong, good-topped colt who moves well and has already shown glimmers of promise, but he's very much one for the second half of the season. He has got his father's front legs, but I understand that Earthlight also has them, and it certainly didn't stop him last year! I think this could be a nice horse if he continues to go the right way."

UNNAMED (IRE)   Neptunes Wonder

24/3 b f Kodiac - Prance (Danehill Dancer)
Owner: Dr Ali Ridha
Sales price: 120,000gns (Rabbah Bloodstock)

First foal of a maiden half-sister to Vertem Futurity Trophy/2019 2000 Guineas winner Magna Grecia and useful Irish triple 7f winner Invincible Ryker out of an Irish 7f 2yo Group 3 winner who was a half-sister to smart 7-10f winner (including at Group 3 level) Drumfire and Group 2-placed UK/Hong Kong 6f-1m winner (including at Listed level) Ho Choi; the family of Prix Vermeille winner Pearly Shells and Irish 7f 2yo Group 3 winner Ugo Fire.

"It has been a bit stop-start with her so far as she has coughed. Hopefully we will get a better idea of what she's all about once getting a clear run with her, but she is an attractive, typically mature Kodiac who should make a two-year-old."

UNNAMED (IRE)   The Rosstafarian

28/2 ch c Starspangledbanner - Via Lattea (Teofilo)
Owner: Middleham Park Racing LXXXVII
Sales price: €57,000 (Avenue Bloodstock/Hugo Palmer)

Half-brother to useful French 6f 2yo winner Double Kodiac. Dam a French 7f 3yo winner who was a sister to Group 3-placed Irish 7f 2yo winner What Style out of an unraced half-sister to Group 3-placed French 10.5f 3yo winner Nobilis, Group 2/Listed-placed 10-12f Flat/useful 2m-2m 4f hurdle winner Drill Sergeant and 7f 2yo winner Sergeant Ablett; the family of Dewhurst Stakes winner Intense Focus and Moyglare Stud Stakes winner Skitter Scatter.

"I adored this colt at the sales and thought he was very well bought at €57,000. The only other Starspangledbanner I have trained is Home Of The Brave and this colt reminds me of him quite a bit, though he is a bit bigger and not as wired. Mares from the Sadler's Wells line clearly work well with the sire - John Quinn's Coventry winner The Wow Signal would be another example of that - and hopefully it clicks again as I have very high hopes for this is colt."

UNNAMED
8/3 b f The Gurkha - Wild Storm (Dubawi)
Owner: Vefa Ibrahim Araci
Sales price: 20,000gns (Rob Speers)

First foal of a useful dual 10f 3yo winner who was a sister to UK 7f/UAE 1m winner Conquerant and a half-sister to useful French 11-12.5f 3yo winner Cosmic Flame out of a French 10f 3yo winning half-sister to Queen Elizabeth II Stakes winner Poet's Voice, the dam of UAE 1m 1f Group 1 winner Blair House and 10f 3yo Listed winner Key Victory and grandam of Japanese 11f Group 1 winner Mozu Katchan and French 6f 2yo Group 3 winner Sporting Chance.

"This filly is the surprise package of my two-year-old crop. She was a cheap foal and I think the plan was to sell her on last autumn, but I am pleased that didn't materialise as she has thrived since coming here and is just beginning to catch the eye in what she does. The Gurkha has been talked up by all the right people and this is a lovely, long-striding filly who I hope will be capable of doing something this year."

Marten writes:

I was tempted to nominate Echo Beach, a daughter of Adaay out of Last Echo, as this is the title of a favourite song of mine, recorded in the late '70s by Canadian band Martha and the Muffins.

Echo Beach doesn't actually exist, to the best of my knowledge, so somebody in the syndicate that owns him must also share my fondness for the song.

I wish them good fortune with him, but from a bunch of very well-bred sorts I am keen to side with **Set Point**, a son of Sea The Stars who the trainer says is "working with the sprinters".

That is certainly encouraging because Set Point's pedigree is all about stamina and next year. He is the first foal of a daughter of Peintre Celebre named Hot Sauce, a winner and Listed-placed half-sister to middle-distance winner and hurdle winner Cardinal Palace. There is speed in the family, through Group 1 sprinter Prohibit and Prior Warning, but I would expect this colt to prove at his most effective over a mile or more.

Set Point is one of a handful of promising two-year-olds in the yard.

JONATHAN PORTMAN

BELAFONTE
27/4 b c Twilight Son - Scarlet Royal (Red Ransom)
Owner: Laurence Bellman
Sales price: 13,000gns (J Portman)

Half-brother to very useful 5-7f winner Baron Bolt, Listed-placed 6f 2yo winner Momalorka and 10f 3yo Flat/fairly useful dual 2m 4f hurdle winner Red Royalist. Dam a maiden daughter of an unraced half-sister to very smart 7f-1m winner (including at Group 1 level) Where Or When, smart 10-12f winner (including at Listed level)/St Leger fourth All The Way and the dam of Group 2/3-placed 5-6f winner (including at Listed level) Danehill Destiny.

"He looks a hardy sort who should develop into a nice-three-year-old, but I would hope he can show something during the second half of this season."

FULL APPROVAL (IRE)
24/2 b f Mehmas - Drifting Spirit (Clodovil)
Owner: Laurence Bellman
Sales price: £15,000 (Stroud Coleman/Johnny Portman)

First foal of a useful 7-7.5f 2yo winning daughter of a maiden half-sister to 1m 3yo Group 1 winner Nahoodh (later dam of 1m Listed winner Hawkesbury), useful 7f-1m winner Silver Games (later dam of Listed-placed UK/US 6-7.5f winner Chiringuita), useful UK/Qatari multiple 6f winner Thahab and useful 2019 5.5-6f 2yo winner Makyon out of an unraced half-sister to French 12f Group 3 winner Not Just Swing and French 10f 3yo Listed winner Minoa.

"Not overly big but very well made and in proportion. She is a wonderfully kind and straightforward filly. I expect she will be an early runner."

HAVE TO HAVE
24/3 gr f Havana Gold - Having A Blast (Exchange Rate)
Owner: A Brooke Rankin
Sales price: 8,000gns (J Portman)

Half-sister to useful Australian 7f-1m winner Succendam. Dam a useful French 1m 3yo winner who was a half-sister to US 6.5-8.5f winner Blasted Boss out of a US 8.5f 2yo winning half-sister to Grade 1-placed US/Canadian 6.5-9.5f winner (including at Grade 3 level) Breaking Lucky and the dam of 2019 Kentucky Derby winner Country House.

"She is coming along all the time and has a good attitude. Under normal circumstances, we would be aiming for her to begin around July time."

HEADORA
2/3 b c Charming Thought - Keladora (Crafty Prospector)
Owner: J F S Laws & Mrs J Laws
Sales price: 15,000gns (Vendor)

Half-brother to 6-7f 3yo winner Mawakib, 12-14f 3yo winner Kelamita and four other winners. Dam a Listed-placed French/US 8-8.5f winner who was a half-sister to Group 1-placed French 7.5f 2yo winner On Verra and Irish 1m 2yo winner Kaminari out of a French 1m 1f 3yo Listed winner/French 1000 Guineas runner-up.

"He was ignored at the sales due to having no 'step' on him at all, but there is much to like otherwise."

HELLAVAPACE
13/4 br/gr f Hellvelyn - Hasten (Lear Fan)
Owner: Portlee Bloodstock
Sales price: 4,500gns (Vendor)

Full sister to Listed-placed 6f 2yo winner Hellofahaste, useful Irish/US 8-8.5f winner Clutchingatstraws, UK/Hong Kong 5-7f winner Great Run and five other winners. Dam a maiden half-sister to smart 7f-1m 2yo winner (including at Group 3/Listed level)/Racing Post Trophy runner-up Fantastic View, Group 2-placed 7f 2yo winner Weald Park and useful 6-7f 2yo winner To The Rescue; the family of smart sprinters Brick By Brick and High Standing.

"She has done really well to catch up with the others, given she came in later than most, and the fact she has done so suggests to me that she might have more to offer than her physical appearance might indicate."

MARK OF RESPECT (IRE)
16/4 b c Markaz - Music Pearl (Oratorio)
Owner: Berkeley Racing, R Dollar, D Powell
Sales price: £6,000 (Vendor)

Three-parts brother to multiple 5.5-6f winner Born To Finish (by Dark Angel) and a half-brother to 6f 2yo winner Arden Pearl. Dam an Irish 8.5f 3yo winner who was a half-sister to high-class 7-9f winner (including at Group 3/Listed level) Haami and useful 8-10f 3yo winner Ayun (later dam of 2m Group 2 winner Akmal) out of an Italian 10f 3yo Group 2 winner who was a half-sister to Derby winner Erhaab; the family of French Oaks winner Star Of Seville.

"Shunned at the Goffs UK Premier Yearling Sale last August, but has changed dramatically in appearance since then and covers twice as much ground as his workmates. He'll take a little time, but is offering us plenty of encouragement."

UNNAMED
10/1 b f Hellvelyn - Arctic Moon (Raven's Pass)
Owner: For Lease
Sales price: £600 (Vendor)

First foal of a lightly-raced maiden half-sister to Grade 3-placed US 8.5-9f winner Try Your Luck and useful US 5-8.5f winner High Quality out of a once-raced US 6f 3yo winner who was a full sister to Stakes-placed US dual 6f winner T S Eliot and US 6f 2yo winner Argentina (grandam of 6f 2yo Group 3 winner La Rioja and great-grandam of 2019 5f 2yo Group 3 winner Liberty Beach) and a half-sister to the dam of Park Hill Stakes winner Eastern Aria.

"Bought very cheaply privately and was put through the ring for a similarly modest amount, but we do like her. She is more of a six and seven-furlong type though, so we won't go rushing in with her just yet."

UNNAMED
6/3 b f Adaay - Fair Maiden (Carnegie)   *Marrance*
Owner: Mrs Mary-Anne Parker
Sales price: £16,000 (Not Sold)

Half-sister to fairly useful 5-6f winner Kapono. Dam an unraced half-sister to smart Australian 5.5f-1m winner (including at Listed level) Premardal and Group 3-placed Australian 1m winner Fallacy out of an unraced half-sister to top-class juvenile Arazi and very smart French/UK 5f-1m winner (including at Group 1 level) Noverre.

"Only small but a forward-going, precocious filly who is keen to get on with things. She should be in action sooner rather than later."

Marten writes:

Few trainers do as well with inexpensive buys as Jonathan Portman.

Last year his Requinto filly Mild Illusion, who cost just 1,000gns as a yearling, won over £66,000 in prize money, narrowly missing out in a valuable sales race before landing a Listed race on her final start.

The filly was sold last December for 160,000gns, a handsome return for her syndicate of owners.

The trainer has been bargain hunting again, with the most expensive of those nominated coming in at 16,000gns.

Of those featured **Mark Of Respect** could be interesting. A son of Markaz, a full brother to Mecca's Angel, he is a three-parts brother to Born To Finish, who won eight of his 57 starts, out of a winning half-sister to Haami from the family of Derby winner Erhaab.

Mark Of Respect is not as precociously bred as the two-year-olds usually associated with this yard, so it's pleasing to learn he's showing something at home. His trainer is sure to get the best out of him.

JOHN QUINN

DISCO BEATS
13/2 b c Pearl Secret - Indigo Beat (Tamayuz)
Owner: John Dance
Sales price: 20,000gns (Creighton Schwartz Bloodstock/John Dance)

First foal of a maiden half-sister to 6f 2yo Group 3 winner Habaayib and dual 5f winner Golden Flower out of a US 6f-1m winning daughter of a US 6.5f 2yo Grade 2 winner who was a half-sister to German 6f 2yo Group 2 winner/ Middle Park Stakes and Dewhurst Stakes runner-up Green Perfume.

"A nice, good-moving colt that is bred to be a two-year-old and looks like being just that. I like the way he goes."

LIBBY AMI (IRE)
19/4 b f The Gurkha - Moore's Melody (Marju)
Owner: S & R Racing Partnership
Sales price: 26,000gns (Sean Quinn)

Half-sister to smart UK/French 7-10.5f winner (including at Group 3/Listed level) Talwar and useful French 6-8.5f winner Dark Orbit. Dam a French 7.5f-1m winner who was a full sister to Irish 7f 2yo Listed winner Bruges out of an unraced close relation to the maiden dam of Irish 6f 2yo Group 2 winner Probably and half-sister to Listed-paced Irish dual 1m 3yo winner Ventura (later dam of six-time French 6f-1m Group 1 winner Moonlight Cloud).

"This an attractive, well put together filly. She is a very good mover who looks as though she will be early enough."

PIXIE K (IRE)
7/2 b f Kodiac - Asrafairy (Zebedee)
Owner: Phoenix Ladies Syndicate
Sales price: 80,000gns (Phoenix Ladies Syndicate)

First foal of an unraced half-sister to high-class 5-6f winner (including twice at Group 1 level) Fairyland, very useful 5-6f winner Atletico (both by Kodiac) and smart Irish/Australian 7f-1m winner (including at Group 2/3 level)/Irish 1000 Guineas third Now Or Later out of an unraced half-sister to Middle Park Stakes/July Cup winner Dream Ahead.

"She isn't overly big, but is well made and has a good mind on her. She moves well and we like what we see."

POSSIBLE AMBITION
27/2 b c Territories - Kotsi (Nayef)
Owner: Phoenix Thoroughbred Limited
Sales price: 52,000gns (West Park Farm)

Half-brother to very useful multiple 1m winner Si Senor and useful 8-11.5f winner Cape Discovery. Dam a Group 2/Listed-placed 7f 2yo winner who was a half-sister to Canadian 10f Grade 1 winner Miss Keller, Group 3/Listed-placed dual 7f 2yo winner Sir George Turner, useful 5-6f 2yo winner Abunai (later dam of St Leger winner Harbour Law) and the dam of smart 5-7f winner (including at Group 2/Grade 3 level) Hatta Fort, 7f 2yo Group 3 winner Blue Bayou and 2019 12f Group 3 winner Spirit Of Appin.

"A good-looking colt who moves very well. He hasn't done anything too serious yet, but we like him."

VIRGINIA PLANE
25/2 b f Mehmas - Flirtinaskirt (Avonbridge)
Owner: Philip Wilkins
Sales price: n/a

Half-sister to Group 2-placed 2019 multiple 5f 2yo winner (including at Group 3/Listed level) Liberty Beach. Dam a 5f 3yo winner who was a half-sister to 6f 2yo Group 3 winner La Rioja, Group 3/Listed-placed 6f 2yo winner Pastoral Girl and Listed-placed triple 5f 2yo winner Lilbourne Lass; the family of Park Hill Stakes winner Eastern Aria.

"A strong, imposing filly who obviously has a good pedigree as a half-sister to our top two-year-old of 2019, Liberty Beach. She didn't come in until fairly recently and hasn't galloped yet, but she's done everything asked of her so far."

UNNAMED (IRE)
30/4 b c Fast Company - Kathy Sun (Intikhab)
Owner: JJ Quinn Racing Ltd
Sales price: 50,000gns (Sean Quinn)

Full brother to French 5.5f 2yo Listed winner Simmie and a half-brother to useful French 6-6.5f 2yo winner Trebtherick and 6f 2yo winner Sunny Harbor. Dam an Italian 5f 2yo winning half-sister to Italian 5f Group 3 winner Kathy College (later dam of Italian triple 6f Group 3 winner Rosendhal), Italian 6f Group 3 winner Kathy Dream and Italian 5.5f 2yo Listed winner Kathy Pekan (later dam of Italian dual 6f Group 3 winner Plusquemavie).

"A nice, good-moving colt. Whilst he hasn't done a load of work yet, the bits he has done have been pleasing."

Marten writes:

I have known John for a number of years, both as a jockey and a trainer. Starting with Edward O'Grady, he later joined Jimmy FitzGerald before turning freelance and ending his career as a jockey with almost 200 winners.

John trained a horse called Mastership for me. The horse had shown plenty of ability for Clive Brittain at Newmarket, but he was quirky and I took the view he would benefit from a change of scene.

I had it in mind that he would be an ideal type for the Bunbury Cup, and we almost pulled it off when he finished fourth after being short of room a furlong from home. He wasn't an easy ride, but things fell into place for him when he won the Beeswing Stakes at Newcastle, ridden by the late Jamie Kyne.

John is now established as one of the country's top dual-purpose handlers. Blythe Knight and Triumph Hurdle winner Countrywide Flame have advertised his skills, while The Wow Signal gave him a Group 1 success when landing the 2014 Prix Morny.

Now ably assisted by his son Sean, John is a quiet, perceptive man with a good eye.

The one I'm keen to propose from the above list is **Possible Ambition**. He may not be the most precocious of the yard's youngsters but I was keen to nominate a two-year-old from the first crop of Territories in the book and he fits the bill.

Territories, who was trained by Andre Fabre, was blessed with a formidable turn of foot. It didn't always win him races, and it should have won him more, but he ran second to Gleneagles in the Guineas and next time out won the Group 1 Prix Jean Prat.

Possible Ambition is out of a Group 2-placed half-sister to Canadian Grade 1 winner Miss Keller and other useful sorts tracing back to the family of St Leger winner Harbour Law. At stud she has produced four-race winner Si Senor and Cape Discovery, winner of three.

This colt is on the cusp of looking well bought at 52,000gns. His pedigree suggests he will come into his own over a mile.

GEORGE SCOTT

BUNGLEDUPINBLUE (IRE)
26/3 b f Bungle Inthejungle - Generous Heart (Sakhee's Secret)
Owner: Christopher Wright
Sales price: £32,000 (JS Bloodstock)

Third foal of a once-raced maiden half-sister to Irish 7f 3yo Group 3 winner/ Irish 2000 Guineas fourth Leitrim House, 5f Listed winner Place In My Heart (later dam of Queen Mary Stakes/Flying Childers Stakes winner Heartache and Listed-placed 5f 2yo winner Heartwarming), very useful 7-9f winner Ace Of Hearts and twice-raced 7f 3yo winner Mulaaseq out of a useful dual 10f

3yo winning half-sister to very useful multiple 5-7f winner Indian Trail and the dam of Group 1-placed multiple 5-5.5f winner (including at Group 2/3 level) Stepper Point and 2019 5.5f 3yo Listed winner Lady In France.

"A precocious filly who is light-framed but sound. She would have been ready to run in the first two-year-old races of the scheduled season. As her pedigree suggests, she has plenty of natural speed, and I would be hopeful she can win a novice event when racing is back."

GREAT VIBES
13/3 b f Showcasing - Whazzat (Daylami)
Owner: W J & T C O Gredley
Sales price: n/a

Half-sister to Group 1-placed 6-7f winner (including at Group 2/3 level) James Garfield, Listed-placed 7.5f-1m winner The Shrew, useful 8-10f 3yo winner Eva Maria and 6-7f winner Theladyinquestion (later dam of Group 3/Listed-placed 6-9f winner Nate The Great). Dam a Chesham Stakes winner who was a half-sister to smart 7f-1m winner (including at Group 3/Listed level) Whazzis and the maiden dam of Group 2-placed 2019 7f 2yo winner Juan Elcano.

"She comes from a family I obviously know well. It all comes very easily to her and she is a typical Showcasing - tall, scopey and incredibly strong. In a normal year I would've hoped to get her going around three or four weeks before Royal Ascot, much like we did with half-brother James Garfield, but that's very unlikely to happen now."

PUNTA ARENAS (USA)
20/2 b c Quality Road - Absolute Crackers (Giant's Causeway)
Owner: Flaxman Stables Ireland Ltd
Sales price: n/a

Third foal of a Listed-placed Irish/US 8-8.5f winner who was a half-sister to Grade 1-placed UK/US 7-12f winner (including at Grade 3/Listed level) Pachattack (later dam of Irish 1m 2yo Group 3 winner Liquid Amber), smart US triple 1m 2yo winner (including at Listed level) La Mina and two other winners out of a Listed-placed 10f 3yo winner.

"He is a bit weak and angular at the moment, but is a very good-looking colt. He's only cantering away at present, but I like him a lot."

RED CARPET QUEEN
10/2 b f Hot Streak - Dark Reckoning (Equiano)
Owner: Ms Luisa Zissman
Sales price: £35,000 (W Jackson-Stops)

Third foal of a 6f 2yo Group 3 winner who was a sister to 5f 2yo winner Alshaqee out of a useful 5-6f winner who was a half-sister to high-class multiple 5-6f winner (including twice at Group 1 level) Reverence, Chesham Stakes winner Helm Bank, useful 5-6f winner Quiet Elegance and five other winners out of a 5f 2yo Group 2 winner.

"It is a speedy family and this filly certainly has the build of a sprinter. All she has done since we bought her is strengthen and grow. She still has a little bit of developing to do even now, but I hope to have her ready for a five or six furlong race by midsummer."

ROHAAN (IRE)
2/3 b c Mayson - Vive Les Rouges (Acclamation)
Owner: H H Shaikh Nasser Al Khalifa & Partner
Sales price: £36,000 (Oliver St Lawrence)

Half-brother to very useful 5.5-7f winner Dougan and 6f 3yo winner/Middle Park Stakes fourth Speedfiend. Dam a Listed-placed 6f 2yo winner who was a half-sister to dual 6f Listed winner Bounty Box and four other winners.

"A tall, athletic colt who is uncomplicated but very immature currently. He will want some cut in the ground when the time comes for him to race, which I hope will be this autumn. A nice three-year-old type who'll want six and seven furlongs."

SIMULATION THEORY (IRE)
7/3 ch c Starspangledbanner - Barawin (Hawk Wing)
Owner: Ms Emma Banks
Sales price: £30,000 (JS Bloodstock/G Scott Racing)

Half-brother to useful 5f-1m winner Family Fortunes and useful 7-12f winner Sir Jack Layden. Dam a 1m 2yo winner who was a half-sister to useful 8.5-12.5f 3yo winner Atkinson Grimshaw out of a maiden half-sister to Group 3/Listed-placed triple 12f 3yo winner Ridaiyma, Listed-placed Irish 8-9f winner Ridiya (grandam of Listed winners Ridaar (11.5f) and Valonia (6f)) and Irish 10f 3yo winner Riyama (later dam of 12f 3yo Listed winner Riyafa).

"He was bought as a project for next year really. He is light-framed, but has improved a huge amount physically since we got him from the sales. He has a nice long stride on him and moves well. I very much doubt we'll see him before the autumn, but is one to keep an eye on for the future as he's a nice horse."

TRIBUNA UFFIZI (IRE)
14/1 b c Zoffany - Bunood (Sadler's Wells)
Owner: E Williams & Partner
Sales price: 35,000gns (JS Bloodstock/G Scott Racing)

Half-brother to Listed-placed 7f-1m winner Lanansaak and useful 2019 11.5-12f 3yo winner Babbo's Boy. Dam a Group 3/Listed-placed 1m 2yo winning half-sister to useful UK/UAE 7f-1m winner Alshawameq and useful 7f 2yo winner Maghanim out of a dual 7f 3yo winning half-sister to 1000 Guineas winner Shadayid (later dam of 7f 2yo Group 3 winner Bint Shadayid, 10/10.5f Listed winner Imtiyaz and 6f 2yo Listed winner Alshadiyah (herself dam of smart pair Farhaan and Haatheq) and great-grandam of US 6f Grade 1 winner Takaful) and 7f Group 3 winner Fath.

"Tall and very handsome, but a late-maturing type who was bought with the long term in mind. He won't be ready to run until much later in the year, but he's a nice horse who finds it all very easy in his slower paces and I am looking forward to stepping up his workload over the coming weeks. Another really nice horse for the future."

WALTER MITTY
14/3 ro c Lethal Force - Furbelow (Pivotal)
Owner: W J & T C O Gredley
Sales price: 75,000gns (Stetchworth And Middle Park Studs)

Full brother to very useful 6-7f winner Flavius Titus and a half-brother to high-class 6-6.5f winner (including three times at Group 1 level) Advertise. Dam a 6f 2yo winner who was a sister to very useful US 5-8.5f winner (including at Listed level) Red Diadem and a three-parts sister to 6f 2yo winner/Cheveley Park Stakes fourth Adorn (later dam of 6f 2yo Group 2 winner Saayerr and Group 2/3-placed multiple 5f winner Ornate) and 6f 2yo winner Red Turban.

"This colt behaved terribly at auction, but Bill Gredley was keen to get him as he liked what he saw physically. He is the heaviest horse I have ever trained, currently weighing in at 524kg, so is obviously very powerful. I think he will make a nice 6f horse from the summer onwards, though is just having a small break at the moment."

WHYZZAT
22/2 b c Dark Angel - Whazzis (Desert Prince)
Owner: W J & T C O Gredley
Sales price: 160,000gns (Stetchworth And Middle Park Studs)

Half-brother to Listed-placed French 1m 2yo winner Whim, very useful 6-7f winner Culturati, useful 10-10.5f 3yo winner Valiant and four other winners. Dam a smart 7f-1m winner (including at Group 3/Listed level) who was a half-sister to several winners including 7f 2yo Listed winner Whazzat (later dam of Group 1-placed 6-7f winner (including at Group 2/3 level) James Garfield) and the maiden dam of 2019 Superlative Stakes runner-up Juan Elcano.

"This colt was quite an expensive purchase and is from the James Garfield family. He is a tall, late-maturing individual who finds life very easy and I wouldn't be at all surprised if he develops into a lovely horse one day. For all he has really come into himself over the past few weeks, it is more about next year with him."

UNNAMED (IRE)
8/4 b f Lope De Vega - Fifth Commandment (Holy Roman Emperor)
Owner: Ms Emma Banks & Mr John O'Connor
Sales price: €160,000 (JS Bloodstock/George Scott Racing)

Full sister to 2019 French 5f 2yo winner Love Vega. Dam a Listed-placed 5-6f winner who was a half-sister to Group 1-placed French 7f-1m 3yo winner (including at Group 3 level) Via Ravenna, smart French 8-9f winner (including at Group 3/Listed level) Via Medici (later dam of Japanese triple 1m Group 1 winner Admire Mars and French Listed winners Via Pisa (1m) and Via Firenze (1m 1f)) and 2019 1m 2yo winner Via De Vega (by Lope De Vega).

"This filly was on the small side when we bought her but has improved markedly ever since. She has a very forward-going nature and a terrific attitude. I haven't pushed any buttons yet, but she looks ready to take on some more work now. If she has ability, this filly is the type to win first time out as she likes to get on with things."

Marten writes:

George Scott has made a good impression since taking out his licence in 2015, notably with Group 2 Mill Reef winner James Garfield, who went on to win the Greenham Stakes.

He has a decent bunch of youngsters to call upon this season and the one I like, with the long term in mind, is **Tribuna Uffizi**.

This son of Zoffany is a half-brother to Lanansaak, a lightly raced daughter of Zamindar who won two of her five starts, out of Bunood, a Group-placed half-sister to the useful Alshawameq from the family of that great mare Shadayid, herself a daughter of the very talented Desirable.

Shadayid won five of her 11 starts, including the Prix Marcel Boussac and the 1000 Guineas and reached the frame in five of her next six starts all at Group 1 level.

This is a very decent bloodline, tracing back to one of the great families, for a relatively inexpensive acquisition. I am pleased to read that the colt will be given the time his pedigree suggests he may need.

Expect him to thrive over a mile and a quarter or more next season.

JAMES TATE

$\bullet \bullet \bullet$

ENCHANTED NIGHT
9/2 ch f Night Of Thunder - Khaseeb (Dutch Art)
Owner: Saeed Manana
Sales price: 37,000gns (Rabbah Bloodstock)

First foal of an unraced half-sister to Group 3-placed 5-6f 2yo winner (including at Listed level) Ventura Mist and very useful 5-5.5f winner Majlaa out of a 5f 2yo winner who was a half-sister to French 10.5/12f 3yo Group 3 winner Lady's Purse and Listed-placed dual 6f 2yo winner Dazilyn Lady out of a Listed-placed 1m 3yo winner.

"A small, strong, speedy filly - very much a two-year-old."

ENTRAPMENT
27/1 b f Iffraaj - Rebecca De Winter (Kyllachy)
Owner: Saeed Manana
Sales price: 25,000gns (Vendor)

Half-sister to smart multiple 5f 2yo winner (including at Group 3/Listed level)
Mrs Danvers. Dam a 5f 2yo winner who was a half-sister to 6f 2yo Listed
winner Izzthatright; family of 2yo Listed winners Soiree (7.5f) and Solaboy (6f).

*"She is a half-sister to Mrs Danvers and is what you'd expect with such a
pedigree: a strong, speedy, medium-sized filly who should be out sooner rather
than later."*

FINAL VOYAGE (IRE)
13/3 b c Camacho - Shamayel (Pivotal)
Owner: Saeed Manana
Sales price: €75,000 (Rabbah Bloodstock)

Half-brother to useful 5-10f winner Mushaakis. Dam a 7f 2yo winning sister to
useful 7-9f winner Karaka Jack and half-sister to four winners out of a 7f 3yo
Listed winning half-sister to Group 3-placed French 10f 3yo winner All Glory
(later dam of Australian 1m Group 2 winner Noble Protector and German 10f
3yo Group 3 winner All Shamar) and Listed-placed 7f-1m 2yo winner Pacific
Grove (later dam of German 6f 2yo Group 2 winner Mokabra).

*"A big, attractive colt. He isn't one you would necessarily pick out on paper, but
on looks and how he goes he'd be one of our better two-year-olds. He is a good
mover who finds it all very easy. Although I suspect he will want six furlongs
sooner rather than later, he almost certainly would have started off over five
furlongs in a normal year."*

GLOBAL RESPONSE
15/5 b c Territories - Terentia (Diktat)
Owner: Sheikh Juma Dalmook Al Maktoum
Sales price: 45,000gns (Rabbah Bloodstock)

Half-brother to Listed-placed multiple 6f winner Crossing The Line, triple 6f
winner Shades Of Silk and 6f 2yo winner Publilia. Dam a very useful multiple
5f winner who was a half-sister to Group 3-placed triple 6f winner (including
twice at Listed level) Cartimandua (later dam of Group 2-placed 6f 2yo winner
Elronaq) out of a 7f 2yo Listed winner.

"Sheikh Juma owned his talented half-sister, Crossing The Line, and that was the rationale behind the purchase of this colt. I am very pleased he bought him as he's a really nice horse who shows plenty of speed. His knees are still open and he's a bit 'up' behind at the moment, so won't be overly early, but I like what I have seen so far. He should do well during the second half of the year once he has developed a bit more."

HIGH SECURITY
8/2 b c Acclamation - Excelette (Exceed And Excel)
Owner: Sheikh Hamed Dalmook Al Maktoum
Sales price: 150,000gns (Stroud Coleman Bloodstock)

Full brother to Group 2/3-placed triple 5f 2yo winner (including twice at Listed level) Well Done Fox and a half-brother to 5f 2yo winner Excellently Poised. Dam a 5f 3yo Listed winning half-sister to Group 3-placed 6f 2yo winner Rapid Applause and useful dual 6f winner Blessington out of an unraced half-sister to Group 1-placed multiple 5f winner (including twice at Group 2 level) Bolshoi, 5f 3yo Listed winner Mariinsky and the dams of 7f Listed winner Mine and Group 2/Listed-placed 5-6f winner Autumn Pearl.

"A brother to a smart juvenile sprinter Richard Hannon trained, and I hope he will prove to be a similar sort of horse. He is a medium-sized, physically mature, very straightforward individual who shows plenty. He is one to follow."

HIT THE HEIGHTS (IRE)
27/3 b c Iffraaj - I'm Yours (Invincible Spirit)
Owner: Saeed Manana
Sales price: 60,000gns (Rabbah Bloodstock)

Third foal of an Irish 9.5f 3yo Listed-winning close relation to Group 1-placed 8-8.5f winner (including at Group 3/Listed level)/Irish 2000 Guineas fourth Recharge and Irish 1m 3yo winner Regalline (later dam of 12f 3yo Group 3 winner Highgarden) and half-sister to 2019 6-7f 2yo winner Grove Ferry out of a high-class Irish 7-10.5f winner (including at Group 1 level) who was a half-sister to smart Irish 5-11f winner (including at Group 2/3 level) Quws.

"He is a strong, muscular colt who comes from a good Lady O'Reilly family. For all it is likely he'll begin over six furlongs, I would say he will be the type to do even better over seven furlongs and a mile later in the year."

PANORAMIC
3/4 ch f Helmet - Jubilant Queen (Kyllachy)
Owner: Saeed Manana
Sales price: 40,000gns (Rabbah Bloodstock)

Half-sister to useful dual 6f winner Royal Residence. Dam a dual 6f 3yo winner who was a three-parts sister to useful 10f 3yo winner Ascot Lime and a half-sister to smart 8-10.5f winner (including at Group 3/Listed level) Class Is Class and useful 11-12.5f winner Magellan out of a Group 3-placed 6f 2yo winner; the family of high-class sprinter College Chapel and Group 2 winners Barrow Creek (6f), Last Resort (7f) and Trans Island (1m).

"She is a half-sister to a fairly decent horse we trained called Royal Residence who wasn't entirely straightforward, and probably didn't win the number of races he should've done. Thankfully this filly has a good temperament and goes particularly nicely in her work."

PUBLICIST
6/2 b f Dark Angel - Diary (Green Desert)
Owner: Saeed Manana
Sales price: 100,000gns (Rabbah Bloodstock)

Half-sister to high-class multiple 5-6f winner (including at Group 1 level) Total Gallery, 13f 3yo Listed winner Tempest Fugit, 5f 2yo winner/Fillies' Mile runner-up Lady Darshaan (later dam of 10f 3yo Listed winner Let's Go) and three other winners. Dam a Greek triple 7f 3yo winner who was a half-sister to Irish 10f Group 1 winner Ambivalent (later dam of 2019 French 12f 3yo Group 2 winner Al Hilalee) and Group 1-placed UK/UAE triple 7f winner Al Waffi.

"A half-sister to a Prix de l'Abbaye winner. A strong, attractive filly, she does it all very easily at the moment."

RISK OF THUNDER (IRE)
21/3 ch f Night Of Thunder - Lady Vyrnwy (Bertolini)
Owner: Saeed Manana
Sales price: £35,000 (Rabbah Bloodstock Ltd)

Fourth foal of a maiden half-sister to French 12.5f Group 2 winner Star Lahib and Listed-placed Irish dual 6f 3yo winner Moone Cross out of an Irish 6f 2yo winning half-sister to Irish five time 9-12f Listed winner Tout A Coup and the dam of Canadian 1m 2yo Grade 3 winner Fearless Flyer (herself later dam of 7f 2yo Group 3 winner Crius).

"Night Of Thunder had an excellent first season last year, and we had a couple of good performers by him in the shape of Magical Journey and Under The Stars. This filly is medium-sized but strong and lengthy with a lovely long stride on her. She goes particularly well and is one to follow when the six furlong races are here."

Under The Stars lands the Group 3 Princess Margaret Keeneland Stakes at Ascot last July. She was one of several by first-season sire, Night Of Thunder, to impress on the track last year.

SENSE OF ROMANCE (IRE)

4/3 ch f Dutch Art - Infatuation (Invincible Spirit)
Owner: Sheikh Juma Dalmook Al Maktoum
Sales price: €75,000 (Rabbah Bloodstock)

First foal of an unraced half-sister to Listed-placed 1m 3yo winner Illusion out of a 1m 3yo Listed winner who was a half-sister to high-class 5-7f winner (including at Group 2/Listed level)/1000 Guineas third Dazzle, 7f 2yo Listed winner Hypnotize (later dam of Cheveley Park Stakes winner Hooray) and the maiden dam of Group 1-placed multiple 5-6f winner (including at Group 2/3 level) Danehurst and French 10.5f 3yo Group 3 winner Humouresque.

"She is a medium-sized filly who is strong and speedy. An out-and-out two-year-old type."

STATE OF PLAY (IRE)
4/1 b c Dark Angel - Ambiguous (Kheleyf)
Owner: Sheikh Rashid Dalmook Al Maktoum
Sales price: n/a

Half-brother to 2019 6f 2yo winner Jamaheery. Dam an unraced half-sister to high-class multiple 5f winner (including at Group 1 level) Alpha Delphini, high-class multiple 5-6f winner (including at Group 1 level) Tangerine Trees, smart triple 5f winner (including at Group 3/Listed level) Kurious, Listed-placed 5f 3yo winner Fairy Falcon, useful multiple 6-7f winner Masai Moon and useful multiple 5-7f winner Galatian.

"A lovely big horse whose half-sister won first time out last year at Yarmouth for Richard Hannon, while the dam's related to Abbaye winner, Tangerine Trees, and Nunthorpe winner, Alpha Delphini. Given his size, he is very much one for the middle part of the season onwards, but does have that bit of star quality about him."

UNNAMED *Illustrator*
26/4 ch c Bobby's Kitten - Amelia May (Dansili)
Owner: Saeed Manana
Sales price: 21,000gns (Rabbah Bloodstock)

Half-brother to once-raced 2019 7f 2yo winner Little Becky. Dam a maiden sister to useful 1m 2yo winner Bartholomew Fair, a three-parts sister to 1m 3yo Listed winner Miss Pinkerton (later dam of 14f Group 3 winner Precious Ramotswe) and a half-sister to smart Irish 7-10f winner Grand Central out of a Coronation Stakes winner.

"His first-season sire won the Breeders' Cup Turf Sprint, and it's a family of milers on the dam's side. He goes nicely enough but we should find out more in the coming weeks. He'll start at six furlongs but will have no issue with going further."

UNNAMED *One over far*
5/3 b c Gleneagles - Cherrington (Lope De Vega)
Owner: Sheikh Juma Dalmook Al Maktoum
Sales price: 50,000gns (Rabbah Bloodstock)

Half-brother to Listed-placed 5f 2yo winner Kemble. Dam an unraced half-sister to very smart 6.5f-1m winner (including twice at Group 1 level) Toronado out of a French 6.5f-1m winning half-sister to high-class 7.5-10f winner (including at Group 1 level) Casamento, very useful 6f-1m winner Inler and Irish 7f 2yo winner Brosna Cry out of a French 1m 2yo Listed winner; the family of Australian Group 1 winners French Clock (6f) and Heart Of Dreams (8/9f).

"A tall colt who has a lovely long stride on him but is still quite babyish. He has a lot of Lope De Vega in him and will be one for later on, but I think he possesses a fair amount of ability and will hopefully show it once growing up a bit."

Marten writes:

Publicist will be given every chance to give his dam yet another winner.

Diary, a daughter of Green Desert, won three times in Greece and since retiring to the paddocks she has produced five winners most notably Total Gallery, winner of six races including the 2009 Prix de l'Abbaye, and Fillies' Mile runner-up Lady Darshaan, both trained by Stan Moore. Tempest Fugit also won for John Gosden.

This daughter of Dark Angel is bred to show plenty of pace and it's encouraging to learn that she is doing everything right at the moment.

MARCUS TREGONING

ALDEENAARY (IRE)
25/4 b c Awtaad - Lucky Clio (Key Of Luck)
Owner: Hamdan Al Maktoum
Sales price: €400,000 (Shadwell Estate Company)

Half-brother to 2019 Irish 2000 Guineas winner Phoenix Of Spain, Listed-placed multiple 5-6f winner Lucky Beggar, very useful triple 10f winner Central Square, very useful 8-10f winner Kingsdesire, useful triple 7f winner Game Player and two other winners. Dam a maiden half-sister to high-class French 7-10f winner (including at Group 2/3 level) Special Kaldoun, Listed-placed Canadian 6.5f 3yo winner Privalova and useful multiple 6f winner Ice Lord.

"He is still with Shadwell and I haven't seen him yet, but it's obviously fantastic to have a half-brother to a horse like Phoenix Of Spain, and also by one of the more exciting first-season stallions around in Awtaad."

ALKUMAIT
18/2 b c Showcasing - Suelita (Dutch Art)
Owner: Hamdan Al Maktoum
Sales price: 220,000gns (Shadwell Estate Company)

Half-brother to very useful Irish 5-5.5f winner (including at Listed level) The Broghie Man and Listed-placed 6f 2yo winner Gloves Lynch. Dam an Italian 5-6f winner who was a half-sister to Group 3-placed multiple 5-7f winner Outer Space and the dam of 2019 Lowther Stakes winner Living In The Past; the family of smart stayer Opinion Poll.

"This colt was bred just down the road at Whitsbury Manor Stud and is a good-looking sort who moves particularly well. He can be a little flighty so needs to try and curb that, but he's very straightforward otherwise and is one of the better-looking Showcasings we have. Everyone here likes him and hopefully he can have a productive campaign."

ENSYAABY (IRE)
23/4 b c Dark Angel - Staceymac (Elnadim)
Owner: Hamdan Al Maktoum
Sales price: £125,000 (Shadwell Stud)

Full brother to Group 2-placed multiple 5f winner (including twice at Listed level) Easton Angel. Dam a 5f 3yo winner who was a half-sister to Group 2/3-placed UK/French 6.5-7f winner (including at Listed level) Kalahari Gold, useful 9.5-12f winner Great Court and three other winners out of an unraced half-sister to US 11f Grade 3 winner Riddlesdown and Listed-placed multiple 6-8.5f winner Vitznau out of a Group 3-placed Irish 6f 2yo winner.

"This is a tallish, leggy colt who has plenty of scope and a nice action. For all his physique doesn't necessarily suggest it, he should be quite a forward type as he shows lots of speed. A very nice horse."

LA FORZA
19/4 b c Shalaa - Seven Magicians (Silver Hawk)
Owner: J A Tabet
Sales price: 45,000gns (MP Tregoning)

Half-brother to Group 3/Listed-placed UK/Hong Kong 7f-1m winner California Disegno, useful Irish 1m-2m winner King's Vow and 7f 2yo winners Magician's Cape and Psychometry. Dam a Listed-placed 10f 3yo winner who was a half-sister to 10f 3yo Listed winner/Yorkshire Oaks runner-up Ocean Silk out of a maiden sister to very smart French 5-10.5f winner (five times at Group 1 level, including the French 1000 Guineas and French Oaks) Divine Proportions.

"A medium-sized colt with a sharp mind who moves well. He looks to be fairly forward."

MOTARAJJA (IRE)
15/5 b c Frankel - Rumoush (Rahy)
Owner: Hamdan Al Maktoum
Sales price: n/a

Full brother to smart triple 1m winner (including at Listed level) Wadilsafa and a half-brother to Group 2-placed UK/UAE 7f-1m winner (including at Group 3/ Listed level) Muntazah, 7f 3yo Group 3 winner/1000 Guineas fourth Talaayeb and Listed-placed 2019 dual 10f 3yo winner Ojooba. Dam a Group 2-placed 8-9f winner (including at Listed level)/Oaks third who was a half-sister to 1000 Guineas winner Ghanaati and Group 1-placed 8-12f winner (including at Group 3 level) Mawatheeq out of a 7/10f Listed winner who was a three-parts sister to four-time 10/10.5f Group 1 winner Nayef.

"A family we obviously know all about and this is the first one from Rumoush that I have trained. She was tall and scopey and this colt is much the same. He will naturally take a bit of time, but has a lovely big stride on him and should be able to do something towards the backend of the season."

MUTASALLEM (IRE)
5/2 b c Showcasing - Bright Glow (Exceed And Excel)
Owner: Hamdan Al Maktoum
Sales price: €240,000 (Shadwell Estate Company)

Half-brother to useful dual 6f 2yo winner Aldana. Dam a dual 7f 3yo winner who was a half-sister to very useful 7f-1m winner Kehaar, useful 5f 2yo winner All For Laura (later dam of 6f 2yo Group 2 winner/Cheveley Park Stakes runner-up Misheer, herself the dam of 6f 3yo Listed winner Mistrusting) and two other winners out of a 1m 3yo winning half-sister to Middle Park Stakes winner First Trump and Group 3-placed 6-7f winner First Veil.

"He is by Showcasing and out of an Exceed And Excel mare, but isn't perhaps as sharp as that sort of breeding would normally suggest. He is a good mover with a sound mind, but I suspect he'll take a little time."

ORIGINATOR (IRE)
26/3 ch c New Approach - Gimasha (Cadeaux Genereux)
Owner: R C C Villers
Sales price: 55,000gns (MP Tregoning)

Half-brother to Listed-placed 6f 2yo winner Samminder, useful triple 6f winner
Queen's Pearl, 7f 3yo winner Platinum Pearl (later dam of 2019 French 7f 3yo
Listed winner Invitational) and 2019 Irish 5f 2yo winner Royal Affair. Dam a
very useful 5-6f winner who was a half-sister to very useful triple 1m Flat/2m-
2m 1f hurdle winner Atlantic Rhapsody, useful 6f 2yo winner Shallal and the
once-raced maiden dam of 7f 3yo Listed winner Telwaar.

*"The dam's page doesn't have a huge amount of black type on it, but they
all seem to be pretty useful with good ratings. This colt is a lovely mover who
is probably one for the autumn, but then aren't they all given the current
situation."*

PEROTTO
28/3 ch g New Bay - Tschierschen (Acclamation)
Owner: Halcyon Thoroughbreds - MT1
Sales price: 28,000gns (MP Tregoning)

First foal of a 5f 2yo winner who was a half-sister to Group 1-placed 6-7f
winner Gallagher, Listed-placed UK/UAE 7-10f winner Quick Wit, Listed-placed
7f 3yo winner New Day Dawn and Listed-placed 5-7f winner Roodeye (later
dam of smart UK/US 6f-1m winner (including at Grade 2/3 level) Prize Exhibit
and dual 7f Group 3 winner Mohaather and grandam of Queen Anne Stakes
winner Accidental Agent) out a Listed-placed 5-6f 2yo winner.

*"We know a bit about this family, given Mohaather is in the pedigree. This is
a quite forward individual who shows good pace, though he has free-going
tendencies which is why we decided to geld him. We have had to knock him
back a bit as we obviously have nowhere to go at present, but he'll be OK to
begin over six furlongs once we're racing again."*

TASFEEQ
14/2 b c Oasis Dream - Blinking (Marju)
Owner: Hamdan Al Maktoum
Sales price: 115,000gns (Shadwell Estate Company)

Half-brother to 14f Listed winner Twitch, useful 1m 2yo winner Kaloor, 10f
3yo winners Maracuja and Myopic, useful 5f 2yo winner Tallulah Rose and the
unraced dam of 2019 German 7.5f 2yo Listed winner Romsey. Dam an unraced

sister to very smart 6-12f winner (including eight times at Group 1 level) Viva Pataca and half-sister to high-class Irish/US 8-11f winner (including twice at Grade 1 level) Laughing and Listed-placed 7f-1m 2yo winner Shambolic.

"This is a particularly nice horse and was in fact my pick of the yearlings from last year. Oasis Dream is still more than capable of producing a good one and this colt is a very nice mover with the temperament to match his good looks. He is doing absolutely everything right and is just the sort of horse I like."

TISTAAHAL

15/2 b c Showcasing - Blue Bayou (Bahamian Bounty)
Owner: Hamdan Al Maktoum
Sales price: 80,000gns (Shadwell Estate Company)

First foal of a Group 2-placed 6-7f 2yo winner (including at Group 3 level) who was a half-sister to smart 5-7f winner (including at Group 2/Grade 3 level) Hatta Fort, 2019 12f Group 3 winner Spirit Of Appin, five other winners and the dam of 13f Group 3 winner/Irish St Leger runner-up Agent Murphy out of a 1m 1f winner who was a half-sister to Canadian 10f Grade 1 winner Miss Keller, Group 2/Listed-placed 7f 2yo winner Kotsi, Group 3/Listed-placed dual 7f 2yo winner Sir George Turner and the dam of St Leger winner Harbour Law.

"I have got a few by Showcasing this year, and although not overly expensive, this colt is another very nice prospect by him. He is a good mover and shows plenty of speed, which one would expect, given he is also out of a Bahamian Bounty mare. I like him and he shouldn't be too long in making an appearance once racing resumes."

Marten writes:

I've long thought that Marcus Tregoning doesn't get the support his talents as a trainer deserve.

He did everything right when winning the Derby narrowly in 2006 with Sir Percy and has also shown he can train horses of lesser ability as his handling of Landue and a few years earlier Lady Hestia, who won six races having started on a mark of 49, prove.

He begins the new season with a team of 55, 22 of them two-year-olds. The one that catches the eye on paper is **Motarajja**, a son of Frankel out of Rumoush, who ran third in the 2010 Oaks to Snow Fairy and has since excelled at stud with four winners including Muntazah, winner of almost £650,000 in prize money, Talaayeb, Ojooba and a full brother Wadilsafa – each of them Group or Listed class performers.

The trainer has sent out five winners of the Hanson and Clark Conditions Stakes at Newbury and this colt could prove the right sort to follow in their footsteps.

ROGER VARIAN

ALBANMAN (IRE)
20/3 b c Lawman - Albanka (Giant's Causeway)
Owner: Nurlan Bizakov
Sales price: n/a

Half-brother to 7f 2yo Group 3 winner/Falmouth Stakes runner-up Altyn Orda. Dam a once-raced maiden sister to US 8.5/9f Grade 2 winner Oonagh Maccool and half-sister to four-time 10/12f Group 1 winner Taipan, 1000 Guineas winner Sleepytime (dam of Group 3 winners Gentleman's Deal (10f) and Hathal (1m)) and Sussex Stakes winner Ali-Royal out of a 7f 3yo Listed winning half-sister to French 9/10.5f Group 1 winner/French Derby second Croco Rouge and the dams of Group 3 winners Centennial and Royal Millennium.

"A big, rangy colt with a sizeable frame to fill. His half-sister was a good horse for us who won the Oh So Sharp Stakes at two and placed in the Falmouth Stakes as a three-year-old. I see this colt as a nice three-year-old prospect, but he should be able do something this year from August onwards."

AQUAMAN (IRE)
10/3 b c Kodiac - Aqualis (Sea The Stars)
Owner: Sheikh Mohammed Obaid Al Maktoum
Sales price: 300,000gns (Roger Varian)

First foal of a 10f 3yo winner who was a half-sister to smart 7f-1m winner (including at Listed level) Pearl Mix and useful UK/French 7f-1m winner Silver Quartz out of a French 7f 2yo winning sister to Group 1-placed French 7f-1m winner (including at Group 2/3 level) Rajsaman and smart French 8-10f winner (including at Listed level) Rosawa (later dam of French 1000 Guineas winner Rosanara) and half-sister to Irish 12f 3yo Listed winner Radanpour.

"This colt has a bit of size to him and is a good-moving sort who is very straightforward. He moves nicely and I hope to see him running in June or July."

ATHERS (IRE)
12/4 ch c Dubawi - Kelly Nicole (Rainbow Quest)
Owner: Sheikh Mohammed Obaid Al Maktoum
Sales price: 320,000gns (Roger Varian)

Full brother to Group 1-placed 6f-1m winner (including at Group 2/Listed level) Aljamaaheer and a half-brother to useful 7f-1m winner Tinkertown. Dam an 8.5-10f winner who was a half-sister to US 11f Listed winner Cold Cold Woman, Listed-placed French 12-12.5f 3yo winner Shada, useful Irish 7-10f winner Robin Hood and Irish 10f 3yo winner Snow Lord; the excellent family of Irish Oaks winner Moonstone and Derby runner-up US Army Ranger.

"A brother to a good horse we used to train called Aljamaaheer. This is a neat colt who has a good temperament and moves nicely. He should be starting over seven furlongs in July."

BELARDIE (FR)
11/3 b f Belardo - Elite (Invincible Spirit)
Owner: Mrs H Varian
Sales price: £11,000 (Ebonos)

Half-sister to French 7-9f winner Different Views and two other winners. Dam a maiden half-sister to French 1m 1f 3yo Group 1 winner Olden Times, 6f 3yo Listed winner/Cheveley Park Stakes third Festoso (dam of 2019 Italian 7.5f 2yo Listed winner Festive Star) and useful 6f 2yo winner Orpha out of a Group 2/3-placed multiple 6f winning half-sister to the dam of smart multiple 1m winner (including at Group 2/Listed level) Dandoun.

"Not overly big but a deep-girthed, well-made filly who is straightforward. She goes very well, and looks a sharp two-year-old type who should be running pretty soon."

BOOMSHALAA
11/3 b c Shalaa - Summer Collection (Teofilo)
Owner: Sheikh Mohammed Obaid Al Maktoum
Sales price: 350,000gns (Roger Varian)

First foal of a maiden sister to Listed-placed dual 7f 2yo winner Monticello and half-sister to Group 2-placed dual 5f winner One Chance out of a maiden half-sister to top-class miler Spinning World, French 1m 3yo Listed winner Visions Of Clarity (later dam of Preakness Stakes winner War Of Will and Irish 7f 2yo Group 1 winner Pathfork and grandam of Listed winners Buying Trouble (6f) and Nucifera (7f)) and Group 3-placed French 7f 3yo winner Rangoon Ruby (later dam of Arc third Sagara).

"This colt moves well and is creating a nice impression so far. One for the summer over six furlongs."

DARK LION (IRE)
29/4 b c Dark Angel - Graciously (Shamardal)
Owner: H H Shaikh Nasser Al Khalifa & Partner
Sales price: €140,000 (Oliver St Lawrence)

Second foal of a French 7-10f winner who was a half-sister to high-class 8-10f winner (including at Group 1 level) Giofra, smart 8-8.5f winner (including twice at Listed level) Big Baz, French 12f Listed winner Gradara and French 1m 2yo Listed winner Gomati out of a 7f 2yo Group 3 winner who was a full sister to 6f Listed winner Lady Grace (later dam of smart pair Glencadam Glory and Penmaen) and Group 3-placed UK/UAE 6-7.5f winner Visionist.

"This is a strong mature colt who shows plenty of natural ability. I could have seen him making it to Royal Ascot in a normal year, and I hope I can get him started over six furlongs in May. A smart horse."

EL DRAMA (IRE)
19/2 ch c Lope De Vega - Victoire Finale (Peintre Celebre)
Owner: Sheikh Mohammed Obaid Al Maktoum
Sales price: 425,000gns (Roger Varian)

Half-brother to 10f 3yo Listed winner/Oaks third Volume (later dam of Irish 7f 2yo Group 1 winner Quorto), Group 3-placed UK/Australian 8-10f winner Velox, very useful dual 1m winner Validus and three other winners. Dam a French 1m 3yo winner who was a half-sister to high-class French 11-15f 3yo winner (including at Group 2/3 level)/St Leger runner-up Vertical Speed; the smart family of Vallee Enchantee, Vespone and Maids Causeway.

"A lovely big colt who will naturally take a bit of time. I hope to see him in action by the late summer or autumn. He is a good prospect, especially for next year."

HAMOUDI

15/3 b c Dark Angel - A Huge Dream (Refuse To Bend)
Owner: Sheikh Mohammed Obaid Al Maktoum
Sales price: 220,000gns (Roger Varian)

Half-brother to smart 5-5.5f winner (including twice at Listed level) Mrs Gallagher and fairly useful 5-6f winners Chasing Dreams and Tone The Barone. Dam a Listed-placed dual 6f winner who was a half-sister to high-class UK/Hong Kong 6f-1m winner (including twice at Group 1 level) Xtension and the dam of very smart multiple 6f winner (including twice at Group 1 level) Harry Angel (by Dark Angel) and 2019 6f 2yo Group 2 winner Pierre Lapin.

"He has the pedigree and is certainly giving us all the right messages so far. He is strong and mature, and has plenty of natural speed. I would like to think he would have been a Royal Ascot two-year-old under normal circumstances. There is a lot to like about him."

The hugely promising Pierre Lapin belies his relative inexperience to win the Group 2 Mill Reef Stakes at Newbury last September. Connections will be hoping Hamoudi can follow in the family footsteps this season.

IMPERIAL YELLOW (IRE)
24/3 b c New Bay - Soteria (Acclamation)
Owner: Varian Racing III
Sales price: £40,000 (Peter & Ross Doyle BS/Ebonos)

First foal of a maiden sister to 5f 2yo winner Tschierschen and a half-sister to Group 1-placed 6-7f winner Gallagher, Listed-placed UK/UAE 7-10f winner Quick Wit, Listed-placed 7f 3yo winner New Day Dawn and Listed-placed 5-7f winner Roodeye (later dam of smart UK/US 6f-1m winner (including at Grade 2/3 level) Prize Exhibit and dual 7f Group 3 winner Mohaather and grandam of Queen Anne Stakes winner Accidental Agent); the family of Middle Park Stakes winner Astaire and Gimcrack Stakes winner Bannister.

"I trained the dam and she could be a bit fiery, but thankfully this colt is straightforward by comparison. New Bay is an interesting first-season sire. Despite him getting better with age and the expectation being his progeny would follow suit, the three we have here by him all look fairly sharp types. This is a medium-sized, strong colt who is well put together and moves smoothly. He will begin over six furlongs and should be out sooner rather than later."

KINDRED SPIRIT (IRE)
15/5 b f Invincible Spirit - Pontenuovo (Green Tune)
Owner: Merry Fox Stud Limited
Sales price: n/a

Fifth foal of a Group 1-placed French 6f 2yo Group 3 winning half-sister to Listed-placed French 6f 2yo winner Ponte Vespucci out of a high-class French 5-6.5f winner (including at Group 1 level) who was a half-sister to Listed-placed French 9.5-12f 3yo winner Ponte Brolla (later dam of French 15f Group 2 winner Ponte Tresa and French 12f Listed winner Pontille) and the maiden dam of Australian 10f Group 1 winner/French 2000 Guineas third Pornichet.

"A nice enough filly who moves well and should come to hand by the summer."

LANEQASH
22/1 b c Cable Bay - Bonhomie (Shamardal)
Owner: Hamdan Al Maktoum
Sales price: £175,000 (Shadwell Stud)

First foal of an 8.5f 3yo winning half-sister to useful 8-10f winner Border Legend out of an unraced half-sister to smart French/US 8-9f winner (including Grade 2/Listed level) Calista and the grandams of French 8/10.5f Group 1 winner/French Derby runner-up Act One, French 1m 2yo Group 1 winner

Ultra and French 12.5f 3yo Group 3 winner Synopsis and 10f 3yo Listed winners Cosmodrome and Splashdown (later dam of Solario Stakes winner Aktabantay); the family of Bosra Sham and Hector Protector.

"A strong, well-made colt with a smooth action. He looks a two-year-old type and should be ready to start by July."

LANKARAN
15/3 gr c Kendargent - Lashyn (Mr Greeley)
Owner: Nurlan Bizakov
Sales price: n/a

Half-brother to useful 1m 2yo winner Lastochka. Dam a 10f 3yo winner who was a three-parts sister to smart 7-9.5f winner (including at Group 3/Listed level) Hathal and US 1m 3yo Listed winner Dame Ellen and a half-sister to smart multiple 7-10f winner (including at Group 3/Listed level) Gentleman's Deal, Group 3-placed Irish 7f 2yo/US 8.5f winner Spanish Harlem and Listed-placed 1m 3yo winners Oh Star and Ry's The Guy.

"A medium-sized, correct colt who moves well. He will definitely improve with age and be even better next year, but I would hope to have him running by July or August time."

LEGEND OF DUBAI
1/3 b c Dubawi - Speedy Boarding (Shamardal)
Owner: Sheikh Mohammed Obaid Al Maktoum
Sales price: 500,000gns (Roger Varian)

First foal of a high-class 10-10.5f winner (including twice at Group 1 level) who was a half-sister to very useful dual 10f 3yo winner Elwazir, useful dual 1m winner Next Stage (by Dubawi) and three other winners including the useful dam of 2019 Queen's Vase winner Dashing Willoughby out of an 11f Listed winner who was a half-sister to Group 1-placed 8-10f winner (including at Listed level) Dash To The Top (later dam of 2019 Oaks winner Anapurna).

"A smart colt with a good temperament who moves well. He cost a lot money, but rightly so as it is a big pedigree. He will obviously need a little time, but I would still hope that he could be running by the backend of the summer."

MILITARY MAN
20/5 ch c Gleneagles - Blue Butterfly (Kyllachy)
Owner: Paul Smith
Sales price: 90,000gns (MV Magnier/Roger Varian)

Second foal of an unraced sister to Group 3/Listed-placed 6f 2yo winner Highland Daughter (later dam of Australian 6f Listed winner Highland Beat) and half-sister to Italian 14/15f Listed winner Ryan, useful 1m 3yo winner Rive Gauche (later dam of wide-margin 2019 6f 2yo debut winner Ultra Violet (by Gleneagles)) and three other winners; the good family of Group 1 winners Laurens (six times, 8-10.5f), Helene Mascot (8/10f) and Kinnaird (10f).

"A lovely colt that has a nice, fluent action. He should be running by July or August and I quite like him."

MOVIN TIME
29/4 b c Fastnet Rock - Time On (Sadler's Wells)
Owner: Sheikh Mohammed Obaid Al Maktoum
Sales price: 170,000gns (Roger Varian)

Half-brother to 7f 2yo Group 3 winner Mot Juste and 1m 2yo winner Moontime. Dam a smart 9.5-12f 3yo winner (including at Group 2/Listed level) who was a full sister to 10.5f 3yo winner Time Control (later dam of Irish 7f 2yo Group 1 winner Cursory Glance and grandam of 2019 US 8.5f 3yo Grade 2 winner Digital Age) and a half-sister to very useful 2019 dual 7f 3yo winner Posted; the family of Queen Mary Stakes winner Best Terms.

"We have enjoyed recent success with the family via Cursory Glance and Mot Juste. This is a very uncomplicated colt who has plenty of size and scope. He is another that I hope to see running by the second half of the summer."

PAPACITO (IRE)
20/2 br c Estidhkaar - Out Of Time (Anabaa)
Owner: Sheikh Mohammed Obaid Al Maktoum
Sales price: 140,000gns (Roger Varian)

Half-brother to Group 3-placed Irish 7f 2yo winner What Style, French 7f 3yo winner Via Lattea and two other winners. Dam an unraced half-sister to Group 3-placed French 10.5f 3yo winner Nobilis and Group 2/Listed-placed 10-12f Flat/useful 2m-2m 4f hurdle winner Drill Sergeant out of an Irish 10/12f Listed winner; the family of Irish Derby winner Solider Of Fortune, Dewhurst Stakes winner Intense Focus and Moyglare Stud Stakes winner Skitter Scatter.

"A good-moving colt who has done everything asked of him to this point. He shows a bit of pace and should be running over six furlongs in June or July."

THE TWO-YEAR-OLD GUIDE 2020

ROYAL CHAMPION (IRE)
28/2 b c Shamardal - Emirates Queen (Street Cry)
Owner: Sheikh Mohammed Obaid Al Maktoum
Sales price: n/a

Half-brother to Listed-placed 12-13.5f winner Outbox. Dam a smart 10-12f winner (including at Group 2 level) who was a half-sister to very smart 6f-1m winner (three times at Group 1 level, including the Irish 2000 Guineas) Dubawi and Group 2-placed 8-10f 3yo winner (including at Listed level) Princess Nada (later dam of smart duo Jordan Princess and Qewy and 2019 7f 2yo debut winner Magnetised (by Shamardal)).

"A lovely big horse who will be one for the autumn and particularly next year."

THIRD REALM
2/3 b c Sea The Stars - Reem Three (Mark Of Esteem)
Owner: Sheikh Mohammed Obaid Al Maktoum
Sales price: n/a

Half-brother to high-class 10-12f winner (including at Group 1 level) Ajman Princess, high-class multiple 1m winner (including at Group 2 level) Ostilio, high-class 6f-1m winner (including at Group 3 level) Cape Byron, Group 1-placed 7f 2yo winner Imperial Charm and very useful UK/UAE 7-12f winner Naqshabban. Dam a Listed-placed 8.5-10.5f 3yo winner who was a half-sister to Group 1-placed 8-10f winner (including at Group 2/3 level) Afsare.

"A nice, medium-sized colt with a good action. He is by Sea The Stars and from a slow-maturing family, but he should be running in the autumn."

ZABEEL QUEEN (IRE)
15/4 b f Frankel - Dubai Queen (Kingmambo)
Owner: Sheikh Mohammed Obaid Al Maktoum
Sales price: n/a

Half-sister to useful 7.5-10f winner Sharja Queen. Dam a Listed-placed 1m 3yo winner who was a half-sister to very smart 6f-1m winner (three times at Group 1 level, including the Irish 2000 Guineas) Dubawi, Lancashire Oaks winner Emirates Queen, Group 2-placed 8-10f 3yo winner (including at Listed level) Princess Nada (later dam of smart duo Jordan Princess and Qewy) and Listed-placed 11.5f-2m winner UAE King (by Frankel) out of an Italian Oaks winner.

"A strong, medium-sized filly with a good mind. She moves well and I hope to see her in action by the summer."

UNNAMED

18/2 b c Kingman - Brevity (Street Cry)
Owner: H H Shaikh Nasser Al Khalifa & Partner
Sales price: 425,000gns (Oliver St Lawrence)

Three-parts brother to useful multiple 5f winner Saaheq (by Invincible Spirit) and a half-brother to fairly useful dual 10f winner Brief Visit. Dam a 6f 2yo Listed winner who was a half-sister to Grade 1-placed UK/US 8-12f winner Concise and very useful Irish 10.5-12.5f winner Fog Of War out of a 1m 3yo winning sister to 6/7f 2yo Group 2 winner Daggers Drawn; the family of Irish 2000 Guineas winner Indian Haven and St Leger runner-up Kite Wood.

"A nice stamp of a colt with a lot of presence about him. He has got a good mind and moves particularly well. I imagine he will be one for the autumn."

UNNAMED

22/1 ch c Frankel - Vasilia (Dansili)
Owner: King Power Racing Co Ltd
Sales price: 260,000gns (SackvilleDonald)

Half-brother to Group 1-placed multiple 6-7f winner (including twice at Listed level) Dream Of Dreams, Group 2/Listed-placed UK/French multiple 5f-1m winner Silverheels, Listed-placed 5f 2yo winner Lasilia and useful 6f-1m winner Candelisa. Dam an unraced half-sister to high-class UK/Irish 5f-1m winner (including the Cheveley Park Stakes) Airwave (later dam of Irish 5f 2yo Listed winner/Queen Mary Stakes runner-up Meow, herself dam of top-class 2yo/2000 Guineas winner Churchill and Cheveley Park Stakes winner Clemmie) and Nunthorpe Stakes winner Jwala.

"A medium-sized colt who is well proportioned. Although it is all speed on the dam's side, Frankel is a stamina influence and therefore he will probably not be seen until the autumn. He will want seven furlongs to start with."

Marten writes:

I could have gone for any of a dozen or so of the horses nominated above but I've decided to side with **El Drama**, by a sire that I like and from a family that I remember well.

El Drama is by dual French Classic winner Lope De Vega out of a half-sister to St Leger runner-up Vertical Speed from a family packed with winners.

The dam Victoire Finale won the first of only three starts and has done better at stud, producing Oaks third Volume and other useful sorts including Velox, Validus and Vuela – all trained by Luca Cumani.

Volume is the dam of Quorto, who I was hoping could go close in last season's Derby only for injury to keep him off the track.

Quorto beat the subsequent Derby winner Anthony Van Dyck by a length and a quarter in the National Stakes at the Curragh so it was very disappointing he didn't appear as a three-year-old. I am encouraged to see that he is listed as remaining in training this season.

One would not expect a son of Lope De Vega out of a mare by Peintre Celebre to be early but El Drama is in the right hands and I will be keeping him in mind for a back-end maiden.

ED VAUGHAN

BRIDLINGTON BOBBY
20/1 b g Swiss Spirit - Primrose Valley (Pastoral Pursuits)
Owner: A M Pickering
Sales price: n/a

First foal of a very useful multiple 5-6f winner who was a full sister to triple 6f winner Costa Filey out of a multiple 5-5.5f winning half-sister to Listed-placed French 6f 3yo winner Newcastle and French 5.5-6f 3yo winner Kentucky Beauty (later dam of French 1m 1f 3yo Group 3 winner Bodhi); the family of smart sprinters King's Signet and Sicyos.

"A strong, mature two-year-old. He is already gelded and, like his mother, has his fair share of quirks. However, that didn't stop her from winning six races and ending up racing at a good level. He looks nice and will make a two-year-old, but it will be more about whether or not his temperament gets the better of him."

VOICE OF GLORY
4/5 b f Poet's Voice - Vanity Rules (New Approach)
Owner: Anthony Oppenheimer
Sales price: 115,000gns (Not Sold)

Half-sister to 2019 5f 2yo winner Xcelente. Dam a Listed-placed 8.5f 3yo winner who was a three-parts sister to 14f Group 3 winner Precious Ramotswe and a half-sister to Listed-placed 10-10.5f winner This Is The Day and the maiden dam of Group 3-placed US 5f 2yo winner Elizabeth Darcy out of a 1m 3yo Listed winning daughter of a Coronation Stakes winner who was a half-sister to the dam of top-class middle-distance performer Golden Horn.

"She isn't here yet but the reports from her pre-trainer, Malcolm Bastard, have been encouraging. I trained the dam in the latter part of her career and she placed at Listed level a couple of times as a four-year-old. She was a fine big sort and this filly is much the same. One for the backend and next year."

UNNAMED (IRE)

14/4 b c Free Eagle - Alice Treasure (Canford Cliffs)
Owner: Lee, Moroney, Singh & Partner
Sales price: 12,000gns (Paul Moroney Bloodstock/Ed Vaughan)

First foal of an unraced half-sister to useful Irish 7-10.5f winner Major Reward out of an unraced half-sister to Group 2-placed 7-12f winner (including at Group 3/Listed level) Rabah, dual 6f 2yo winner/Cheveley Park Stakes third Najiya (later dam of Swedish two-time 6f Listed winner Bush Baby), useful 7f 2yo winner Nayyel and the dam of Irish 12f 3yo Group 3 winner/Irish Oaks runner-up Ice Queen; the excellent family of 2019 English and Irish 1000 Guineas winner Hermosa, French 1000 Guineas winner Valentine Waltz and Coronation Stakes winner Immortal Verse.

"A lovely horse physically who is looking like he will come to hand earlier than his pedigree suggests. He will undoubtedly need seven furlongs to begin with, but should be pretty much ready to go once those races are here."

UNNAMED (IRE) Miss Chess

20/1 b f Zoffany - Chenchikova (Sadler's Wells)
Owner: Phoenix Thoroughbred Limited
Sales price: €220,000 (Phoenix Thoroughbred/D Farrington)

Closely related to fairly useful 7-10f winner Unex Michelangelo (by Dansili) and a half-sister to Irish 7f 2yo Group 3 winner Smuggler's Cove, French 12/12.5f Listed winner Casterton and 2019 Irish 1m 2yo Listed winner Fancy Blue. Dam a useful Irish 7.5f 2yo winner who was a sister to top-class middle-distance performer High Chaparral, Dante Stakes winner Black Bear Island and Listed-placed Irish 10f 3yo winner Helena Molony and a half-sister to the unraced dam of Australian 12.5f Group 2 winner Hunting Horn and Irish 1m 2yo Group 2 winner David Livingston.

"A lovely, athletic filly that has a nice way of going. She has done a couple of bits of work and we like what we see. I imagine she will be racing in July or August and will want seven furlongs to begin with - being out of a Galileo mare."

UNNAMED

10/2 b f Mayson - Kaminari (Sea The Stars)
Owner: The Machell Place Partnership
Sales price: 20,000gns (Paul Moroney Bloodstock/Ed Vaughan)

Half-sister to 2019 12f 3yo winner Glorious Dane. Dam an Irish 1m 2yo winner who was a half-sister to Group 1-placed French 7.5f 2yo winner On Verra and Listed-placed French/US 8-8.5f winner Keladora out of a French 1m 1f 3yo Listed winner/French 1000 Guineas runner-up who was a half-sister to French 1m 3yo Listed winner Kart Star.

"She is on a break at the moment but will be back in by May. Not the biggest but has quite a nice page - the dam was a winner at two in Ireland and there are a couple of relations in France who placed in the Prix Marcel Boussac and 1000 Guineas over there. One for the six and seven furlong races whenever she is ready to race."

UNNAMED

18/2 b f Kingman - Madam President (Royal Applause)
Owner: Phoenix Thoroughbred Limited
Sales price: 270,000gns (Phoenix Thoroughbreds)

Half-sister to high-class Irish 5-6f 2yo winner (including at Group 3/Listed level)/Coventry Stakes runner-up Cappella Sansevero. Dam a 10f winner who was a half-sister to 7f 3yo winner/Ribblesdale Stakes second Eldalil, useful 9-14f winner High Office and 10f winners Bronze Star and Monicalew out of a 10f 3yo winning half-sister to 12f Group 2 winner Little Rock, French 13.5f Group 2 winner/Yorkshire Oaks second Whitewater Affair (later dam of Dubai World Cup winner Victoire Pisa), 10.5/12f Group 3 winner/Oaks third Short Skirt and 5f 2yo Listed winner Seductress.

"A sizeable but typically athletic Kingman filly. She has a great mind on her and goes very nicely, though she had a little niggle which was to do with immaturity more than anything. Her half-brother was a very good two-year-old and although she will take more time than he did, I hope she is one to look forward to later on in the year."

Marten writes:

I will be keen to see how the unnamed Free Eagle colt gets along.

Not dear at just 12,000gns as a yearling, this first foal of a daughter of Canford Cliffs is by Free Eagle, who won three races for Dermot Weld including the Group 1 Prince of Wales's Stakes on his four-year-old seasonal debut. He was a little unlucky when short of room in the Irish Champion Stakes and the Arc and has since made a steady start at stud, with Listed winner and Group-placed Beauty Smile his highest earner.

The dam Alice Treasure never ran but has had two winners at stud with Major Reward and Mister Jo. She comes from the family of the very useful Rabah, Cheveley Park third Najiya from the family of Irish Oaks runner-up Ice Queen and English and Irish Guineas winner Hermosa. The line traces back further to a French Guineas winner and Coronation Stakes winner Immortal Verse.

You don't often see names of this quality on the page of a 12,000gns colt and his trainer believes he may come to hand earlier than his pedigree suggests.

He looks well bought.

TOM WARD

AMAZALI (IRE)
31/3 b f Elzaam - Taffetta (Paco Boy)
Owner: Altitude Racing 1
Sales price: 15,000gns (Marcus Collie/Tom Ward Racing)

First foal of a dual 5f winner who was a half-sister to Group 2-placed 7-10f winner (including at Group 3 level) Enforcer, useful UK/UAE 5-7f winner Zalzilah, useful dual 5f 2yo winner Lord Of The Inn, six other winners and the maiden dam of 2019 Norfolk Stakes/Prix Robert Papin winner A'Ali.

"She is very sharp and would have been amongst our first runners if we were racing. She shows plenty of speed and has trialled well."

AUSSIE RASCAL (IRE)
29/4 ch c Australia - Refusetolisten (Clodovil)
Owner: Charlie Rosier & Mrs Julia Rosier
Sales price: 45,000gns (Stroud Coleman Bloodstock/Tom Ward)

Half-brother to useful 6-7f winner Dirty Rascal and 2019 6f 2yo winner Stormy Girl. Dam an Irish 7f 3yo winning daughter of a maiden half-sister to US 6.5-8.5f Grade 3 winner Snowdrop (later dam of Group 2-placed 7-8.5f winner (including at Group 3/Listed level) Tawhid) out of a Listed-placed UK/US 6f-1m winner; the family of 1m 2yo Group 1 winner Tenby, 12f Group 2 winner Exosphere and 10f 3yo Listed winner/Oaks runner-up Something Exciting.

"He is a half-brother to the same owners' Dirty Rascal, but was never going to be as precocious as that one, being by Australia. He is well put together, but we've not pushed any buttons yet. One for the seven furlong races a bit later on."

BILANDY
1/2 b f Adaay - Showstoppa (Showcasing)
Owner: Ontoawinner & Whitsbury Manor Stud
Sales price: 35,000gns (Stroud Coleman/Ward/Ontoawinner)

Half-sister to 2019 Italian 6f 2yo Listed winner Avengers Queen. Dam a useful 5-6f winner who was a half-sister to 6f 2yo Group 2 winner Temple Meads, Group 3/Listed-placed 6f 2yo winner Sneak Preview, useful 5-6f winner O'Gorman and dual 6f winner Exist out of a useful dual 5f 2yo winner; the family of 5f 2yo Listed winner Fortunately.

"She is starting to learn what it's all about now and ought to be a relatively early type. She will likely start out over six furlongs and is sure to improve with racing."

DIAMOND BAY
11/2 ch c New Bay - Amarillo Starlight (Dalakhani)
Owner: Ebury Racing 5
Sales price: 17,000gns (Will Edmeades Bloodstock/Tom Ward)

Third foal of an unraced half-sister to six winners out of a Group 3-placed 10-12f 3yo winner (including at Listed level) who was a sister to 12f 3yo Listed winner Peach Out Of Reach and a half-sister to top-class 10-12f winner (including six times at Group/Grade 1 level) Pilsudski, Irish 1m 2yo Group 3 winner Glowing Ardour, Lingfield Oaks Trial winner Baraka and the grandam of dual 12f Group 1 winner/three-time Arc runner-up Youmzain.

"He has size but needs to fill out a bit. I'm happy with how he's going though, and he should be starting out over seven furlongs during the middle part of the season."

FILLE D'OR (IRE)
3/2 b f Dandy Man - Frabrika (Intense Focus)
Owner: Mrs Elaine Roberts
Sales price: £42,000 (Will Edmeades)

First foal of a maiden half-sister to very useful 7f-1m winner Temptress, useful 6f 3yo winner Shahzan, dual 7f 3yo winner Dream Date (later dam of Group 1-placed multiple 5f winner (including at Group 3/Listed level) Extortionist (by Dandy Man)), 7f 2yo winner Sadie Thompson and three other winners out of a 6f 2yo Listed winning half-sister to dual 10f 3yo Listed winner Foodbroker Fancy (later grandam of Nassau Stakes winner Sultanina).

"This is a strong, well put together individual who looks like an early runner. She has plenty of boot and will more than likely start out over five furlongs when we return to action. I hope she can contest some nice races later on."

FLIRTY RASCAL
2/2 b f Acclamation - Enliven (Dansili)
Owner: Charlie Rosier & Mrs Julia Rosier
Sales price: €37,000 (Stroud Coleman Bloodstock/Tom Ward)

Half-sister to 2019 5f 2yo winner Iva Go and 6f 2yo winner Windy Guest. Dam a 7f 3yo winning daughter of a half-sister to French Oaks winner/Arc runner-up Aquarelliste (later dam of Group 1-placed French 9.5-10f winner (including at Listed level) Ame Bleue and grandam of Listed winners Art Du Val (1m) and Maqsad (10f)), US 10f Grade 1 winner Artiste Royal and Group 1-placed French/Australian 8-12f winner (including at Listed level) Annenkov.

"This filly is coming along nicely and shows plenty of speed. She should be ready to roll whenever racing resumes, and will almost certainly begin over five furlongs."

LITTLE MISS RASCAL
21/1 b f Zoffany - Hibiscus (Galileo)
Owner: Charlie Rosier & Mrs Julia Rosier
Sales price: £32,000 (SackvilleDonald/Tom Ward)

First foal of a Listed-placed Irish 10f 3yo winner who was a sister to Breeders' Cup Juvenile Turf winner Line Of Duty and Irish 9.5f 3yo winner World War out of a 7f 2yo winner/1000 Guineas runner-up who was a half-sister to Listed-placed 10-12f winner Mam'selle out of a 12f-2m 1f winning half-sister to Group 2-placed 8.5-10f winner (including twice at Group 3 level) Regime and Group 2/3-placed dual 5f 2yo winner (including at Listed level) Salut D'Amour.

"It is a slow-maturing family but one that has done well recently, with Line Of Duty especially smart. This filly is very much one for the future and is essentially a three-year-old type, but I hope we can get a run into her at two."

MERRY SECRET (IRE)
8/2 b c Elzaam - Secret Liaison (Dandy Man)
Owner: Ontoawinner & Matthew Webber
Sales price: £37,000 (Stroud Coleman Bloodstock/Tom Ward)

Half-brother to useful 2019 5-6f winner Dazzling Des. Dam a useful 5f 2yo winner who was a half-sister to useful 8-10.5f winner Desert Kiss out of a maiden sister to Group 2-placed Irish 5-6f 2yo winner (including at Group 3/ Listed level) Raphane and half-sister to Listed-placed French 6f 2yo winner Nellie Nolan and Listed-placed French 1m 1f 3yo winner Where's Dave; the family of US 6.5f 2yo Grade 2 winner All Chatter.

"A strongly-built, straightforward individual who looks like being the early type his pedigree suggests he should be. He loves his job and is showing all the right signs currently. Will kick off over five furlongs."

RAGING RASCAL (IRE)
22/3 b c Coulsty - Limousine (Beat Hollow)
Owner: Charlie Rosier & Mrs Julia Rosier
Sales price: 30,000gns (Stroud Coleman Bloodstock/Tom Ward)

Half-brother to Listed-placed 2019 dual 7f 2yo winner Sesame Birah. Dam a 12f 3yo winner who was a half-sister to four winners including Italian 10f Group 3 winner Distain out of a Listed-placed 12-15f winning half-sister to 7f 2yo Listed winner Protectress and useful 12-14f winner Acquisition (later dam of French 10.5f Group 3 winner Gainful).

"This is a really nice colt. His sire was a good-looking, talented horse who was at Richard Hannon's when I was there, and the mare also comes from a very good family. He is a strong sort with plenty of scope and is uncomplicated. I think he will prove best at six and seven furlongs this year."

SPRING TIME BAY (IRE)
24/1 b f Fascinating Rock - Serenity Dove (Harbour Watch)
Owner: Cormac Doyle
Sales price: €25,000 (Stroud Coleman Bloodstock/Tom Ward)

First foal of a maiden half-sister to French 1m 3yo Listed winner Madhya, French 6f 2yo Listed winner Wilki and useful French 6f-1m winner Jodphur out of a Grade 2-placed French/US 5.5-9f winner (including at Grade 3 level).

"I love this filly. Her sire is something of a stamina influence, but she's not short of speed and should do something over sprint distances this season. She has a terrific attitude and a nice action. I have high hopes for her."

STAR OF DEAUVILLE (IRE)
24/4 b f Dandy Man - Happy Land (Refuse To Bend)
Owner: Daniel McAuliffe, Anoj Don & Partners
Sales price: €38,000 (Stroud Coleman Bloodstock/Tom Ward)

Half-sister to very useful multiple 1m winner Bless Him and four other winners. Dam an unraced half-sister to US 8.5f 2yo Grade 1 winner Creaking Board, German 1000 Guineas winner Dakhla Oasis, Group 2-placed 5.5-6f winner (including twice at Group 3 level) Dyhim Diamond and German 11f 3yo Listed winner Santenay.

"She won't be overly early but is showing all the right signs. She comes from a decent family and can hopefully make up into a useful filly. Will likely want six and seven furlongs."

UNNAMED (IRE)
11/3 b f Vadamos - La Marchesa (Duke Of Marmalade)
Owner: M H Dixon & Luke Lillingston
Sales price: 30,000gns (Stroud Coleman/Tom Ward)

Half-sister to 2019 Italian 1m 2yo winner Laurus Nobilis. Dam an unraced half-sister to six winners including 12f Listed winner Livia's Dream out of a 1m 3yo Listed winning half-sister to very useful 8.5f 3yo winner La Spezia (later dam of smart dual-purpose performer Thomas Hobson); the family of Oaks winner/St Leger runner-up Talent.

"A sizeable filly with plenty of scope who will want seven furlongs at least. Her half-sister in Italy looks a promising sort and could be a black type performer in the making."

UNNAMED (IRE)

21/2 b c Belardo - No Such Zone (Oasis Dream)
Owner: Matthew Webber, M T Ward, Schiff Family
Sales price: £15,000 (SackvilleDonald/Tom Ward)

Fourth foal of an unraced sister to Listed-placed 1m-2m 2f winner Address Unknown and half-sister to smart UK/US 6f-1m winner (including at Listed level) To Sender and 10f 3yo winner Coming Back (later dam of smart stayer Withhold) out of a 10f 3yo winner who was a sister to Derby runner-up/St Leger third Dushyantor and a half-sister to Derby winner Commander In Chief, Sussex Stakes winner Warning and US 10f Grade 1 winner Yashmak.

"A strong, well put together colt that has a bit of class about him. He has blossomed since we purchased him last autumn and should do well over six and seven furlongs this year."

Marten writes:

Tom Ward, who started out as a trainer last autumn, can call upon a wide range of experience to guide him through his new career.

Four years as assistant to Richard Hannon, before that he worked for Darley, Mark Johnston, Pat Chamings, spent time in France with Alain de Royer-Dupre and Francis Graffard and a period with Kiaran McLaughlin in the States.

He joined Hannon after working with John O'Shea in Australia and he's already had a handful of winners to get his name on the board.

Judging by the above list a few more will be coming his way this season because he has a mix of precocity and stamina, with some strong names on the page.

Little Miss Rascal has a strong bottom line.

A daughter of Phoenix Stakes winner Zoffany, who ran Frankel to three-quarters of a length in the St James's Palace Stakes, she is the first foal of Hibiscus, a winning daughter of Galileo out of Henry Cecil's disqualified 1000 Guineas winner Jacqueline Quest.

Hibiscus, who cost 625,000gns as a yearling, is a sister to Godolphin's Breeders' Cup Juvenile Turf winner Line Of Duty, who last year ran down the field in the Derby before reaching the frame in two Group 1s and a Group 2.

This filly has a lot on the page for the £32,000 she cost at the sales. Let's hope she proves as well bought as it appears.

SECTION TWO

We were delighted that a selection of owners, syndicate managers, breeders and bloodstock agents shared with Dan the following thoughts on the two-year-olds they consider to be of particular interest for the coming year.

Ashbrittle Stud/M H Dixon

Many thanks to representative, Barry Thompkins, for offering the following trio of homebreds from James Rowsell's Ashbrittle Stud in Somerset, owned and bred in partnership with Mark Dixon.

Although still early days, and with all three hailing from the same excellent family that thrives with age, Barry comments: *"My favourite of the three at this stage would be **Sibling**, who has made huge improvement of late and has got the looks to be up there with her Oaks-winning sister, Talent. **Fiesty** is pretty well named but has lots of quality and is bigger and stronger than her mother, while **Pretty Fair** looks very similar to her smart sister, Ambition."*

FIESTY
22/2 ch f Siyouni - Forte (New Approach)
Trainer: Ralph Beckett
Sales price: n/a

First foal of a useful 1m 2yo winner who was a full sister to Oaks winner/St Leger runner-up Talent (later dam of 2019 French 10.5f 3yo Group 3 winner Ambition) and a half-sister to Listed-placed 7f-1m winner Skilful out of a Listed-placed 12f 3yo winning half-sister to Listed-placed 11.5f 3yo winner Genoa (later dam of 1m Listed winner Brindisi and grandam of smart dual purpose performer Thomas Hobson) and Listed-placed 1m 2yo winner Clipper.

Talent winning the 2013 Oaks. Her daughter, Pretty Fair, and full sister, Sibling, will hope to carry on the strong family tradition of success at a smart level that goes right back to 1980 Oaks winner Bireme.

PRETTY FAIR (IRE)
16/4 ch f Dubawi - Talent (New Approach)
Trainer: Simon Crisford
Sales price: n/a

Full sister to 2019 French 10.5f 3yo Group 3 winner Ambition. Dam an Oaks winner who was a full sister to useful 1m 2yo winner Forte and a half-sister to Listed-placed 7f-1m winner Skilful and fairly useful 6f 2yo winner Much Promise out of a Listed-placed 12f 3yo winner who was half-sister to Listed-placed winners Clipper (1m) and Genoa (11.5f).

SIBLING
12/4 ch f New Approach - Prowess (Peintre Celebre)
Trainer: Ed Walker
Sales price: n/a

Full sister to high-class 7-12f winner (including the Oaks)/St Leger second Talent (later dam of 2019 French 10.5f 3yo Group 3 winner Ambition) and useful 1m 2yo winner Forte and a half-sister to Listed-placed 7f-1m winner Skilful. Dam a Listed-placed 12f 3yo winner who was a half-sister to Listed-placed 11.5f 3yo winner Genoa (later dam of 1m Listed winner Brindisi) and Listed-placed 1m 2yo winner Clipper (later dam of Irish 7f 2yo Listed winner Mister Tee) out of a 7f 2yo Group 3 winner who was a half-sister to the dam of 1m Listed winner Staying On.

Clipper Logistics (Joe Foley)

RUNWAY QUEEN
8/4 ch f Kitten's Joy - Puzzled Look (Sakhee's Secret)
Trainer: Archie Watson
Sales price: 50,000gns (Joe Foley)

First foal of a 7f 2yo winner who was a half-sister to Group 3-placed 6-6.5f winner Laugh A Minute, Group 3-placed 2019 6f 2yo winner Endless Joy and useful dual 7f 3yo winner Horroob out of a thrice-raced maiden half-sister to smart 6f-1m winner (including at Listed level) Oasis Dancer, Group 3-placed UK/Swedish multiple 1m winner (including at Listed level) Smart Enough and useful 7f-1m winner Sufficient; the family of smart stayer Jardine's Lookout.

"We have got her relation, Endless Joy, who is a useful performer also with Archie Watson. This filly has shown up well in her early work."

SOUTHERN VOYAGE (FR)
5/5 b c Wootton Bassett - Blue Blue Sea (Galileo)
Trainer: Archie Watson
Sales price: €120,000 (Joe Foley)

Half-brother to French 7.5-9f winner Khorodov. Dam a useful French 1m 3yo winner who was a half-sister to French 7f-1m winner Onirique and French 9-10.5f winner Blink out of a Group 3-placed French 5-7f 2yo winner (including at Listed level) who was the daughter of a maiden half-sister to French 1000 Guineas winner Bluemamba.

"A quality colt by a good sire and out of a Galileo mare (like our 2019 Group 2 and Group 3 winner Space Traveller). He moves nicely and has taken pre-training well."

UNNAMED (IRE)   *Escape Route*

22/2 b c Dandy Man - Elaysa (Shamardal)
Trainer: Richard Fahey
Sales price: 50,000gns (Joe Foley)

Second foal of a German 7-7.5f 3yo winner who was the daughter of a 7f
3yo winning half-sister to very smart multiple 5-6f winner (including twice
at Group 1 level) Kingsgate Native and Stakes-placed UK/US 5-6.5f winner
Vanishing Grey (later dam of Group 1-placed 7f-1m 3yo winner (including at
Listed level) First Contact); the family of 1000 Guineas winner Las Meninas,
Queen Mary Stakes winner Signora Cabello and Flying Childers Stakes winner
Sheer Viking.

*"A really attractive colt out of a Shamardal mare we bought from Tally-Ho Stud
at Book 2. He is a strong, powerful individual who does everything with ease at
the moment."*

UNNAMED

2/3 b f Frankel - Noozhah (Singspiel)
Trainer: William Haggas
Sales price: n/a

Half-sister to Group 1-placed Spanish/French 4f-1m winner (including at Listed
level) Noozhoh Canarias, French 5f 2yo Listed winner Money Maker, Listed-
placed Spanish 5.5f 2yo winner Corazon Canarias, useful 6-7f winner Wise
Counsel and once-raced 2019 7f 2yo winner Higher Kingdom. Dam a Spanish
8-11f winning daughter of an unraced half-sister to French 12f Listed winner
Gallery God, the dam of 12f Group 3 winners St Mawes and Steppe Dancer
and the great-grandam of Group 1-placed multiple 5-6f winner (including at
Group 2/3 level) Utmost Respect.

*"A homebred from Branton Court, she has been a beautiful filly right from the
start and is impressing in her early work. A fine big individual, she looks a nice
prospect for a late summer and autumn campaign."*

UNNAMED (IRE)

15/3 b f Ajaya - Thousandfold (Giant's Causeway)
Trainer: Kevin Ryan
Sales price: 55,000gns (Joe Foley)

Half-sister to Grade 2/Listed-placed US 5.5-8.5f winner Kazan and 2019 7f 2yo
winner Good Job Power. Dam an unraced half-sister to Listed-placed French
1m 2yo winner Secret Admirer and the unraced dam of US 8.5f 3yo Listed

winner Mo d'Amour out of a Group 2/3-placed dual 5f 2yo winner (including at Listed level) who was a half-sister to dual 10f Group 3 winner Regime and Listed-placed Irish 10f 3yo winner Coquette Rouge (later dam of 7f 2yo winner/1000 Guineas second Jacqueline Quest, herself dam of Breeders' Cup Juvenile Turf winner Line Of Duty).

"This filly was purchased at Book 3 from Rathbarry Stud. She is a sizeable sort with a great action who also shows a lot of athleticism and power. She's out of a Giant's Causeway mare who has already bred a good one in the States."

Matt Coleman (Bloodstock Agent)

STAR OF DEAUVILLE (FR)
24/4 b f Dandy Man - Happy Land (Refuse To Bend)
Trainer: Tom Ward Owner: Daniel McAuliffe, Anoj Don & Partners
Sales price: €38,000 (Stroud Coleman Bloodstock/Tom Ward)

Half-sister to very useful multiple 1m winner Bless Him and four other winners. Dam an unraced half-sister to US 8.5f 2yo Grade 1 winner Creaking Board, German 1000 Guineas winner Dakhla Oasis, Group 2-placed 5.5-6f winner (including twice at Group 3 level) Dyhim Diamond and German 11f 3yo Listed winner Santenay.

"She is a half-sister to Britannia Stakes winner, Bless Him, and has looked smart in her early work for up-and-coming trainer, Tom Ward."

THUNDERCLAP (IRE)
13/5 b c Night Of Thunder - Former Drama (Dynaformer)
Trainer: Hughie Morrison Owner: Sir Thomas Pilkington & Mr R A Pilkington
Sales price: 70,000gns (Stroud Coleman Bloodstock/H Morrison)

Half-brother to five winners including Irish 1m 1f Listed winner Champagne Or Water. Dam a maiden half-sister to Group 1-placed 6f-1m winner (including twice at Group 2 level) Endless Drama and useful multiple 6f winners Always A Drama and Histoire out of a 5f 3yo Listed winner; the family of smart performers Ghaiyyath, King's Drama and Rosinka.

"He is a sizeable individual bred to thrive as a three-year-old, but he has impressed Hughie Morrison so far."

UNNAMED (IRE)

20/5 b c Tamayuz - Marah Dubai (Dubawi)
Trainer: John Joseph Murphy Owner: John Joseph Murphy
Sales price: 43,000gns (Stroud Coleman Bloodstock/John Murphy)

Half-brother to Group 3-placed French 12-15f winner Haky and Australian 7.5-10f winner Malmas. Dam a maiden half-sister to French 10f 3yo Group 1 winner Belle Et Celebre, French/Italian dual 10f Group 2 winner Whortleberry, five-time Swedish/German 9-12f Group 3 winner Appel Au Maitre, French triple 8-9.5f Group 3 winner Valentino and French 1m 2yo winner/French 1000 Guineas third Ysoldina (later dam of Derby winner Wings Of Eagles).

"We thought this colt was one of the best horses at Book 3 of the Tattersalls October Yearling sale. He is a half-brother to a stakes-placed French and Australian winner called Haky and is from a top French family. While very much a middle-distance, three-year-old prospect, he is one to keep an eye on as he matures."

UNNAMED

27/4 b f Sea The Stars - Party (Cadeaux Genereux)
Trainer: John Joseph Murphy Owner: John Joseph Murphy
Sales price: 55,000gns (Stroud Coleman Bloodstock/John Murphy)

Half-sister to smart UK/Australian 8-11f winner (including at Group 3/Listed level) Observational and useful 12-14f winner Party Line. Dam a 7f 2yo Listed winner who was a full sister to useful 7f 2yo winner Jummana (later dam of French 1000 Guineas winner Teppal and Group 3/Listed-placed French 5-6.5f winner Another Party); the family of Group 1 winners Call The Wind, Dominant, We Are and With You and smart pair Lily's Angel and Zurigha.

"One of the cheapest Sea The Stars fillies sold at Book 1 of the Tattersalls October Yearling sale, but initial reports suggest that she will outrun her purchase price."

Sara Cumani (Fittocks Stud)

DREAM A LITTLE

27/2 b f Oasis Dream - Got To Dream (Duke Of Marmalade)
Trainer: Ed Walker Owner: Hot To Trot Racing 1 & Fittocks Stud
Sales price: 45,000gns (Vendor)

Second foal of a 12f 3yo winner who was a half-sister to 10f 3yo Listed winner/ Oaks third Lady Of Dubai, useful 10-12f 3yo winner Saving Grace and French

10-10.5f 3yo winner Indian Skies out of an unraced close relation to Irish 13f Listed winner/Irish Oaks second Roses For The Lady and useful Irish 12f 3yo winner Dance The Classics (later dam of Irish 1m 1f 2yo Listed winner Call To Battle); family of St Leger winner Millenary and Derby third Let The Lion Roar.

"Although physically this filly looks a sharp two-year-old type, I don't think Ed believes she is that precocious and views her as more of an autumn horse, though who knows what the racing calendar is going to look like this year!"

ROOSTER
17/4 ch c Showcasing - Slatey Hen (Acclamation)
Trainer: Hughie Morrison Owner: Michael Kerr-Dineen & Martin Hughes Sales price: 78,000gns (H Morrison)

Half-brother to dual 5f winner Gold Stone and 2019 6f 2yo winner Foad. Dam a 5-6f winner who was a half-sister to smart multiple 5-5.5f winner (including at Group 3/Listed level) Masta Plasta and 5f 2yo winner Kheleyf's Silver (dam of Cheveley Park Stakes winner/1000 Guineas third Tiggy Wiggy) out of a maiden half-sister to Listed-placed 6f 2yo winner Ras Shaikh (dam of 7f Group 3 winner Racer Forever and grandam of 1m 2yo Listed winner Gallic Star).

"Whilst we aren't really known for breeding speedy two-year-olds, we did buy this colt's dam a few years ago specifically because she was tough and had good, fast relations. She has had two winners from three runners to date and we think this colt is the best she has produced so far. He is trained by Hughie Morrison who you wouldn't usually associate with two-year-old types, but that probably won't matter too much given what's happening at present."

UNNAMED
1/3 b c Dubawi - Koora (Pivotal)
Trainer: Charlie Appleby Owner: Godolphin
Sales price: 400,000gns (Godolphin)

First foal of a Group 2-placed 10-12f 3yo winner (including at Group 3 level) who was a half-sister to St Leger winner/Breeders' Cup Turf runner-up Milan, Group 3-placed 7f 2yo winner Go For Gold, Listed-placed 10-14f 3yo winner Kahara (later dam of German 2000 Guineas winner Karpino) and 11.5f 3yo winner Kibara (later dam of 2019 US 8.5f Stakes winner Dubara (by Dubawi)) out of a 12f 3yo Group 3 winner; the family of Derby winner Kahyasi.

"While we are obviously biased, we thought he was a lovely horse and the only reason Luca regretted giving up training was because he didn't get the chance

to train this colt himself! I doubt he will make much of a two-year-old given his pedigree, but we've always liked him and thought he was a fine first foal. He has an equally nice full brother due to sell later this year, and Koora has very recently produced a lovely colt by Galileo."

Dubawi was the top performing son of sire Dubai Millennium's first and only crop. His most notable success came in the 2005 Irish 2000 Guineas.

Alastair Donald (Bloodstock Agent)

BEYOND BOUNDARIES (IRE)
20/3 ch c Australia - What A Treasure (Cadeaux Genereux)
Trainer: Andrew Balding Owner: King Power Racing Co Ltd
Sales price: 280,000gns (SackvilleDonald)

Full brother to smart Irish 7-13f winner (including at Listed level)/Racing Post Trophy third Western Australia and a half-brother to very useful 7-10f winner (including at Listed level) Hoarding. Dam a dual 7f 3yo winner who was a sister to French 7f Group 1 Toylsome and a half-sister to 6f 2yo Group 3 winner Coral Mist; the family of 2013 St Leger winner Leading Light.

"This colt is very much one for next year, but is an unbelievably good mover. An exciting middle-distance prospect for the future."

DILLYDINGDILLYDONG
22/2 b c Territories - Cephalonie (Kris S)
Trainer: Richard Hannon Owner: King Power Racing Co Ltd
Sales price: 110,000gns (SackvilleDonald)

Three-parts brother to French 1m 3yo Listed winner Arctic Gyr, Group 3-placed 6f-1m winner (including at Listed level) Festivale and useful 6f 2yo winner Simple Magic (all by Invincible Spirit) and a half-brother to Group 3/Listed-placed 6f-1m winner Tell. Dam a French 12f 3yo winner from the excellent family of Arc winner Bago, French Oaks winner Senga and very smart French two-year-old performers Denebola and Machiavellian.

"This colt has an excellent outlook, is a super mover and finds life very easy. He is from a good family and should be ready around June or July time for the six and seven furlong races."

FOREVER GLORIOUS
5/2 b c Archipenko - Aksaya (Sea The Stars)
Trainer: Ed Walker Owner: Kangyu International Racing (HK) Limited
Sales price: 80,000gns (SackvilleDonald)

First foal of an unraced half-sister to useful 7.5-8.5f winner Akvavera and two other winners out of a Group 1-placed Irish 8.5-10f winner (including at Group 3/Listed level) who was a half-sister to five winners including the dam of Irish 12f Listed winner Aklan out of a Group 2-placed Irish 12f 3yo winning half-sister to high-class stayer Akbar.

"This colt is very much one for next year, but he should be ready to run come the early autumn when the mile races are here. There is lots to like about him."

MELODY OF LIFE (IRE)
1/3 b c Dark Angel - Tamarisk (Selkirk)
Trainer: Andrew Balding Owner: King Power Racing Co Ltd
Sales price: 425,000gns (SackvilleDonald)

Full brother to smart 6f-1m winner (including at Listed level) Happy Power. Dam an unraced half-sister to 7f 2yo Group 2 winner Cairns, Listed-placed German 11.5f 3yo winner Tanamia, useful UK/UAE 5-6f winner Machynleth and the once-raced maiden dam of high-class French 7.5f-1m winner (including at Group 2/3 level)/French 1000 Guineas and French Oaks runner-up Tamazirte out of a smart 5-6f 2yo winner/Cheveley Park Stakes runner-up.

"He is a full brother to our Listed winner, Happy Power. This is a strong, athletic colt who looks like he will be a mid-season two-year-old. One for the six and seven furlong races."

WINTER POWER (IRE)

16/3 b f Bungle Inthejungle - Titian Saga (Titus Livius)
Trainer: Tim Easterby Owner: King Power Racing Co Ltd
Sales price: €90,000 (SackvilleDonald)

Half-sister to 5f 3yo Listed winner Hay Chewed, Listed-placed 5-7f winner
Flying Sparkle and useful 5f 2yo winner Pres Rapide. Dam a 6f 2yo winner who
was a half-sister to fairly useful multiple 5-6f winner Yungaburra and the dam
of high-class Irish 7-9f winner (including at Group 2/Listed level)/Irish 1000
Guineas third Devonshire and 5f 2yo Listed winner Hurryupharriet.

*"A sharp, precocious filly, and almost all of the family have been very quick. I
expect her to be in action as soon as we are ready to start again. She's highly
regarded by the stable."*

UNNAMED

25/3 b c Camelot - Beach Frolic (Nayef)
Trainer: Sir Michael Stoute Owner: King Power Racing Co Ltd
Sales price: 300,000gns (SackvilleDonald)

Half-brother to 2019 dual 7f 2yo winner Palace Pier and 10f 3yo winner
Tatweej. Dam an unraced half-sister to Group 1-placed UK/Australian 8-12f
winner (including at Group 2/Listed level) Bonfire, 1m Group 2 winner Joviality
and three other winners; the family of smart performers Arethusa, Comicas,
Karen's Caper and Rare Rhythm.

*"A half-brother to an exciting prospect in Palace Pier. This colt is a very athletic
individual, but very much one for the backend of the season. More of a three-
year-old type."*

UNNAMED (FR)   Longlai

22/2 b c Shalaa - Mojo Risin (Lope De Vega)
Trainer: Richard Hannon Owner: King Power Racing Co Ltd
Sales price: €130,000 (SackvilleDonald)

First foal of a French 10.5f 3yo Listed winner who was the granddaughter of
a Listed-placed French 1m 3yo winning half-sister to French 1m 1f 3yo Listed
winner Palacoona (later dam of US 1m 1f Grade 3 winner Diamond Tycoon and
11f Listed winner Cassique Lady), French dual 1m 3yo Listed winner Palafairia
and the dam of the smart Kendargent.

*"This colt is really catching the eye and does everything like a good horse
should. Hopefully he will be ready to contest six and seven furlong races in May
and June."*

UNNAMED (FR)   *Kingofthemidlands*

1/2 b c Kingman - Spin (Galileo)
Trainer: Andrew Balding Owner: King Power Racing Co Ltd
Sales price: €600,000 (SackvilleDonald)

Full brother to 2019 French 8-8.5f 3yo winner Bowled Over. Dam a Group 3/Listed-placed 1m 2yo winner who was a sister to French 12.5f 3yo Listed winner Dirgam and Irish 7f 3yo winner/1000 Guineas third Moth, a three-parts sister to Group 1-placed 8-10f winner (including at Listed level) Rave Reviews, 12f 3yo Listed winner Fermion (later dam of 6f 2yo winner/Coventry Stakes runner-up Roman Soldier) and Cheshire Oaks winner Sail and a half-sister to smart 8-10f winner (including at Group 3/Listed level) Hearthstead Maison.

"A quality individual by an exciting stallion. He will be one for seven furlong and mile races during the second half of the season".

Alex Elliott (Bloodstock Agent)

ASTIMEGOESBY (IRE)

14/2 ch c Mehmas - Chantaleen (Falco)
Trainer: George Boughey Owner: Mrs Susan Roy
Sales price: £40,000 (A C Elliott, Agent)

Half-brother to once-raced 2019 5f 2yo winner Bomb Proof. Dam a French 10f 3yo winner who was a half-sister to Group 2-placed French/Italian 7.5-9f winner (including at Group 3/Listed level) Spoil The Fun out of a once-raced maiden three-parts sister to French 7f 2yo Group 2 winner Roi Gironde and half-sister to smart French 10.5f 3yo Group 3 winner Garendare, 10f 3yo Listed winner Port Vila and Listed-placed French 8-10f winner Glen Falls.

"He is a half-brother to Bomb Proof, who won on his only start at York last season before injuring himself on the eve of Royal Ascot when well-fancied for the Norfolk Stakes. I bought Bomb Proof as a yearling and hopefully this colt will show just as much early on. He is in training with George Boughey who has made a great start to his career as a trainer, having previously been assistant to Hugo Palmer."

BARADAR (IRE)
4/3 b/br c Muhaarar - Go Lovely Rose (Pivotal)
Trainer: Roger Varian Owner: Amo Racing Limited
Sales price: 260,000gns (A C Elliott, Agent)

Half-brother to smart 2019 8-8.5f 3yo winner (including at Listed level) Roseman and Group 3-placed French 10.5-12f 3yo winner Game Zone. Dam a useful French 7.5f 3yo winner who was a sister to dual 1m 3yo Group 1 winner Immortal Verse out of a French 1m 3yo Listed winning sister to 6f 2yo Listed winner Flowerdrum and half-sister to Nunthorpe Stakes/Breeders' Cup Mile winner Last Tycoon, French 5f 2yo Group 2 winner The Perfect Life and the dams of French 1000 Guineas winner Valentine Waltz and French 5.5f 2yo Group 2 winner/Middle Park Stakes runner-up Zipping.

"Muhaarar was ice cold at last year's yearling sales after a lacklustre first season, and this is essentially what allowed us to buy this colt. If he had been by a 'sexier' sire, he would have brought in at least double what he went for given his pedigree and physique. He's out of a Pivotal mare who's a sister to a Group 1 winner and has already produced two stakes horses from three runners. This colt will be a late-summer two-year-old, but is doing everything right."

GOLDEN BEAR (IRE)
6/5 b c Kodiac - Golden Flower (Royal Applause)
Trainer: Charlie Fellowes Owner: Mrs Susan Roy
Sales price: 100,000gns (A C Elliott, Agent)

Full brother to useful 6f 2yo winner Mutawaffer and 2019 5f 2yo winner Harswell. Dam a dual 5f winner who was a full sister to 6f 2yo Group 3 winner Habaayib out of a US 6f-1m winning daughter of a US 6.5f 2yo Grade 2 winner.

"His brother, Mutawaffer, won on his second start before going on to contest the Windsor Castle at Royal Ascot, and I'd like to think that sort of programme would have been on this colt's agenda under normal circumstances. Mutawaffer's temperament was his biggest downfall so that will have to be minded, but Charlie Fellowes reports him to be doing well so far. Although a May foal, he is very typical of one by his sire, looking a sharp, quick horse."

JUST TELLEM (IRE)

20/4 b c Bungle Inthejungle - Art Of Gold (Excellent Art)
Trainer: Ralph Beckett Owner: Peter Mellett
Sales price: 80,000gns (A C Elliott, Agent)

Half-brother to very useful 7f-1m winner Kynren. Dam a maiden half-sister
to a 6f 2yo winner out of a Listed-placed triple 5f 2yo winning half-sister to
Group 1-placed Irish/UAE 5-6f winner (including twice at Listed level) Balmont
Mast, Group 1-placed 6f 2yo winner Crazee Mental (later dam of multiple
7f/1m Group 2 winner Premio Loco) and the dam of high-class 7-8.5f winner
(including at Group 2/3 level) Gregorian, Group 2-placed UK/Australian 7-12f
winner (including at Listed level) Naval Warfare and Listed-placed 8.5f 2yo
winner/1000 Guineas fourth Manderley.

*"He is a half-brother to David Barron's smart handicapper, Kynren, and is a
horse that has been stuck in my mind since we bought him. I am a big fan of
the sire, and this colt looks typically a fast, hardy type by him. He wouldn't
be the usual sort of horse that Ralph Beckett gets to train, inasmuch as he's a
precocious two-year-old. I think he will make an instant impact and be able to
hit his window of opportunity without too much fuss."*

MR RYDER

20/4 b c Pearl Secret - Jackline (Diktat)
Trainer: Michael Bell Owner: Amo Racing Limited & A C Elliott
Sales price: 25,000gns (A C Elliott, Agent)

Half-brother to Italian multiple 5-7f winner Excellent Jack, 6f 2yo winner
Epona and two other winners. Dam a maiden half-sister to smart 5-6f winner
(including at Group 3/Listed level) Elnawin, useful multiple 5f winner Normal
Equilibrium and useful multiple 5f-1m winner Elna Bright out of a useful 5-6f
2yo winner; the family of 2019 1m Group 2 winner Move Swiftly, 6f/1m Group
3 winner Satchem and 10.5f 3yo Group 3 winner Mulaqat.

*"A horse I took a real shine to in the back ring at Tattersalls, so I went in and
bought him without a client. I loved everything about him. He looked the
sort of tank that Wesley Ward brings over to Royal Ascot every summer. He
is showing up well at home, and although not bred in the purple looks like a
horse that may outrun his pedigree."*

MR SENSIBLE (USA)
12/5 b c Street Sense - Laura's Pleasure (Cactus Ridge)
Trainer: Roger Varian Owner: Amo Racing Limited
Sales price: $210,000 (Amo Racing)

Half-brother to useful UK/UAE 6-7f winner Important Mission. Dam a US 5-5.5f winner who was a half-sister to US 1m Grade 2 winner Withgreatpleasure, US 6f Stakes winner Sea Of Pleasure and four other winners.

"Street Sense is a horse I have admired ever since I was present to see him win the 2007 Kentucky Derby under Calvin Borel. After we purchased this colt, the sire's Maxfield won the Breeders' Futurity and was favourite for the Breeders' Cup Juvenile before being scratched on the eve of the race. If he had been sold later in the year after Maxfield's exploits, I am sure this colt would've gone for more money. He is now in training with Roger Varian and is a big, raw horse who probably won't be seen until the backend of the year, but is one to keep an eye on for the future."

Angus Gold (Hamdan Al Maktoum)

LANEQASH
22/1 b c Cable Bay - Bonhomie (Shamardal)
Trainer: Roger Varian
Sales price: £175,000 (Shadwell Stud)

First foal of an 8.5f 3yo winning half-sister to useful 8-10f winner Border Legend out of an unraced half-sister to smart French/US 8-9f winner (including Grade 2/Listed level) Calista and the grandams of French 8/10.5f Group 1 winner/French Derby runner-up Act One, French 1m 2yo Group 1 winner Ultra and French 12.5f 3yo Group 3 winner Synopsis and 10f 3yo Listed winners Cosmodrome and Splashdown (later dam of Solario Stakes winner Aktabantay); the family of Bosra Sham and Hector Protector.

"This colt was bought at Doncaster last summer and is by a sire who got plenty of winners with his first crop of two-year-olds last year. He is currently giving Roger Varian all the right signs at home."

MAWKEB

15/4 b/gr c Dark Angel - Best Terms (Exceed And Excel)
Trainer: William Haggas
Sales price: 425,000gns (Shadwell Estate Company)

Half-brother to Group 2/3-placed 7-12f winner (including at Listed level) Star Terms and French 10f 3yo Listed winner Fresh Terms. Dam a high-class 5-6f 2yo winner (including twice at Group 2 level) who was the daughter of an unraced half-sister to French 11f 3yo Group 2 winner Anton Chekhov, 2m Group 2 winner First Charter and 12f 3yo Listed winner/Italian Derby runner-up Private Charter; the family of Moyglare Stud Stakes winner Cursory Glance.

"A half-brother to a pair of Listed winners who was bought at Book 1 of the Tattersalls October Yearling sale last autumn. William Haggas reports that he goes up the hill very sweetly already, and he shouldn't be long in appearing once racing resumes."

MUTASALLEM (IRE)

5/2 b c Showcasing - Bright Glow (Exceed And Excel)
Trainer: Marcus Tregoning
Sales price: €240,000 (Shadwell Estate Company)

Half-brother to useful dual 6f 2yo winner Aldana. Dam a dual 7f 3yo winner who was a half-sister to very useful 7f-1m winner Kehaar, useful 5f 2yo winner All For Laura (later dam of 6f 2yo Group 2 winner/Cheveley Park Stakes runner-up Misheer, herself the dam of 6f 3yo Listed winner Mistrusting) and two other winners out of a 1m 3yo winning half-sister to Middle Park Stakes winner First Trump and Group 3-placed 6-7f winner First Veil.

"This horse was bought at the Goffs Orby sale last autumn and certainly looks like he should be a two-year-old."

UNNAMED   Alanmar

1/3 b c Siyouni - America Nova (Verglas)
Trainer: William Haggas
Sales price: 800,000gns (Shadwell Estate Company)

Half-brother to Group 1-placed UK/Australian 6-7.5f winner (including at Group 2/3 level) Weary, smart 6f-1m winner (including at Group 2/3 level) Nyaleti and smart French/US 7-8.5f winner (including at Grade/Group 3 level) Stellar Path. Dam a French 1m 2yo Listed winner who was a half-sister to French 12.5f 3yo Listed winner Cat Nova.

"This colt cost a great deal of money at Book 1, but he was an outstanding individual as a yearling and is a half-brother to a trio of high-class performers including Weary (previously known as Sir Patrick Moore in Europe)."

UNNAMED   *Hasenaat*

23/3 b f Oasis Dream - Hedaaya (Indian Ridge)
Trainer: Owen Burrows
Sales price: n/a

Sister to 1m 3yo winner Bawaasil, three-parts sister to Listed-placed Irish dual 7f winner Tamadhor (by Arcano) and a half-sister to two winners. Dam an Irish 8.5f 3yo winner who was a half-sister to 6f 2yo Group 2/3 winner Memory (later dam of smart stayer Call To Mind and Acomb Stakes winner Recorder), Irish 7f 2yo Group 3 winner Remember Alexander and useful 6-7f winner Kafuu; the family of Group 3 winners Bin Rosie (7f) and Generous Rosi (10f).

"Homebred filly out of a half-sister to Memory. She looks like making up into a very nice summer two-year-old."

Bill and Tim Gredley

Many thanks to Tim for offering the following trio of homebreds from the Gredley's breeding operation at Stetchworth & Middle Park Stud.

Tim says: *"While it is still early days, all three seem to be handling everything really well at home so far. They each have strong pedigrees, so fingers crossed they can live up to them at some point."*

AESTHETE
5/4 b c Muhaarar - Miss Brown To You (Fasliyev)
Trainer: Michael Bell
Sales price: n/a

Half-brother to very smart 10f-2m 4f winner (including the Ascot Gold Cup) Big Orange and useful triple 12f 3yo winner India. Dam a 1m 3yo winner who was a half-sister to very smart 8-10f winner (including twice at Group 1 level) Military Attack, Group 2-placed multiple 5f winner (including at Group 3/Listed level) Almaty, very useful 7-10f winner Impeller and the maiden dam of Hong Kong Vase winner/Melbourne Cup runner-up Red Cadeaux.

GREAT VIBES
13/3 b f Showcasing - Whazzat (Daylami)
Trainer: George Scott
Sales price: n/a

Half-sister Group 1-placed 6-7f winner (including at Group 2/3 level) James Garfield, Listed-placed 7.5f-1m winner The Shrew, useful 8-10f 3yo winner Eva Maria and 6-7f winner Theladyinquestion (later dam of Group 3/Listed-placed 6-9f winner Nate The Great). Dam a Chesham Stakes winner who was a half-sister to smart 7f-1m winner (including at Group 3/Listed level) Whazzis and the maiden dam of Group 2-placed 2019 7f 2yo winner Juan Elcano.

STANLEY BALDWIN
7/3 br c Showcasing - Madame Defarge (Motivator)
Trainer: Michael Bell
Sales price: n/a

Half-brother to useful 2019 14f-2m 2f winner Land Of Oz. Dam a Listed-placed 1m 2yo winner who was a three-parts sister to useful 7f-1m winner Foolin Myself and a half-sister to US 1m 1f Grade 3 winner Gender Agenda, Listed-placed 7-12f UK/Bahraini winner Unex El Greco and the dam of high-class triple 6f 2yo winner (including at Group 1 level)/Irish 1000 Guineas runner-up Pretty Pollyanna out of a half-sister to Oaks/St Leger winner User Friendly.

Ed Harper (Whitsbury Manor Stud)

RUNWAY QUEEN
8/4 ch f Kitten's Joy - Puzzled Look (Sakhee's Secret)
Trainer: Archie Watson Owner: Clipper Logistics
Sales price: 50,000gns (Joe Foley)

First foal of a 7f 2yo winner who was a half-sister to Group 3-placed 6-6.5f winner Laugh A Minute, Group 3-placed 2019 6f 2yo winner Endless Joy and useful dual 7f 3yo winner Horroob out of a thrice-raced maiden half-sister to smart 6f-1m winner (including at Listed level) Oasis Dancer, Group 3-placed UK/Swedish multiple 1m winner (including at Listed level) Smart Enough and useful 7f-1m winner Sufficient; the family of smart stayer Jardine's Lookout.

"When we sold her for 20,000 guineas as a foal, I was very disappointed with the result as I really liked her. Then I saw that she had developed into a very nice filly as a yearling, but she was catalogued at the end of a three-day sale. I think she was very well bought, given it's a family that improves with time."

STEP SISTER
7/3 b f Twilight Son - Sacre Coeur (Compton Place)
Trainer: Clive Cox Owner: Mainline Racing
Sales price: n/a

Three-parts sister to Group 1-placed multiple 5-5.5f winner (including at Group 2/3 level) Stepper Point (by Kyllachy) and a half-sister to three winners including 2019 5.5f 3yo Listed winner Lady In France. Dam a 6f 2yo winner who was a half-sister to very useful 5-7f winner Indian Trail and useful dual 10f winner Lonely Heart (later dam of Irish 7f 3yo Group 3 winner/Irish 2000 Guineas fourth Leitrim House and 5f Listed winner Place In My Heart, herself later the dam of Queen Mary Stakes/Flying Childers Stakes winner Heartache and Listed-placed 5f 2yo winner Heartwarming).

"If racing was decided on how good-looking a horse is, this filly would be unbeatable. She is from our favourite female line, being a three-parts sister to Group 1-placed sprinter, Stepper Point, and having Queen Mary winner, Heartache, further back in the pedigree. She has been leased to a syndicate called Mainline Racing, who had a Group winner named Streamline with Clive in their first year."

Highclere Thoroughbred Racing (Harry Herbert)

CIRRUS
4/3 ch f Starspangledbanner - Callendula (Halling)
Trainer: Richard Hannon
Sales price: £40,000 (Peter & Ross Doyle Bloodstock)

First foal of an 11.5-12f 3yo winner who was a half-sister to eight winners and out of a dual 5f 3yo winning sister to useful 6f 2yo winner High Sevens and half-sister to Lingfield Derby Trial winner Munwar, Group 1-placed 10-14f winner (including at Listed level) Hateel and useful prolific 5-7f winner Alpen Wolf; the family of Cherry Hinton Stakes winner/Cheveley Park Stakes runner-up Torgau and Duke Of York Stakes winners Grey Desire and Steenberg.

"This is a very racy filly who is forward going and one who really catches the eye out at exercise. Under normal circumstances she would be a May or June starter."

DIGITAL (IRE)
23/1 b c Kodi Bear - Notte Illuminata (Acclamation)
Trainer: Kevin Ryan
Sales price: £52,000 (Hillen/Ryan)

First foal of a 1m 3yo winner who was a full sister to Irish 6f 2yo Group 2 winner/Middle Park Stakes runner-up Lilbourne Lad and a half-sister to Group 3/Listed-placed 7-10f winner Bobbyscot, useful Irish dual 12f 3yo winner Robertstown and useful Irish 7f 2yo winner Bluebell out of an Irish 1m 1f 3yo winning close relation to Irish 12f Listed winner Chatres (later dam of UAE 2m Group 2 winner Certerach) and half-sister to Group 1-placed Irish 10-14f winner (including at Listed level)/Irish Derby fourth Pugin out of a smart Irish 7f 2yo winner/Irish Oaks third.

"A really strong, well-made son of first-season sire, Kodi Bear. I was looking at our other Highclere horses with Kevin back in January and asked whether he had any unsold yearlings. He showed me this belter of a colt and it was a no-brainer as he ticked all the right boxes. Under normal circumstances I suspect he would be a candidate for one of those good six furlong races at York in May and June that Kevin likes to target."

HOST (IRE)
22/1 b c Mehmas - Mistress Makfi (Makfi)
Trainer: Richard Hannon
Sales price: £52,000 (John & Jake Warren)

First foal of a twice-raced maiden half-sister to Group 2-placed Irish 7f-1m winner/Irish 1000 Guineas fourth Rare Ransom and Listed-placed Irish 10-10.5f 3yo winner Ransomed Bride out of a Group 3-placed Irish 10f 3yo winner who was a half-sister to Group 3-placed Irish dual 6f 2yo winner (including at Listed level) Warrior Queen (later dam of US dual 8.5f 3yo Grade 2 winner A. P. Warrior and grandam of US 8.5f 3yo Grade 2 winner Global View).

"He is so typical of his sire in that he is very strong, and looks to be a precocious two-year-old in the making. Also like his sire - who I knew well when I was with Al Shaqab - he has a great temperament and does everything with the minimum amount of fuss. A real summer two-year-old in the making."

IMMACULATE
10/4 b f Invincible Spirit - Coquette Noire (Holy Roman Emperor)
Trainer: Mark Johnston
Sales price: 82,000gns (John & Jake Warren)

Half-sister to useful 8.5-9.5f winner Thunderbolt Rocks. Dam an Irish 7f 3yo winning three-parts sister to 7f 2yo winner/1000 Guineas second Jacqueline Quest (later dam of Breeders' Cup Juvenile Turf winner Line Of Duty) and half-sister to Listed-placed 11.5-12f 3yo winner Mam'selle out of a Listed-placed Irish 10f 3yo winning half-sister to dual 10f Group 3 winner Regime and Group 2/3-placed dual 5f 2yo winner (including at Listed level) Salut d'Amour.

"I love this filly. She has developed into the most lovely, strong individual who moves well and looks sure to be a first half of the season starter. Both Mark and Charlie seem more than happy with her progress and I think she could be a bit special."

OPERATIC (IRE)
2/3 ch f Showcasing - Dream Dana (Dream Ahead)
Trainer: Simon Crisford
Sales price: €78,000 (John & Jake Warren)

First foal of a 6f 3yo winner who was a half-sister to smart UK/UAE 5-7.5f winner (including at Listed level) Yaa Wayl, Listed-placed Irish 6.5f winner Lidanski (later dam of Prix de l'Abbaye winner Wizz Kid and French 1m 1f 3yo Listed winner Mustaheel), Listed-placed Irish/Hong Kong 5f-1m winner Sounds Best, very useful 6-8.5f winner Robert The Painter and three other winners out of a smart Irish 5-6f winner (including at Group 3/Listed level).

"This filly is bred to be a fast and precocious two-year-old, and at this stage Simon reckons she will be exactly that. She has done extremely well physically and is very forward going. She will be ready to roll as soon as racing resumes."

TITLE (IRE)
29/4 b c Camelot - Danehill's Dream (Danehill)
Trainer: Roger Varian
Sales price: €175,000 (John & Jake Warren)

Three-parts brother to very useful 12-14f winner Viking's Storm (by Hurricane Run) and a half-brother to 2019 US 1m 2yo Listed winner Yesterdayoncemore, useful Irish/Australian 9.5-11f winner Birth Of Venus and useful Irish 10.5f 3yo winner Moldowney. Dam an unraced sister to Group 1-placed UK/Hong Kong 6-10f winner Summerland and Irish 7f 3yo winner Last Love (later dam of Irish 14f 3yo Group 3 winner/St Leger third Fields Of Athenry); the family of Derby winner Dr Devious, Oaks winner Dancing Rain and Racing Post Trophy/2000 Guineas winner Saxon Warrior.

"Jake Warren and I fell in love with this colt when we saw him at the Goffs sale in Ireland. He simply oozes class and very much reminds me of Telescope at the same stage of his career, and he was, of course, such a star for Highclere. Title is all about next year, but like all those classy middle-distance prospects, he does everything asked of him at this early stage very easily indeed. A backend two-year-old who could be anything!"

TRUST (IRE)
29/1 b f Kingman - Split Decision (Teofilo)
Trainer: John Gosden
Sales price: €165,000 (John & Jake Warren)

First foal of an unraced sister to very smart 8-12f winner (including the Irish Derby) Trading Leather and Listed-placed Irish/Australian 11-12.5f winner Wexford Town out of an unraced daughter of a French 7f 2yo winning sister to 1000 Guineas/Champion Stakes winner Hatoof and Breeders' Cup Mile winner Irish Prize and half-sister to French dual 10f 3yo Listed winner Insijaam (later dam of 10f Group 3 winner/Oaks third Pictavia and Irish 10f 3yo Group 3 winner Maputo).

"I cannot believe this filly fell into our price bracket at the Goffs sale in Ireland as she is a serious beauty who boasts the most terrific pedigree. She was broken in by Malcolm Bastard and has stayed with him throughout. Physically she has done extremely well and to my eye looks something a bit special. She will move to John's Clarehaven base in Newmarket when we know more about when racing will recommence, but I wouldn't expect to see her on a racecourse until the latter part of the summer anyway. She quite honestly could be anything!"

Jan Hopper (Owner/Breeder)

ISOLA ROSSA
14/4 b f Iffraaj - Isola Verde (Oasis Dream)
Trainer: James Fanshawe Owner: Mr & Mrs P Hopper, Mr & Mrs M Morris
Sales price: n/a

Half-sister to useful triple 1m winner Merchant Of Venice and useful 5f 2yo winner Glory Fighter. Dam a 6f 3yo winning three-parts sister to fairly useful 5-6f winner Green Monkey and half-sister to Group 3-placed UK/UAE multiple 5-6f winner Mazzini and very useful multiple 5-6f winner Harry's Bar out of a dual 6f Listed winning sister to July Cup winner Frizzante and half-sister to Group 3-placed multiple 6f winner (including at Listed level) Zidane.

"Isola Verde is a young Oasis Dream mare out of Firenze. This filly was bred in partnership with Mike and Michelle Morris and it was decided that we'd retain her to race. She is a half-sister to our three-time winner, Merchant Of Venice (by Bated Breath), and a two-year-old winner called Glory Fighter (by Kyllachy), and this is the fourth generation of the family that James has trained. This a well-grown, forward-going filly with a good attitude, and hopefully she will begin her racing career during the second half of the season."

UNNAMED
9/3 ch f Twilight Son - Firenze (Efisio)
Trainer: James Fanshawe Owner: Sheikh Juma Dalmook Al Maktoum
Sales price: 50,000gns (Rabbah Bloodstock)

Half-sister to Group 3-placed UK/UAE multiple 5-6f winner Mazzini, very useful multiple 5-6f winner Harry's Bar, fairly useful 5-6f winner Green Monkey and two other winners. Dam a Group 2-placed multiple 6f winner (including twice at Listed level) who was a sister to high-class multiple 5-6f winner (including the July Cup) Frizzante (grandam of 2019 French 7f 2yo Group 2/3 winner/ Cheveley Park Stakes third Tropbeau) and 6f Listed winner Zidane.

"She is a big, strong filly - very typical of the family. Firenze's progeny have won 20 races between them to date, including talented all-weather performers Mazzini and Harry's Bar, while she has a promising maiden named Lady Eleanor who ran twice as a two-year-old last year. Tropbeau is also in the family and enjoyed a very good first season in 2019, winning Group 2 and 3 races in France before finishing third in the Group 1 Cheveley Park Stakes. This filly is going well at home for James Fanshawe, who has of course, successfully trained so many of the family."

Hot To Trot Racing (Sam Hoskins)

DAISY WARWICK
26/3 b f Kingman - Our Poppet (Warning)
Trainer: Andrew Balding
Sales price: n/a

Half-sister to high-class sprinter Overdose, French 7.5f Listed winner Majestic Mount, Listed-placed French 6-6.5f winner Poppet's Treasure, useful triple 7f winner Poppet's Lovin and five other winners. Dam a once-raced maiden half-sister to 1m Listed winner Musicanna (later dam of UAE 1m Group 2 winner One Man Band), eight other winners including the great-grandam of 2019 Queen Mary Stakes winner/Cheveley Park Stakes runner-up Raffle Prize and the maiden dam of Group 3-placed 2019 dual 5f 2yo winner (including at Listed level) Alligator Alley (by Kingman).

"This filly is a half-sister to the 'Budapest Bullet,' Overdose, and is by one of the most exciting young sires in Europe. She is one for the second half of the season, but has impressed pre-trainer, Hetta Stevens, with what she has done to date. She's a good-moving filly who appears to want to be a racehorse."

INTOXICATION
11/2 b f Havana Gold - B Berry Brandy (Event Of The Year)
Trainer: David Menuisier
Sales price: 12,000gns (Redwall Bloodstock)

Half-sister to 10.5f 3yo Flat/Listed-placed dual 2m hurdle winner Act Of Valour, useful multiple 7f-1m winner Cricklewood Green and US 8-8.5f 3yo winner Hy Point Player. Dam a lightly-raced maiden half-sister to Group 1-placed 6-7f winner (including at Group 2/3 level) Strong Suit; the family of 1m 3yo Listed winner Silver Pivotal.

"This filly is a very fluent mover who David likes at this early stage. She is a half-sister to the useful Act Of Valour, and out of a half-sister to a Coventry Stakes winner in Strong Suit. She looks an ideal candidate for those median auction novice events during the second half of the season."

PERSARIA
3/5 b f Equiano - Persario (Bishop Of Cashel)
Trainer: James Fanshawe
Sales price: 150,000gns (Vendor)

Full sister to very smart multiple 6f winner (including three times at Group 1 level) The Tin Man and a half-sister to very smart multiple 5-6f winner (including at Group 2/3 level) Deacon Blues, Listed-placed multiple 5f winner Holley Shiftwell and useful multiple 6f winner If So. Dam a useful 6-7f winner who was a full sister to very useful 6f-1m winner Heretic and a half-sister to triple 7f Group 3 winner/Lockinge Stakes second Warningford.

"Obviously this filly boasts a wonderful pedigree, being a sister to The Tin Man and a half-sister to Deacon Blues. She moves well and appears more forward compared to some of her siblings. We are certainly excited to have her."

Kennet Valley Thoroughbreds (Sam Hoskins)

DUAL IDENTITY (IRE)
5/3 b c Belardo - Teide Lady (Nashwan)
Trainer: William Knight
Sales price: 50,000gns (Kern/Lillingston Association)

Half-brother to German 7f 2yo Group 3 winner Ayaar, fairly useful 5-5.5f winner Albany Rose and 6f winner Torreon. Dam a 1m 1f 3yo winner who was a half-sister to smart 5-7f winner (including at Group 2/Grade 3 level) Hatta Fort, Group 2-placed 6-7f 2yo winner (including at Group 3 level) Blue Bayou, 2019 12f Group 3 winner Spirit Of Appin and the unraced dam of 13f Group 3 winner/Irish St Leger runner-up Agent Murphy.

"This colt is a very likeable individual who moves easily at home. He is from the first crop of the supremely-talented two-year-old and older horse, Belardo. We have high hopes for him."

EQUALITY
27/2 b c Equiano - Penny Drops (Invincible Spirit)
Trainer: Charlie Hills
Sales price: £50,000 (Kern/Lillingston Association)

Closely related to useful 2020 6-7f 3yo winner Badri (by Dark Angel). Dam a Listed-placed 6f 3yo winner who was a half-sister to Group 3-placed 7f 2yo Flat/2m hurdle winner Prompter out of a Listed-placed 7-8.5f 3yo winner who was a half-sister to high-class multiple 7f-1m winner (including at Group 2/Listed level) Priors Lodge.

"This is a powerful colt who appears fast and relatively precocious. Charlie speaks highly of him and feels he is one of his smarter two-year-old colts at this stage."

NOVELTY
13/5 b f New Approach - Welsh Angel (Dubai Destination)
Trainer: Mark Johnston
Sales price: 60,000gns (Kern/Lillingston Association)

Half-sister to Group 3-placed 7-12f Flat/smart dual 2m hurdle (including at Listed level) winner Scarlet Dragon, useful 7-10f winner Commander Cole and useful 10f 3yo winner Welsh Lord. Dam an unraced half-sister to Group 2-placed 6f-1m winner (including at Listed level) Nantyglo, useful 8-12f winner Resplendent Light, fairly useful 11-12f winner Ride The Lightning and five other winners; the excellent family of Honolulu, L'Ancresse, Moonstone etc.

"A really nice filly who was always going to be more of a three-year-old type. However, she moves well and the Johnston team like what they have seen so far. The mare has already produced the likes of Scarlet Dragon and Commander Cole at stud, and hopefully this filly can be another smart performer for her."

Mark McStay (Avenue Bloodstock)

CASSOWARY (IRE)
10/2 ch f Australia - Arose (Fastnet Rock)
Trainer: Marco Botti Owner: Saveall-Green & James 1
Sales price: €15,000 (Avenue Bloodstock/Marco Botti)

First foal of an unraced half-sister to smart UK/US 6f-1m winner (including at Grade 2/3 level) Up In Time out of a maiden half-sister to Listed-placed 6-7f winner Wake Up Call (later dam of UAE 1m 3yo Listed winner Zaman), useful 6-10f winner Take It To The Max and UAE Oaks winner Tamarillo (later dam of 7f 3yo Group 3 winner Summer Fete, herself dam of 2019 Queen Mary Stakes winner/Cheveley Park Stakes runner-up Raffle Prize); the family of high-class sprinter Overdose.

"She is quite backward at this stage but should furnish into a nice middle-distance filly in time. I believe Australia has gone a bit under the radar as he is fully capable of producing a good horse."

GLESGA GAL (IRE)
14/3 ch f Lope De Vega - Crystany (Green Desert)
Trainer: Hugo Palmer Owner: New Wave Racing & Partners
Sales price: €120,000 (Avenue Bloodstock/Hugo Palmer)

Three-parts sister to French 1m winner Sapphirine (by Shamardal) and a half-sister to useful Irish 1m 3yo winner Vivianite and multiple 7f winner Smugglers Creek. Dam a Listed-placed 6f 2yo winning half-sister to very useful 8-10f 3yo winner High End, useful UK/US 7-11f winner Treasury Devil and the unraced dams of French 10f 3yo Group 2 winner Ocovango and Group 3/Listed-placed 6.5-7f 2yo winner Glitter Girl out of a Fillies' Mile winner/Irish 1000 Guineas runner-up who was a half-sister to 12f Group 3 winner Dubai Success.

"A lovely, balanced filly who possesses a lot of quality. One for the second half of the season."

KNOCKNAKILLA (IRE)
2/3 b c Holy Roman Emperor - Star Of Spring (Iffraaj)
Trainer: Ger O'Leary Owner: Lance Bloodstock Limited
Sales price: €45,000 (Avenue Bloodstock)

First foal of a 1m winner who was a full sister to useful 7f 2yo winner Musharakaat (later dam of Listed-placed 6f 2yo winner Alqubbah) out of a maiden half-sister to several winners including useful 6-7f 2yo winner Witch Of Fife (later dam of Solario Stakes winner Drumfire, Hong Kong 1m Listed winner/Gimcrack Stakes runner-up Ho Choi and Irish 7f 2yo Group 3 winner Cabaret, herself the dam of last year's 2000 Guineas winner Magna Grecia).

"This colt would probably be the value purchase of everything we bought last year. He is a really nice horse and obviously the pedigree is very active with Magna Grecia on the page."

NOMAN (IRE)
28/2 b c Shalaa - Mathool (Alhaarth)
Trainer: Hugo Palmer Owner: Al Shaqab Racing
Sales price: 70,000gns (Avenue Bloodstock/Hugo Palmer)

Half-brother to Irish 8.5f 3yo Listed winner Erysimum, very useful 10f-2m winner Rhombus and two other winners. Dam a maiden three-parts sister to Group 2-placed 8-12f winner (including at Listed level) Sahool (later dam of 12f Group 3 winner Laraaib) and a half-sister to the dams of Italian 12f 3yo Group 1 winner/St Leger runner-up Ventura Storm, two-time Hardwicke Stakes winner Maraahel, 5/5.5f 2yo Group 2 winner Gutaifan and 2019 French 5f 3yo Listed winner/Queen Mary Stakes third Shades Of Blue and the grandam of 2019 Lockinge Stakes winner Mustashry.

"We bought this colt on spec and I was delighted to see him taken by Al Shaqab. He was the nicest yearling from last year and came highly recommended by Michael Carty. Physically he looks a sprinter and ought to be quick given who his sire is. He could quite literally be anything."

SET POINT (IRE)
4/2 b c Sea The Stars - Hot Sauce (Peintre Celebre)
Trainer: Hugo Palmer Owner: John Livock
Sales price: 220,000gns (Vendor)

First foal of a Listed-placed Irish 9.5f 3yo winning half-sister useful Irish 10.5-12f Flat/Grade 2-placed 2m 1f hurdle winner Cardinal Palace out of an unraced half-sister to high-class multiple 5-6f winner (including at Group 1 level) Prohibit, French 6/6.5f 3yo Listed winner Prior Warning and Group 3-placed

French dual 7f 3yo winner (including at Listed level) Emergency out of a Group 2/3-placed 6f 2yo winning sister to 1m 3yo Listed winner Out Of Reach.

"This colt wouldn't be too far behind Noman, and is as nice a middle-distance prospect as I've ever purchased. He is the kind of horse you dream could make a classic contender one day."

UNNAMED (IRE)
4/5 b c Kingman - I Am Beautiful (Rip Van Winkle)
Trainer: Jim Bolger Owner: A Partnership
Sales price: €65,000 (Avenue Bloodstock/Vincent Tam)

Third foal of an Irish 6f 2yo Group 3 winning half-sister to high-class 6f-1m 2yo winner (including twice at Group 1 level) Rumplestiltskin (later dam of Yorkshire Oaks winner/Irish Oaks runner-up Tapestry and Irish 7f 2yo Group 3 winner John F Kennedy), Group 2-placed Irish 1m 2yo winner Tower Rock and the unraced dams of UAE 1m 1f Group 1 winner Real Steel and Irish 8.5f 3yo Listed winner/French 1000 Guineas third Wild Wind; the family of very smart miler Kingmambo.

"His dam won a Group 3 and the third dam is the brilliant Miesque. I thought he was a particularly cheap purchase given the page and his physique, and although he will need a bit of time, he has every chance of making it."

UNNAMED (IRE)
1/3 b/br f Iffraaj - Isobel Archer (Oasis Dream)
Trainer: Hugo Palmer Owner: A Partnership
Sales price: 87,000gns (Avenue Bloodstock/Hugo Palmer)

Full sister to useful 7-7.5f winner Bow And Arrow. Dam a French 10f 3yo winner who was a full sister to very smart French 6.5-7f 2yo winner (including at Group 1 level) Naaqoos and a half-sister to French 10f 3yo Group 3 winner Barastraight, useful 2019 French 6f 2yo winner Golden Boy and the unraced dam of French 6f 2yo Group 3 winner Mazameer and grandam of French 10f 3yo Group 3 winner/Prix Saint Alary runner-up Vue Fantastique.

"Hugo has done well with the progeny of Iffraaj. This filly's brother was held in high regard by Charlie Appleby when I was there."

UNNAMED (FR)

6/2 b f Olympic Glory - Ornelia Ruee (Sea The Stars)
Trainer: Hugo Palmer Owner: A Partnership
Sales price: €31,000 (Avenue Bloodstock/Hugo Palmer)

Second foal of an unraced sister to Group 2/Listed-placed French 9-12f winner
Migwar and half-sister to the unraced dam of French 7f 2yo Group 3 winner
Sacred Life and Group 2-placed 2019 French 12f 3yo winner Khagan out of an
unraced sister to St Leger winner/Derby runner-up Rule Of Law, three-parts
sister to Listed-placed Irish 8.5f 3yo winner Totally Devoted (later dam of 7f
Group 3 winner Tomyris) and half-sister to useful 7f 2yo winner Cast In Gold
(later dam of UAE 1000 Guineas winner Wedding Ring).

"A very nice filly with a fantastic page. I think she could be quite smart in time."

UNNAMED

19/4 ch f Australia - Queens Park (King's Best)
Trainer: George Boughey Owner: George Boughey
Sales price: 33,000gns (Avenue Bloodstock/George Boughey)

Half-sister to 2019 Irish 6f 2yo Listed winner Sir Boris. Dam an 8.5-9f 3yo
winning half-sister to useful Irish 7f 2yo winner Singing Bird out of an unraced
half-sister to French 10.5f 3yo Group 3 winner/French Oaks runner-up
Abbatiale (later dam of four-time 6/7f Group 3 winner Bewitched), French
10.5f 3yo Listed winner Aubergade and the dam of high-class Irish/Australian
12-14f winner (including at Group 2/3 level)/St Leger third Southern France.

*"A lovely half-sister to a stakes winner. She is still growing and one for the
backend, but she moves nicely and is well liked at home."*

Middleham Park Racing (Tim Palin)

LEXINGTON FURY (IRE)

20/2 br c Footstepsinthesand - Majraa (Invincible Spirit)
Trainer: Richard Hannon
Sales price: €90,000 (Peter & Ross Doyle Bloodstock/MPR)

Half-brother to very useful 6-7f winner Intuitive. Dam a French 7.5f 2yo winner
who was a half-sister to Listed-placed French/Qatari 10f-2m winner Duke Of
Dundee out of a lightly-raced maiden half-sister to French 12.5f 3yo Group

3 winner Maroussies Wings, 7f 3yo Listed winner Mamounia and French 12f Listed winner Lago Minto.

"A beautifully put together son of Footstepsinthesand, who is one of the most prodigious sires of the last two years, having produced the likes of Marie's Diamond, Threat and Mums Tipple in that time, with the latter pair trained by this colt's trainer, Richard Hannon. He is a half-brother to a 113 Timeform-rated horse called Intuitive, and is an athletic colt who could be a potentially high-class recruit for the second half of the season and beyond."

VENTURA MUTINY
1/4 b c Showcasing - Ealaan (Invasor)
Trainer: Richard Fahey
Sales price: 85,000gns (Aidan O'Ryan/Middleham Park/Richard Fahey)

Second foal of an unraced half-sister to Group 3-placed 6f-1m winner (including at Listed level) Shabiba (later dam of Group 1-placed UK/UAE multiple 5-7f winner (including at Group 2/3 level) Ertijaal) and Group 3/Listed-placed 6f 2yo winner Darajaat out of a smart 6-7f winner (including at Group 3/Listed level) who was a sister to useful 5-12f winner Mustajed and half-sister to 6f 2yo winner Muqtarb; the family of Juddmonte International Stakes/Prix de l'Arc de Triomphe winner Sakhee.

"A particularly well put together son of Showcasing who went through the ring for €135,000 as a foal, but we picked him up for 85,000gns last autumn. He is bred along the same lines as high-class sprinter, Ertijaal, and is taking everything in his stride so far by all accounts."

VENTURA TORMENTA (IRE)
10/2 b c Acclamation - Midnight Oasis (Oasis Dream)
Trainer: Richard Hannon
Sales price: £95,000 (Peter & Ross Doyle Bloodstock)

Three-parts brother to very useful multiple 6f winner George Bowen (by Dark Angel) and a half-brother to very useful 6-7f winner Mr Win, useful 6f-1m winner Mutahaady and two other winners. Dam a maiden three-parts sister to the dam of French 5f 2yo Group 3 winner Fly On The Night and a half-sister to smart 5-6f winner (including at Group 3/Listed level) Miss Anabaa (grandam of 6f 2yo Listed winner Enjazaat (by Acclamation)) and very useful 5-6f winners Move It and Out After Dark; the family of July Cup winner Owington and French 1000 Guineas second Nathra.

"A strong, straightforward son of the fabulous Acclamation. Given the success the Hannons have had with the sire's progeny, and the fact he is closely related to the very classy George Bowen, everything looks in place for him to make up into a smart two-year-old performer."

VENTURA VISION (FR)
18/2 b f No Nay Never - Great Trip (Lemon Drop Kid)
Trainer: Mark Johnston
Sales price: €120,000 (Mandore International Agency)

First foal of a French 1m 3yo winning daughter of a Group 3/Listed-placed US 6.5f winner who was a sister to Group 2-placed 5-7f winner (including at Group 3/Listed level) Iron Mask and half-sister to the dams of French 5f 2yo Listed winner Beautifix (herself dam of French 7f 2yo Group 3 winner Sofast and French Listed winners Eyeful (1m), Spiritfix (5.5f) and Spaday (6.5f)) and French 7f 2yo Group 3 winner Ameenah; the family of Dayjur.

"This filly is by the most up-and-coming sire around at the moment, and the second dam's a full sister to a high-class two-year-old called Iron Mask. She is a quality filly with plenty of scope who is shaping up especially well on the gallops at Middleham. Her pedigree strongly suggests she will be fully effective at two, and she is one to keep on the right side of when the six furlong races begin."

Liam Norris (Bloodstock Consultant)

HIGHLAND ROCKER (FR)
18/4 gr c Gleneagles - Cay Dancer (Danehill Dancer)
Trainer: John Gosden Owner: Roy Van Gelder
Sales price: 105,000gns (Norris/Huntington)

Second foal of a Grade 3-placed UK/US 7-12f winner who was a half-sister to smart 8-10f winner Dynamic out of a French 8-9f 3yo winning half-sister to Coronation Stakes winner Balisada (later dam of 12f Listed winner Galactic Star and grandam of UAE 10f Group 3 winner Folkswood) and Listed-placed 7-7.5f winner Stirring Ballad.

"A quality colt consigned by Newsells Park. He looks sharp and the reports from his pre-trainer, Malcolm Bastard, are very positive. He should be more than capable of winning a race this year."

UNNAMED
9/4 b f Havana Gold - Salome (Fuisse)
Trainer: n/a Owner: n/a
Sales price: 15,000gns (Vendor)

Half-sister to 2019 1m 2yo winner Mazikeen. Dam a maiden half-sister to smart French multiple 6f winner (including twice at Listed level) Silva, Group 3-placed French dual 7f winner Sylvestre and the dams of French 11/12f Group 2 winner Silver Pond and French 9.5f 3yo Listed winner Savoie (herself dam of 10.5/12f Listed winner Fire Fighting).

"A filly that I bred myself. She is in the Craven breeze-up sale and Malcolm Bastard says she goes well. Her half-sister won at Chelmsford at two despite not looking an early type. This filly, in contrast, is athletic and racy so should have no problem making a more immediate impact. I like the sire and will race her myself if it comes to that."

UNNAMED
23/1 br c Showcasing - Zora Seas (Marju)
Trainer: Richard Hughes Owner: The Heffer Syndicate & P Merritt
Sales price: 110,000gns (Richard Hughes Racing)

Second foal of a 1m 3yo winner who was a half-sister to Listed-placed dual 6f 2yo winner Al Aasifh, useful triple 5f winner Cowboy Soldier, useful 6-7f 2yo winners Chicago May and Invincible Gold and useful triple 1m winner Cordell out of a French 1m 3yo Listed winning daughter of a Listed-placed French 7f-1m winner who was a half-sister to French 10f Group 2 winner Gunboat Diplomacy and Listed-placed French dual 12f 3yo winner Honeytrap.

"A magnificent colt bred by Ben Sangster, who we sold to Richard Hughes. He is a powerful individual who is a fabulous mover. He takes his work well, and is another that really ought to be winning at two."

Ontoawinner (Chris Patten)

AMOR DE MI VIDA (FR)
28/3 b f Dabirsim - Troiecat (One Cool Cat)
Trainer: Archie Watson
Sales price: €48,000 (Blandford Bloodstock)

Half-sister to Norsk Derby/Norsk 1000 Guineas winner High As A Kite, Listed-placed French 6.5f-1m winner London Protocol and useful French 7f 2yo winner Crown Vallary. Dam a maiden daughter of a half-sister to Ribblesdale

Stakes winner Mont Etoile and the dam of high-class miler Cesare and French Derby runner-up Nowhere To Exit.

"A good-looking filly who is the third horse we've had from the mare, with Crown Vallary and London Protocol both winning for us. She qualifies for the excellent French premiums, so it's more than likely she will travel over there at some point. She is cantering away at the moment, shows plenty of speed and will head for a barrier trial soon."

ANDALASKA BEAR (IRE)
26/3 b f Kodiac - Well Focused (Intense Focus)
Trainer: Richard Fahey
Sales price: £65,000 (Robin O'Ryan/Ontoawinner)

Third foal of an unraced half-sister to Australian 12f Group 1 winner Opinion, smart 10-14f winner (including twice at Group 3 level) Fox Hunt and Irish 7.5f 3yo Group 3 winner Anam Allta out of a French 12f 3yo Listed winning daughter of an Irish 7f 2yo Group 1 winner who was a half-sister to Italian 10f Group 1 winner Eva's Request, Irish 7f 3yo Group 3 winner Wild Bluebell and the dam of Fillies' Mile/Breeders' Cup Juvenile Fillies Turf winner Chriselliam.

"All the right people were in for her at the sale and we were delighted to get her. She is ready to start galloping on grass and is doing very well."

BILANDY
1/2 b f Adaay - Showstoppa (Showcasing)
Trainer: Tom Ward
Sales price: 35,000gns (Stroud Coleman/Ward/Ontoawinner)

Half-sister to 2019 Italian 6f 2yo Listed winner Avengers Queen. Dam a useful 5-6f winner who was a half-sister to 6f 2yo Group 2 winner Temple Meads, Group 3/Listed-placed 6f 2yo winner Sneak Preview, useful 5-6f winner O'Gorman and dual 6f winner Exist out of a useful dual 5f 2yo winner; the family of 5f 2yo Listed winner Fortunately.

"Her dam won at two and her only previous foal to race was a good juvenile in Italy. She is in full work and everyone likes her. She has a touch of class, a wonderful attitude and ought to be out fairly early."

BRUTAL LION (IRE)

14/3 b c Estidhkaar - Eleganza (Balmont)
Trainer: Richard Fahey
Sales price: £15,000 (Robin O'Ryan/Richard Fahey)

Half-brother to Listed-placed 5f 2yo winner It Don't Come Easy. Dam an unraced half-sister to smart 5-7f winner (including four times at Listed level) Rolo Tomasi, Grade/Group 2-placed German/US 6.5-8.5f winner Elegant Ridge (later dam of 1m 3yo Group 3 winner Montiridge), Listed-placed Irish 1m 2yo winner Summer Sunset and very useful 9-12f winner Eastern Breeze; the family of 5f 2yo Listed winner/Cheveley Park Stakes third Good Girl.

"His dam has produced a couple of winners from her only two previous foals to race, including a horse Richard trained called It Don't Come Easy, who finished second in the Rockingham Stakes before sadly passing away. This colt has impressed Richard with his work, and is developing into a really nice horse."

DENZIL'S LAUGHING (IRE)

9/3 b c Mehmas - Question (Coronado's Quest)
Trainer: Keith Dalgleish
Sales price: £28,000 (Ontoawinner/Keith Dalgleish)

Half-brother to Group 2/3-placed dual 5f 2yo winner (including at Listed level) Clem Fandango and two other winners. Dam a thrice-raced maiden half-sister to Listed-placed 7f-1m winner Commander Cave, useful Irish/Bahraini 8-8.5f winner Van Rooney and 5f 2yo winners Jillnextdoor and Kaiulani out of a 6f 2yo winner/Cheveley Park Stakes third who was a half-sister to 6f 2yo winner/ Coventry Stakes third Missel.

"Keith knows this family well, having trained half-sister Clem Fandango to win a Listed Race and finish third in the Queen Mary. This colt is currently leading the other two-year-olds at home and Keith likes him a lot."

DEREKSSON (IRE)

17/2 b c Mayson - Sampleur (Canford Cliffs)
Trainer: Tim Easterby
Sales price: £18,000 (Ontoawinner/Tim Easterby)

Second foal of an unraced half-sister to Group 3/Listed-placed UK/French 7-10.5f winner Al Waab and the maiden dam of Hong Kong 1m Group 1 winner Waikuku out of a Listed-placed 10f 3yo winning daughter of an unraced half-sister to dual 12f Listed winner Xtra and the unraced dam of US 1m Grade 1 winner Grand Arch.

"This colt looks great and is doing very well. He has a lovely temperament, and looks well bought at £18,000. He is doing steady canters at present and has gone upsides."

MERRY SECRET (IRE)
8/2 b c Elzaam - Secret Liaison (Dandy Man)
Trainer: Tom Ward
Sales price: £37,000 (Stroud Coleman Bloodstock/Tom Ward)

Half-brother to useful 2019 5-6f winner Dazzling Des. Dam a useful 5f 2yo winner who was a half-sister to useful 8-10.5f winner Desert Kiss out of a maiden sister to Group 2-placed Irish 5-6f 2yo winner (including at Group 3/Listed level) Raphane and half-sister to Listed-placed French 6f 2yo winner Nellie Nolan and Listed-placed French 1m 1f 3yo winner Where's Dave; the family of US 6.5f 2yo Grade 2 winner All Chatter.

"We are all incredibly pleased with his progress and he hasn't missed a day so far. He is really starting to understand the job and enjoys his work. Tom Marquand has ridden him at home and says he should sharpen up further still with a few more bits of work. He'll be ready to tackle the earlier five and six furlong races when we're back racing. Has a touch of quality."

MISS MILBY (IRE)
24/2 b f Camacho - Miss Huffey (Acclamation)
Trainer: Karl Burke
Sales price: €5,800 (Karl Burke)

Fourth foal of a twice-raced maiden three-parts sister to useful 7f-1m winner Passing Star and half-sister to four winners including UK/UAE 5-6f winner Sixty Minutes out of a 1m 3yo winner who was a sister to Queen Mary Stakes winner Shining Hour and Group 1-placed 1m 2yo winner Titian Time; the family of Italian 1m Group 1 winner Le Vie Dei Colori and Princess Margaret Stakes winner Soraaya.

"A strong, compact filly who looks sharp and ought to be early."

MISTER B
7/3 ch c Dandy Man - Days Of Summer (Bachelor Duke)
Trainer: Karl Burke
Sales price: £48,000 (Karl Burke)

Half-brother to 6f 2yo winner Serradura. Dam a 6f 2yo winning half-sister to Irish 6f 2yo Listed winner Pharmacist (dam of US 11/12f Grade 1 winner Red

Rocks and 10f 3yo Listed winners Galvaun and Medicinal), Listed-placed 7f 2yo winner Phariseek and the dam of 9/10.5f Group 3 winner Frankuus and French 1m 2yo Group 3 winner US Law.

"This colt came highly recommended and we certainly had to fight to get him. So far, he has justified it as his work has been very nice. We are delighted with his progress. He is a strong, athletic type who we are hoping can make up into an above-average horse in time. He holds a whole host of sales entries and is also Plus10 qualified."

MOONLITE JEWEL
13/3 b f Garswood - Dangerous Moonlite (Acclamation)
Trainer: Karl Burke
Sales price: £27,000 (Barberini/Ontoawinner/Burke)

Second foal of a dual 5f winner who was closely related to UK/Jersey 5-7f winner Limelite out of a maiden half-sister to South African 6f Group 3 winner Purple Orchid; the family of very useful sprinters Connemara and Presentation.

"Her dam was a sharp juvenile who won on debut and achieved a peak rating of 96. This filly is coming along nicely and is well liked by Karl. She is a typical Garswood - tough as nails and easy to deal with. I imagine she will need further than five furlongs in time, but does hold a Weatherbys Super Sprint entry."

MY BEST FRIEND (IRE)
22/2 b/gr g Gutaifan - School Holidays (Harlan's Holiday)
Trainer: David O'Meara
Sales price: £40,000 (Ontoawinner/O'Meara)

Half-brother to Listed-placed Italian 6f 2yo winner Nonna Grazia, dual 6f winner Parkour and 7-14f winner Herm. Dam an Irish 7f 3yo winner who was a half-sister to Group 3/Listed-placed 6-8.5f winner One More Round out of a maiden daughter of 6/7f Group 3 winner/French 1000 Guineas runner-up; the family of US triple 7f/1m Grade 1 winner Affirmed Success and US 10f Grade 1 winner/2000 Guineas runner-up Exbourne.

"The dam has had three winners from three runners so far. He has been gelded already, but is tough and hardy - a proper two-year-old type. David has said he would be surprised if he wasn't up to winning a race or two."

SECRET HANDSHEIKH
29/4 b c Mayson - Descriptive (Desert King)
Trainer: Archie Watson
Sales price: €32,000 (Blandford Bloodstock)

Half-brother to Group 2-placed dual 6f winner (including at Listed level) Valonia and useful multiple 6-7f winner Explain. Dam an Irish 6f 2yo winner who was a half-sister to useful Irish 1m 3yo winner Ridiyara (later dam of French 11.5f 3yo Listed winner Ridaar) and the dam of Listed-placed multiple 7-9f winner Bronze Angel out of a Listed-placed Irish 8-9f winner; the family of French 10f Group 1 winner Ridasiyna.

"This colt goes very well and leads the other youngsters at home. He shows plenty of speed and is well regarded by Archie. He would've been ready to run in April, and was actually going to follow a similar route to the one taken by Corinthia Knight during his two-year-old campaign."

UNNAMED (IRE)
19/3 b f Prince Of Lir - Pilot Hill (Intikhab)
Trainer: Archie Watson
Sales price: €5,000 (Archie Watson)

First foal of an unraced sister to useful 5-6f winner National Anthem, useful 7-10f 2yo winner Crafty Choice and 6f 2yo winner The Clan Macdonald out of a useful 6-7.5f winner who was a half-sister to Group 1-placed 5f-1m winner (including at Group 2/3 level) Hurricane Alan, Listed-placed 8.5f-2m 2f Flat/3m hurdle winner Aaim To Prosper and the maiden dam of Listed-placed 5-7f winner Squats.

"She was consigned by Ballyhane Stud and was only a cheap purchase, but she shows plenty of speed and goes well at this stage. I'd say she is almost certain to begin over five furlongs."

Qatar Racing Limited (David Redvers)

LOUISVILLE
26/2 b c Charm Spirit - Likely (Exceed And Excel)
Trainer: Joseph O'Brien
Sales price: n/a

Second foal of a 5f 2yo winning three-parts sister to Group 3/Listed-placed German 9.5f 2yo winner La Merced out of a maiden half-sister to US 12f Grade

3 winner La Luna De Miel, German 7f 2yo Listed winner La Salvita and Listed-placed 11f 3yo German winner La Sabara out of a Listed-placed German 1m 2yo winner; the family of German triple 12f Group 1 winner/German Derby second Lomitas.

"He is a homebred colt who finds Joseph's hill at home pretty easy to climb, which obviously bodes well."

SCIENCE (IRE)
30/1 b c No Nay Never - Princess Desire (Danehill)
Trainer: Archie Watson
Sales price: 170,000gns (David Redvers Bloodstock)

Half-brother to Listed-placed 6f 2yo winner Mappa Mundi, Listed-placed Italian 6-7.5f winner Bloody Love and dual 6f 2yo winner Lady Desire. Dam a Japanese 7f 3yo winning daughter of an unraced half-sister to 1m 2yo Group 3 winner Intimate Guest and eight other winners including the dam of Irish 7f 2yo Group 1 winner Kingsfort.

"This colt is a very smart prospect who is expected to hit the ground running when racing resumes. I hope he'd have made a Royal Ascot two-year-old under normal circumstances."

TERRIFY (IRE)
5/2 b f Galileo - Terror (Kodiac)
Trainer: David Simcock
Sales price: 550,000gns (David Redvers Bloodstock)

Second foal of a Group 3-placed dual 6f 2yo winner (including at Listed level) who was a half-sister to fairly useful multiple 5f winner Sonko out of a 7f-1m winner who was the daughter of a maiden half-sister to several winners, notably Group 1-placed multiple 6f winner (including at Group 2/Listed level) Indian Rocket and 6f 2yo Listed winner/Norfolk Stakes runner-up The Bonus King; the family of smart milers Forjatt and Sovereign Debt.

"She is out of a fast filly we had with David, and is a gorgeous-looking individual."

Kirsten Rausing (Lanwades Stud)

ALAMBRISTA
28/4 ch f Bobby's Kitten - Almiranta (Galileo)
Trainer: Sir Mark Prescott

Half-sister to smart 12-14.5f winner (including at Group 2/Listed level) Alyssa, French 1m 2yo Group 3 winner Alea Iacta and 2019 10f 3yo Listed winner Aloe Vera. Dam a once-raced maiden half-sister to Irish 10f 3yo Group 3 winner Alla Speranza (later dam of 2019 7f 3yo Group 2/Listed winner Shine So Bright) and Group 3-placed Irish 11-12f winner (including at Listed level) Altesse out of a French 10.5f 3yo Listed winner.

"A relatively late foal, she defies her foaling date by looking quite forward. The dam's previous three foals, all fillies, are all black type winners over different distances: Alea Iacta (1m as a 2yo, defeating colts), Alyssa (14.5f as a 4yo) and Aloe Vera (10f as a 3yo). An interesting prospect for her first-season sire."

ALETOILE
1/2 ch f Sea The Stars - Alamode (Sir Percy)
Trainer: Mark Johnston

First foal of a Group 3-placed 6f 2yo winner who was a half-sister to dual 2m winner Alternate Route and 11.5f 3yo winner Aloha out of a maiden half-sister to Group 2-placed Irish/Australian 7-10f winner (including at Group 3/Listed level) My Nordic Hero, French 10.5f 3yo Group 3 winner Alvarita (later dam of Irish 10f 3yo Group 3 winner Alla Speranza and Irish 12f Listed winner Altesse) and Group 2/3-placed French 10-10.5f winner Albion out of a two-time Champion Stakes winner who was a full sister to German triple 12f Group 1 winner Albanova.

"Seemingly stoutly bred, this filly would appear to be speedier and more forward than some might expect. Her dam, whose first foal she is, was a good 2yo (Timeform rating 101) and only just beaten in the Group 3 Oh So Sharp Stakes at Newmarket. Expected to be a turf runner, she is already showing promise."

ALVARINO
17/3 b c Bobby's Kitten - Alinstante (Archipenko)
Trainer: Jamie Osborne

First foal of a useful 6f-1m 2yo winning daughter of a useful 8-10.5f winner who was a half-sister to South African 14f Group 2 winner Kingston Mines, Listed-placed 11.5-12f 3yo winner Allannah Abu and useful 12-14f winner

Alambic out of a 10-13f winning half-sister to Nassau Stakes/Sun Chariot Stakes winner Last Second (later dam of French 1000 Guineas winner Aussie Rules and grandam of French 10/12f Group 1 winner Coronet, Irish Derby/ St Leger second Midas Touch and 11f 3yo Listed winner/St Leger third Michelangelo) and excellent broodmares Alouette and Jude.

"First foal of a useful three-time winner as a 2yo (Timeform rating 100+ at two) who was badly injured in her first Group race start and never regained her form afterwards. This is a nice, well-balanced colt who is a good representative of his first-season sire, Breeders Cup Turf Sprint winner Bobby's Kitten, himself a son of perennial Champion US Turf sire Kitten's Joy. I expect this colt to need seven furlongs, but he could go on either turf or AW. He is much liked for his easy action, good temperament and all-round professionalism."

NASTASIYA
21/4 ch f Archipenko - Nezhenka (With Approval)
Trainer: Ed Walker

Full sister to useful multiple 12f-2m 4f winner Timoshenko and 2020 9.5f 3yo winner Nikolayeva. Dam a useful 12f-2m winner who was a half-sister to Group 3/Listed-placed 6f 2yo winner Nataliya and Grade 2-placed UK/US multiple 12f winner Nadeszhda out of a Group 3-placed dual 12f 3yo winner (including at Listed level); the family of Hong Kong 10f Group 1 winners Time Warp (three times) and Glorious Forever (both by Archipenko).

"This big filly is a Lanwades product, through and through. Whilst I would not expect to see her until the autumn, she is one to keep in mind when appearing. Bred on similar lines to Group 1-winning brothers Time Warp and Glorious Forever, she is much-liked by her connections. She will need a minimum of seven furlongs."

ORIENTAL ART
27/2 b c Archipenko - Robe Chinoise (Robellino)
Trainer: David Simcock

Full brother to smart 8-12f winner (including at Group 1 level) Madame Chiang, useful 1m-2m winner Mister Chiang and 1m 2yo winner Chinoiseries and a half-brother to useful 8-8.5f winner Oriental Scot. Dam a 10-11.5f 3yo winner who was a half-sister to German 14f Listed winner Kiswahili (later dam of 7f 2yo Listed winner Kinetica).

"A charming, elegant colt with a good action. He looks a more forward type than his Group 1-winning sister Madame Chiang, who was also trained by his handler."

SANDS OF TIME
20/3 b f Bobby's Kitten - Starlit Sands (Oasis Dream)
Trainer: Mark Johnston

Half-sister to useful 6-7f winner Seychelloise and fairly useful 2019 10f 3yo winner Starfighter. Dam a Group 2-placed 5-5.5f 2yo winner (including at Group 3 level) who was a half-sister to four-time 6f Listed winner Sea Dane, very useful 6-7f winner Sheltering Sky, useful dual 1m winner South Atlantic, 6f 3yo winner Summer Night (later dam of French 1m 2yo Group 3 winner Songerie, French 9.5f 3yo Listed winner Soft Morning, Swedish 8.5f 3yo Listed winner Sourire and German 12f Listed winner Souvenance) and the unraced dam of 1m Group 3 winner Chigun.

"A filly bred to be speedy, by a Breeders Cup Turf Sprint winner and out of a 5f Group 3 (Prix d'Arenberg) winner at two. The dam has bred three useful winners from her first four foals and will also be represented by an unraced three-year-old colt by Galileo named Sidereal (Andrew Balding) this year. This filly was always a forward-looking, well-balanced type, and we hope that she will add to her family's glory - in the same ownership for 45 years."

Oriental Mystique successfully builds on her debut promise with a comfortable win at Kempton last November in the famous Kirsten Rausing silks.

Sam Sangster (Bloodstock Agent)

MUHA
20/1 b c Muhaarar - Cut Short (Diesis)
Trainer: Brian Meehan Owner: Martin Hughes & Michael Kerr-Dineen
Sales price: 40,000gns (Sam Sangster Bloodstock)

Half-brother to 6f 2yo Listed winner Brevity, Grade 1-placed UK/US 8-10f winner Concise, useful Irish 10.5-12.5f winner Fog Of War, useful 2019 7f 3yo winner Rux Power and two other winners. Dam a 1m 3yo winner who was a sister to high-class 6-7f 2yo winner (including twice at Group 2 level) Daggers Drawn and a half-sister to dual 6f 2yo winner/Lowther Stakes fourth Enemy Action (later dam of 1000 Guineas third Super Sleuth and grandam of 5f 2yo Listed winner Shadow Hunter).

"He was bought from Book 2 and looks an absolute steal. It is a lovely pedigree that Brian Meehan knows all about, having trained Brevity to win the Dick Poole Stakes as a two-year-old. This colt is shaping up to be a mid-season type, and has a great attitude and sound mind on him. He has taken everything that's been thrown at him in his stride."

UNNAMED (IRE) *Jimmy Sparks*
5/2 b c Zoffany - Gale Song (Invincible Spirit)
Trainer: Brian Meehan Owner: Manton Thoroughbreds V
Sales price: £60,000 (Sam Sangster Bloodstock)

First foal of a 6f 3yo winning three-parts sister to Grade 3-placed 2019 US 8.5f 3yo winner Good Governance and half-sister to very useful 6f-1m winner Four Seasons out of a 6f 2yo Group 2 winner who was a half-sister to Group 1-placed 7-10f winner Mountain Song, Group 3/Listed-placed 6f 2yo winner Raindancing (grandam of French 7f 2yo Group 3 winner Great Page) and the dam of 2019 Breeders' Cup Turf Sprint winner Belvoir Bay.

"This is a very nice individual. I love the stallion as he has been so consistent for us, and this colt looks another success story. He is forward and has already been to a barrier trial at Lingfield, where he fell out of the stalls before making up the best part of 15 lengths in the home straight, which certainly raised a few eyebrows. He'll be an early runner."

UNNAMED (IRE)

15/1 b c Kodiac - Shared Experience (Raven's Pass)
Trainer: Brian Meehan Owner: Manton Thoroughbreds V
Sales price: 52,000gns (Sam Sangster Bloodstock)

Half-brother to useful Irish 6f 2yo winner Decisive Action. Dam an unraced half-sister to Group 2-placed multiple 10-12.5f winner (including at Group 3/ Listed level) Gatewood out of a 10f 3yo Group 3 winner who was a full sister to smart 10-12f winner (including at Group 2/Listed level) Aiken and a half-sister to high-class 7f-1m winner (including at Group 2/3 level) Sleeping Indian, 1m Listed winner Nationalism and French 12.5f 3yo Listed winner La Paz.

"A particularly smart colt who has a wonderful attitude and is doing everything right at the moment. He is thriving physically and is a powerful-looking individual who we hope to see from the middle of the season onwards."

Alan and Mike Spence

BREAKAWAY

1/4 b f Muhaarar - Cloud's End (Dubawi)
Trainer: Clive Cox
Sales price: 65,000gns (Clive Cox Racing)

Half-sister to fairly useful multiple 5-6f winner Zamjar and 2019 5f 2yo winner Ishvara. Dam a 6-7f winner who was a half-sister to high-class UK/Irish 5f-1m winner (including the Cheveley Park Stakes) Airwave (later dam of Irish 9.5f 3yo Listed winner Aloof and Irish 5f 2yo Listed winner/Queen Mary Stakes runner-up Meow, herself dam of top-class 2yo/English and Irish 2000 Guineas winner Churchill and Cheveley Park Stakes winner Clemmie), Nunthorpe Stakes winner Jwala and the dam of Group 1-placed 6-7f winner (including twice at Listed level) Dream Of Dreams.

"A strong filly from a very fast family. She does everything really easily at the moment and, all being well, should be ready to run at the end of May over six furlongs."

FIRE DANCING

4/3 b f Iffraaj - Street Fire (Street Cry)
Trainer: Mark Johnston
Sales price: n/a

Half-sister to smart UK/UAE 7f-1m winner (including at Group 3 level) Salute The Soldier, useful 7f 2yo winner Way Too Hot and three other winners. Dam an unraced half-sister to useful 6-7f 2yo winner Seeking Star out of a maiden half-sister to US 1m 1f Grade 1 winner Monzante and French 7f 2yo Listed winner Alpha Plus.

"She is co-owned and bred with the Hargreaves, and is from a family we've had success with in the past. The mare has produced some decent performers when crossed with speed and Iffraaj would be the best stallion she has visited so far. This filly is very much like her half-brother, Salute The Soldier, in terms of looks - she's very strong, weighing nearly 500kg. The early signs have been encouraging. She should be ready to go in the second half of the season."

PINBALL WIZARD (IRE)
3/4 b c Dark Angel - Alsalwa (Nayef)
Trainer: Clive Cox
Sales price: 60,000gns (Clive Cox Racing)

Half-brother to smart 8-8.5f winner (including at Listed level) Another Touch and useful Irish 7f-1m winner Spiorad Saoirse. Dam a useful Irish dual 1m 3yo winner who was a half-sister to Group 3/Listed-placed triple 6f winner/2000 Guineas fourth Bossy Guest and 5f 2yo winners Liberating and Kate The Great (later dam of good sprinters Eastern Impact, Miss Katie Mae (by Dark Angel) and Summerghand); the family of Japanese Triple Crown winner Deep Impact and Breeders' Cup Turf winner Talismanic.

"This is a big horse that still has plenty of growing to do. He was a relatively cheap purchase as he was far from the finished article at the sales, and is also an April foal. He has done well so far, but his knees are still very open, so we are just giving him more time to mature. Hopefully he will be out during the second half of the season."

ROSÉ ALL DAY
27/3 b f Oasis Dream - May Rose (Lawman)
Trainer: Clive Cox
Sales price: 75,000gns (Clive Cox Racing)

First foal of a 5-6f winner who was a three-parts sister to Group 1-placed 6-7f winner (including at Group 2/3 level) Cable Bay, Irish 6f 2yo Listed winner Indigo Balance and two other winners and a half-sister to smart 5f-1m winner (including at Group 2/3 level) Mister Sea Wolf out of a maiden half-sister to French 1m 3yo Group 3 winner/French 2000 Guineas third Bowman, Group 1-placed multiple 5f winner Ahtoug and the dam of St Leger/Hong Kong Vase winner Mastery and Italian 1m 2yo Group 1 winner Kirklees and grandam of Eclipse Stakes winner Mukhadram.

"She is a first foal but a good size and well put together. We were surprised to get her for the price we did as there was nothing to dislike at the sales. She comes from a really good family that has plenty of speed in it and, though not a very early sort, I think she will be running around June or July time."

UNNAMED

8/4 b f Muhaarar - Clarietta (Shamardal)
Trainer: Mark Johnston
Sales price: 50,000gns (Johnston Racing)

Half-sister to Lingfield Oaks Trial winner Perfect Clarity, Italian 10f Listed winner Law Power and Listed-placed dual 1m 3yo winner Clarentine. Dam a Listed-placed dual 7f 2yo winner who was a half-sister to Group 1-placed UK/US 7-11.5f winner (including at Grade 3/Listed level) Cassydora (later dam of smart trio Ernest Hemingway, South Sea Pearl and Toulifaut) and 10f 3yo Listed winner Classic Remark; the family of Irish 6f 2yo Group 1 winner Zoffany.

"A big, strong filly. Her dam has already produced three black type performers from just four foals, all of whom were by unfashionable sires. Muhaarar would be the best stallion she has visited so far, and we were quite surprised to get this filly for as little as we did. She had a superficial cut above her knee earlier in the year which held her up, but she's doing everything right at the moment and should be hitting the track in June or July."

Positive (right) on his way to a battling success in the Group 3 Betway Solario Stakes at Sandown last August, defeating subsequent Group 1 Vertem Futurity Trophy Stakes winner, Kameko.

Titanium Racing Club (Megan O'Brien)

H BOMB
26/3 ch c Pearl Secret - Mothers Finest (Tamayuz)
Trainer: Karl Burke
Sales price: £20,000 (Larry Stratton)

First foal of a useful dual 1m winner who was a half-sister to useful 10-12f winner Dame Lucy out of a maiden half-sister to US 1m 1f Grade 3/Irish 6f 2yo Listed winner Coney Kitty and four other winners including the dam of Dante Stakes winner/Derby second Libertarian, 10f Group 3 winner Prince Siegfried and French 12.5f Listed winner Bigzam.

"It is a family Karl knows well as he trained both the dam and a notable relation in Libertarian, who was second in the 2013 Derby. This colt has seemingly inherited his first-season sire's speed, and is easily the most forward of our three juveniles. He is a medium-sized, attractive sort who should be ready to roll when racing eventually resumes."

HOLY ENDEAVOUR (IRE)
26/2 b f Holy Roman Emperor - Incoming Call (Red Ransom)
Trainer: Richard Fahey
Sales price: 50,000gns (Creighton Schwartz Bloodstock/Titanium Racing)

Half-sister to Group 3-placed 10-12f winner (including at Listed level) Missed Call. Dam a once-raced maiden half-sister to smart French 7-10.5f 3yo winner (including at Group 3/Listed level) Dance Dress (later dam of US 8/9f Grade 2 winner/French 1000 Guineas fourth Costume) and Listed-placed 1m 3yo winner Discuss (grandam of French 10f 2yo Group 1 winner Epicuris); good family of French 1000 Guineas winner Matiara, French 1m 2yo Group 1 winner Indonesienne and 7f 2yo Group 3 winner Thousand Words.

"This filly was bought from Book 1 and is a lovely individual - sizeable and scopey with a bit of quality. She is very straightforward and should be one for the seven furlong races from the middle of summer onwards. The Danehill sireline has had good results with this family in the past with the likes of Costume (by Danehill himself), Epicuris (by Rail Link) and Thousand Words (by Dansili) all winning at Group level for Juddmonte, so hopefully it can work once again."

L'UN DES CINQ
24/3 b c Acclamation - Danat Al Atheer (Shamardal)
Trainer: Jedd O'Keeffe
Sales price: 25,000gns (Creighton Schwartz Bloodstock/Titanium Racing)

Third foal of a useful 6-10f winner who was a half-sister to Group 3-placed 7-10f winner Dynamism, useful UAE 8-10f winner Blue Sea and four other winners out of a maiden half-sister to US 10/11f Grade 1 winner Lahudood (later dam of French 10f 3yo Listed winner Aghareed) and French 10f 3yo Listed winner Kareemah; the excellent family of Derby winner Nashwan and 1000 Guineas winner Ghanaati.

"He isn't your typical Acclamation and seems to take after the dam's side of the family, which is more about stamina. He is still in pre-training and I would say at this stage it's unlikely we'll see much of him at two. One for next year."

Mark Weinfeld (Meon Valley Stud)

KING OF CLUBS
19/4 b c Intello - Queen Arabella (Medicean)
Trainer: Hughie Morrison Owner: Castle Down Racing
Sales price: 19,000gns (Not Sold)

Half-brother to 10f 3yo winner Garden Oasis. Dam an unraced half-sister to smart 8-10.5f Flat (including at Group 3/Listed level)/2m hurdle winner Poet, Group 3-placed French dual 6f 2yo winner Hothaifah and five other winners including the dam of Irish 7f 3yo Group 3 winner/Irish 2000 Guineas runner-up France and 10.5f Listed winner Hippy Hippy Shake (herself later dam of 2019 French 1m 3yo Listed winner Twist 'N' Shake) and grandam of Oaks second Shirocco Star (later dam of 2019 Dante Stakes winner Telecaster and Group 3-placed 2019 7f 2yo winner Al Suhail).

"He is currently going very well at home and we like him. His dam was unraced but is very well bred. Incidentally, Telecaster - who is a member of the extended family - is still with Hughie Morrison and seems to be in good form."

UNNAMED
23/3 b f Lope De Vega - Miss Dashwood (Dylan Thomas)
Trainer: James Fanshawe Owner: Helena Springfield Ltd
Sales price: n/a

Half-sister to 2019 Queen's Vase winner Dashing Willoughby. Dam a useful 8.5-12f winning half-sister to high-class 10-10.5f winner (including twice at Group

1 level) Speedy Boarding, very useful dual 10f 3yo winner Elwazir, useful dual 1m winner Next Stage and useful 13-14f 3yo winner Joshua Reynolds out of an 11f Listed winning half-sister to Group 1-placed 8-10f winner (including at Listed level) Dash To The Top (later dam of 2019 Oaks winner Anapurna).

"A very nice filly. She is out of a half-sister to Speedy Boarding, and is currently in pre-training with Ed Peate. Like the aforementioned King Of Clubs, she isn't really a two-year-old type but that won't really be a problem this year!"

THE WEEKEND CARD

Issued every Wednesday, The Weekend Card is our specialist publication offering professional updates, views and recommendations from our select team of experts.

The Card covers the next six days racing with the emphasis firmly focused upon the key weekend action. The importance of continuity is the heartbeat of this service. So not only do you receive all the latest news on key horses from our various publications which are declared to run but also informed comments on selected horses from previous editions. And we also provide you with honest and accurate feedback on all the previous week's selections – win or lose.

The Card, which includes a quick reference selection sheet, is available as a download, hard copy (by post) or both and you receive a Welcome Pack when you subscribe. Please visit our website or contact us for more information.

SECTION THREE

The stables featured below are those that, for one reason or another, didn't contribute to the book this year. Here is a look at some of the more interesting two-year-olds on paper from the selected operations.

Charlie Appleby

AL MEBRAH
14/4 ch c Dubawi - Rumh (Monsun)
Owner: Godolphin
Sales price: n/a

Full brother to high-class 8-10f winner (including three times at Group 1 level) Wild Illusion and a half-brother to 1m 2yo Listed winner Really Special and Group 3-placed 7f 2yo winner Ceratonia. Dam a 10f 3yo Listed winner who was a three-parts sister to German 10f 3yo Listed winner Realeza out of a German 1m 2yo Group 3 winning half-sister to US 9.5f Grade 1 winner Royal Highness (later dam of French 10/11f Group 2 winner Free Port Lux).

MODERN NEWS
11/4 ch c Shamardal - Modern Ideals (New Approach)
Owner: Godolphin
Sales price: n/a

Third foal of a twice-raced maiden half-sister to French 1m 2yo Group 1 winner Ultra, French 12.5f 3yo Group 3 winner Synopsis and Listed-placed French 12f 3yo winner Epic Simile (later dam of Group 2/3-placed 6f 2yo winner Figure Of Speech); the family of French 1m 2yo/10.5f 3yo Group 1 winner/French Derby runner-up Act One and 1000 Guineas/Champion Stakes winner Bosra Sham.

UNNAMED Visionary Ruler
15/4 b c Dubawi - Alessandria (Sunday Silence)
Owner: Godolphin
Sales price: n/a

Half-brother to very smart French/Australian 8-12f winner (including three times at Group 1 level) Avilius, Group 1-placed French 9-10f 3yo winner (including at Group 2/3 level) Saint Baudolino, Group 2/3-placed French 7-9f winner (including at Listed level) Army Bulletin and Group 3-placed 5f-1m winner (including twice at Listed level) Well Of Wisdom. Dam a useful 8-12f winner who was the daughter of a French 6f 2yo Group 3 winning sister to Middle Park Stakes winner/2000 Guineas runner-up Lycius.

UNNAMED (IRE)
20/2 b c Dubawi - Chachamaidee (Giant's Causeway)
Owner: Godolphin
Sales price: 200,000gns (Godolphin)

Half-brother to 2019 12f Group 3 winner Klassique. Dam a high-class 6f-1m winner (including at Group 1 level) who was a full sister to high-class 6-7f winner (including twice at Group 3 level) J Wonder (dam of 2019 dual 7f 2yo winner Boccaccio (by Dubawi)), a three-parts sister to smart UK/Hong Kong 6-7f winner (including at Group 3 level) California Whip and a half-sister to the dam of 1m 2yo Listed winner/Racing Post Trophy third Celestial Path.

UNNAMED *Desert Star*
18/1 b f Dubawi - Desert Blossom (Shamardal)
Owner: Godolphin
Sales price: n/a

Full sister to Group 3-placed 7f-1m winner (including at Listed level) Duneflower and a half-sister to once-raced 2019 7f 2yo winner Spring Of Love. Dam a Group 2-placed 7f 2yo winner who was a three-parts sister to smart 6f-1m winner (including at Listed level) Flaming Spear and a half-sister to UAE 5f Listed winner Taqseem out of a Listed-placed 7f 2yo winner.

UNNAMED
11/2 b c Dubawi - First Victory (Teofilo)
Owner: Godolphin
Sales price: n/a

First foal of a 7f 2yo Group 3 winner who was a half-sister to high-class 6-10f winner (including four times at Group 1 level) Thunder Snow, Group 1-placed 7-9.5f winner (including at Group 2/3 level)/1000 Guineas third Ihtimal, Group 1-placed 6-8.5f winner (including at Listed level) Always Smile and UAE 1000 Guineas winner Winter Lightning.

UNNAMED (IRE)
19/2 b c Kingman - Kamakura (Medaglia d'Oro)
Owner: Godolphin
Sales price: 625,000gns (Godolphin)

First foal of an unraced sister to Grade 3-placed US 8-9f winner Bay Of Plenty
and half-sister to Grade 2-placed US 6.5f-1m winner Fortify out of a maiden
sister to Grade 3-placed US 8-9f winner Anasheed and half-sister to Listed-
placed French/US 8-9.5f winner Dubai Belle (later dam of US 8.5f 3yo Grade 1
winner Little Belle, herself dam of US 8.5f Grade 1 winner Dickinson) and the
dam of 6f 2yo Group 3 winner Newfangled.

UNNAMED (IRE) *Creative Silence*
22/4 b f Exceed And Excel - Veil Of Silence (Elusive Quality)
Owner: Godolphin *Miss Jingles*
Sales price: n/a

Full sister to smart 5-6f 2yo winner (including at Group 3/Listed level) Sound
And Silence and dual 7f 2yo winner Silent Bullet and a half-sister to 8.5f 2yo
winner Stay Silent. Dam an unraced half-sister to Racing Post Trophy winner
Ibn Khaldun who was herself the daughter of a Fillies' Mile/Irish 1000 Guineas
winning sister to very smart miler Barathea.

UNNAMED (IRE)
28/2 ch f Dubawi - Winters Moon (New Approach)
Owner: Godolphin
Sales price: n/a

Half-sister to 2019 Prix Morny/Middle Park Stakes winner Earthlight. Dam a 7f
2yo winner/Fillies' Mile third who was a half-sister to French 1m 2yo Group 1
winner Mandaean, French 10f 3yo Group 1 winner Wavering and the maiden
dam of Group 2-placed 2019 6f 2yo winner Maxi Boy out of a French 1m 2yo
Group 3 winner; the family of Irish 1m 3yo Group 3 winner Be My Guest.

UNNAMED
19/3 b c Dubawi - Zibelina (Dansili)
Owner: Godolphin
Sales price: n/a

Full brother to 2019 7f-1m 3yo winner Severnaya and a half-brother to Group
2/3-placed 2019 7f 2yo winner Royal Crusade. Dam a smart 7f-1m 3yo winner
(including at Group 3/Listed level) who was a sister to useful 6f 3yo winner
Ihtifal and a half-sister to 6f 2yo Listed winner Floristry (later dam of French

6f 3yo Listed winner Inspiriter and useful 2019 dual 6f 2yo winner Lazuli (by Dubawi)) out of a 7f 2yo winning half-sister to Group 1-placed 8-10.5f winner (including at Group 2/3 level)/Derby third Carlton House.

Pinatubo was the standout two-year-old performer of 2019, bursting onto the scene at Royal Ascot last June. The son of Shamardal would go on to record a further three victories last season, including a nine-length win in the Goffs Vincent O'Brien National Stakes, before rounding off his perfect 6-6 juvenile campaign by winning the Darley Dewhurst Stakes at Newmarket.

Saeed Bin Suroor

HIDDEN WORLD (IRE)
14/5 b/br c Teofilo - Haughtily (Invincible Spirit)
Owner: Godolphin
Sales price: n/a

Second foal of an unraced half-sister to high-class 6f-1m winner (including twice at Group 1 level) Lillie Langtry (later dam of 1000 Guineas/Oaks winner Minding and Irish 1m 3yo Group 3 winner Kissed By Angels), Irish 1m 3yo Listed winner Count Of Limonade, Grade 3-placed UK/US 8-8.5f winner (including at Stakes level) Danilovna and the maiden dam of 10f 3yo Group 3 winner Master Apprentice.

LOST GOLD (IRE)
20/5 b/br c Dark Angel - Windsor County (Elusive Quality)
Owner: Godolphin
Sales price: n/a

Half-brother to 2019 French 1000 Guineas winner Castle Lady, smart UK/ UAE 6-7f winner (including at Listed level) Top Score and useful 2019 dual 6f 2yo winner Eton College. Dam an unraced sister to top-class 7-10f winner (including the Breeders' Cup Classic) Raven's Pass and half-sister to US 1m Grade 3 winner Gigawatt.

Opening Scene

UNNAMED
9/3 b f Territories - Beautiful Ending (Exceed And Excel)
Owner: Godolphin
Sales price: n/a

Half-sister to useful 2019 6f 2yo winner Story Of Light. Dam an 8.5f 2yo winner who was a half-sister to Group 1-placed multiple 7-10f winner (including at Group 2/3 level) Nayyir, high-class multiple 10-12f winner (including at Group 2/3 level)/French Derby third Sky Hunter, Group 1-placed triple 12f winner (including at Group 3 level)/St Leger runner-up Highest, 14f Listed winner Shamaiel (later dam of 10f Listed winner Shamali) and the dam of German 12f 3yo Group 2 winner Parvaneh.

Deep Thoughts

UNNAMED (IRE)
6/3 gr c Dark Angel - Betimes (New Approach)
Owner: Godolphin
Sales price: n/a

Half-brother to 2019 6f 2yo winner Theory Of Time. Dam a Listed-placed 7f 2yo winner who was a half-sister to smart multiple 5-6f winner (including at Listed level) Aahayson, very useful UK/UAE multiple 5-6f winner (including at Listed level) Take Ten and very useful multiple 6-7f winner Thebes out of a Listed-placed dual 5f winning half-sister to 7f 2yo Group 3 winner Peak To Creek and dual 6f Listed winner Ripples Maid.

Underwater Attack

UNNAMED
26/4 b c Dawn Approach - Inner Secret (Singspiel)
Owner: Godolphin
Sales price: n/a

Half-brother to French 1m 2yo Group 1 winner Royal Marine, 2019 UAE 1m Group 3/Listed winner Secret Ambition and French 1m 1f 3yo Listed winner Crystal River. Dam a once-raced maiden half-sister to 1m Group 1 winners

Librettist (twice) and Dubai Destination and high-class middle distance performer Secret Number.

UNNAMED (IRE) *Next Victory*
25/3 b f Shamardal - Inspiriter (Invincible Spirit)
Owner: Godolphin
Sales price: n/a

Half-sister to Group 3/Listed-placed UK/UAE 5-6f winner Leading Spirit. Dam a French 6f 3yo Listed winner who was a half-sister to Listed-placed French 5.5f 3yo winner Bouquet De Flores, useful 2019 dual 6f 2yo winner Lazuli and 7f 2yo winner Efflorescence out of a 6f 2yo Listed winner who was a half-sister to smart 7f-1m 3yo winner (including at Group 3/Listed level) Zibelina (dam of Group 2/3-placed 2019 7f 2yo winner Royal Crusade (by Shamardal)).

UNNAMED (IRE) *Dubai Lady*
10/4 b f Invincible Spirit - Long Lashes (Rock Hard Ten)
Owner: Godolphin
Sales price: n/a

Half-sister to 2020 8-9.5f 3yo winner Beautiful Illusion. Dam a Group 2-placed 6f-1m winner (including at Group 3/Listed level) who was a half-sister to 2020 US 10f Grade 1 winner Combatant and Group 2-placed 5f 2yo winner Mythical Border; the family of 1m 2yo winner/Craven Stakes runner-up Dancing David.

UNNAMED (IRE) *Navy Blue*
17/3 b c Invincible Spirit - New Style (Street Cry)
Owner: Godolphin
Sales price: n/a

Second foal of a maiden half-sister to top-class 6-7f winner (including five times at Group 1 level) Dream Ahead, Group 3-placed 10-12f winner (including twice at Listed level) Into The Dark, very useful UK/UAE 6-12f winner Bin Battuta, useful Irish 7f 2yo winner Only Make Believe and the unraced dam of Cheveley Park Stakes winner Fairyland out of a high-class 5-6f winner (including at Group 2/3 level).

UNNAMED *Heroic Soldier*
27/2 ch c Iffraaj - Show Day (Shamardal)
Owner: Godolphin
Sales price: n/a

First foal of a German 1m 1f 3yo Listed winner who was a full sister to high-class 7-9.5f winner (including twice at Group 2 level) Usherette and a half-sister to 2019 1m 3yo Listed winner Magnetic Charm and useful 12f-2m winner African Jazz out of a Listed-placed French 9.5-10.5f winning sister to US 11f Grade 2 winner Expansion.

UNNAMED *Storm Damage*
27/4 b c Night Of Thunder - Sundrop (Sunday Silence)
Owner: Godolphin
Sales price: n/a

Closely related to 2020 French 7.5f Listed winner Nature's Colors and 6f 2yo Listed winner Whitman (both by Poet's Voice) and a half-brother to a very useful French 8-9f winner Mount Pelion and the dam of 2020 French 6.5f 3yo Listed winner Quiet Times. Dam a Group 1-placed 7-10f winner (including at Grade/Group 3 level)/1000 Guineas runner-up.

Clive Cox

FERNANDO RAH
23/3 b c Lethal Force - Lacing (Equiano)
Owner: Peter Ridgers
Sales price: 50,000gns (Clive Cox Racing)

First foal of a useful 6f 2yo winner who was a half-sister to Group 3-placed triple 5f 2yo winner (including at Listed level)/Cheveley Park Stakes fourth Miss Work Of Art (dam of 2019 7f 3yo Listed winner Tapisserie) and Group 3-placed 8-9f winner Romantic Settings out of a useful 7-10f winning daughter of a dual 5f 2yo winner who was a half-sister to 6f 2yo Group 2/3 winner Soar (dam of Group 2/Listed-placed 5f 2yo winner Konchek (by Lethal Force)).

KOHINOOR
7/2 b f Adaay - Satsuma (Compton Place)
Owner: AlMohamediya Racing
Sales price: £100,000 (Clive Cox Racing)

Half-sister to Group 2-placed 2019 triple 5f 2yo winner (including at Group 3/Listed level) Good Vibes. Dam a useful 5f 2yo winner who was a half-sister to

Group 2-placed 5-6f winner Astrophysics out of a maiden full sister to Grade 1-placed Irish/US 7-9f winner Sebastian Flyte and half-sister to Irish 6f 3yo Group 3 winner Age Of Chivalry.

NIGHT NARCISSUS (IRE)
20/1 b f Kodi Bear - Midnight Martini (Night Shift)
Owner: AlMohamediya Racing
Sales price: £90,000 (Clive Cox Racing)

Half-sister to useful prolific 5f winner Midnight Malibu and fairly useful 5-6f winner Mr Pocket. Dam a Group 3-placed 5-6f 2yo winning daughter of an unraced half-sister to Listed-placed 10.5f 3yo winner Sues Surprise out of an unraced half-sister to 1m 3yo Listed winner Well Beyond (later dam of 1m 3yo Listed winner Out Of Reach and grandam of King's Stand Stakes winner Prohibit); the family of Dewhurst Stakes/2000 Guineas winner Zafonic.

NIKULINA
10/3 ch f Dutch Art - Osipova (Makfi)
Owner: Cheveley Park Stud
Sales price: n/a

Full sister to Group 2-placed 2019 dual 7f 2yo winner (including at Group 3 level) Positive. Dam a useful dual 12f 3yo winner who was a half-sister to Group 2-placed 7f-1m winner (including at Group 3/Listed level) Zonderland and useful dual 10f 3yo winner Whitlock (both by Dutch Art) out of a maiden sister to Listed-placed 7f 3yo winner Safina (later dam of 7f 3yo Group 3 winner Marenko) and the unraced dam of 7f Group 3 winner Spangled.

PROP FORWARD
16/3 b c Iffraaj - My Propeller (Holy Roman Emperor)
Owner: Jeff Smith
Sales price: 75,000gns (Littleton Stud)

Second foal of a smart multiple 5-6f winner (including twice at Listed level) who was a half-sister to useful 5-7f winner Cut Across out of a Listed-placed 5f 2yo winning half-sister to Duke of York Stakes winner Twilight Blues.

ROYAL SCIMITAR (IRE)
7/2 b c Territories - Prequel (Dark Angel)
Owner: AlMohamediya Racing
Sales price: 80,000gns (Clive Cox Racing)

First foal of an unraced sister to 6f 2yo Group 2 winner Alhebayeb and useful UK 7f 2yo/UAE 1m winner Azmaam and half-sister to Group 3-placed multiple 5-6f winner (including at Listed level) Humidor out of a lightly-raced maiden half-sister to 10f 3yo Listed winner/Oaks fourth Musetta; the family of Canadian 7f Grade 2 winner Vanderlin.

SUNSET GLOW (IRE)
20/2 b c Pride Of Dubai - Golden Shine (Royal Applause)
Owner: Julie Deadman & Stephen Barrow
Sales price: £68,000 (Clive Cox Racing)

Half-brother to useful 5-6f winner Chagatai, dual 5f winner Moondyne Joe and 6f 2yo winner Arthur Martinleake. Dam a 5f 2yo winner who was a half-sister to smart 5-6f winner (including twice at Listed level) Falcon Hill, Listed-placed 5f-1m 2yo winner Raine's Cross and the grandam of 5f Group 3 winner Dutch Masterpiece out of a Group 3-placed dual 5f 2yo winning close relation to 1m Group 2 winner Desert Deer.

SUPREMACY (IRE)
28/3 b c Mehmas - Triggers Broom (Arcano)
Owner: J Goddard
Sales price: £65,000 (Clive Cox Racing)

Half-brother to useful dual 6f 2yo winner Triggered and 2019 5f 2yo winner Star Alexander. Dam a maiden half-sister to high-class UK/Hong Kong 6f-1m winner (including twice at Group 1 level) Xtension, Listed-placed French dual 6f winner A Huge Dream (later dam of 5/5.5f Listed winner Mrs Gallagher) and the maiden dam of very smart multiple 6f winner (including twice at Group 1 level) Harry Angel and 2019 6f 2yo Group 2 winner Pierre Lapin.

TOP OF THE SHOP (IRE)
20/2 b c Mehmas - Oh Simple Thing (Compton Place)
Owner: Julie Deadman & Stephen Barrow
Sales price: £34,000 (Clive Cox Racing)

First foal of a maiden half-sister to German 6f Group 2/3 winner Donnerschlag, French 7f 2yo Listed winner Izzy Bizu and Group 3-placed Irish 6f 2yo winner Da Boss Man out of a useful Irish 8-9.5f winning half-sister to Group 2-placed 5-6f winner Funny Valentine and the dam of smart 5-6f winner (including at

Group 3/Listed level) Resplendent Glory and grandam of Norfolk Stakes winner Prince Of Lir and 2019 Irish 5f 3yo Listed winner Nitro Boost.

UNNAMED (IRE)
12/2 ch f Night Of Thunder - Exempt (Exceed And Excel)
Owner: Sheikh Rashid Dalmook Al Maktoum
Sales price: 110,000gns (Blandford Bloodstock)

Half-sister to useful dual 8.5f winner Guvenor's Choice. Dam a maiden half-sister to Grade 1-placed US 6-8.5f winner (including at Grade 2 level) Three Degrees, Group 3-placed 6-7f winner (including at Listed level) Mehronissa and US 8-8.5f 3yo winner Vapour Musing.

Golden Horde on his way to a commanding win at Windsor last June. The son of Lethal Force subsequently landed the Group 2 Richmond Stakes at Goodwood, before acquitting himself with credit at the highest level in the Darley Prix Morny and Juddmonte Middle Park Stakes.

Simon Crisford

LATEST GENERATION
2/2 b c Frankel - Rizeena (Iffraaj)
Owner: Sheikh Rashid Dalmook Al Maktoum
Sales price: n/a

First foal of a high-class 5f-1m winner (including twice at Group 1 level) who was a half-sister to Group 3-placed 2019 dual 6f 2yo winner (including at Listed level) Summer Romance out of a 5f 2yo winner who was a half-sister to high-class 8-9f winner (including at Group 1 level) Zabeel Prince, Group 1-placed Australian 7-13f winner (including at Group 2/3 level) Puissance De Lune, 2019 10f 3yo Listed winner Queen Power and five other winners.

LORD LOVELACE
26/2 b c Invincible Spirit - Fond Words (Shamardal)
Owner: Godolphin
Sales price: n/a

Second foal of a French 6.5f 3yo Listed winning daughter of a Group 3-placed multiple 7-10f winner (including four times at Listed level) who was a half-sister to French 1m 1f 3yo Listed winner Ighraa, 1m 2yo Listed winner Streets Ahead and Listed-placed UK/Hong Kong 6-8.5f winner Sabre And Gold; the family of Canadian 12f Grade 1 winner Forte Dei Marmi, 14f 3yo Listed winner Savarain and 1m 2yo winner/English and Irish Oaks third Harlequeen.

MABDAA
14/5 b c Oasis Dream - Darajaat (Elusive Quality)
Owner: Hamdan Al Maktoum
Sales price: n/a

Full brother to 7f 3yo winner Fakhoor and a half-brother to useful Irish 5f winner Amthaal and dual 5f winner Buniann. Dam a Group 3/Listed-placed 6f 2yo winner who was a half-sister to Group 3-placed 6f-1m winner (including at Listed level) Shabiba (later dam of Group 1-placed UK/UAE multiple 5-7f winner (including at Group 2/3 level) Ertijaal (by Oasis Dream)) out of a smart 6-7f winner (including at Group 3/Listed level).

MASTER OF COMBAT (IRE)
7/3 b c Invincible Spirit - Sharja Queen (Pivotal)
Owner: Sheikh Mohammed Obaid Al Maktoum
Sales price: n/a

First foal of a useful 7.5-10f winning daughter of a Listed-placed 1m 3yo
winner who was a half-sister to very smart 6f-1m winner (three times at
Group 1 level, including the Irish 2000 Guineas) Dubawi, Lancashire Oaks
winner Emirates Queen, 10f 3yo Listed winner Princess Nada and several other
winners including Listed-placed 8.5f 3yo winner Suba (grandam of Group
2-placed 2019 7f 2yo winner Cloak Of Spirits (by Invincible Spirit)).

NOORJIHAN
3/2 b f Kingman - Comic (Be My Chief)
Owner: Hussain Alabbas Lootah
Sales price: 200,000gns (Richard Knight BS Agent)

Half-sister to very smart UK/Hong Kong 6-12f winner (including eight times at
Group 1 level) Viva Pataca, high-class Irish/US 8-11f winner (including twice at
Grade 1 level) Laughing, Listed-placed 7f-1m 2yo winner Shambolic, useful UK/
UAE 7-10f winner George Villiers, five other winners and the unraced dam of
14f Listed winner Twitch. Dam a 10-11.5f 3yo winner who was a half-sister to
smart UK/US 7-10f winner (including at Grade 2/3 level) Brave Act.

SENSE OF HUMOUR
23/1 b f Dark Angel - Golden Laughter (Bernardini)
Owner: Godolphin
Sales price: 150,000gns (Stroud Coleman Bloodstock)

Second foal of a thrice-raced maiden half-sister to 2000 Guineas winner
Footstepsinthesand, Irish 6f 2yo Group 1 winner Pedro The Great, 1m 3yo
Listed winner Belle D'Or and the dam of Irish 2000 Guineas winner Power,
Canadian 10f Grade 1 winner/Irish Oaks third Curvy and Ribblesdale Stakes
winner Thakafaat out of a 7f 2yo Group 3 winning half-sister to Cheshire Oaks
winner Rockerlong and the dam of high-class sprinter Superstar Leo.

UNNAMED
4/2 b f Kingman - Lustrous (Champs Elysees)
Owner: Mrs Poilin Good
Sales price: 100,000gns (Vendor)

First foal of a Group 2-placed 7-12f winner (including at Listed level) who was
a half-sister to 6f 2yo Group 3 winner Melody Of Love and useful 6-7f winner
Nobleman's Nest out of an unraced half-sister to Group 2-placed multiple

7f-1m winner (including at Group 3/Listed level) Ordnance Row; the family of French Derby winner Holding Court, French 7f Group 1 winner Tomba and Duke of York Stakes winner/2000 Guineas runner-up Delegator.

UNNAMED (IRE)
6/2 b c Acclamation - Medicean Queen (Medicean)
Owner: Hamdan Al Maktoum
Sales price: £110,000 (Shadwell Stud)

First foal of a maiden half-sister to very useful 5-6f winner Justice Good (by Acclamation) out of a 10f 3yo winner who was a half-sister to German 1000 Guineas/German Oaks winner Que Belle, US 8.5f Listed winner Alybgood, German 12f 3yo Listed winner Quartier Latin and the dams of German 11f 3yo Group 2 winner Quelle Amore and Australian 12f Group 2 winner Muir; the family of 1m Group 2 winner Emperor Jones, 6f 2yo Listed winner/Middle Park Stakes third Majlood and Group 2/3-placed 6f 2yo winner Qui Danzig.

UNNAMED (IRE)
10/5 b f Shamardal - Red Dune (Red Ransom)
Owner: Sheikh Ahmed Al Maktoum
Sales price: n/a

Half-sister to Group 3/Listed-placed 7f-1m 2yo winner Feedyah and Listed-placed 7f-1m winner Red Mist. Dam a Listed-placed 7f-1m 3yo winner who was a half-sister to Japanese 1m Listed winner Hyblon and the unraced dam of Melbourne Cup winner Fiorente out of a useful 7f-1m winning close relation to French 12f Group 1 winner Mountain High and a half-sister to Breeders' Cup Filly & Mare Turf/dual Yorkshire Oaks winner Islington.

UNNAMED (IRE)
13/3 b c Sepoy - Tantshi (Invincible Spirit)
Owner: Sheikh Ahmed Al Maktoum
Sales price: n/a

Half-brother to useful 2019 dual 1m 3yo winner Motawaj. Dam a very useful 6-7f winner (including at Listed level) who was a half-sister to smart UK/UAE 7-10f winner (including at Listed level) Toolain out of a Group 3/Listed-placed 7f 2yo winner; the family of French 10f Group 1 winner Ajman Princess and 1m Group 2 winners Afsare and Ostilio.

Andre Fabre

AGES OF MAN (IRE)
4/5 ch c New Approach - Antiquities (Kaldounevees)
Owner: Godolphin SNC
Sales price: n/a

Three-parts brother to Irish 10f 3yo Listed winner/Irish Oaks third Mary
Tudor (by Dawn Approach) and a half-brother to 2019 French 1m 2yo Group
1 winner Victor Ludorum. Dam a Group 3/Listed-placed French 10-10.5f 3yo
winner who was a half-sister to very useful 7.5-12f winner Space Age (by
New Approach) out of a French 10.5f 3yo Listed winning half-sister to US 1m
1f Grade 1/UAE 10f Group 1 winner Street Cry, the dam of four-time 7-10.5f
Group 1 winner Shamardal and great-grandam of French 1m 3yo Group 1
winner/2000 Guineas second Territories.

AMBOSELI
25/3 b f Kingman - Alla Speranza (Sir Percy)
Owner: Khalid Abdullah
Sales price: n/a

Half-sister to smart 5-7f winner (including at Group 2/Listed level) Shine So
Bright. Dam an Irish 10f 3yo Group 3 winner who was a half-sister to Irish 12f
Listed winner Altesse, five other winners and the once-raced maiden dam of
Park Hill Stakes winner Alyssa, French 1m 2yo Group 3 winner Alea Iacta and
2019 10f 3yo Listed winner Aloe Vera out of a French 10.5f 3yo Listed winner.

CHERIE AMOUR (FR)
15/5 b f Shalaa - Angel Falls (Kingmambo)
Owner: Lady Bamford
Sales price: €250,000 (Charles Gordon Watson Bloodstock)

Three-parts sister to French 1m 2yo Group 1 winner National Defense (by
Invincible Spirit) and a half-sister to Listed-placed 12f 3yo winner Cascading.
Dam an unraced close relation to Group 3-placed French 8-10f winner
(including four times at Listed level) Advice and half-sister to French 1m
3yo Group 3 winner/Irish 1000 Guineas runner-up Anna Salai and Group
2/3-placed UK/UAE 7f-1m winner (including at Listed level) Iguazu Falls.

EGOT (IRE)
24/3 b c Invincible Spirit - Entertains (Street Cry)
Owner: Godolphin SNC
Sales price: n/a

Half-brother to 2019 UK 7f 2yo/2020 UAE 9.5f 3yo winner Laser Show. Dam a Group 3-placed Australian 7-9f winner who was a half-sister to Group 2-placed Australian 7.5f-1m winner Minnesinger and Australian 6.5-7f winner Outdoor (later dam of Australian 7f Group 1 winner Trekking) out of an Australian triple 10-12.5f Group 1 winner.

ERASMO
26/2 b c Oasis Dream - Sant Elena (Efisio)
Owner: Godolphin SNC
Sales price: 140,000gns (Rabbah Bloodstock)

Half-brother to Prix Morny/Middle Park Stakes winner Reckless Abandon, Japanese 12f Listed winner Best Approach and the dam of 2019 7f 2yo Group 3 winner West End Girl. Dam a Listed-placed UK/Canadian 6f-1m winner who was a half-sister to US 9/10f Grade 1 winner Ticker Tape (grandam of 7f 2yo Group 2 winner War Decree) and French 6.5f Group 1 winner Brando out of a maiden half-sister to Racing Post Trophy winner Crowded House.

GOLDEN GLITTER
17/3 b f Dubawi - Golden Lilac (Galileo)
Owner: Gestut Ammerland
Sales price: n/a

Second foal of a French 1000 Guineas/French Oaks winner who was a full sister to Group 2-placed French/Australian 8-12.5f winner (including at Group 3/Listed level) Grey Lion and a half-sister to French 12f 3yo Listed winner Golden Guepard out of a French 1m 3yo Group 1 winner/French 1000 Guineas second/French Oaks third.

GRETA HELLSTROM
17/3 ch f Pivotal - Gonfilia (Big Shuffle)
Owner: Godolphin SNC
Sales price: n/a

Full sister to very useful French/UK 7-9f winner (including at Listed level) Glen Shiel and a half-sister to useful dual 6f winner Signs In The Sand and useful dual 10f winner Greek War. Dam a smart 6-9f winner (including at Group 3/Listed level) who was a half-sister to German dual 12f Group 1 winner

Gonbarda (later dam of Lockinge Stakes/Champion Stakes winner Farhh and 10f Group 3 winner Racing History (both by Pivotal)).

LYRA STAR (IRE)
2/2 b f Frankel - Light The Stars (Sea The Stars)
Owner: Gestut Ammerland
Sales price: n/a

Half-sister to useful 2019 6f 2yo winner Light Angel. Dam a Listed-placed German 7.5f 2yo winner who was a half-sister to French 2000 Guineas/ French Derby winner Lope De Vega, smart French 7.5-10f winner (including at Group 3/Listed level) Bal de La Rose (later dam of German 10f Group 1 winner Danceteria) and Group 1-placed French dual 1m 3yo winner (including at Group 3 level) Lady Frankel (by Frankel).

PARIS (FR)
4/3 b f Shalaa - Treve (Motivator)
Owner: Al Shaqab Racing
Sales price: n/a

Second foal of a top-class French 8-12f winner (including the Prix de l'Arc de Triomphe twice) who was a full sister to French 1m 3yo winner Terre and a half-sister to French 10f 3yo Listed winner Trois Rois and smart US 9-11f winner Trophee out of a French 5.5f 2yo winning half-sister to Grade 1-placed French/US 6f-1m winner (including at Listed level) Tsigane.

PIMENTO
5/2 b c Iffraaj - Chili Dip (Alhaarth)
Owner: Godolphin SNC
Sales price: 115,000gns (Stroud Coleman Bloodstock)

Half-brother to Listed-placed 6f 3yo winner White Bullet and 7f-1m 2yo winner Zakreèt. Dam an unraced sister to Lingfield Oaks Trial winner Birdie (dam of 2019 US 1m 1f 3yo Grade 3 winner Hostess (by Iffraaj)) and half-sister to 10f 3yo Listed winner Fickle (later dam of 1m 1f Group 3 winner Tarfah, herself dam of 2000 Guineas/Derby winner Camelot) and Group 3/Listed-placed 1m 2yo winner Fading Light (later dam of triple 7-12f Listed winner Fireglow).

SATONO CASTLE (FR)
16/3 b c Shalaa - Maiden Tower (Groom Dancer)
Owner: Satomi Horse Company Ltd
Sales price: €600,000 (Narvick International Inc)

Half-brother to Group 2-placed 1m-2m 2f Flat (including at Listed level)/very useful 2m-2m 5f hurdle winner Penglai Pavilion, Listed-placed French 7.5f 3yo winner Picture Hat, useful dual 1m winner Kiz Kulesi and the dam of US 12f Listed winner Creative Thinking. Dam a French 1m 3yo Group 2/3 winner/French 1000 Guineas runner-up who was a half-sister to French 7f 3yo Listed winner Tokyo Rose (dam of Group 3/Listed-placed 7f-1m winner Salsabeel).

SENTIMENTAL MAMBO
4/2 b f Deep Impact - Stacelita (Monsun)
Owner: Teruya Yoshida
Sales price: n/a

Full sister to Japanese 1m 2yo Group 3 winner Schon Glanz and a half-sister to Japanese Oaks winner Soul Stirring. Dam a high-class 9-12f winner (six times at Group/Grade 1 level, including the French Oaks) who was the daughter of a German 7.5f 2yo Listed winning half-sister to German dual 11f Group 2 winner Simoun and German 11f Listed winner Soudaine.

URBANIA
18/4 b f Sea The Stars - Plumania (Anabaa)
Owner: Wertheimer & Frere
Sales price: n/a

Sister to useful French 8-10.5f winner Starmaniac and a half-sister to smart French 8-10.5f winner (including at Group 2/3 level) Plumatic and French 12.5f 3yo Listed winner Maniaco. Dam a French 12f Group 1 winner who was a half-sister to French 12.5f 3yo Group 2 winner Balladeuse (dam of French 12f 3yo Group 1 winner/French Oaks runner-up Left Hand) and the dams of 2019 French 1m 1f 3yo Group 3 winner Flap Shot and 2019 Irish 12f 3yo Listed winner Solage; the family of French 2000 Guineas winner Falco.

VERDERON (IRE)
27/3 ch c Lope De Vega - Indigo Lady (Sir Percy)
Owner: Godolphin SNC
Sales price: 500,000gns (Stroud Coleman Bloodstock)

Half-brother to 10f 3yo winner Expensive Liaison and 2019 1m 2yo winner Indie Angel. Dam a Group 3-placed 7-10f winner (including at Listed level) who was a half-sister to smart multiple 6f 2yo winner (including at Listed level) Prism out of a useful 10.5-12f winner who was a half-sister to Listed-placed Irish 1m 3yo winner Gorgeous Dancer (later dam of Italian 10f Group 1 winner Imperial Dancer); the excellent family of 1000 Guineas winner Harayir.

UNNAMED
2/5 b f Galileo - Waldlerche (Monsun)
Owner: Newsells Park Stud & Gestut Ammerland
Sales price: n/a

Full sister to 2019 Prix de l'Arc de Triomphe winner Waldgeist, a three-parts sister to French 12f 3yo Group 2 winner Waldlied (by New Approach) and a half-sister to very useful 8-10f winner Waldstern and once-raced 2019 8.5f 2yo winner Waldkonig. Dam a French 10.5f 3yo Group 3 winning three-parts sister to the dam of 2019 7f 2yo Listed winner Al Dabaran and half-sister to St Leger winner Masked Marvel and German 1m 3yo Listed winner Waldnah.

Richard Fahey

AL SHOUGHOR
11/3 b f Shalaa - Full Mandate (Acclamation)
Owner: Al Shaqab Racing
Sales price: 160,000gns (Al Shaqab Racing)

Closely related to useful 7-7.5f 3yo winner Dan Troop (by Lawman). Dam a Group 3-placed 6f 2yo winner who was a full sister to very useful 6-6.5f winner Badr Al Badoor (dam of 2019 6f 3yo Listed winner Archer's Dream) and useful multiple 5f winner Acclaim The Nation and a half-sister to very smart multiple 5f winner (including at Group 1 level) Profitable, smart multiple 5-6f winner (including at Group 3/Listed level) Ridge Ranger, Group 3-placed 6-7f winner Crafty Madam and Group 3-placed 6f 2yo winner Danidh Dubai.

BABY BEAMER (IRE)
23/2 ch f Iffraaj - Classic Falcon (Dubawi)
Owner: Mrs Helen Steel
Sales price: €20,000 (Aidan O'Ryan)

Half-sister to 7f 2yo winner Balance Of Power. Dam a 7.5f-1m 3yo winner who was a half-sister to Irish 6f 2yo Group 3 winner Dingle View, Listed-placed prolific 5-7f winner Vhujon and fairly useful 6f 2yo winner An Chulainn.

BEECHWOOD DAVE (IRE)
13/2 b c No Nay Never - The Tempest (Mastercraftsman)
Owner: Middleham Park Racing CXVIII
Sales price: 65,000gns (Bobby O'Ryan/Middleham Park)

Second foal of a 12f 3yo winner who was a half-sister to Listed-placed triple 6f winner Marie Of Lyon out of a Group 3-placed 5f-1m winner (including at Listed level) who was a half-sister to Group 2-placed 5.5-6.5f 2yo winner (including at Group 3 level) Violette, smart 5-7f winner (including at Group 3/Listed level) Silca's Gift and the dams of Group 3-placed 5-6f winner Red Balloons and Listed-placed 5-6f 2yo winner/Norfolk Stakes fourth Nosedive.

CHILLSEA (USA)
5/2 ch f Mshawish - Sandiva (Footstepsinthesand)
Owner: Al Shaqab Racing
Sales price: n/a

First foal of a Grade 2-placed UK/US 5-8.5f winner (including five times at Grade/Group 3 level) who was a half-sister to smart UK/Danish 7-9f winner (including at Listed level) Wentworth and Listed-placed Spanish/French 5f-1m winner Irish Cliff out of an Italian 7-11f winner; the family of Derby winner/2000 Guineas runner-up Sir Percy.

FAYATHAAN (IRE)
28/1 b c Mehmas - Beauty Of The Sea (Elusive Quality)
Owner: H H Shaikh Nasser Al Khalifa & Partner
Sales price: £35,000 (Oliver St Lawrence)

Second foal of a maiden half-sister to Listed-placed 6f 2yo winner Make Fast and 2019 7f 2yo winner Cranberry out of a smart 5-7f winner (including at Group 3/Listed level) who was a half-sister to several winners including useful 8.5f 2yo winner Big Challenge and useful Irish 11.5f 3yo winner Hikari (dam of 2019 10f 3yo Listed winner Raise You).

IN PARADISE
7/2 ch f Twilight Son - Resort (Oasis Dream)
Owner: Cheveley Park Stud
Sales price: n/a

Three-parts sister to Listed-placed 5f 2yo winner Secret Venture (by Kyllachy) and a half-sister to useful multiple 7-8.5f winner Supersta. Dam a 7f-1m 3yo winner who was a three-parts sister to high-class 6-7f winner (including twice at Group 2 level) Byron and two other winners and a half-sister to five winners and Cheshire Oaks runner-up Gay Heroine out of a Cheveley Park Stakes winning half-sister to the dam of Royal Lodge Stakes winner Al Jadeed.

INTERNATIONALDREAM (IRE)
14/2 b c Acclamation - Komedy (Kodiac)
Owner: P D Smith Holdings Ltd
Sales price: €60,000 (A O'Ryan/Richard Fahey)

First foal of a maiden sister to Group 3-placed 6f-1m winner (including twice at Listed level) On Her Toes and half-sister to Group 3-placed 5-6f winner (including at Listed level) Jane's Memory out of an 8-10f winning half-sister to smart multiple 5-7.5f winner (including at Group 2/3 level) The Kiddykid and useful 10-12f winner Mezzanisi.

INTERNATIONAL GIRL (IRE)
2/2 ch f Camacho - Lady Arabella (Dark Angel)
Owner: P D Smith Holdings Ltd
Sales price: £35,000 (Robin O'Ryan/Richard Fahey)

Half-sister to Italian 5-6.5f winner Bella Senz'anima. Dam a 9.5f 3yo winner who was a half-sister to Group 1-placed 5-7f winner (including twice at Listed level)/1000 Guineas fourth Winning Express (by Camacho).

NURSE DEE (IRE)
3/2 b f Kodiac - Party Whip (Whipper)
Owner: Anthony O'Callaghan
Sales price: 52,000gns (Highflyer Bloodstock)

Full sister to Irish 7f 3yo winner Shatharaat and a half-sister to 7f 2yo Group 3 winner Nations Alexander. Dam a once-raced maiden half-sister to 6f 2yo Group 2 winner/Middle Park Stakes third Always Hopeful, Listed-placed 6-7f winner Nacho Libre, very useful multiple 6f-1m winner Extraterrestrial and useful dual 6f 2yo winner Enford Princess.

RHYTHM MASTER (IRE)
5/3 b c Dark Angel - Pastoral Girl (Pastoral Pursuits)
Owner: John Dance
Sales price: 210,000gns (Creighton Schwartz Bloodstock/John Dance)

First foal of a Group 3/Listed-placed 6f 2yo winner who was a sister to Listed-placed triple 5f 2yo winner Lilbourne Lass and a half-sister to 6f 2yo Group 3 winner La Rioja and 5f 3yo winner Flirtinaskirt (dam of Group 2-placed 2019 multiple 5f 2yo winner (including at Group 3/Listed level) Liberty Beach); the family of Park Hill Stakes winner Eastern Aria.

ROOSEVELT'S GRIT
6/2 b c Showcasing - Ziefhd (Haafhd)
Owner: W J & T C O Gredley
Sales price: 100,000gns (A C Elliott, Agent for Tim Gredley)

Fourth foal of a 6-7f winner who was a half-sister to multiple 7f winner Zing Wing, dual 7f 3yo winner Ziekhani, three other winners and the maiden dam of Group 2-placed Irish 6-8.5f winner (including at Group 3/Listed level) Psychedelic Funk, useful 6-9f winner Gurkha Friend (by Showcasing) and useful multiple 6f winner Gale Force Maya out of a dual 1m Listed winning half-sister to Listed-placed 7f-1m winner Welenska; the family of Derby winner Shaamit.

SACRISTY
24/3 b f Twilight Son - Pious (Bishop Of Cashel)
Owner: Cheveley Park Stud
Sales price: n/a

Three-parts sister to high-class prolific 7-8.5f winner (including at Group 2/3 level) Penitent and smart 5-6f 2yo winner (including at Group 2/Listed level) Supplicant (both by Kyllachy) and a half-sister to useful prolific 5f winner Solemn, useful multiple 6f winner Dalton, useful 7f 3yo winner Blithe and 5f 2yo winner My Boy Bill. Dam a dual 6f winner from the family of King's Stand Stakes winner Dominica, 7f 3yo Group 3 winner/Cheveley Park Stakes runner-up Rimth, 6f 2yo Group 2 winner Classic Blade, 6/7f Group 3 winner Kiyoshi and 5f 2yo Group 3 winner Abel Handy.

UNNAMED
13/5 b c The Last Lion - Anadolu (Statue Of Liberty)
Owner: Sheikh Juma Dalmook Al Maktoum
Sales price: 72,000gns (Rabbah Bloodstock)

Half-brother to 2019 5f 2yo winner Istanbul and two other winners. Dam an Irish 5f 2yo Listed winner who was a half-sister to Listed-placed French/Italian 8-13f winner Libero Mercato and the dam of smart Italian 7-12f winner (including at Group 2/Listed level) Chestnut Honey and Listed-placed Irish prolific 7f-1m winner Captain Joy.

UNNAMED (IRE) *Midge*
13/4 ch c Anjaal - Conversational (Thousand Words)
Owner: Mrs Janis Macpherson
Sales price: 26,000gns (Jill Lamb Bloodstock)

Three-parts brother to useful 5f 2yo winner Simmy's Copshop (by Bahamian Bounty) and a half-brother to useful 2019 triple 5f 2yo winner Electric

Ladyland and useful 5-6f winner Thegreatestshowman. Dam a 7f-1m winner who was a half-sister to 7f 3yo Listed winner Kamakiri and Listed-placed 8.5-10f winner Road To Love.

UNNAMED (IRE) *State Patrol*

26/4 b c Zoffany - Mala Mala (Brief Truce)
Owner: Clipper Logistics
Sales price: €50,000 (Joe Foley)

Half-brother to high-class multiple 5-6f 2yo winner (including the Middle Park Stakes) The Last Lion, smart UK/UAE prolific 5-6f winner (including twice at Listed level) Russian Rock, Group 3-placed multiple 5-6f winner (including twice at Listed level) Contest and six other winners. Dam an Irish 5f 3yo winner/Cheveley Park Stakes third who was a half-sister to Irish 1000 Guineas winner Tarascon (later dam of 6f 2yo Listed winner High Award) and high-class 7-10.5f winner (including at Group 2/3 level) Mister Monet.

John Gosden

ALJARDAA (IRE)

4/4 b f Muhaarar - Yasmeen (Sea The Stars)
Owner: Hamdan Al Maktoum
Sales price: n/a

Second foal of a Listed-placed 7f 3yo winner who was a three-parts sister to Group 3-placed 6-7f 2yo winner (including at Listed level) Mudaaraah and a half-sister to 6f 3yo Listed winner Ethaara (later dam of 1m 3yo Listed winner Etaab), 7f 2yo Listed winner Sudoor (later dam of French 10.5f 3yo Group 3 winner Raseed), Group 3-placed dual 7f winner/French 2000 Guineas fourth Muwaary and the dam of Listed-placed 6f 2yo winner Mutaaqeb.

ALMAAN (IRE)

16/3 b c Muhaarar - Seagull (Sea The Stars)
Owner: Hamdan Al Maktoum
Sales price: 360,000gns (Shadwell Estate Company)

Half-brother to useful 2019 7f 2yo winner Wasaayef and 2019 10f 3yo winner Whimbrel. Dam a useful 12f 3yo winner who was a half-sister to Irish 1000 Guineas winner Nightime (dam of 2019 German 12f Group 1 winner Ghaiyyath and US 11f Grade 1 winner Zhukova), Listed-placed Irish 1m 2yo winner Mermaid Island and six other winners out of an Irish 1m Listed winner.

ALPHA KING
5/5 br c Kingman - Kilo Alpha (King's Best)
Owner: Khalid Abdullah
Sales price: n/a

Full brother to 2019 1m 2yo winner Tsar and a half-brother to Grade 1-placed UK/US 7-9.5f winner (including at Grade 3 level) Juliet Foxtrot, Listed-placed French 6f 2yo winner Bravo Sierra and useful French 1m 2yo winner Alpha Bravo. Dam a French 1m 3yo Listed winner who was a sister to Group 1-placed French 7-10f winner (including three times at Listed level) Runaway out of a maiden three-parts sister to 2000 Guineas/Prix de l'Arc de Triomphe winner/Derby runner-up Dancing Brave and French Oaks winner Jolypha (grandam of Canadian 12f Grade 1 winner Redwood).

ALTO VOLANTE
3/3 b c Kingman - Disco Volante (Sadler's Wells)
Owner: Anthony Oppenheimer
Sales price: n/a

Half-brother to smart 7f-2m winner (including twice at Group 3 level) Namibian, useful 7f-1m winner Westwood Hoe, once-raced 2019 1m 2yo winner Domino Darling and four other winners. Dam a Listed-placed 1m 3yo winning half-sister to Group 1-placed 6-7.5f winner/French 2000 Guineas third Valentino out of a Group 1-placed French 5-6f winner (including at Group 2/3 level) who was a half-sister to French 6.5f Group 2 winner/2000 Guineas third Pursuit Of Love and the great-grandam of Oaks winner Look Here.

ATTENDANT
27/3 ch f Frankel - Zuhoor Baynoona (Elnadim)
Owner: Cheveley Park Stud
Sales price: n/a

Half-sister to 2019 6f 2yo winner Custodian. Dam a very useful triple 5f winner (including at Listed level) who was a half-sister to high-class multiple 6f winner (including the 2019 Haydock Sprint Cup) Hello Youmzain and Italian 7.5f 2yo Group 2 winner Royal Youmzain out of an unraced half-sister to 10f 3yo Listed winner Persian Majesty.

BLUE DIAMOND (IRE)
11/5 b f Galileo - Pearling (Storm Cat)
Owner: Imad Al Sagar
Sales price: 1,700,000gns (Blue Diamond Stud Farm UK)

Full sister to very smart 8-10.5f winner (including three times at Group 1 level) Decorated Knight. Dam an unraced sister to six-time 7-10.5f Group 1 winner/2000 Guineas runner-up Giant's Causeway and 6f 2yo Group 2/3 winner You'resothrilling (later dam of 2000 Guineas winner Gleneagles and Irish 1000 Guineas winner Marvellous (both by Galileo)) and half-sister to the unraced dam of Great Voltigeur Stakes winner/Irish Derby runner-up/Derby third Storm The Stars.

CHIASMA (IRE)
27/2 b f Galileo - Kind (Danehill)
Owner: Khalid Abdullah
Sales price: n/a

Full sister to outstanding 7-10.5f winner (ten times at Group 1 level, including the Dewhurst Stakes, 2000 Guineas, Sussex Stakes (twice) and Juddmonte International Stakes) Frankel and high-class 8-12f winner (including three times at Group 1 level) Noble Mission, a three-parts sister to Lingfield Derby Trial winner Bullet Train (by Sadler's Wells) and a half-sister to Group 3-placed triple 6f winner (including twice at Listed level) Joyeuse. Dam a 5/6f Listed winning close relation to UK 12f 3yo Group 2/US dual 11f Grade 2 winner Riposte and a half-sister to 10f Grade 1 10.5f Group 1 winner Powerscourt.

CIVIL CODE
8/3 b c Muhaarar - Helleborine (Observatory)
Owner: Khalid Abdullah
Sales price: n/a

Half-brother to high-class triple 6f winner (including at Group 2/3 level) Calyx. Dam a Group 1-placed French 6f-1m 2yo winner (including at Group 3/Listed level) who was a full sister to very smart 6-7f winner (including at Group 1 level) African Rose (later dam of 6f 2yo Group 3 winner Fair Eva) out of a Group 3/Listed-placed 10f 3yo winner.

DERAB
1/3 b c Sea The Stars - Concentric (Sadler's Wells)
Owner: Khalid Abdullah
Sales price: n/a

Half-brother to top-class 8-12f winner (ten times at Group/Grade 1 level, including the Oaks, Prix de l'Arc de Triomphe (twice) and Breeders' Cup Turf) Enable, Group 3-placed 1m 2yo winner Entitle and Group 3-placed French 12-15f 3yo winner Contribution. Dam a Group 3-placed French triple 10f 3yo winner (including at Listed level) who was a sister to French 12.5f 3yo Group 3 winner Dance Routine (later dam of five-time 10-12f Group/Grade 1 winner Flintshire and grandam of 2019 French dual 10f 3yo Group 2 winner Headman) and a three-parts sister to French dual 1m Group 3 winner Apsis.

EBNZAIDOON
19/3 b c Siyouni - Moonlit Garden (Exceed And Excel)
Owner: Hamdan Al Maktoum
Sales price: 600,000gns (Shadwell Estate Company)

Half-brother to Group 3-placed 5-6f winner Mokaatil and Listed-placed French triple 1m winner Dan. Dam a Listed-placed Irish 6f 2yo winner who was closely related to useful multiple 5-6f winner Profile Star out of an Irish 6-7f winner; the family of Chesham Stakes/Mill Reef Stakes winner Red Cross.

ENTHRAL (IRE)
26/1 b f Exceed And Excel - Aurora Leigh (Dubawi)
Owner: The Queen
Sales price: n/a

First foal of an unraced sister to French 8-8.5f 3yo winner Emirates Rewards and half-sister to high-class 7f-1m 2yo winner (including the Breeders' Cup Juvenile Turf) Outstrip (by Exceed And Excel) out of a US 1m 1f Grade 1 winner.

EXISTENT
3/3 b c Kingman - Entity (Shamardal)
Owner: Cheveley Park Stud
Sales price: n/a

Second foal of a dual 10f 3yo winner who was a half-sister to high-class multiple 1m winner (including twice at Group 1 level) Integral, Listed-placed 7f-1m 3yo winner Provenance and two other winners out of a high-class multiple 6-9f winner (including at Group 1 level) who was a half-sister to dual

1m Group 2 winner Chic; the family of 2000 Guineas winner Entrepreneur, Lockinge Stakes winner Virtual and Coventry Stakes winner Iceman.

FUTURE (IRE)

4/4 b f Galileo - Question Times (Shamardal)
Owner: Qatar Racing Limited
Sales price: 800,000gns (David Redvers Bloodstock)

Half-sister to Irish Derby winner Latrobe, 2019 Irish 10f 3yo Listed winner/ Oaks runner-up Pink Dogwood and Grade 2-placed Irish 6-7f winner (including at Group 3 level) Diamond Fields. Dam a Listed-placed 6f 3yo winner who was a half-sister to 7f 3yo Group 3 winner/Cheveley Park Stakes runner-up Sunday Times (later dam of Breeders' Cup Juvenile Fillies Turf winner Newspaperofrecord and 6f Listed winner Classical Times).

JACK KENNEDY

17/2 b c Galileo - Jack Naylor (Champs Elysees)
Owner: Denford Stud
Sales price: n/a

First foal of a Group 1-placed Irish 7-9.5f winner (including at Group 3/Listed level)/Irish Oaks runner-up who was a half-sister to useful 7-10f winner Hollydaze out of a 10f 3yo Listed winner; the family of Group/Grade 1-placed 2019 6-7f 2yo winner (including at Group 2/3 level) Daahyeh, Group 1-placed 2019 Irish triple 7f 2yo winner (including at Group 2/3 level) Armory (by Galileo) and 7f Group 3 winner So Beloved.

KING LEO

14/3 ch c The Last Lion - Dijarvo (Iceman)
Owner: Sheikh Hamdan Bin Mohammed Al Maktoum
Sales price: 170,000gns (Stroud Coleman Bloodstock)

Half-brother to Group 1-placed multiple 5f 2yo winner (including at Group 2/3 level) Soldier's Call. Dam a French 5f 2yo Listed winner who was a half-sister to seven winners including the dam of Group 2/3-placed Irish 5f 2yo winner Mamba Noire out of a 5f 2yo winning granddaughter of a Queen Mary Stakes winner/Cheveley Park Stakes third.

THE TWO-YEAR-OLD GUIDE 2020

MAHOMES
26/1 b c Dubawi - The Fugue (Dansili)
Owner: Qatar Racing Ltd And Watership Down Stud
Sales price: 1,000,000gns (David Redvers Bloodstock)

Third foal of a very smart multiple 7-12f winner (including four times at Group 1 level) who was a full sister to useful UK/UAE 9.5-10.5f winner Ducab and a half-sister to useful French 1m 3yo winner Excellency out of a 1m 1f 3yo winner/Ribblesdale Stakes runner-up who was a half-sister to Eclipse Stakes winner Compton Admiral, Queen Elizabeth II Stakes winner Summoner and the unraced grandam of July Cup/Prix de la Foret winner Limato.

PARLIAMENT
26/3 b c Fastnet Rock - Starlet's Sister (Galileo)
Owner: Qatar Racing Limited
Sales price: €700,000 (David Redvers)

Half-brother to high-class French/US multiple 8.5-11f winner (seven times at Grade 1 level, including the Breeders' Cup Filly & Mare Turf) Sistercharlie, 2019 French Derby winner/2019 Arc third Sottsass and French 1m 3yo Group 3 winner My Sister Nat. Dam a maiden sister to French 10.5f 3yo Group 3 winner Leo's Starlet and half-sister to Grade 1-placed French 8-9f 2yo winner (including at Group 3 level) Anabaa's Creation (later dam of US 1m 2yo Listed winner/Albany Stakes fourth Create A Dream).

SAEIQA
2/2 b c Shalaa - Present Danger (Cadeaux Genereux)
Owner: Al Shaqab Racing
Sales price: £130,000 (Al Shaqab Racing)

Half-brother to Greek 7f 3yo winner Patriot Game. Dam a useful 6f-1m winner who was a full sister to very useful 7f-1m winner Kehaar and useful 5f 2yo winner All For Laura (later dam of 6f 2yo Group 2 winner/Cheveley Park Stakes runner-up Misheer, herself the dam of 6f 3yo Listed winner Mistrusting) out of a 1m 3yo winner who was a half-sister to Middle Park Stakes winner First Trump; the family of July Cup/Prix de l'Abbaye winner Mr Brooks.

SALAASA (IRE)
6/4 br f Teofilo - Gharaaneej (Pivotal)
Owner: Hamdan Al Maktoum
Sales price: n/a

First foal of a 7f 3yo winner who was a half-sister to German 6f 3yo Listed winner Best Regards and useful 7f 2yo winner Outlaw Country (by Teofilo) out of a dual 5f 3yo winning three-parts sister to 5/6f Group 3 winner Tickled Pink and Group 3/Listed-placed Irish 5f 2yo winner Fantasy and a half-sister to Irish 1000 Guineas/Nassau Stakes winner Halfway To Heaven (dam of four-time 10-12f Group 1 winner Magical and 8/10f Group 1 winner/Oaks runner-up Rhododendron) and 6f 3yo Group 3 winner Theann (dam of US 8/10f Grade 1 winner Photo Call and 6f 2yo Group 2 winner Land Force).

SEVENTH KINGDOM
24/4 b c Frankel - Nayarra (Cape Cross)
Owner: Prince A A Faisal
Sales price: n/a

Half-brother to Listed-placed 5-7f winner Lahore, useful 2019 dual 1m 3yo winner Magical Rhythms and 2019 10f 2yo winner Colonize. Dam an Italian 1m 2yo Group 1 winner who was a half-sister to 7f 2yo Group 2 winner Gustav Klimt, Irish 7f 2yo Group 3 winner Wonderfully, Irish 6f 2yo Listed winner Cuff, 2019 Irish 7f 2yo Listed winner Blissful and Irish 1m 2yo winner/St James's Palace Stakes third Mars; the family of Invincible Spirit and Pinatubo.

SIDE SHOT
27/3 b c Frankel - Photographic (Oasis Dream)
Owner: Khalid Abdullah
Sales price: n/a

Half-brother to smart 8-10.5f winner (including at Group 3 level)/French Oaks fourth Shutter Speed. Dam a useful dual 1m 3yo winning half-sister to Australian triple 8-10f Group 1 winner Foreteller, high-class French 7f-1m winner (including at Group 2/3 level) Modern Look and 6f 3yo Listed winner Arabesque (later dam of Gimcrack Stakes winner Showcasing and 6f 3yo Listed winner/Jersey Stakes second Camacho) out of a Cheveley Park Stakes winner.

SOCIAL STATUS
28/2 b f Frankel - Household Name (Zamindar)
Owner: Lordship Stud
Sales price: 500,000gns (One Agency)

Half-sister to Irish 6f 2yo Listed winner Gobi Desert. Dam a maiden half-sister to Prix du Cadran winner/Ascot Gold Cup runner-up Reefscape, high-class French 12-15.5f winner (including at Group 2/3 level)/Ascot Gold Cup third Coastal Path, high-class French 8-14f winner (including at Group 2/3 level) Martaline and the maiden dam of French 15f 3yo Group 2 winner Doha Dream; the family of Beat Hollow, Kingman, Oasis Dream etc.

TAWLEED (IRE)
2/4 b c Exceed And Excel - Terhaab (Elusive Quality)
Owner: Hamdan Al Maktoum
Sales price: n/a

Third foal of a 6f 2yo winner who was a full sister to Prix Morny winner/Middle Park Stakes third Elusive City and a three-parts sister to US 5f Stakes winner Parisian Affair (later dam of US 8.5f 2yo Stakes winner Crimson China and grandam of Grade 2/3-placed US 1m 2yo winner Belle Laura); the family of US 1m 1f 2yo Grade 3 winner Millions.

THUNDER DRUM (IRE)
16/4 b f Dubawi - Great Heavens (Galileo)
Owner: Nat Rothschild
Sales price: n/a

Full sister to very useful UK/UAE 1m-2m winner Dubhe and a half-sister to useful 8.5-11.5f winner Great Bear. Dam an Irish Oaks winner who was a sister to King George VI And Queen Elizabeth Stakes/Eclipse Stakes winner Nathaniel, a three-parts sister to high-class 7-12f winner (including at Group 1 level)/Irish Oaks runner-up Playful Act, Yorkshire Cup winner/Derby fourth Percussionist and US 11/12f Grade 3 winner Changing Skies and a half-sister to Sun Chariot Stakes/Park Hill Stakes winner Echoes In Eternity.

UNDER WRAPS
14/4 b f Kingman - Confidential Lady (Singspiel)
Owner: Cheveley Park Stud
Sales price: n/a

Half-sister to 1m 3yo Listed winner Red Box, useful French/UAE 8-10f winner Untold Secret, 2019 7.5f-1m 2yo winner Tell Me All and the maiden dam of French 6f 2yo Listed winner Private Matter. Dam a very smart 7-10.5f winner (including the French Oaks)/1000 Guineas runner-up who was the daughter of a Listed-placed dual 7f 3yo winning half-sister to 7f 2yo Group 3 winner White Crown and Group 3/Listed-placed 6f 2yo winner Wind Cheetah.

ZAGATO
15/4 b c Frankel - Izzi Top (Pivotal)
Owner: Castle Down Racing
Sales gns: 725,000gns (Vendor)

Half-brother to smart 6-7f winner Dreamfield, Group 3-placed 7f 2yo winner Prince Eiji and Listed-placed 7-10f winner Willie John. Dam a high-class 9-10.5f winner (including twice at Group 1 level)/Oaks third who was a half-sister to

Group 1-placed 8-10f winner (including at Group 2/Listed level) Jazzi Top and Grade 2-placed UK/US 7-8.5f winner Emaraaty.

ZAHAA
15/2 br f Kingman - Maktaba (Dansili)
Owner: Hamdan Al Maktoum
Sales price: n/a

Second foal of an unraced sister to 12f 3yo winner/Queen's Vase fourth Almoghared and half-sister to Oaks/King George VI and Queen Elizabeth Stakes winner/Arc third Taghrooda out of a Group 2-placed Irish 8-14f winner (including three times at Listed level) who was a full sister to Irish 12f 3yo winner Gentle On My Mind (later dam of 7f 3yo Listed winner Solomon's Bay and 2019 French 1m 2yo Listed winner Tammani).

UNNAMED
12/4 b f Dubawi - Dar Re Mi (Singspiel)
Owner: Lord Lloyd-Webber
Sales price: n/a

Full sister to very smart multiple 7f-1m winner (three times at Group 1 level, including the Dewhurst Stakes and Sussex Stakes) Too Darn Hot, high-class 10-12f winner (including at Group 2/Listed level)/St Leger runner-up Lah Ti Dar and high-class 8-10.5f winner (including at Group 3/Listed level) So Mi Dar. Dam a very smart multiple 10-12.5f winner (including three times at Group 1 level) who was a half-sister to very smart French/UK 8-12f winner (including twice at Group 1 level)/Derby third Rewilding.

UNNAMED (USA)
29/3 b f Medaglia d'Oro - Debonnaire (Anabaa)
Owner: Qatar Racing Limited
Sales price: $300,000 (David Redvers)

Half-sister to high-class UK/Australian prolific 7-12f winner (including four times at Group 1 level) Hartnell, 7f 2yo Listed winner/Fillies' Mile runner-up Roz, 2019 US 6f 2yo winner Ursula and two other winners. Dam a 7f-1m winner who was a three-parts sister to Listed-placed 6-7f winner Proceed With Care out of a Group 3-placed French dual 1m 3yo winning half-sister to French Derby/Prix de l'Arc de Triomphe winner Suave Dancer.

UNNAMED

24/2 b f Galileo - J Wonder (Footstepsinthesand)
Owner: Andrew Rosen
Sales price: n/a

Half-sister to 2019 dual 7f 2yo winner Boccaccio. Dam a high-class 6-7f winner (including twice at Group 3 level) who was a full sister to high-class 6f-1m winner (including at Group 1 level) Chachamaidee (dam of 2019 12f Group 3 winner Klassique (by Galileo)), a three-parts sister to smart UK/Hong Kong 6-7f winner (including at Group 3 level) California Whip and a half-sister to the dam of 1m 2yo Listed winner/Racing Post Trophy third Celestial Path.

Charlie Hills

ALTAAYSHAH (IRE)

22/1 b f Dark Angel - Anna Law (Lawman)
Owner: Hamdan Al Maktoum
Sales price: 800,000gns (Shadwell Estate Company)

Full sister to very smart prolific 5f winner (including twice at Group 1 level) Battaash. Dam a lightly-raced maiden half-sister to Group 1-placed 6-7f winner (including at Group 2/Listed level) Etlaala, Listed-placed dual 6f winner Button Moon, very useful 7f-1m winners Back On Top, Limitless and Selective and the once-raced maiden dam of Group 1-placed 6-7f winner (including at Group 2/3 level) Tasleet and Listed-placed 2019 6f 2yo winner Lady Light.

AMLWCH (IRE)

19/3 b/gr c Muhaarar - Nations Alexander (Dark Angel)
Owner: Dan Hall
Sales price: 80,000gns (Jill Lamb Bloodstock)

First foal of a 7f 2yo Group 3 winning daughter of a once-raced maiden half-sister to 6f 2yo Group 2 winner/Middle Park Stakes third Always Hopeful, Listed-placed 6-7f winner Nacho Libre, very useful multiple 6f-1m winner Extraterrestrial, useful Irish 6.5f-1m winner Monkeylou and useful dual 6f 2yo winner Enford Princess.

DISCOTEQUE (IRE)
7/3 b f Acclamation - Party For Ever (Iffraaj)
Owner: John Dance
Sales price: 185,000gns (Creighton Schwartz Bloodstock/John Dance)

First foal of an unraced close relation to French 6f 2yo Listed winner Corsario and half-sister to smart multiple 5-6f winner (including at Listed level) Line Of Reason, very useful 6-7f winner Bentong and 6.5f 2yo winner Noafal out of a French 1m 3yo winning half-sister to five winners including US 6.5f 2yo Grade 2 winner All Chatter; the family of US 8.5f 3yo Grade 1 winner Caline and Irish 5f 2yo Group 3 winner/Norfolk Stakes runner-up Raphane.

IBIZA ROCKS
10/4 gr c Dark Angel - The Thrill Is Gone (Bahamian Bounty)
Owner: Christopher Wright
Sales price: 70,000gns (Vendor)

Half-brother to dual 7f 3yo winner No More Thrills. Dam a Listed-placed 5f 2yo winner who was a half-sister to high-class UK/UAE prolific 5-7f winner (including at Group 1 level) Muarrab, two-time 5f 2yo Group 3 winner Bungle Inthejungle, 6f Listed winner Waveband, Group 2/3-placed multiple 5f winner Group Therapy, Group 3-placed dual 5f winner Classic Encounter, Listed-placed multiple 5-6f winner Moonraker and the dam of 2019 UAE 5f Listed winner Thammin (by Dark Angel).

MOBARHIN (IRE)
9/4 b c Muhaarar - Fadhayyil (Tamayuz)
Owner: Hamdan Al Maktoum
Sales price: n/a

Second foal of a Group 2/3-placed dual 7f winner (including at Listed level) who was a half-sister to very useful 6-7f winner (including at Listed level) Athenian, very useful French 8-10f winner (including at Listed level) Zipzip, French 7f 2yo Listed winner Cold Stare and useful multiple 7f winner Zacynthus out of a smart French 4.5-5f winner (including at Group 3/Listed level); the family of 1m Group 2 winner/Lockinge Stakes third Swallow Flight.

MOQADAMA (IRE)
16/2 b f Dark Angel - White Daffodil (Footstepsinthesand)
Owner: Hamdan Al Maktoum
Sales price: 390,000gns (Shadwell Estate Company)

Full sister to 6f 2yo Listed winner/Norfolk Stakes runner-up Log Out Island and 2019 6f 3yo Listed winner Khaadem. Dam a 5-6f winner who was a half-sister to dual 6f Listed winner Lady Links (later dam of 7f/1m Listed winner Selinka, herself the dam of Irish dual 5f Group 3 winner Hit The Bid), Group 3-placed 6f 2yo winner Umniya and Listed-placed 6f 2yo winner King Malachi out of a 10-12f winning half-sister to French 6.5f Group 1 winner Bold Edge.

MUJBAR
12/3 b c Muhaarar - Madany (Acclamation)
Owner: Hamdan Al Maktoum
Sales price: n/a

Half-brother to 6f 3yo Group 1 winner Eqtidaar, Group 1-placed dual 7f winner (including at Group 2 level)/2000 Guineas runner-up Massaat and very useful UK/Irish 5-6f winner Hathiq. Dam a dual 6f 2yo winner who was a half-sister to French 5f 2yo Group 3 winner Dolled Up and French 6f 2yo Listed winner Zeiting (later dam of smart performers Bikini Babe, Combat Zone, Royal Empire and Scottish); the family of Lowther Stakes winner Infamous Angel.

MUTARABES (IRE)
23/1 br c Dark Angel - Relation Alexander (Dandy Man)
Owner: Hamdan Al Maktoum
Sales price: £145,000 (Shadwell Stud)

Third foal of a dual 7f winner who was a half-sister to smart 6f-1m winner (including at Listed level) Flaming Spear and seven other winners including UAE 5f Listed winner Taqseem and Group 2-placed 7f 2yo winner Desert Blossom out of a Listed-placed 7f 2yo winner who was a half-sister to the dam of 6f 2yo Listed winner Master Of War.

MUTASAABEQ
29/3 br c Invincible Spirit - Ghanaati (Giant's Causeway)
Owner: Hamdan Al Maktoum
Sales price: n/a

Full brother to 2019 1m 3yo winner Alandalos, closely related to very useful multiple 1m winner Afaak (by Oasis Dream) and a half-brother to three winners, most notably 2020 UAE 6f Group 3 winner Wafy. Dam a 1000 Guineas winner who was closely related to the dam of Queen Mary Stakes winner Maqaasid and a half-sister to 12f Group 3 winner/Champion Stakes runner-up Mawatheeq and 1m 1f 3yo Listed winner/Oaks third Rumoush (later dam of smart performers Muntazah, Talaayeb and Wadilsafa).

TANMAWWY (IRE)
12/4 b c Invincible Spirit - Rufoof (Zamindar)
Owner: Hamdan Al Maktoum
Sales price: n/a

Half-brother to 2019 8.5-10f 3yo winner Muhaarar's Nephew. Dam a dual 7f 3yo winner who was a half-sister to top-class sprinter Muhaarar, 6f 2yo Listed winner Sajwah, Group 3-placed UK/UAE 6-7f winner Tamaathul, useful 1m 3yo winner Raasekha, 7.5f 3yo winner Wufud and 7f 2yo winner Mootaharer out of a Listed-placed dual 7f 3yo winner.

Ger Lyons

ANGEL PALM
24/4 br f Dark Angel - Palmette (Oasis Dream)
Owner: Khalid Abdullah
Sales price: n/a

Half-sister to useful dual 6f 2yo winner Partitia. Dam a 6f 3yo winning sister to Gimcrack Stakes winner Showcasing, Group 3/Listed-placed 6f 2yo winner Tendu and Listed-placed triple 6f winner Bouvardia and half-sister to Group 3-placed dual 6f winner (including at Listed level) Camacho out of a 6f 3yo Listed winning half-sister to Australian triple 8-10f Group 1 winner Foreteller, high-class French 7f-1m winner (including at Group 2/3 level) Modern Look and the dam of Musidora Stakes winner/French Oaks fourth Shutter Speed.

DRESS KODE
19/4 b f Kodiac - Enigmatique (Arcano)
Owner: H Rogers
Sales price: n/a

Second foal of an unraced close relation to very useful multiple 5-6f winner Furious and half-sister to Group 1-placed multiple 5f-1m winner (including at Group 3/Listed level) Lily's Angel and Group 2-placed 7f-1m winner (including at Listed level) Zurigha out of an unraced half-sister to French 10.5f 3yo Group 3 winner In Clover (later dam of French Group 1 winners Call The Wind (2m 4f), We Are (10f) and With You (1m)), French 10f 3yo Listed winner Bayourida and French 10.5f 3yo Listed winner Bellona (grandam of Hong Kong 12f Group 1 winner Dominant).

FLEUR DELACOUR (IRE)
31/3 b f Kodiac - She Bu (Bushranger)
Owner: Miss Kerri Lyons
Sales price: £14,000 (Kerri Lyons)

First foal of an unraced three-parts sister to Irish 6f 2yo Listed winner Alexander Alliance and half-sister to Group 3-placed multiple 6f winner (including twice at Listed level) Ruby Rocket (later dam of Prix de l'Abbaye winner Maarek), German 7.5f 2yo Listed winner Inzar's Best, Listed-placed dual 7f winner Cool Panic and the dam of 5f 2yo Group 2 winner Ardad (by Kodiac); the family of smart sprinters Swiss Spirit, Yalta and Kier Park.

FRENETIC (IRE)
9/4 b f Kodiac - Moojha (Forest Wildcat)
Owner: SBA Racing Limited
Sales price: 170,000gns (SackvilleDonald)

Half-sister to Grade 2-placed US 5-7f winner (including at Stakes level) Big Handsome. Dam a US 6f 3yo winner who was a half-sister to smart US 6-8.5f winner (including at Grade 3 level) Kiss Moon, Grade 3-placed US multiple 8-8.5f winner (including four times at Listed level) Kiss Mine and the unraced dam of high-class 5-6f 2yo winner (including at Group 2/3 level)/Cheveley Park Stakes third Besharah (by Kodiac).

IDES OF AUGUST (USA)
10/4 b/br c More Than Ready - Alina (Came Home)
Owner: Newtown Anner Stud Farm Ltd
Sales price: $420,000 (Not Sold)

Full brother to Group/Grade 1-placed 6.5f-1m winner (including at Group 3/ Listed level) Nemoralia and fairly useful dual 7f 3yo winner Blue On Blue and a half-brother to US 5-6.5f 2yo winner Cynical Storm and US 6f 2yo winner Stormalina. Dam a smart US 5.5f-8.5f winner (including at Listed level) who was a half-sister to six winners.

MASEN
13/3 b c Kingman - Continental Drift (Smart Strike)
Owner: Khalid Abdullah
Sales price: n/a

Third foal of a 6f 2yo winner who was a half-sister to Listed-placed 7.5-8.5f winner Abseil out of a US 8/10f Grade 1 winning sister to Breeders' Cup Filly And Mare Turf winner Banks Hill (later dam of French 10f Group 1 winner

Romantica and grandam of 2019 10f 3yo Group 3 winner Sangarius (by Kingman)), Canadian/US triple 12f Grade 1 winner Champs Elysees, US 10/11f Grade 1 winner Cacique and very smart miler Dansili and half-sister to US 8/9.5f Grade 1 winner Heat Haze (later dam of smart pair Forge and Mirage Dancer) and US 1m 1f Grade 3 winner Deluxe.

Aidan O'Brien

APOLLO THIRTEEN (IRE)
10/2 b/br c No Nay Never - Nasty Storm (Gulch)
Owner: Mrs John Magnier, Michael Tabor & Derrick Smith
Sales price: n/a

Half-brother to Group 1-placed Irish 5-6.5f 2yo winner (including twice at Group 3 level) Actress and the dams of 2019 US 12f Grade 3 winner Causeforcommotion and Italian 8/10f Listed winner Aury Touch. Dam a Grade 1-placed US 5-8.5f winner (including at Grade 2/3 level) who was a half-sister to US 1m 3yo Stakes winner Born Winner and the unraced dam of 6f 2yo Listed winner Sir Edwin Landseer.

BRAZIL (IRE)
6/3 b c Galileo - Dialafara (Anabaa)
Owner: Derrick Smith, Mrs John Magnier & Michael Tabor
Sales price: n/a

Full brother to high-class 7.5-14.5f winner (including the Irish Derby and St Leger) Capri, Irish 2m 3yo Group 3 winner Cypress Creek, useful 7f 2yo winner Jamaica and 2019 Irish 1m 2yo winner Passion. Dam a French 12.5f 3yo winner who was a half-sister to Group 3-placed French 7f 2yo winner Diaghan out of a Group 1-placed French 10-12.5f 3yo winner (including at Group 2/3 level) who was a half-sister to French 7f 2yo Group 3 winner/French 2000 Guineas runner-up Diamond Green.

COUNTY WICKLOW (USA)
18/2 b c War Front - Coolmore (Galileo)
Owner: Michael Tabor, Mrs John Magnier & Derrick Smith
Sales price: n/a

First foal of a Grade 1-placed Irish 7f 2yo Group 3 winner who was a sister to 2000 Guineas winner Gleneagles, Irish 1000 Guineas winner Marvellous (dam of 2019 Irish 7f 2yo Listed winner Fort Myers (by War Front)), 7f/1m 2yo Group 1 winner/1000 Guineas third Happily and Australian dual 12f Group 2 winner The Taj Mahal out of a 6f 2yo Group 2 winning sister to six-time 7-10.5f Group 1 winner/2000 Guineas runner-up Giant's Causeway.

ELIZABETHAN (USA)
31/3 b f War Front - Misty For Me (Galileo)
Owner: Michael Tabor, Derrick Smith & Mrs John Magnier
Sales price: n/a

Full sister to very smart multiple 6-7f winner (including the Middle Park Stakes and Dewhurst Stakes) U S Navy Flag and very smart 5f-1m winner (including three times at Group 1 level)/Irish 1000 Guineas runner-up Roly Poly. Dam a very smart 6-10f winner (four times at Group 1 level, including the Irish 1000 Guineas) who was a sister to high-class 7f-1m 2yo winner (including at Group 1 level)/1000 Guineas runner-up Ballydoyle out of an unraced half-sister to dual 6f 2yo Group 1 winner Fasliyev.

GIORGIO VASARI (IRE)
29/1 b c Air Force Blue - Dream The Blues (Oasis Dream)
Owner: Mrs John Magnier, Michael Tabor & Derrick Smith
Sales price: n/a

Half-brother to smart 5-6f winner (including at Group 1 level) Sioux Nation. Dam a once-raced 6f 3yo winner who was a full sister to useful 6-7.5f winner Bean Uasal and a half-sister to Listed-placed 7-8.5f winner Colour Blue, 7f 2yo winner Blue Mirage, three other winners and the maiden dam of French 6f 2yo Group 3 winner My Catch and French 6f 2yo Listed winner Vladimir out of a Group 1-placed 5-7f winner (including at Group 3 level).

GREAT SUGAR LOAF (IRE)
23/4 b c Galileo - How's She Cuttin' (Shinko Forest)
Owner: Michael Tabor, Mrs John Magnier & Derrick Smith
Sales price: n/a

Three-parts brother to 6f-1m winner Cuttin' Edge (by Rip Van Winkle) and a half-brother to Group 1-placed 5-7f winner (including at Group 3/Listed level) Washington DC. Dam a Listed-placed multiple 5f winner who was a half-sister to fairly useful Irish 6-7f winner Like Magic out of an Irish 5-6f winning half-sister to Listed-placed dual 6f 2yo winner Escape Plan and the unraced dam of 6f 2yo Group 3 winner/Cheveley Park Stakes runner-up Aspen Darlin.

HYDE PARK BARRACKS (USA)
14/3 b c Air Force Blue - Secret Charm (Green Desert)
Owner: Michael Tabor, Derrick Smith & Mrs John Magnier
Sales price: €250,000 (M V Magnier)

Half-brother to Grade 1-placed 6f-1m winner (including at Listed level) Hidden Message, very useful French/UAE 7f-1m winner Encipher and very useful UAE 9-10f winner Respect Me. Dam a 7f 2yo Listed winner who was a half-sister to 7f 2yo Listed winner/Oaks third Relish The Thought (later dam of US 1m 1f 3yo Grade 2 winner My Gi Gi).

IOWA (IRE)
2/4 b c Galileo - Bridal Dance (Danehill Dancer)
Owner: Mrs John Magnier, Michael Tabor & Derrick Smith
Sales price: n/a

Three-parts brother to 2019 Royal Lodge Stakes winner Royal Dornoch (by Gleneagles) and a half-brother to Group/Grade 1-placed UK/US 7-10f winner (including at Grade 2/Group 3 level) Hawksmoor, Group 2-placed Irish 6f 2yo winner Magical Fire and the maiden dam of 2019 French 5f 2yo Listed winner Flaming Princess. Dam a maiden half-sister to Grade 1-placed UK/US 7f-1m winner (including at Grade 3/Listed level) Millennium Dragon.

MADONNA (IRE)
4/2 b f Galileo - You'resothrilling (Storm Cat)
Owner: Michael Tabor, Derrick Smith & Mrs John Magnier
Sales price: n/a

Full sister to very smart 7f-1m winner (four times at Group 1 level, including the 2000 Guineas) Gleneagles, Irish 1000 Guineas winner Marvellous, 7f/1m 2yo Group 1 winner/1000 Guineas third Happily, Australian dual 12f Group 2 winner The Taj Mahal and Grade 1-placed Irish 7f 2yo Group 3 winner Coolmore. Dam a 6f 2yo Group 2/3 winning sister to six-time 7-10.5f Group 1 winner/2000 Guineas runner-up Giant's Causeway.

MERCHANTS QUAY (FR)
13/3 ch c No Nay Never - Painting (Peintre Celebre)
Owner: Mrs John Magnier, Michael Tabor & Derrick Smith
Sales price: €300,000 (Michael Vincent Magnier)

Half-brother to 2020 French 1m 3yo Listed winner Pisanello, French 6f 2yo winner Pauline and the maiden dam of Group 3-placed French 6f 2yo winner Kilfrush Memories. Dam a maiden half-sister to smart French 5-5.5f 2yo winner (including at Group 2/3 level) Beauty Is Truth (later dam of 2019

English and Irish 1000 Guineas winner Hermosa, 8/12f 3yo Group 1 winner Hydrangea and Australian 10f Group 1 winner The United States) and French 1m 1f 3yo Listed winner/French 1000 Guineas second/French Oaks third Glorious Sight.

MILITARY STYLE (USA)
8/2 b c War Front - Together Forever (Galileo)
Owner: Derrick Smith, Mrs John Magnier & Michael Tabor
Sales price: n/a

Full brother to 2019 7f 2yo winner King Of Athens. Dam a Fillies' Mile winner who was a full sister to Oaks winner Forever Together and a half-sister to high-class 6f-1m winner (including at Group 1 level) Lord Shanakill out of an unraced half-sister to US 10f Grade 1 winner Spanish Fern, the dam of US 10f Grade 1 winner Heatseeker and grandam of Italian 1m 2yo Group 1 winner Hearts Of Fire.

MONDAY (USA)
23/2 b/br f Fastnet Rock - Ballydoyle (Galileo)
Owner: Michael Tabor, Derrick Smith & Mrs John Magnier
Sales price: n/a

First foal of a high-class 7f-1m 2yo winner (including at Group 1 level)/1000 Guineas runner-up who was a sister to very smart 6-10f winner (four times at Group 1 level, including the Irish 1000 Guineas) Misty For Me (later dam of very smart multiple 6-7f winner (including three times at Group 1 level) U S Navy Flag and very smart 5f-1m winner (including three times at Group 1 level)/Irish 1000 Guineas second Roly Poly).

MORE BEAUTIFUL (USA)
22/4 b f War Front - Maybe (Galileo)
Owner: Derrick Smith, Mrs John Magnier & Michael Tabor
Sales price: n/a

Half-sister to very smart multiple 1m winner (including the 2000 Guineas) Saxon Warrior. Dam a very smart 6-7f winner (including at Group 1 level)/1000 Guineas third who was a full sister to Group 1-placed Irish 7-7.5f 2yo winner (including at Group 3 level) Promise To Be True out of a 5f 2yo Listed winning close relation to Oaks winner Dancing Rain (later dam of UAE 8/9f Group 2 winner Magic Lily and 2019 French 12f 3yo Listed winner Jalmoud).

SAN MARTINO (IRE)
15/3 ch c The Gurkha - Euphrasia (Windsor Knot)
Owner: Mrs John Magnier, Michael Tabor & Derrick Smith
Sales price: €260,000 (M V Magnier)

Third foal of a smart Irish 9-10f winner (including at Group 3/Listed level) who
was a half-sister to five winners including Listed-placed 5f 2yo winner Langavat
out of a Listed-placed 6f 2yo winning half-sister to Group 3-placed 6-7f winner
(including at Listed level) Intense Pink, 6f 2yo winner/Racing Post Trophy third
Henrik, Group 2/Listed-placed 6-6.5f winner Sir Reginald and the unraced dam
of 1m 3yo Listed winner/2000 Guineas third Van Der Neer.

SNOWFALL (JPN)
9/2 b f Deep Impact - Best In The World (Galileo)
Owner: Michael Tabor, Derrick Smith & Mrs John Magnier
Sales price: n/a

First foal of an Irish 12f 3yo Group 3 winner who was a full sister to very smart
8-12f winner (including the Prix de l'Arc de Triomphe)/Irish 1000 Guineas
runner-up Found, Irish 7f 2yo Group 3 winner Magical Dream and three other
winners out of a Lockinge Stakes winner.

ST MARK'S BASILICA (FR)
18/3 b c Siyouni - Cabaret (Galileo)
Owner: Derrick Smith, Mrs John Magnier & Michael Tabor
Sales price: 1,300,000gns (M V Magnier)

Half-brother to Vertem Futurity Trophy/2019 2000 Guineas winner Magna
Grecia and useful Irish triple 7f winner Invincible Ryker. Dam an Irish 7f 2yo
Group 3 winner who was a half-sister to several winners including smart 7-10f
winner (including at Group 3 level) Drumfire and Group 2-placed UK/Hong
Kong 6f-1m winner (including at Listed level) Ho Choi.

SWEET MOLLY MALONE (USA)
30/1 b f American Pharoah - Cherry Hinton (Green Desert)
Owner: Michael Tabor, Derrick Smith & Mrs John Magnier
Sales price: n/a

Half-sister to high-class 7-12f winner (including the Irish Oaks) Bracelet, US
10f 3yo Grade 1 winner Athena, 7f 2yo Group 2 winner Wading (later dam
of Rockfel Stakes winner Just Wonderful) and 2019 Irish 1m 1f 3yo Group
3 winner Goddess. Dam a Group 3/Listed-placed maiden close relation to
exceptional 7-12f winner (six times at Group 1 level, including the 2000
Guineas, Derby and Arc) Sea The Stars and Irish 6f 2yo Listed winner Born

To Sea and a half-sister to several smart winners, notably Derby, Irish Derby and King George VI and Queen Elizabeth Stakes winner Galileo and the great-grandam of Derby winner Masar.

SWISS ACE
11/2 b c Kingman - Swiss Lake (Indian Ridge)
Owner: Mrs John Magnier, Michael Tabor & Derrick Smith
Sales price: 400,000gns (M V Magnier)

Three-parts brother to Group 2-placed 5-6f winner (including at Group 3/Listed level) Swiss Spirit (by Invincible Spirit) and a half-brother high-class multiple 5-6f winner (including at Group 3/Listed level) Swiss Diva (dam of French 5f 2yo Listed winner Poetry (by Kingman)), smart 5-6f winner (including three times at Listed level) Swiss Dream (later dam of 6f 3yo Group 3 winner Yafta), very useful dual 5f winner/Coventry Stakes runner-up Swiss Franc and six other winners. Dam a Group 2-placed triple 5f winner (including twice at Listed level) who was a half-sister to Listed-placed 5-6f winner Dubai Princess.

WILLOW (IRE)
9/3 b f American Pharoah - Peeping Fawn (Danehill)
Owner: Michael Tabor, Derrick Smith & Mrs John Magnier
Sales price: n/a

Half-sister to Group/Grade 1-placed dual 7f 2yo winner (including at Listed level) September and Irish 6f 2yo winner/Coventry Stakes third Sir John Hawkins. Dam a very smart 8-12f winner (four times at Group 1 level, including the Irish Oaks)/Oaks runner-up who was a half-sister to French 1m 2yo Group 1 winner Thewayyouare out of an Irish 7f 2yo winner/Fillies' Mile runner-up who was a half-sister to French 1m 3yo Group 2 winner/Coronation Stakes second Smolensk, Irish 1m 2yo Group 3 winner Turnberry Isle and the dam of Belmont Stakes winners Jazil and Rags To Riches.

UNNAMED (IRE)   *The Orient*
23/3 b c Gleneagles - Obama Rule (Danehill Dancer)
Owner: Mrs John Magnier, Derrick Smith & Michael Tabor
Sales price: €170,000 (M V Magnier)

Half-brother to 7f 3yo winner Yamarhaba Malayeen. Dam an Irish 1m 1f 3yo Group 3 winner who was a full sister to Grade 1-placed 6f-1m winner (including at Group 3/Listed level) Osaila and a three-parts sister to Australian 1m Group 3 winner Dawn Wall out of an unraced half-sister to Arc winner Carnegie, French 10f 3yo Group 2 winner Antisaar, 12f Group 3 winner Lake Erie and the grandam of Ribblesdale Stakes winner Banimpire.

Joseph O'Brien

BOYNE RIVER
24/1 b f Kingman - Adonesque (Sadler's Wells)
Owner: Sun Bloodstock Sarl
Sales price: 120,000gns (Sun Bloodstock)

Half-sister to Listed-placed French 8-8.5f winner Bergamask (later dam of Coventry Stakes winner Buratino), Listed-placed UAE 7-10f winner Busker, dual 1m 2yo winner Fareej, 5f 2yo winner Split Rock and 6f 2yo winner Alderney. Dam an Irish 10f 3yo Listed winner who was a half-sister to very smart 6-7f winner (including twice at Group 1 level) Danehill Dancer, 6f 2yo Group 3 winner Unilateral and Irish 6f 2yo Listed winner Colossus.

COMICAL (IRE)
15/4 b f No Nay Never - Veronica Falls (Medicean)
Owner: Mrs A M O'Brien
Sales price: 375,000gns (Joseph O'Brien)

Half-sister to Listed-placed Irish dual 6f 2yo winner Chicas Amigas. Dam an Irish 1m 3yo winner who was a half-sister to five winners and the daughter of a Group 3/Listed-placed 7-12f winning half-sister to the unraced dam of smart 7-10f winner (including at Group 3/Listed level) Red Badge; the family of Fillies' Mile winner Red Bloom.

EQUUS DEUS (IRE)
21/2 b c Galileo - Mystical Lady (Halling)
Owner: Rectory Road Holdings Ltd/Mrs Magnier & O'Brien
Sales price: n/a

Full brother to smart 8.5-14f winner (including twice at Listed level)/Irish Derby and Ascot Gold Cup runner-up Kingfisher, Group 3-placed Irish 1m 2yo winner Finn McCool and Listed-placed Irish 1m 2yo winner Cocoon. Dam an Irish 1m 3yo Listed winner who was a half-sister to Irish 1m 3yo Group 3 winner/French 2000 Guineas third Furner's Green, Irish 1m 2yo Listed winner Lady Lupus and Irish 8.5f 3yo Listed winner Palace (dam of 2019 Irish 1m 2yo Group 2 winner/Vertem Futurity Trophy runner-up Innisfree (by Galileo)).

LIFFEY RIVER (FR)
2/4 b c Lope De Vega - Black Dahlia (Dansili)
Owner: Sun Bloodstock Sarl
Sales price: €380,000 (Private Sale)

Full brother to smart 2019 Irish 6-7f 2yo winner (including at Group 3 level) Lope Y Fernandez, Listed-placed French 7.5f 3yo winner Al Hayyah and useful dual 10f winner Another Eclipse and a half-sister to smart 6-7f 2yo winner (including at Group 3 level) Dark Vision. Dam a Listed-placed 7-10f winning daughter of a French 7f 3yo Listed winning half-sister to the dam of 6f 2yo Group 3 winner Majestic Dubawi.

UNNAMED (IRE)   *Hype* (handwritten)
19/2 b c Siyouni - Eavesdrop (Galileo)
Owner: Lloyd J Williams
Sales price: 150,000gns (Joseph O'Brien)

First foal of a maiden half-sister to high-class multiple 5-6f winner (including twice at Group 1 level) Kingsgate Native and Stakes-placed UK/US 5-6.5f winner Vanishing Grey (later dam of French 1m 3yo Listed winner First Contact); the family of 1000 Guineas winner Las Meninas and Queen Mary Stakes winner Signora Cabello.

UNNAMED (CAN)   *Early Warning* (handwritten)
13/4 ch c Air Force Blue - Orchard Beach (Tapit)
Owner: Qatar Racing Ltd/Mrs A M O'Brien
Sales price: $400,000 (David Redvers)

Half-brother to Group 2-placed multiple 5-5.5f 2yo winner (including at Group 3/Listed level) Sergei Prokofiev. Dam a twice-raced maiden half-sister to US 6f 2yo Grade 3 winner Necessary Evil and three other winners out of a once-raced maiden half-sister to US 5f 2yo Stakes winner Forest Danz; the family of US 6/7f 2yo Grade 1 winner Over All.

Kevin Ryan

BERGERAC (IRE)
7/4 b c Kodi Bear - Fancy Vivid (Galileo)
Owner: Mrs Angie Bailey
Sales price: £75,000 (Hillen/Ryan)

Half-brother to smart Irish 7f-1m winner (including at Group 3 level) Zihba. Dam a maiden sister to useful Irish dual 10f 3yo winner Great Explorer and half-sister to useful Irish 8-10f winner Tobar Na Gaoise, useful multiple 6-7f winner Bungee Jump and 5f 2yo winner Somebody To Love; the family of Middle Park Stakes/July Cup winner Dream Ahead, Cheveley Park Stakes winner Fairyland and Princess Margaret Stakes winner/Cheveley Park Stakes second Princess Noor.

BROOMY LAW
9/2 b c Gleneagles - Hooray (Invincible Spirit)
Owner: Sheikh Mohammed Obaid Al Maktoum
Sales price: 200,000gns (Kevin Ryan)

Three-parts brother to useful dual 1m 3yo winner Restive Spirit (by Intello) and a half-brother to fairly useful 6-7f 3yo winner Boost. Dam a Cheveley Park Stakes winner who was a three-parts sister to Listed-placed 6f-1m winner Mazyoun and a half-sister to French 1m 2yo Listed winner Hypnotic, 6f 2yo winner Hip and 1m 2yo winner Notorize out of a 7f 2yo Listed winning half-sister to Cherry Hinton Stakes winner/1000 Guineas third Dazzle.

CAIRN ISLAND (IRE)
21/3 b c Kodiac - Landmark (Arch)
Owner: Sheikh Mohammed Obaid Al Maktoum
Sales price: 525,000gns (Kevin Ryan)

Closely related to useful dual 10f winner Sour Mash (by Danehill Dancer) and a half-brother to smart 10-11.5f winner (including twice at Listed level) Cameron Highland, Group 2/Listed-placed 12f 3yo winner Field Of Miracles (dam of 2019 Chester Cup winner Making Miracles), useful 7-10f winner Solid Stone and 2019 7f 2yo winner Rovaniemi. Dam a US 1m 2yo winning full sister to US 1m 1f/Canadian 10f Grade 1 winner Arravale.

DARVEL (IRE)
24/3 b c Dark Angel - Anthem Alexander (Starspangledbanner)
Owner: Sheikh Mohammed Obaid Al Maktoum
Sales price: 380,000gns (Kevin Ryan)

Half-brother to 2019 6.5f 2yo winner Full Verse. Dam a Group 1-placed 5-6f winner (including at Group 2/3 level) who was a half-sister to Group 1-placed 5-6f winner (including at Group 3/Listed level) Dandy Man, useful 6-7f winner Good Authority and the dams of 6f Group 3 winner Hamza and Irish 7f 3yo Listed winner Alkasser out of a 5/6.5f 2yo Group 3 winner who was a half-sister to the dam of 5f 2yo Listed winner Patience Alexander.

HELLO ZABEEL (IRE)
7/3 b c Frankel - Lady Of The Desert (Rahy)
Owner: Jaber Abdullah
Sales price: n/a

Full brother to high-class 5-6f winner (including at Group 2/Listed level) Queen Kindly and a half-brother to useful 6-7f winner Marhaba Milliar. Dam a Group 1-placed 5-6f winner (including at Group 2/3 level) who was a half-sister to eight winners including very useful 9-14f winner King's Advice (by Frankel) out of a Cheveley Park Stakes winning half-sister to top-class middle distance performer Dylan Thomas and 1000 Guineas winner Homecoming Queen.

HOPE OF LIFE (IRE)
13/3 b f Kodiac - Bobby Jane (Diktat)
Owner: Sheikh Abdullah Almalek Alsabah
Sales price: 80,000gns (Sheikh Abd. Al-Malek Al-Sabah)

Full sister to Group 2-placed multiple 6f-1m winner (including three times at Listed level) Second Thought and useful UK/Hong Kong 5-6f winner Forever Red. Dam a maiden daughter of a useful dual 5f 2yo winning half-sister to very smart multiple 6f-1m winner (four times at Group 1 level, including the 1000 Guineas) Sky Lantern, Irish 6f 2yo Group 3 winner Arctic, Queen's Vase winner Shanty Star and 6/7f Listed winner Hinton Admiral.

MANASSAS
22/5 b c Dubawi - Without You Babe (Lemon Drop Kid)
Owner: Sheikh Mohammed Obaid Al Maktoum
Sales price: 1,000,000gns (Kevin Ryan)

Half-brother to high-class 7f-1m winner (including at Grade 1 level) Tamarkuz, high-class multiple 1m winner (including at Group 1 level) Without Parole, Listed-placed 7f-1m winner She's Got You and two other winners. Dam an unraced half-sister to US 8/10f Grade 1 winner Stay Thirsty and US 1m 1f 3yo Grade 3 winner Andromeda's Hero.

PRINCE OF PEARLS
15/2 b c Kingman - Martha Watson (Dream Ahead)
Owner: Sheikh Mohammed Obaid Al Maktoum
Sales price: 550,000gns (Kevin Ryan)

First foal of an unraced half-sister to Group 1-placed 5-6f winner (including at Group 2/3 level) Anthem Alexander, Group 1-placed 5-6f winner (including at Group 3/Listed level) Dandy Man, five other winners including the dam of Irish

7f 3yo Listed winner Alkasser and maiden dam of 6f Group 3 winner/Prix de l'Abbaye third Hamza.

SEACLUSION

20/5 b f Fountain Of Youth - On The Brink (Mind Games)
Owner: T G & Mrs M E Holdcroft
Sales price: n/a

Half-sister to 6f Listed winner Aetna, Listed-placed triple 6f winner Shabaaby and four other winners. Dam a 5f 2yo Listed winner who was a full sister to Listed-placed 5-7f winner Silaah and the dam of 2019 Prix de l'Abbaye winner Glass Slippers and 7f 2yo Listed winner Electric Feel and a half-sister to French 5f 2yo Listed winner Eastern Romance, Listed-placed prolific 5-6f winner Blue Tomato and very useful UK/UAE 5-7f winner Sea Hunter.

TRILOGY

7/2 b c Dark Angel - Shaden (Kodiac)
Owner: Sheikh Mohammed Obaid Al Maktoum
Sales price: 210,000gns (Kevin Ryan)

First foal of a 6f 2yo Group 3 winner who was a half-sister to Irish 10-10.5f Flat/dual 2m hurdle winner I'll Be Your Clown out of a Listed-placed 5f 2yo winning daughter of a maiden half-sister to Listed-placed 6f 2yo winner Shuhrah (later dam of Listed-placed UK/UAE 6-9f winner Iqte Saab); the family of Queen Elizabeth II Stakes/Queen Anne Stakes winner Lahib.

Richard Spencer

BIG NARSTIE (FR)

4/3 b/br c Cable Bay - Granadilla (Zafonic)
Owner: Rebel Racing Premier III
Sales price: €52,000 (Arthur Hoyeau, Agent)

Half-brother to French 7f 2yo Listed winner Aktoria, Group 3-placed French dual 5f 2yo winner Galaktea, Listed-placed Irish 5f 3yo winner Now You're Talking and the dam of French 10.5f 3yo Listed winner Sweet Charity. Dam a 7f 3yo winning daughter of a Group 3-placed 6-7f winner (including at Listed level) who was a half-sister to the dam of high-class sprinter Ialysos; the family of Irish Derby winner Tyrnavos, Dewhurst Stakes winner Tromos and Middle Park Stakes winner Tachypous.

HAROLD SHAND (IRE)
6/3 b c Acclamation - Shy Audience (Sir Prancealot)
Owner: Rebel Racing Premier III
Sales price: £70,000 (Bobby O'Ryan/Richard Spencer)

First foal of an unraced half-sister to very smart 6f-1m winner (including at Group 1 level) Toormore, smart 6.5f-1m winner (including at Group 2/Listed level) Estidhkaar, useful 5.5-7f winner Try The Chance and the unraced dam of 2019 5f 2yo Listed winner Orlaith out of an unraced half-sister to Group 3-placed UK/UAE 7-8.5f winner Easaar.

IVAN DRAGO
6/4 br c Equiano - Tesary (Danehill)
Owner: Rebel Racing Premier III
Sales price: £46,000 (Bobby O'Ryan/Richard Spencer)

Three-parts brother to fairly useful multiple 5-6f winner Englishwoman (by Acclamation) and a half-brother to useful prolific 5-6f winner Englishman, useful 5-6f winner Verbeeck and 6.5f 2yo winner Thrilla In Manila. Dam a useful 5-7f winning daughter of an unraced half-sister to French 5.5f 2yo Group 1 winner Balbonella (later dam of July Cup winner Anabaa, French 1000 Guineas winner Always Loyal and French 5f 2yo Group 3 winner Key Of Luck).

OCEAN EYES (IRE)
18/3 b f Mehmas - Rise Up Lotus (Zebedee)
Owner: Phil Cunningham
Sales price: £34,000 (Bobby O'Ryan/Richard Spencer)

Half-sister to 5f 2yo winner Mawde. Dam a dual 5f 2yo winner who was a half-sister to Group 2-placed 5-7f winner Roi De Vitesse and Listed-placed 6-7f winner Rebel Surge out of a 1m 2yo winner who was a half-sister to 10f 3yo Listed winner Santa Isobel (later dam of smart stayer Whiplash Willie).

WINGS OF A DOVE (IRE)
22/1 gr f Dark Angel - Silk Bow (Elusive City)
Owner: Phil Cunningham
Sales price: £82,000 (Bobby O'Ryan/Richard Spencer)

First foal of a Listed-placed 5f 2yo winner who was the daughter of a 1m 3yo winning half-sister to smart 6f-1m winner (including at Listed level) Flaming Spear, smart Irish/UAE 5-6.5f winner (including at Listed level) Taqseem, Group 2-placed 7f 2yo winner Desert Blossom (dam of 2019 1m 3yo Listed winner

Duneflower and once-raced 2019 7f 2yo winner Spring Of Love) and useful Irish 7.5-10.5f 3yo winner Aqraan out of a Listed-placed 7f 2yo winner.

Sir Michael Stoute

CRYSTAL STARLET
21/2 b f Frankel - Crystal Zvezda (Dubawi)
Owner: Sir Evelyn de Rothschild
Sales price: n/a

First foal of a 10f 3yo Listed winner who was a half-sister to very smart 10-12f winner (including the 2019 Prince Of Wales's Stakes) Crystal Ocean, high-class 7-12f winner (including at Grade 1 level) Hillstar and high-class 10-12f winner (including at Group 2/3 level) Crystal Capella out of a Group 3-placed dual 7f 2yo winner (including at Listed level) who was a half-sister to 12f 3yo Listed winner Waila; the family of French 1000 Guineas winner Rose Gypsy.

DEGREE
16/2 b f Dubawi - Echelon (Danehill)
Owner: Cheveley Park Stud
Sales price: n/a

Half-sister to high-class multiple 1m winner (including twice at Group 1 level) Integral, Listed-placed 7f-1m 3yo winner Provenance and three other winners. Dam a high-class multiple 6-9f winner (including at Group 1 level) who was a half-sister to Group 1-placed multiple 7f-1m winner (including at Group 2/3 level) Chic and the dam of 6f Listed winner Don't Touch out of a Coronation Stakes winner who was a half-sister to 2000 Guineas winner Entrepreneur and Cheshire Oaks winner/Oaks runner-up Dance A Dream.

DIVINE HERALD
2/4 b f Frankel - Heaven Sent (Pivotal)
Owner: Cheveley Park Stud
Sales price: n/a

Full sister to Listed-placed UK/Hong Kong 6-7f winner Seven Heavens and a half-sister to very useful multiple 7f-1m winner Firmament and useful 7-11.5f winner You're Hired. Dam a Group 1-placed 7-9f winner (including at Group 3/Listed level) who was a sister to US dual 10f Grade 1 winner Megahertz, Listed-placed dual 1m winner Heavenly Dawn and very useful multiple 5-7f winner Orion's Bow and a half-sister to the dam of Grade 3-placed UK/Canadian dual 7f winner (including at Stakes level) Endless Light.

KING CAPELLA
24/1 b c Kingman - Crystal Capella (Cape Cross)
Owner: Sir Evelyn de Rothschild
Sales price: n/a

Half-brother to useful dual 10f 3yo winner Crystal Moonlight. Dam a high-class 10-12f winner (including at Group 2/3 level) who was closely related to very smart 10-12f winner (including at Group 1 level) Crystal Ocean and a half-sister to high-class 7-12f winner (including the Canadian International) Hillstar and 10f 3yo Listed winner Crystal Zvezda.

MASNOON
14/3 br/gr c Shalaa - Vayasa (Zamindar)
Owner: Hamdan Al Maktoum
Sales price: 110,000gns (Shadwell Estate Company)

Third foal of a once-raced maiden half-sister to French 7f 2yo Group 3 winner Visionario, Group 2-placed French 11-12f 3yo winner Vision Celebre, Group 3-placed French dual 1m winner Visiyani and the maiden dam of 2019 6f 2yo winner/July Stakes third Visinari out of a French 1m 3yo winner/French Oaks third who was a sister to French 10.5f 3yo Group 3 winner Visorama (later dam of very smart stayer Vazirabad) and a half-sister to French 7f Group 1 winner Varenar and French 10f 3yo Group 2 winner Visindar.

MAXIMAL
3/3 b c Galileo - Joyeuse (Oasis Dream)
Owner: Khalid Abdullah
Sales price: n/a

Half-brother to 2019 6-7f 3yo winner/Coronation Stakes third Jubiloso and 2019 dual 6f 2yo winner Jovial. Dam Group 3-placed triple 6f winner (including twice at Listed level) who was a sister to useful 8-8.5f winner Morpheus and a half-sister to outstanding 7-10.5f winner (including ten times at Group 1 level) Frankel, high-class 8-12f winner (including three times at Group 1 level) Noble Mission (both by Galileo) and Lingfield Derby Trial winner Bullet Train.

POTAPOVA
21/5 b f Invincible Spirit - Safina (Pivotal)
Owner: Cheveley Park Stud
Sales price: n/a

Full sister to 6f 2yo winner Panova and a half-sister to Group 2-placed 7f-1m winner (including at Group 3 level) Marenko, useful 6f 2yo winner Vesnina (dam of Group 3-placed 2019 6f 2yo winner Nina Ballerina), useful 2019 8-10f winner Davydenko and 2019 7f 2yo winner Melnikova. Dam a Listed-placed 7f 3yo winning half-sister to the dam of Group 2-placed 7f-1m winner (including at Group 3/Listed level) Zonderland out of a 1000 Guineas winner.

QUEEN'S FAIR
16/4 b f Dansili - Queen's Best (King's Best)
Owner: Cheveley Park Stud
Sales price: n/a

Sister to Breeders' Cup Filly & Mare Turf winner Queen's Trust and useful dual 7f 3yo winner Royal Seal. Dam a Group 2-placed 6-12f winner (including at Group 3/Listed level) who was a half-sister to French 12f Listed winner Reverie Solitaire (later dam of German 1m Group 2 winner Royal Solitaire), 13f Listed winner Urban Castle and the dam of Group 1-placed triple 7f winner (including at Group 3 level) Dabyah; the family of French 1000 Guineas/French Oaks winner Avenir Certain and smart trio Blue Monday, Hattan and Tastahil.

SATONO CHEVALIER (IRE)
22/2 b c Invincible Spirit - Albisola (Montjeu)
Owner: Satomi Horse Company Ltd
Sales price: €450,000 (Narvick International Inc)

Half-brother to useful French 9-10f winner Louversey. Dam a smart French 9-10.5f winner (including at Group 3/Listed level) who was a half-sister to Group 1-placed 7f-1m winner (including at Group 3 level) Johnny Barnes, Listed-placed French dual 1m winner Bufera (dam of French 1m 3yo Listed winner Chartreuse) and the dams of French 1m 2yo Group 1/US 12f Grade 1 winner Ectot and St James's Palace winner Most Improved and 7f 3yo Group 3 winner/1000 Guineas third Daban and 1m 3yo Group 3 winner Thikriyaat.

Satono Japan announces himself a colt of significant potential with an impressive debut success at Kempton last autumn. The same connections will be hoping that Satono Chevalier can make a similarly favourable impression in his first season.

SUNRISE VALLEY (USA)
6/3 b f Karakontie - Story (War Front)
Owner: Flaxman Stables Ireland Ltd
Sales price: n/a

First foal of an unraced sister to US 1m 3yo winner Scandaleuse out of a US 1m 1f Grade 1 winner who was a half-sister to US 1m 1f Grade 2 winner Hoop Of Colour, Listed-placed US 8-8.5f winner Namaskara, once-raced 7f 2yo winner Spy Eye and French 9.5f 2yo winner Loverdose out of a US 8.5f Grade 2 winning three-parts sister to the dam of 1m 3yo Listed winner Consort; the family of US six-time 7-8.5f Grade 1 winner Miss Oceana.

THALER
2/3 b c Dubawi - Timepiece (Zamindar)
Owner: Khalid Abdullah
Sales price: n/a

Fourth foal of a high-class 8-11f winner (including at Group 1 level) who was a half-sister to high-class 7-10.5f winner (including at Group 1 level) Passage Of Time (later dam of Grade 1-placed 7-10.5f winner (including at Group 2/3 level) Time Test (by Dubawi)) and smart 8-12f winner (including at Group 2 level)/St Leger fourth Father Time.

UNNAMED (FR)
19/2 ch c Le Havre - Al Jassasiyah (Galileo)
Owner: Al Shaqab Racing
Sales price: n/a

Half-brother to Group 3-placed 2019 French 10-12f 3yo winner (including at Listed level) Mashael. Dam an unraced sister to Oaks winner Was, Irish 10f 3yo Group 3 winner Douglas Macarthur and Group 3/Listed-placed French 7f 2yo winner Al Naamah and half-sister to 7f 2yo Listed winner Janood out of a Listed-placed Irish 6f 2yo winning half-sister to Dewhurst Stakes/Derby winner New Approach and Irish 1m 3yo Group 3 winner/Irish 1000 Guineas third Dazzling Park (grandam of Irish 6f 2yo Group 1 winner Alfred Nobel).

UNNAMED (FR)
26/1 b c Siyouni - Bal de La Rose (Cadeaux Genereux)
Owner: Saeed Suhail
Sales price: 450,000gns (Blandford Bloodstock)

Half-brother to high-class 8-10f winner (including at Group 1 level) Danceteria and French 1m 3yo Listed winner Blossomtime. Dam a smart French 7.5-10f winner (including at Group 3/Listed level) who was a half-sister to French 2000 Guineas/French Derby winner Lope De Vega, Group 1-placed French dual 1m 3yo winner (including at Group 3 level) Lady Frankel and Group 3-placed 6.5f-1m winner (including at Listed level) Lord Of The Land.

UNNAMED (FR)
1/2 b f Shalaa - Iltemas (Galileo)
Owner: Al Shaqab Racing
Sales price: n/a

Second foal of a French 12f 3yo Listed winner who was a half-sister to US 11f Grade 3 winner Guilty Twelve out of a Group 3/Listed-placed Irish 9.5f 3yo winning close relation to Moyglare Stud Stakes/Irish 1000 Guineas winner Again (later dam of Irish 7.5f 2yo Listed winner Indian Maharaja and 2019 13f 3yo Listed winner Delphinia) and Listed-placed Irish 7f 3yo winner Aris (later dam of French 7f Group 1 winner Aclaim); the family of top-class middle-distance performer Montjeu, 2000 Guineas winner Galileo Gold and King's Stand Stakes/Prix de l'Abbaye winner Goldream.

UNNAMED (IRE)
4/4 b c Kingman - Toquette (Acclamation)
Owner: Saeed Suhail
Sales price: 380,000gns (Blandford Bloodstock)

Half-brother to Group 2-placed UK/UAE triple 6f winner (including at Listed level) Platinum Star and 2019 French 1m 3yo Listed winner Tifosa. Dam an unraced half-sister to Prix Morny winner Arcano out of an unraced half-sister to Listed-placed Irish 9-12f 3yo winner Tarwila and the dams of Irish 14f 3yo Group 2 winner Sword Fighter and 7f/1m 2yo Listed winner Big Audio and Prix de l'Abbaye winner Gilt Edge Girl (herself later dam of French 6f Listed winner Time's Arrow) and Flying Childers Stakes winner Godfrey Street.

Others

BASEMAN
19/1 b c Kingman - Big Break (Dansili)
Trainer: Dermot Weld Owner: Khalid Abdullah
Sales price: n/a

Half-brother to very useful 2019 Irish 8.5-10f 3yo winner Georgeville. Dam a smart Irish 7-7.5f winner (including twice at Group 3 level)/Irish 1000 Guineas fourth who was a sister to Group 1-placed Irish prolific 6-10f winner (including at Group 2/3 level) Famous Name and Irish 10f 3yo Listed winner Discipline, closely related to US 12f Grade 3 winner Renown and a half-sister to Group 3-placed Irish 7-10f winner (including at Listed level) Zaminast.

FREAK OUT (IRE)
2/3 b c Kodiac - Herridge (Bahamian Bounty)
Trainer: Declan Carroll Owner: John Dance
Sales price: 105,000gns (Creighton Schwartz Bloodstock/John Dance)

Second foal of a 7f 2yo winner who was a full sister to useful multiple 6f winner Hairspray (later dam of smart 7-8.5f winner (including at Group 3/Listed level) Epsom Icon) and a half-sister to Listed-placed 6-8.5f winner Medieval (by Kodiac), fairly useful 6f-1m winner Watneya and four other winners out of a 1m 2yo winning half-sister to Grade 1-placed UK/US 8-12f winner (including at Listed level) Red Fort and 12f Listed winner Red Carnation.

LULLABY MOON

4/4 b f Belardo - Bold Bidder (Indesatchel)
Trainer: Joseph Tuite Owner: Phillip Cove & GB Horseracing
Sales price: 16,000gns (D Tunmore/GB Horseracing)

Half-sister to useful multiple 5-7f winner Celebration and fairly useful dual 6f 3yo winner Gaval. Dam a useful dual 5f 2yo winner who was a half-sister to Listed-placed 5f 2yo winner Right Answer (later dam of Listed-placed UK/Hong Kong multiple 5-6f winner Sea The Pearls), Listed-placed Swedish/Norwegian 5.5f-1m winner Better Built and once-raced Irish 5f 2yo winner Twenty Questions out of a 7f 3yo winning half-sister to high-class multiple 5f winner (including at Group 2/3 level) Mind Games.

ONES ARE WILD

5/2 ch c Bated Breath - Bouvardia (Oasis Dream)
Trainer: Donnacha O'Brien Owner: J Carthy & Mrs A M O'Brien
Sales price: £52,000 (Aidan O'Ryan/Joseph O'Brien)

Sixth foal of a Listed-placed triple 6f winning sister to Gimcrack Stakes winner Showcasing, Group 3/Listed-placed 6f 2yo winner Tendu and 6f 3yo winner Palmette (later dam of useful dual 6f 2yo winner Partitia (by Bated Breath)) and a half-sister to Group 3-placed dual 6f winner (including at Listed level) Camacho out of a 6f 3yo Listed winner.

PERFECT SIGN (IRE)

18/4 b f Charm Spirit - Exceedingly Rare (Lope De Vega)
Trainer: Johnny Murtagh Owner: Qatar Racing Limited
Sales price: n/a

Second foal of a once-raced French 7f 2yo winner who was a half-sister to Group 3-placed French 7.5f-1m winner (including at Listed level) Sunday Nectar and Listed-placed French 6f 2yo winners Aseena and Pestagua out of a twice-raced maiden half-sister to Listed-placed French dual 12f winner Reve Parisien and the dam of French 7f 2yo Group 3 winner Gwenseb (herself dam of French dual 1m 3yo Group 2 winner Impassable, French triple 7f/1m Group 3 winner Attendu and 2019 UAE 10f Group 3 winner Spotify).

SIR TITUS (IRE)

24/2 ch c Dandy Man - Moss Top (Moss Vale)
Trainer: Bryan Smart Owner: Michael & Terry Moses
Sales price: 38,000gns (B Smart)

Half-brother to fairly useful 6f-1m winner Caustic Love. Dam a maiden half-sister to Group 2-placed 6f 2yo winner Crown Dependency and useful 6f-1m

2yo winner Motown Mick out of a lightly-raced maiden half-sister to smart 5-7f 2yo winner (including at Group 3/Listed level) Rag Top, Listed-placed 7.5f 3yo winner Red Top, useful dual 6f winner Democretes and the dams of Windsor Castle Stakes winner Elhamri and Coventry Stakes third Rakaan.

TATSTHEWAYTODOIT
28/2 b c Mayson - Resist (Rock Of Gibraltar)
Trainer: Keith Dalgleish Owner: Middleham Park Racing CXIX & Partner
Sales price: £20,000 (F Barberini/Middleham Park)

Third foal of a maiden half-sister to Group 3-placed 5-6f winner Red Balloons out of a 5-6f winner who was a half-sister to Group 2-placed 5.5-6.5f 2yo winner (including at Group 3 level) Violette, smart 5-7f winner (including at Group 3/Listed level) Silca's Gift, Group 3-placed 5f-1m winner (including at Listed level) Virginia Hall (later dam of 6f 3yo Listed winner Marie Of Lyon) and the dam of Listed-placed 5-6f 2yo winner/Norfolk Stakes fourth Nosedive.

THREAD COUNT
13/3 b f Adaay - Wigan Lane (Kheleyf)
Trainer: Archie Watson Owner: Hambleton Racing Ltd XXXI and Partner
Sales price: 28,000gns (Blandford Bloodstock)

Half-sister to useful multiple 5f winner Lathom. Dam a 6f 2yo winner who was a half-sister to Group 3/Listed-placed 5-6f winner Hoh Hoh Hoh and 5f 2yo winner Miss Otis out of a thrice-raced maiden half-sister to the dams of 5f 2yo Group 2 winner/Middle Park Stakes runner-up Wi Dud and 7f Group 2 winner/ Coventry Stakes third Tariq and the grandams of Irish 6f Group 2 winner Mobsta and French 6f 3yo Group 3 winner Snazzy Jazzy.

UNNAMED (IRE)
13/5 b c Iffraaj - Annie The Doc (Nayef)
Trainer: Peter Chapple-Hyam Owner: Phoenix Thoroughbred Limited
Sales price: €200,000 (Phoenix Thoroughbred/D Farrington)

Full brother to French 6f 2yo Listed winner Biraaj and a half-brother to French dual 7f Listed winner Lida and useful 2019 6f 2yo winner Cobra Eye. Dam a maiden half-sister to Listed-placed 1m 1f 3yo winner Balladonia (later dam of French 7f 2yo Group 1 winner Wootton Bassett (by Iffraaj)) and Listed-placed 6f 2yo winner Tioga.

UNNAMED (FR)

19/5 br c Invincible Spirit - Magic Mission (Machiavellian)
Trainer: David Simcock Owner: Sheikh Juma Dalmook Al Maktoum
Sales price: 120,000gns (Vendor)

Half-brother to high-class French/US 9.5-14f winner (including at Grade 1 level) Talismanic and five other winners including 7.5f 2yo winner Witnessed (later dam of French 1m 2yo Group 3 winner Stage Magic). Dam a US 1m Grade 3 winning sister to 6f 2yo winner Dream Scheme and three-parts sister to 7f 2yo winner Box Office; the family of Japanese Triple Crown winner Deep Impact and 1m Group 2 winner Jeremy.

HORSE INDEX

TRAINER INDEX

DAM INDEX

SIRE INDEX

—•—